VOICES FROM THE SOVIET EDGE

VOICES FROM THE SOVIET EDGE

Southern Migrants in Leningrad and Moscow

Jeff Sahadeo

CORNELL UNIVERSITY PRESS   ITHACA AND LONDON

First published 2019 by Cornell University Press

Printed in the United States of America

Library of Congress Cataloging-in-Publication Data

Names: Sahadeo, Jeff, 1967– author.
Title: Voices from the Soviet edge : southern migrants in Leningrad
    and Moscow / Jeff Sahadeo.
Description: Ithaca : Cornell University Press, 2019. |
    Includes bibliographical references and index.
Identifiers: LCCN 2018045871 (print) | LCCN 2018047146 (ebook) |
    ISBN 9781501738210 (pdf) | ISBN 9781501738227 (epub/mobi) |
    ISBN 9781501738203 | ISBN 9781501738203 (cloth : alk. paper)
Subjects: LCSH: Migration, Internal—Soviet Union—History. |
    Migration, Internal—Caucasus, South—History—20th century. |
    Migration, Internal—Asia, Central—History—20th century. | Saint Petersburg
    (Russia)—Ethnic relations. | Moscow (Russia)—Ethnic relations.
Classification: LCC HB2067 (ebook) | LCC HB2067 .S34 2019 (print) |
    DDC 304.80947/0904—dc23
LC record available at https://lccn.loc.gov/2018045871

Image Permissions

The RIA Novosti archives project on Wikimedia Commons can be accessed through commons.wikimedia.org/wiki/Commons:RIA_Novosti.

The photography collection of Thomas T. Hammond on Wikimedia Commons can be accessed through commons.wikimedia.org/wiki/Category:Hammond _Slides_Moscow.

To Petra, Caroline, Andrew, Brahm, and Judie

My address is not my house or my street.
My address is the Soviet Union.

—David Tukhmanov, Soviet composer, 1973

Contents

Acknowledgments

Many years went into the making of this book, and I have many people to thank. An incomplete list begins with the seventy-five citizens of the Soviet Union who gave their time and thoughts for the oral histories that lie at the heart of the project. Equally important were colleagues and graduate students who assisted in the interview process. Together, we tracked down Armenians, Azerbaijanis, Buryats, Georgians, Kazakhs, Kyrgyz, North Caucasus peoples, Tajiks, and Uzbeks. Interviews took place over crackly phone lines, but mostly in person, in Ottawa, New York, St. Petersburg, Moscow, Baku, Lenkoran, Almaty, Tashkent, Bishkek, small Kyrgyz villages, Tbilisi, and Kutaisi. Those who located or interviewed these subjects from 2005 to 2011 include Lisa Greenspoon, Allison Keating, Altynay Teshebaeva, Shakhnoza Matnazarova, Rauf Garagazov, Tair Faradov, Mehrigiul Ablezova, Gulmira Churokova, Akamral Arzybaeva, Ryan Buchanan, and Ia Eradze. Bruce Grant and Madeleine Reeves served as excellent cultural mediators as I undertook my fieldwork in rural Azerbaijan and Kyrgyzstan. I count myself extremely fortunate to have gained access to vivid personal memories and glimpses of both the ordinary and the extraordinary in later Soviet society and culture.

The Social Sciences and Humanities Research Council of Canada provided the principal funding for this project. Internal grants from Carleton University assisted in realizing initial fieldwork and completing finishing touches. The Institute of European, Russian, and Eurasian Studies, and its superb administrators, Ginette Lafleur and Krysia Kotarba, provided solid technical help. I received support also as part of South Ural State University's Laboratory of Migration Studies, with special thanks to Yulia Khmelevskaya and Olga Nikonova. The Azerbaijani embassy to Canada, the Uzbek embassy to Canada and the United States, and the University of Central Asia also assisted with logistics during research trips.

The search for published documents on late Soviet migration also took me near and far. At Carleton University, Aleksandra Blake and our excellent library staff tracked down sources worldwide. Yulduz Kutlieva spent many hours combing through Soviet newspapers at our university library, and Patryk Reid mined the collections of Indiana University. Helen Sullivan, Jan Adamczyk, and Kit Condill at the Slavic Reference Service of the University of Illinois at Urbana-Champaign worked with me from beginning to end. I also consulted Terri Miller at Michigan State University. Erik Scott, Krista Goff, Patryk Reid, and Ryan Buchanan aided with archival research in Baku and Moscow. Saadat Mammadova, Farid Shafiyev, and Aimee Dobbs helped me settle into library work in Baku, even as I could not crack the code for archival access to a project that seemed strange, perhaps suspicious for some reason, to Azerbaijani staff. Ben Loring and Gulmira Musuralieva oriented me to Kyrgyzstani archive and library collections. Mira Kalilova was part of a crack team at the Central State Archive of Political Documentation of the Kyrgyz Republic who took the time to understand how and why I might label movement inside the Soviet Union as "migration." In Tashkent, the Institute of Strategic and Regional Studies mobilized librarians at the Alisher Navoi National Library of Uzbekistan to assist me in finding material on the republic's relationship to Leningrad and Moscow.

I am grateful to colleagues who provided intellectual support over the years, indeed more than a decade, of thinking for this project. My first discussions about this as a research endeavor came when I served as Diane Koenker's research assistant at the University of Illinois at Urbana-Champaign. Her patience and excellence as a supervisor offered me a model as a scholar and a person. I gained initial inspiration from Antoinette Burton, Keith Hitchins, Adeeb Khalid, and Mark Steinberg. As I moved to life as a professor, Lewis H. Siegelbaum acted as superb combination of mentor and colleague as we both recognized the importance of studying mobility from the bottom up in the Soviet Union. Adrienne Edgar and I have shared multiple important conversations on intercultural contact. In addition to the colleagues I have mentioned, I thank for their advice and encouragement Sergei Abashin, Laura Adams, Sara Brinegar, James Casteel, Heather Coleman, Emily Elliott, Yulia Gradskova, Ali Igmen, Ablet Kamalov, Marianne Kamp, Adeeb Khalid, Masha Kirasirova, Nathaniel Knight, Denis Kozlov, Marlène Laruelle, Maike Lehmann, Terry Martin, Maxim Matusevich, David McDonald, Leslie Page Moch, Alexander Morrison, Sarfaroz Niyozov, Douglas Northrop, Sebastien Peyrouse, James Pickett, John Randolph, Blair Ruble, Isaac Scarborough, Ed Schatz, Charles Shaw, Mireya Tinoco, Anna Marie Whittington, and Arif Yunusov. My field research was greatly facilitated by the advice and friendship of colleagues, old and new: Irina Levin, as well as Aimee Dobbs and Bruce Grant, in Baku, and Elmira Kuchumkulova, Duishon Shamatov, Maria Louw, and Maya Peterson, in Bishkek.

I received excellent feedback at several workshops: the Central Eurasia Working Group at the University of California, Berkeley, in 2008; the Midwest Russian History Workshops at Michigan State University in 2009 and the University of Toronto in 2015; the InterAsia Speaker Series at Yale University in 2015; and the Contact Zones Symposium at Seton Hall University in 2015. I also presented portions of this project at more Central Eurasian Studies Society and Association for Slavic, East European, and Eurasian Studies annual conventions than I care to remember. Other venues included Association for the Study of Nationalities conferences and invited talks at Binghamton University, University of Toronto, the Caucasus Resource Research Center in Baku, the University of Central Asia, South Ural State University, Södertörn University, Dalhousie University, Boğaziçi University, the Slavic Research Center at Hokkaido University, and Oxford University. I also thank editors and copy editors—Jan E. Goldstein, Jane Hedges, Adeeb Khalid, Mary Leas, Madeleine Reeves, and Mark Steinberg—and the anonymous reviewers who advanced articles that preceded this manuscript. Initial outlines for the project appeared as "*Druzhba narodov* or Second-Class Citizenship? Soviet Asian Migrants in a Post-Colonial World," *Central Asian Survey* 26, no. 4 (December 2007): 559–79. An early version of chapter 6 was published as "The Accidental Traders: Marginalization and Opportunity from the Southern Republics to Late Soviet Moscow," *Central Asian Survey* 30, nos. 3–4 (2011): 521–40. Chapters 3 and 5 include material that first appeared in "Soviet 'Blacks' and Place Making in Leningrad and Moscow," *Slavic Review* 71, no. 2 (Summer 2012): 331–58. Chapter 4 is based on "Black Snouts Go Home! Migration and Race in Late Soviet Leningrad and Moscow," *Journal of Modern History* 88, no. 4 (2016): 797–826.

Roger Haydon has provided helpful advice and encouragement in equal measure throughout the publication process. His quick responses and thorough readings of the manuscript improved its quality immensely. I thank him also for finding two thoughtful anonymous reviewers and carefully considering their suggestions. Paul Gosselin assisted with the final touches before submission, giving the work a last read before submission. He also helped to collect the photographs for the book. Jane Lichty's and Michelle Witkowski's care and attention to detail helped this enduring project over the finish line.

Petra Alince has been integral to this project at every stage, and in almost every way. Her love and support has been at the foundation of my life and career. Our children, Caroline Alince and Andrew Sahadeo, have seen their father disappear physically to faraway lands or mentally as he sought to hold this project together in his head. My father, Brahm Sahadeo, whose experiences in London after the Second World War helped me consider this work in a global context, passed away before we could talk about my findings. He and my mother, Judie Sahadeo, complete the circle of those closest to me, to whom I dedicate this book.

Abbreviations

BAM Baikal–Amur Mainline (railway)

GUM State Universal Store

KUTV Kommunisticheskii universitet trudiashchikhsia Vostoka (Communist University of the Toilers of the East)

LKN *litsa kavkazskoi natsional'nosti* (individuals of Caucasian nationality)

PTU professional-technical institute

RSFSR Russian Soviet Federated Socialist Republic

SSR Soviet Socialist Republic

USSR Union of Soviet Socialist Republics

VDNKh Exhibition of Achievements of the National Economy

Note on Terminology

The Union of Soviet Socialist Republics consisted of fifteen union republics from 1956 to 1991. These included the Russian Soviet Federated Socialist Republic (RSFSR) and fourteen "national" or Soviet Socialist Republics (SSRs). Official documents generally referred to these regions using their Russian-language names: the Georgian SSR (*Gruzinskaia Sovetskaia Sotsialisticheskaia Respublika*), the Uzbek SSR (*Uzbekskaia Sovetskaia Sotsialisticheskaia Respublika*), and so forth. In this book, I have decided to follow the appellations for the republics used by my interview subjects. These reflect more simplified labels, which were also used in the Soviet period: Russia; Georgia, Armenia, and Azerbaijan; Kazakhstan, Kyrgyzstan, Tajikistan, and Uzbekistan; and, when my subjects traveled, Belarus, Ukraine, Latvia, and Lithuania. I do retain the SSR form when discussing institutional bodies. In the case of Kyrgyzstan, I use the translation directly from modern Kyrgyz to English (so not the Russian Kirgiz).

All interview translations are mine, with assistance from members of my interview team. All translations from published sources are mine, unless otherwise indicated.

JOURNEYS TO THE CORE(S)

Seeking help for his critically ill sister, Jasur Haydarov left his wife and seven children behind in an Uzbek village near Osh, Kyrgyzstan in 1982.[1] That same year, Elnur Asadov, assuming responsibility for his family following his father's death, abandoned Baku for greener economic pastures. Their paths followed an intensifying movement from the Soviet Union's southern republics and eastern regions, encompassing hundreds of thousands of people, including Tajiks, Georgians, Kyrgyz, Buryats, and other local nationalities, as well as Russians. The dynamism produced by this mobility intertwined state and society, formal and informal economies, center and periphery, and drove individual, family, and network plans in the late Union of Soviet Socialist Republics (USSR). Leningrad and Moscow, the USSR's "two capitals," with their availability of goods, services, and work opportunities, emerged as the most attractive destinations for southern and eastern migrants. A chance encounter and friendship with a vacationing Russian woman led Maia Asinadze to forsake her seaside Georgian village and pursue dreams of a top-flight education in the Soviet capital. Abdul Khalimov, a "scared country boy" from rural Tajikistan, began his studies in Dushanbe in 1978 before prejudice from ethnic Russians drove him to the more "international" city of Moscow.[2] He encountered students from dozens of ethnic groups in the Soviet Union and beyond, all seeking upward mobility at the center of their part of the world.

Groundwork for these students, workers, traders, and others was laid by an earlier postwar generation, on all manner of state-sponsored programs. Sevda Asgarova came to Moscow in 1952 to be groomed for a leadership position after having studied at the High Party School in Baku. She regularly hosted relatives in her shared dormitory room, allowing them to test their own fortune in the Soviet capital. Akmal Bobokulov arrived in Leningrad in 1971 to serve in the Baltic Fleet, where he would spend his entire career. His parents, a collective farm bookkeeper and a teacher, swelled with pride at his personal success and patriotism, and he assisted many others who came from his Uzbek hometown of Andijon. The USSR's top coaches spotted Shuhrat Kazbekov's figure skating talents in Tashkent and brought him to Leningrad, where he won several competitions before making a career as a stuntman at the Leningrad Film Studios (Lenfilm). Taking a more orthodox route to the heart of the USSR, Lali Utiashvili and her husband obtained positions through a 1979 recruitment drive in Georgia for "economist-organizers" in Moscow.[3] The two-story house they received on arrival, located on the outskirts, became home to friends and relatives seeking a taste of life in the big city.

Movement invigorated the late Soviet Union. Soviet citizens from the Caucasus, Central Asia, and the Asian regions of Russia brought energy and entrepreneurship to Leningrad's and Moscow's universities, workplaces, factories, and streets.[4] The oral histories that I and my research team conducted highlight the roles of initiative, skill, and hard work in a combined social and geographic mobility that transformed local and migrant lives alike. Words and actions of new arrivals, alongside ambivalent state policies toward movement, remain hidden in contemporary and scholarly accounts of the USSR's last decades. Migrant dynamism, I argue, challenges the perception of stagnation that predominated among Western and Soviet observers of the time and is only now being questioned.[5] Examining the late Soviet Union from the outside in and the bottom up, as in a state of motion instead of stasis, exposes its vibrancy and hope, alongside challenges, through its very last years.

Life stories expose the intricate nature of networks, intimate and large-scale, unofficial and official, and their role in setting the people of the late USSR on the move. New and old friends, immediate and extended families, fellow villagers and flatmates alike provided connections that drove dreams and realities of long-distance movement. Framing individual strategies were myriad state policies and institutions—from professional and labor recruitment drives to guaranteed spots for students in each republic at top central universities, from the multinational nature of the Soviet army and the Communist Youth League (Komsomol) to cheap and easy travel. The USSR emerged in migrant stories as a place of safety and freedom, as compared to the lack of personal security and the restrictions of the first two post-Soviet decades. Many, at the same time, recognized that Soviet-era south-north and east-west movement reflected core-periphery imbalances and triggered nationalism and racism within the Russian host society. Perestroika, its opportunities and uncertainties, unleashed an even larger wave of migration to the USSR's privileged cities. Nationalist feeling and economic discrepancies strengthened and their effects moved from the edges of the union inward at the turn of the 1990s, when societal dynamism overwhelmed an eroding state.

Late Soviet mobility remade center and periphery alike. Leningrad and Moscow grew reliant on the human capital and resources that came increasingly from the farms, industrial towns, small villages, and large cities of the USSR's eastern and southern edges. As demographers sounded alarm bells over a graying population in the USSR's two capitals, residents witnessed a browning one. Tatars, Georgians, Azerbaijanis, Kyrgyz, Tajiks, Buryats, and others made central spaces of Leningrad and Moscow their own, for one or several trading seasons, for the length of a university degree, or for a career or a lifetime. Merchants and construction workers, students and professionals connected their ability to succeed at the heart of the USSR to their equality as citizens; only a few condemned the inequalities that had prompted such moves. Soviet citizens had imbibed since the 1930s, from mass education, media, and other channels, the belief that modernization meant urbanization, that large cities were symbols of a brighter future.[6] Increased wealth at the center seemed the natural order of things. Leningrad and Moscow appeared as spaces for all willing to work hard, overcome challenges of integration and sometimes fierce competition, and lead society and state to prosperity.[7] Ideas, values, and rubles learned or earned at the USSR's core redounded to distant villages and cities. Urban hierarchies and discrepancies deepened as economic opportunities in the 1980s and 1990s simultaneously constricted and, through informal as well as formal networks and movement, spread.

Communist Party leaders had global aspirations for Leningrad and Moscow, as centers of an expanding socialist world. Caucasus and Central Asian peoples played unique and important roles in these pretensions, as models and mediators for Asians and Muslims targeted for pro-Soviet campaigns during the Cold War. Multinational universities, parades honoring their contributions, and even mosques offered official visibility to non-Slavic citizens of eastern Russia as well as the union's southern republics. Global, socialist cities presented distinct models of integrating peoples of former colonies—of, first, the tsarist empire and, then, those of other European states.[8] Absent from Leningrad and Moscow were the residential segregation, political debates over immigration, and sporadic racial riots that marked late twentieth-century postcolonial London, Paris, and other hubs of past empires. Absent too was formal associational life, which might allow schools, newspapers, and other organizations to represent minority communities. Even as Caucasus and Central Asian peoples did not have to cross international borders to move to "their" privileged global cities, they were subject to registration requirements through the residence permit (*propiska*) system. Transnational mobility required awareness of the formal mechanisms of movement as well as the ability and energy to convert the USSR's global power and ambitions, concentrated in its two capitals, toward individual gain.[9]

Mobility tested emotional states as well as practical strategies for integration into the centers of Soviet life. Migrants' oral histories signal the importance and range of emotional lives and communities across time and space.[10] Even as differentials in investment and attention between the center and periphery mounted, Caucasus and Central Asian peoples held fast to the regime's underlying and universalizing rhetoric of family and, especially, friendship. The *druzhba narodov* (friendship of peoples), far from one of the Soviet slogans that Alexei Yurchak declared as frozen and empty, remained a critical component of identity for southern migrants.[11] Mobility allowed them to test the friendship and to make it their own. Contentment—even if mixed, on a few occasions, with resentment at having to move so far from home—proliferated among those newcomers who found themselves at the USSR's core, even if their aspirations were not fully realized. Happiness and compassion emerged as emotional yardsticks for migrants who sought to improve their lives and connect to each other, their own ethnic groups, the host society, a broader Soviet family, and, to varying degrees, the regime itself, all the while maintaining links to home. Adherence to the friendship of peoples became a strategy to hold the state to account, to harangue officials when migration experiences produced unfavorable results. A dynamic maxim, friendship abetted practical strategies for mobility as well as fostered positive emotions that combated potential isolation, thousands of kilometers from home.

Intercultural contact emerged as a defining feature of identity and status in Leningrad and Moscow, as it did across the late Soviet Union. Migrants and locals alike used encounters to frame personal, professional, ethnic, and Soviet senses of belonging in a Russian-dominated but multinational state. Cultural associations and differences evolved within a complicated blend of horizontal linkages and vertical hierarchies. Social, educational, and national background and achievement; original and adopted homes; religion; gender—sometimes, sex—and positioning vis-à-vis the state played important roles as Soviet citizens assessed themselves and each other. Were the two capitals the domain of privileged, urban Russians, of anyone with fair skin, or of those, regardless of background, willing to contribute to a modern society? Could men and women, Christians, Muslims, or atheists, Komsomol or party members or not, equally power, and profit from, a modernizing state? Amid ambiguous official messages, answers varied based on the nature of intercultural encounters, as well as individual perceptions of them. Migrant life stories underscore the complex, personal nature of engagements and their connections to broader Soviet worlds, all within a global context of late twentieth-century periphery-core movement.

Racism challenged migrant integration. Caucasus and Central Asian peoples, as they appeared in greater numbers in northern Russian cities, including Leningrad and Moscow, heard calls denigrating them as "blacks" (*chernye*). In the USSR as across North America and Europe, ideas of race shifted post-Holocaust from biological to cultural criteria, but fomented alongside increased movement of those considered non-white from former imperial peripheries to major Western cities.[12] Race's, and racism's, core concepts remained that "humankind [exists] in distinct groups, each defined by inborn traits that its members share and that differentiate them from the members of other distinct groups of the same kind but of unequal rank."[13] Race contested the friendship of peoples, whereby migrants, and all Soviet citizens, could identify themselves as component, if not completely equal, parts of the same whole. "Black" migrants linked everyday racism in Leningrad and Moscow to the host society's perceptions of their appearance, speech, and behavior. They saw it manifested in slights, stares, patronizing or demeaning language, and occasional violence, even as attacks never approached the level of those in Western cities that greeted their own so-called blacks.[14] The proliferation of Caucasus and Central Asian traders on street corners and at bus and metro stations in the 1980s heightened tensions in the two capitals. Market exchanges could turn violent, and militia behavior toward merchants grew increasingly aggressive. "Individuals of Caucasian nationality" (*litsa kavkazskoi natsional'nosti*), generally shortened to *LKN*, joined black as an epithet and applied ever more broadly to darker-skinned or dark-haired Soviet peoples, much to the chagrin of Leningrad's and Moscow's well-established Tatar communities. Soviet-era epithets endured and would accompany deadly racial violence in St. Petersburg and Moscow in the first decade of the 2000s, when many interviews for this project took place.[15]

Racism occupied a highly charged and emotional, but limited, place in migrant narratives of life in Leningrad and Moscow. Newcomers considered the certain prices they had to pay for the ability to succeed at the heart and summit of the Soviet Union. They concentrated on networks and relationships, formal and informal, that would "bind migrants and non-migrants in a complex web of social roles and interdependent relationships."[16] Leningrad's and Moscow's residence permit system remained leaky by design, with various categories and exceptions. Municipal leaders allowed, or failed to halt, the growing street trade and other paths to mobility through service and construction as well as professional sectors. Young, dynamic migrants charged these aging cities with energy, provided goods and services more effectively than the state, and expressed and spread their loyalty to the Soviet system. Urban informalities, more than strict regulation, characterized the two capitals in the late Soviet period.

Ideas of home—their hometowns, thousands of kilometers away, adopted homes in Leningrad and Moscow, and a broader Soviet home—predominated in migrant memories. Homes in eastern regions and southern republics served as places of imagined solace, but also as reminders that time in Leningrad and Moscow linked to broader, family, and perhaps regional strategies of mobility. Common citizenship and new or existing networks eased initial adaptation to Leningrad and Moscow, but newcomers dealt with everything from cold weather to cold residents. Absent ethnic neighborhoods, which in the West could at once offer reminders of home as well as isolate them from the host society, faraway Soviet migrants carved out their own spaces. Individual flats, multiethnic student or worker dormitories, restaurants, Lenin's mausoleum, and even Moscow's Exhibition of Achievements of the National Economy (VDNKh) became sites where newcomers animated memories of local, national, and Soviet homes and eased integration into cities to which they believed all peoples of the USSR, if not the world, had a right.

Soviet dreams of accomplishment, comfort, status, and inclusion within a collective spirit occupied migrant expectations and thoughts, and remained emblazoned in their memories.[17] Aspirations embraced visions of mobility—social and spatial—and the freedom to choose a career, if not for them, for their children, within a color-blind state. In a way, these mobile citizens realized Nikolai Bukharin's early Soviet vision as "conscious producers of their own fate [and] real architects of their own future."[18] Their ideas of individual rights, privileges, and ambitions, of qualification for the Soviet dream, could at once enforce and challenge official conceptions of a future state and society. Migrants believed state agents were, or should be, duty-bound to help them realize their objectives, which flowed into visions of an advanced society. Popular conceptions of modern, privileged citizens favored the urban professional over workers and peasants.[19] Education and desire could trump social or ethnic background. In the Soviet Union as well as across the industrialized world, migrants reshaped ideas of progress to allow them to abandon "Asia" and join "Europe."[20]

Migrant stories decenter state- and Russia-based narratives to reveal how ordinary and extraordinary individuals union-wide understood and fashioned the late Soviet Union. Listening to what made one person leave a small Kyrgyz village, a comfortable Georgian town, or a cosmopolitan Azerbaijani or Tajik city is to understand how periphery and core, individual and official, emotional and practical became mutually constitutive. Policies and networks, ambition and opportunity originating thousands of kilometers away supplied Leningrad's and Moscow's universities and workplaces with talent and labor, fed their stomachs with food, and filled their homes with flowers. Central Asian and Caucasus traders exposed the bottom-up and outside-in energy that propelled, as coined by

James Millar, the "little deal." The state offered, albeit inconsistently and not always willingly, the space, but not the work and goods, for a tacit accord that allowed the satiation of the needs and desires of increasingly acquisitive populations in Brezhnev-era large, central cities.[21]

The intertwined nature of the Soviet center and its margins, the complexity of networks and relationships between them, complicates understandings of the Soviet Union as, or as not, an empire. Erik Scott's valuable contribution on Moscow's Georgian community, even as it exposes intricate political as well as cultural, social, and economic linkages between the center and the republic, defaults to characterizing the USSR as an empire, albeit one of "mobile diasporas."[22] Adeeb Khalid prefers to label the Soviet Union a "modern mobilizational state"; migrant oral histories show mobilization emerging from below as well as above.[23] Conceptions and practices of empire and modernization worked hand in glove in the Soviet Union. Privileges accumulated at the center relied on energy from all citizens and resources from all regions. These privileges diffused—albeit unevenly—to locals and sojourners across the USSR, through official and unofficial avenues.[24] A decade-plus after the collapse, Soviet migrants themselves, with some notable exceptions, hesitated to characterize their former state as an empire. They argued that ease of movement and equal citizenship overrode differential wealth and investments that tied southern republics to raw material production and, certainly, perpetuated imperial ideas and practices of Russian superiority. The Soviet Union remains a unique human as well as state experiment, at once challenging and perpetuating regional, imperial, and global inequities that persisted, and worsened, in the late twentieth-century postcolonial world.

Migrant stories, alongside official, if incomplete, statistics and press and archival sources, also offer new ways to periodize the late Soviet era. Soviet concentrations of investment in the European core and new resource-rich areas in Russia's east, which started late in the Khrushchev period, began to bite in Central Asia and Caucasus villages and cities alike at the end of the 1970s. Economic migration, as southern residents sought to supplement incomes, fueled a rise in so-called black traders on the streets of Leningrad, Moscow, and other major Russian cities.

Their presence altered streetscapes and fueled a backlash from urban residents, even as the quality and prices of their goods were appreciated. Militia sweeps highlighted a municipal campaign to cleanse Moscow's streets before the 1980 Olympics. "Black" traders were "taken to the 101st kilometer"[25]—beyond where residence permission was required. Campaigns began simultaneously to relocate populations, from Central Asia especially, to labor-deficit regions, primarily in Russia's Far East, as officials union-wide concluded that the Soviet economy could no longer support growing populations in the south. The next turn came not with the advent of perestroika but with the turbulence of 1990. Increased hardship on the periphery, as policies restricted state spending on poorer republics, presaged nationalist agitation and violent state reactions. Movements for greater autonomy within the USSR now considered independence. Migrants who came to Leningrad and Moscow before and during the wave of the 1980s weighed staying or leaving amid political uncertainty as well as the growing challenges of everyday life. Feelings of security faded amid food shortages, and a 1990 round of media reforms unleashed nationalist and racist discourse. That year, before the formal dissolution, marks migrants' memories of when their idea of the USSR, as a state that rewarded energy and mobility, ended.

Leningrad's and Moscow's "politics of unrecognition" of ethnic minorities complicate understandings and calculations of their multinational character.[26] Annual, detailed municipal census counts did not include statistics on ethnic background.[27] Official publications designed for broader consumption showed residents as uniquely white and Slavic.[28] Skills attained or money earned in Leningrad and Moscow by Caucasus, Central Asian, or other travelers from less-developed regions of the USSR, in the minds of Soviet administrators, would be transferred home. Russians were to play their role as "elder brother" in the friendship of peoples, spreading their advancement to distant republics. All-union census figures give the only official tallies by ethnicity. Tatars, with a longer history of incorporation and relative geographic proximity, dominated early counts: in 1959 Moscow, they totaled 80,500, with smaller populations of over 5,000 Armenians, Georgians, Chuvash, and Mordvins.[29] Numbers from the Soviet south continually increased, with the 1989 all-union census registering over 30,000 Central Asians in Leningrad and Moscow, respectively, in addition to over 30,000 from Azerbaijan.[30] Government statistics, which relied on self-identification, almost certainly undercounted minorities, who might categorize themselves as Russian or, more likely, avoid participation at all.[31] Undercounting increased in the last decade or so of the Soviet Union, when, as Vera Glubova notes, migration rates from Soviet Asia to Moscow were two to three times higher than from other European areas.[32] Olga Vendina writes that Caucasus and Central Asian nationalities constituted a substantial portion of the 20 percent non-Russian population in Moscow's core by the end of the Soviet era.[33]

Oral histories for this project recorded seventy-five Soviet citizens, among them students, professionals, traders, shopkeepers, skilled and unskilled workers, tourist agents, and demobilized soldiers.[34] They included Buryats, North Caucasus peoples, Armenians, Azerbaijanis, Georgians, Kazakhs, Kyrgyz, Tajiks, and Uzbeks who spent months or years in Leningrad and Moscow from the 1950s to the 1990s—the significant majority in the last two decades of the USSR. The study also employs oral histories conducted by other scholars and journalists.[35] The interview set is meant to be illustrative, not representative. I sought to capture as many facets as possible of the migration experience through the eyes, words, and memories of those who instigated and lived it in Leningrad, Moscow, and points near and far in the late Soviet Union.

These oral histories offer unparalleled access to Soviet daily life. In a dynamic process such as migration, listening to voices of those on the move shows how "matrices of social forces impact and shape individuals, and how individuals, in turn, respond, act, and produce change in the social arena."[36] These sources gain added value in modern states, like the USSR, which conceal the scope and importance of human mobility, formal and especially informal.[37] The appendix elaborates on the background of these interviews, as well as their challenges. Language, situation, and perceptions of, or relationships with, the interviewer, for example, influence responses.[38] Subjects frame words, as well as broader biographies, within narrative strategies. Past and present intermingle in migrants' memories. They compared Leningrad's and Moscow's Soviet past favorably to a post-Soviet present, when racial violence was claiming, during the interview period of 2005–11, dozens of lives annually.[39] Contrasts offered in interviews between Soviet and post-Soviet migration experiences—even though the assignation of blame for the xenophobia and violence of the first decade of the 2000s shifted in unexpected ways—underlined the well-documented wistfulness for an "imaginary affective geography" of the USSR, on which ex-Soviet citizens map ideas of stability, community, and mutual trust.[40] Nostalgia emerges most powerfully in these interviews, however, in relation to ideas of mobility and success tied, almost universally, to youth. Migrants fondly recalled a time when they considered no barrier too large or structure too foreboding.[41]

A wide variety of printed sources accompanies migrant voices and offers insight into official practices and reactions to late Soviet movement. Archival research was conducted at the State Archive of the Russian Federation, the Russian State Archive of Social and Political History, the Central State Archive of the City of Moscow, and the Central State Archive of Political Documentation of the Kyrgyz Republic; I was denied access at archives in Azerbaijan. Leningrad, Moscow, and Tashkent newspapers offered official representations of national relationships and movement in the USSR. Discussions of Soviet economics, mobility, and ethnic relations loosened during the glasnost era, although a large gap remained between the established press and the overtly nationalist, racist publications that found their way to Leningrad's and Moscow's streets in 1990–91. Lively debates on the consequences of Soviet investment policy, demographics, and the roles of, and relationships in, multicultural cities marked academic Soviet and Western studies alike. Leningrad's and Moscow's "ethnosociologists," who emerged in the 1980s, provided contemporaneous views of movement and integration, alongside studies conducted by historians, demographers, and other scholars.[42] They counterpoised the uniquely and astonishingly rosy views of Leningrad's and Moscow's place in the USSR in publications designed for a popular audience, often expressed through personal testimonies, that I read in Baku's, Bishkek's, and Tashkent's libraries. As complex a picture as this study presents, it can only offer slices of daily life and partial perspectives on Leningrad's and Moscow's multi-ethnic, global worlds. No late twentieth-century state, continuing to the present, has successfully managed, much less openly discussed or studied, flows from outside, primarily from poorer or former colonial territories, to its largest cities.[43]

This book consists of seven chapters, roughly organized into three sections. Chapters 1 and 2 establish the imperial, Soviet, and global contexts for movement and the foundations of interethnic relationships in the USSR. Common citizenship jockeyed with Russian primacy as Caucasus, Central Asian, and Asian Russian peoples weighed their place, both home and away, in the Soviet Union. Chapters 3–5 follow Soviet migrants through the incorporation process in Leningrad and Moscow. Individual motivations and pathways, alongside initial encounters, shaped the entire migrant experience. New arrivals battled to overcome, rather than be defined by, difference. Once established, they became integral parts of the two capitals' cityscapes.

Chapters 6 and 7, which constitute the last section, focus on two major turning points in the last decade-plus of Soviet rule. Four traders, one from Azerbaijan and three from Central Asia, effectively narrate chapter 6. Their voices highlight the scope of Soviet entrepreneurship at the turn of the 1980s within poignant life stories that underscore the emotional and practical challenges of informal movement. The optimism that greeted Mikhail Gorbachev's policy of perestroika opens chapter 7. Could societal dynamism now be accommodated, instead of dissimulated? The turn to the 1990s marked a rapid and intense erosion of the state. As shortages and violence worsened, decisions to stay in Leningrad and Moscow or go home assumed new meanings and urgency. The conclusion mines migrants' memories for ideas of home and their wistfulness for the Soviet Union decades after its collapse. Soviet discourses appear throughout the book as powerful shapers not just of individual, national, or supranational identities but also of a broader collective that sought to make sense of connections between home and away. Soviet policies, even when recalled as distant from many migrants' daily lives, shaped choices and behaviors then, and their ghostlike presence infuses itself into narratives of lives now.

GLOBAL, SOVIET CITIES

The Soviet Union set in motion peoples from all corners of the state and beyond. Leningrad and Moscow emerged as the Communist world's "global" or "gateway" cities.[1] Internal—increasingly from east and south—as well as international movement underpinned the privileged position of the "two capitals" and highlighted intertwined paths of social and geographic mobility. Post–Second World War rebuilding and development enforced the status of major European metropolitan centers as bastions of economic opportunity and modern culture. Leningrad's and Moscow's global aspirations blended with boundaries on behavioral norms, appearance, and language. Leaders worldwide expected or, given piecemeal planning, hoped that late twentieth-century arrivals, from near and far, would integrate seamlessly into modern, European urban spaces.[2] Local and state governments in Leningrad, Moscow, and elsewhere grappled with newcomers who brought their own cultural, economic, and professional dynamics and vigor, often outside official pathways of movement.

Seeing the spires of its skyscrapers, the clothing of its inhabitants, and the quality and availability of its high culture and goods, Jyldyz Nuriaeva called 1978 Moscow "Babylon."[3] She had followed family members and colleagues from Kyrgyzstan's capital of Frunze and would inspire others.[4] Students like Nuriaeva, alongside workers, traders, and professionals across the Soviet Union, as well as growing numbers in Asia and Africa, sought their own Babylon in one of the USSR's two capitals. Common institutions and citizenship, endowed to those from the Caucasus, Central Asia, and the eastern regions of Russia, softened differences with a white host society. Even so, as Lewis H. Siegelbaum and Leslie Page Moch point out, the flows, causes, and outcomes of Soviet movement reflected its practice of "transnational politics within national borders."[5] Official efforts to control and channel mobility had limited success when met with migrant determination, individually and through networks, established and new.

Early networks formed in the crucible of tsarist empire-building, binding core and periphery. Over time, they evolved within and beyond ambiguous and changing state designs. Modernization and postimperial processes in many ways strengthened and expanded these networks—in part due to greater differentials of growth and investment between the center and edges of former imperial holdings. Just as Kirsten McKenzie and others have argued that global networks made empires, I argue that postimperial networks, alongside postwar urbanization and modernization, made global cities—in this case, Leningrad and Moscow.[6] Cities both shaped and were shaped by the cultural, social, and economic systems of empire.[7] Many considered European capitals as "escapes" from legacies of "draconian colonial rule," evident in the continued privileges of urban white settler populations in British, French, and Russian/Soviet postcolonies alike.[8] Migrants—and regimes—take "calculated risks," moving or not moving, encouraging or limiting movement, to gain personal, professional, or political advantages through human and economic development.[9] Intense debate ensued in postwar states over whether to restrict the privileges and power of showcase cities or to accept migrants—unofficial as well as official—needed to perpetuate these privileges, as urban, Western populations aged and cities grew.

Mobility remains underestimated in understanding the power of world cities. Finance and business sectors power Western metropolises, Doreen Massey and Saskia Sassen contend, through their capital and ability to command and control across state borders.[10] Information is concentrated, interpreted, and distributed, almost facelessly. Migrants appear as instruments of state- or privately controlled agencies and enterprises.[11] Sassen sees global cities using two streams of migrants: the first, with "official" status, work in professional or knowledge economies; the second join a shrinking but still substantial industrial workforce or, more likely, seek employment in low-skill service economies.[12] Massey sees similar streams of "post-industrial migration."[13] Migrant origins, and how newcomers shape urban spaces, appear irrelevant; calls to include them in studies of global cities still appear only sporadically in scholarly literature.[14]

Leningrad's and Moscow's socialist nature offers numerous paths to broaden conceptions of global cities. Massey underlines "neoliberal globalization" in building these spaces.[15] Jennifer Robinson, who criticizes world city literature for ignoring the metropoles of the "global South," which emerged as nodes of regional and world economies, maintains the central role of capitalism.[16] Only in the post-Soviet era does Moscow enter into the global city conversation, and, even then, as an example of "competing globalities."[17] I argue here against the idea of competition, even in the Cold War. Including Soviet Leningrad and Moscow as global cities expands understandings of the scope of modern development—capitalist or not—worldwide. Their state institutions and agencies, populated by citizens from across the USSR, exercised command and control functions extending beyond state borders, to the "Second World" and beyond. Deepening core-hinterland disparities enforced parallels of economic development between a capitalist West and socialist East and conditioned migrant flows.[18]

Struggles to balance the economic dynamism that accompanied migration with political controls over the types of people who should be allowed residence epitomize global cities. The USSR's planned economy placed it on a distinct path, although the state exercised far less control over movement than it advertised. Popular and official conceptions of place and progress intertwined and transformed through mobility. As Nina Glick Schiller and Ayşe Çağlar note, "locality matters" in migration, but in a more nuanced way than existing scholarship has acknowledged.[19]

Imperial and global networks strengthened St. Petersburg/Leningrad and Moscow from the beginning of the twentieth century. Newcomers from distant peripheries weighed economic opportunities as well as the play of power in the two capitals. The Soviet Union's rise as a postwar superpower elevated Leningrad's and Moscow's status, within and beyond Soviet borders. The dynamic between state efforts to develop an advanced, socialist economy through planned movement and the multitude of paths—official and unofficial—drove distant newcomers to the two capitals. Retrenchment produced consequences, as the Soviet state belatedly followed global patterns of concentrating investment and development in core European regions. Migration patterns nonetheless ensured Leningrad's and Moscow's globality, even if not in ways the regime intended.

From Empire to Union

Early generations of newcomers from points east and south tested opportunities in imperial St. Petersburg and Moscow. They interacted with, learned from, and shaped spaces and cultures far removed from those of their homelands. The two capitals retained their privileged status throughout the turbulent transition from tsarist to Soviet rule, offering, alternately, political and administrative connections, economic prospects, and a "pathway to European [and, later, socialist] modernity."[20] The USSR considered its most powerful cities as global hubs; Petrograd/Leningrad and Moscow emerged as centerpieces of official strategies to attract diverse peoples from within and beyond the borders of their young state.[21]

Their opportunities and status also attracted growing numbers—some welcome, some not—outside of the plans or reach of the regime.

Movement toward tsarist centers followed the routes—in reverse—of conquest. Imperial administrators invited select elites in recently subject, non-Russian lands to visit or reside at the heart of empire. These newcomers served as evidence of the empire's greatness and could prove useful as loyal mediators with now colonized peoples.[22] Early networks focused on these political figures as well as trade. Small Tatar neighborhoods emerged from the seventeenth century in Moscow, and early St. Petersburg had its own "Tatar Lane."[23] In early nineteenth-century Moscow, a Georgian Orthodox church became the center of a small community. Armenian circles clustered around Chernyshevsky Street, with schools and three churches.[24] Across imperial Russia, younger members of privileged families, or those who had drawn the attention of tsarist administrators, studied at Oriental institutes or other branches of academies or universities in the two capitals.[25] Knowledge of the empire, in the European tradition, could improve, it was hoped, control from an imperial center.[26] The come and go of academics, students, and tsarist functionaries catalyzed imperial core-periphery linkages, laying a foundation for Soviet-era networks.

Growing numbers of generally privileged, influential representatives from imperial peripheries pursued higher education in European capitals, from St. Petersburg and Moscow to Paris and London, at the turn of the twentieth century. They sought engagement with European ideas of progress in order to lead their own peoples in a modernizing world. Mustafa Choqay, a prominent modernist intellectual in Russian Turkestan, studied law in St. Petersburg and remained to draft speeches in the imperial duma for Muslim deputies after the 1905 revolution.[27] Budding Georgian socialists pursued contacts and knowledge in St. Petersburg. Like Indians in London or North Africans in Paris, they saw in imperial capitals the formation of a critical, empire-wide intellectual mass that could offer pathways to softening, if not overturning, imperial rule.[28] These capitals became junction boxes for networks of colonized intellectuals and elites determined to assimilate and transmit ideas of development, as well as to implement reform or revolution, to transform their own lands and leave their mark at the heart of empire.

Beyond privileged tiers, national groups incorporated into the empire gained reputations for specific skills in imperial St. Petersburg and Moscow. Tatars became known as doormen, Caucasus peoples as cobblers and construction workers, Bashkirs as horse-keepers.[29] Tatar, Caucasus, and Central Asian traders occupied stalls at city marketplaces, selling food, silk, horses, and other goods. Mosques, built in Moscow in the early nineteenth century and St. Petersburg in the early twentieth, along with trade fairs and streets dominated by peoples from eastern and southern stretches of the empire, played important roles in Russia's imperial image.[30] Ethnic neighborhoods dissipated at the turn of the twentieth century, as waves of primarily Russian and other Slavic workers swept over rapidly industrializing St. Petersburg and Moscow. A 1912 Moscow census nonetheless recorded 17,200 Tatars, 10,400 "Muslims" (likely Azerbaijanis, before the label became officially used in the 1930s, and Central Asians), and 6,800 Armenians among 1.5 million residents.[31] The Muslim Charitable Society in Moscow joined others assisting First World War victims. Ethnic cuisine, especially Caucasus and Central Asian kebabs, entered popular consciousness alongside the ostensible sectoral workforce aptitudes of various nationalities.[32]

Moscow emerged as the capital of a new Soviet state and quickly became, in the words of Erik Scott, a "self-consciously multiethnic metropolis."[33] V. I. Lenin and other Bolshevik leaders considered the city the hub of an international socialist revolution. Higher education in Petrograd as well as Moscow remained a vehicle for networks, mobility, and influence for subjects-turned-citizens of the new state, and now for subject and colonized peoples worldwide. Both streams flowed into the Communist University of the Toilers of the East (Kommunisticheskii universitet trudiashchikhsia Vostoka, or KUTV), which opened in Moscow in 1921.[34] G. I. Broido, its first rector, pronounced the university's mission: "to prepare cadres for Soviet and party construction and flow into local organization and strengthen Soviet power of the workers in the faraway steppes and mountains of Asia."[35] Named after Joseph Stalin in 1925, the university reflected his conception of a separate Soviet East and a colonized and dependent East, both of which required assistance from Moscow's educators. In one stream studied dozens to hundreds of each officially recognized nationality within the bounds of the USSR, from the Caucasus to the Far East.[36] Another, moving beyond Broido's vision, was recruited globally—Moscow had become a "coveted destination" for foreigners who were inspired by communist ideas and wanted to see the world, escape poverty and imperial subjugation, and receive a free education.[37] These students, who composed one-third of KUTV's enrollment, arrived from the Arab states, India, China, and Africa; African Americans were also included in the nebulous Bolshevik understanding of the foreign "East."

Azerbaijan and Central Asia became not just the Soviet East in the 1920s; the regime designated their peoples as "backward" (otstal'nye). Recently reconquered by Red Army troops, these overwhelmingly Muslim regions had offered significant local and nationalist resistance to the Russian-dominated Bolsheviks. Their economies, producing primarily raw materials, from oil to cotton, were reincorporated into the former imperial system, which remained largely intact in the Soviet Union.[38] By virtue of low education levels and purported lack of awareness of socialism, Azerbaijanis and Central Asians required special assistance to allow them to contribute to state and societal modernization.[39] In addition to two- or three-year programs offered by KUTV, the Ia. M. Sverdlov Communist University put forward specific short courses on administration, to quickly train new cadres of these "backward" peoples in Soviet rule and jumpstart the modernization process.

Other educational establishments appealed to broader categories of "eastern" peoples. In 1921, the Institute of Oriental Studies opened in Moscow. Strong contingents of Tatars and Armenians, among others, enrolled at engineering and teaching academies in Petrograd and Moscow. The Bolsheviks established a quota system to reserve spaces at top institutes of higher education in European Russia for all designated national groups and territories throughout the Soviet Union. A centerpiece of what Francine Hirsch labeled the USSR's "state-sponsored evolutionism," the quota strategy altered the careers and lives of millions of Soviet citizens from the Caucasus and Central Asia.[40] Moscow immediately, and consistently throughout the Soviet period, faced demands to raise quota numbers for institutions deemed prestigious in the name of uplifting less-privileged regions.[41] Educational policies were, from the beginning, designed to send newly trained cadres home to develop and Sovietize their republics. A handful of KUTV graduates worked in Leningrad or Moscow as translators or editors of propaganda journals, but there was no system to incorporate them into predominantly Russian cities.[42]

Moscow's status as capital of a young, dynamic state—"a source of inspiration" for would-be Communists and modernizers alike—attracted intellectuals from across the so-called east, with goals beyond joining the Soviet mission.[43] Uzbeks studied at institutes of drama and journalism, using new ideas and contacts to shape literary and political ideals for their young nation. By the mid-1920s, the city emerged, Adeeb Khalid argues, as a "hub of Uzbek cultural life."[44] Moscow's pull linked it to other major European cities and empires. Cultural and educational opportunities drew ever-greater numbers to London and Paris from African and Asian colonies—these sojourners sought to connect their peoples and lands to imperial and global power.[45] As the Depression struck the West and racism and fascism rose, Moscow became, for left-wing intellectuals and others worldwide, alternately "the future" and humanity's "only hope."[46]

Information on interwar interactions between arrivals from the Soviet "East" and Slavic residents of modernizing, industrializing Leningrad and Moscow is sparse. Tatars remained the largest minority. Numbers in Leningrad climbed from 1,200 in 1920 to 31,500 in 1939.[47] Moscow was home to over 100,000 Tatars as well as smaller groups from the Caucasus and Central Asia.[48] Oksana Karpenko writes that Tatars who worked in service industries, and were connected to pre-revolutionary networks, experienced significant dislocation. Newcomers often brought their entire families to preserve language and culture.[49] Five of the eleven "national" schools in interwar Moscow operated in the Tatar language, though many Tatars educated their children in Russian.[50]

"National" institutions—schools, theaters, and clubs—fell victim to official campaigns against non-state organizations in the 1930s. Leningrad's council shuttered national associations, fixing two "cultural" spaces for non-Russian citizens of the Soviet Union in 1933. Finns, Jews, Poles, Belarusians, and other European minorities shared one building. The second was reserved as a "house of enlightenment for Tatars and peoples of the East."[51] The division created and enforced a civilizational divide. Georgians and Armenians found themselves in liminal positions, as Christians and self-considered "Europeans" but from imperial lands with mixed populations, discussed by travel writers and policymakers as on the edges of Asia.[52] Scott noted that Georgians constituted "the easternmost fringe of nations classified as Western," though some migrants—particularly those in menial professions and traders—considered themselves as the westernmost fringes of those considered by host populations as eastern.[53]

In 1936–38, "a purposeful, comprehensive, and carefully targeted institutional Russification" of the RSFSR, according to Terry Martin, "had been set into motion."[54] Stalin's "Caucasian group," having solidified its hold on top political positions in Moscow, sought to soothe Russian feelings of inferiority within a multinational union. Moscow's municipal authorities followed Leningrad's lead in Russifying cultural and institutional life. All remaining non-Russian national schools, periodicals, and cultural organizations closed. Two Armenian churches were destroyed. Stalin scaled back earlier Bolshevik anti-imperial efforts to promote peripheral, non-Russian peoples to positions of influence, particularly in their home regions, through a policy known as korenizatsiia (indigenization). Arrests of those suspected of spying for foreign powers in the purge era, outmigration, and the Second World War significantly reduced Leningrad's and Moscow's minorities.[55]

Cities, States, and Movement after the Second World War

The Second World War transformed Leningrad and Moscow. Leningrad, the now largely depopulated "hero-city," having survived a 900-day siege, and Moscow, now the capital of a global superpower, required significant reconstruction and renovation. Nearby rural areas provided an initial workforce, with migrants increasingly arriving from all corners of the Soviet Union. Caucasus and Central Asian peoples—sometimes with official blessing, sometimes without—arrived in ever-greater numbers, especially as initial postwar investment in southern peripheries faded. The two capitals became Cold War showcases, dueling with London, Paris, New York, and Washington, D.C., for the allegiance of the nonaligned, or "Third World." Leningrad and Moscow unrolled welcome mats not only to citizens of the new Communist Eastern Bloc but also to those in Central and Latin America, Asia, and Africa. The presence of those from Stalin's internal East showcased the diversity of a postcolonial, socialist state with global aspirations but became a symbol of imperfect planning in a socialist system that at once sought to control movement and unleash the power of its citizens to advance modern cities in their own republics.

Leningrad and Moscow approached postwar construction in the manner of major capitals across Europe. Urban centers became nodes to deliver better standards of living for societies traumatized by the conflict. Soviet leaders envisaged socialist planning as best able to place resources and people to realize this promise. Their "distinct expressions of urbanity" would outstrip the West.[56] Concentrations of services and expertise in the two capitals from across the USSR intensified prewar trends of focusing attention toward the core. Leningrad and Moscow had become hubs of Soviet and global identities, enforced by their critical importance in wartime and their growing political, ideological, and economic significance, through education and planning agencies as well as industry. Their image spread through the Soviet Union, across the Communist "Second World," centered in Eastern Europe, and beyond.[57] A four-day television quiz sponsored by the Soviet-Czechoslovak Friendship Society in 1957 delved into contestants' knowledge of "Leningrad-Moscow: Centers of the Great October Socialist Revolution."[58] Elevating the two capitals became a strategy to enforce a cohesive socialist world. Moscow's international youth festival in 1957 greeted thirty thousand foreign visitors and highlighted its cosmopolitan character. A true global city opened its arms to, among others, former colonized peoples who were facing economic distress, isolation, or violence.[59] The festival moved the newspaper *Komsomol'skaia pravda* "to feel the love of the world for Moscow, fully and clearly."[60]

Postwar development strategies marked Leningrad's and Moscow's unique trajectories as multiethnic as well as global cities. Substantial peasant populations and demobilized soldiers in the Russian heartland remained despite the war's horrific human cost and allowed for "homegrown" labor forces even as Great Britain and France were compelled to turn to overseas, soon-to-be-former, colonies for workers to rebuild and advance their capitals.[61] The Soviet Union invested in its southern peripheries, following party decisions to build on the wartime relocation of industry, where hundreds of factories had decamped to Central Asia and exploited its abundant natural resources.[62] Hydroelectric, coal, and chemical factories sprouted across the 1950s and 1960s Soviet south.[63] The state designated resources for social services, including literacy and education programs. Soviet attention forestalled larger rates of migration to powerful state centers, while West Indians, South Asians, and Africans decamped to the hearts of their imperial systems in London and Paris, believing that the imminent end to empire would produce substantial economic damage.[64]

Central Asian party leaders highlighted these divergent paths, which enforced socialism's ostensible superiority, as they sought increased funding from Moscow. Nikita Khrushchev had made regional equality a cornerstone in his own bid to replace Stalin at the pinnacle of Soviet leadership, and was anxious to spread Soviet influence abroad. Gaining Khrushchev's ear, these Central Asian heads argued that Moscow could show a unique socialist trajectory to global development, overcoming the inequities that were driving south-north migrations in North America and Western Europe.[65] Persistent accusations from within and beyond Central Asia that the USSR had, in effect, recolonized the region as a giant cotton collective, however, continued to hinder Soviet outreach to the Middle East and Africa.[66] In the mid-1950s, both the United States and the Soviet Union considered the Third World solidarity movement crucial as they jockeyed for global economic and ideological preeminence.[67]

Soviet development policies accompanied another practice capable of stemming the early postwar movement that immersed western European capitals, which grew far beyond state designs.[68] In the 1930s, Soviet leaders had expressed significant anxiety over the composition of large cities, the nodes from which a modern, socialist culture would develop.[69] Planners designed a residence permit system to regulate all those within major urban boundaries. Those discovered without a *propiska* (plural: *propiski*), a document verifying official city residence, especially so-called alien elements—criminals, Roma, wealthy peasants (*kulaks*), and others—could be not only expelled but also sent to work camps in the Far East or elsewhere.[70] Massive efforts were undertaken to "passportize" Leningrad and Moscow. Citizens or not, residence of any length in the two capitals required another layer of documentation.[71]

The propiska epitomized the Soviet state's efforts to institute a "scientific, predictable, and planned" migration process in the postwar years.[72] Initial labor recruitment in larger cities revolved around the practice of "organized enlistment" (*orgnabor*). After economic planners determined targets and "control figures," agents from the Labor Ministry sought to allocate, and, if necessary, relocate, potential personnel from across the USSR. Enterprises could apply for extra working forces to relieve shortages or to produce at "optimal" rates. In this way, Soviet citizens were ostensibly delivered to appropriate sectors of the economy.

Professionals or workers recruited to large cities were given temporary or permanent propiski, with employers generally responsible for the new arrivals' housing. In this way, as demographer N. A. Tolokontseva argued, individuals would not become "lost" in large cities and succumb to social problems and dangers, as in the West.[73]

The *orgnabor* system, however, lacked the flexibility to meet labor needs in rapidly developing Leningrad and Moscow. Managers and other local officials, unwilling to await the results of a creaky and unpredictable allocation process, recruited labor outside of official channels in the 1950s and beyond. They turned first to surrounding rural areas, which continued to suffer from a lack of economic opportunities or social mobility while absorbing demobilized soldiers. Vera Isaeva recalled an older man driving into her village outside the capital and recruiting farmers on the spot to build the Leningrad Hotel, across from the Kazan station in Moscow, in the early 1950s.[74] Informal hiring increased as confusion reigned over the propiska process—who needed one, what type they needed, and who ruled on these needs. Officially, those not born in "regime zones"—Soviet cities where propiski were required—needed to apply, with their passport and a letter of employment, to the housing department of a local council (soviet). The tie between employment and propiski was summed up in the Soviet saying: *Propiski net, raboty net; raboty net, propiski net* (No propiska, no work; no work, no propiska).[75] Collective farm members, most of whom lacked a passport until the 1970s, needed a village council's letter of permission. Applications did not guarantee success; regulations for approval, hidden from the public and continually tweaked over the Soviet period, offered more than twenty categories of rejection.[76] A propiska could take years to issue, and the wait for state-approved housing, in cases where enterprises lacked their own dormitories, even longer.[77]

As Soviet enterprises and projects in Leningrad and Moscow remained short of labor, confusion and waits produced chaos as citizens—some with propiski, some without—flowed in and out of cities.[78] In the 1950s, Azamat Sanatbaev, on his first trips from southern Kyrgyzstan to Moscow as a child, recalled the dirtiness, crowds, and chaos of train stations, with hundreds sleeping on the floor as hundreds of thousands moved in and out of the city.[79] Leading Soviet figures, including Deputy Premier Lavrentii Beria, condemned the cumbersome registration system as preventing an efficient distribution of labor. In 1954, however, "zones of special regime" were extended to dozens of cities, due to the continued fear of an internal enemy and belief that this was the only path to manage population flows in a rapidly urbanizing society.[80] The expansion also recognized that consumer allocation polices favored major cities and sought to stem numbers of traders who operated on gray or black markets. Cities retained their cultural importance; those who violated behavioral norms—including Muscovite women accused of sleeping with foreigners in 1957—were expelled.[81]

Even as the propiska controlled movement, official discourse discussed migration to large cities in uniquely positive terms. Party leaders and Soviet planners considered large urban spaces as ideal engines of social and ethnic mixture and modernization, as they worked toward the realization of a new Soviet man. All citizens could contribute to, and benefit from, the building of modern cities.[82] Such a common enterprise would incorporate, instead of—as they believed occurred in the West—isolate new urban residents. Soviet commentators noted with pride that Caucasus and Central Asian nationalities were urbanizing at a faster pace than all other national groups in the USSR in postwar decades, even if overall numbers remained below average.[83] Urbanization was the most effective path to overcome backwardness and erode traditions as eyes were opened to a "broader world."[84] At the same time, this discourse centered on major republican capitals, such as Tbilisi, Georgia; Alma-Ata, Kazakhstan; or Tashkent, Uzbekistan, where ethnic Russian dominance in administrative and skilled positions, a holdover from the tsarist era and enforced by Stalin's preferential trust, remained.[85] Leningrad and Moscow offered shining examples of the Soviet Union's promise, but careful limits remained on movement toward them. Azamat Sanatbaev, who led Central Asian tour groups to Moscow in the 1970s, recalled his task: "to instruct how Communism could connect Central Asians to urban life and that there would eventually be one Soviet people."[86] First, however, the periphery needed to be elevated to the center's level.

Ambivalent Soviet views and practices toward mixture and movement subsumed Leningrad and Moscow. The two capitals operated as, in Oren Yiftachel's labeling based on studies of major privileged cities worldwide, "gray zones."[87] Gray zones emerge as state and urban leaders struggle to reconcile the limitations of official channels to provide appropriate or sufficient human capital to modern cities with a desire for control over treasured, central spaces. In the 1950s and beyond, hundreds of thousands of Soviet citizens streamed in and out of Leningrad and Moscow, as well as Tbilisi and Tashkent, daily—working, shopping, studying, sightseeing, visiting friends or relatives, short- or long-term. They brought skills and energy, enforcing the status and desirability of Soviet capitals. Enforcement for lack of residence documentation was sporadic and penalties arbitrary. Those discovered without a permit could be warned; dropped, in the case of Moscow, at the "101st kilometer" just outside the propiska zone; imprisoned; or sent to internal exile in faraway cities. The propiska did not fulfill its fundamental goal of cleansing cities of "undesirables." Some who arrived in Leningrad and Moscow sought to avoid persecution or prosecution in their home

FIGURE 1   Man from the Caucasus in traditional headdress, in front of Moscow's Hotel Metropol in 1954. Attribution: Henri Cartier-Bresson / © Magnum Photos

territories. Reza Ahmedova, whose father was purged and shot in Baku, Azerbaijan, in 1937 when she was six, applied to a technical institute in Leningrad, hoping, successfully as it turned out, that no one would ask for or examine her distant file.[88] A blackballed father used a connection to place his son, expelled from the Yerevan Art Institute due to unreliable family connections, in a similar institution in Moscow.[89] Soviet citizens, near and far, saw central urban spaces as potential refuges as well as places of opportunity. They could melt away and avoid the stain of personal or family misdeeds documented in distant, home republics.

Education provided a pathway to incorporation for southern and eastern non-Russian, Soviet citizens in Leningrad and Moscow. The 1959 census registered 80,500 Tatars in Moscow, as well as around 5,000 Armenians and Georgians respectively.[90] Soviet ethnologist Iu. V. Bromlei noted that postwar Tatar migrants, many who had served in the Soviet army, became increasingly bilingual. Newcomers tended to join more integrated networks in the two capitals, including students who had attended Russian-language schools.[91] Large numbers of Tatar students now stamped the diaspora as privileged in the eyes of the host population. Student and professional arrivals to Leningrad and Moscow also increased from Azerbaijan, the product of a society that had significantly urbanized in the 1930s, led by the burgeoning oil industry.[92] Party schools in the two capitals continued to train future leaders of all Soviet republics, as postwar Soviet policy sought once more to "nativize" republican administration through korenizatsiia.[93]

Students from across the Soviet Union became a common sight in Leningrad and Moscow in the 1950s and beyond. Growing education systems in the Caucasus and Central Asia, now stretching to rural regions, increased youth numbers proceeding to secondary and then to tertiary education. Russian-language schooling in these southern republics expanded from cities with substantial Russian populations to the countryside, where an education in Russian quickly became associated with social mobility.[94] Aibek Botoev recalled the popularity of his Russian school in a 1950s Kyrgyz village, over one hundred kilometers from the capital, Frunze, and Eliso Svanidze stated that in her village in the Abkhaz region of Georgia all parents with aspirations for their children sent them to a Russian school.[95] Such beliefs redounded across the Soviet Union. As Russian gained a recognition as the language of science, technology, and intercultural communication, the Soviet state sought to ensure that all students who desired an education in its privileged tongue could do so, even if it meant the closure of "national" schools.[96]

Russian-language instruction and higher education in Russia became keys to social and professional mobility union-wide. Leningrad's and Moscow's institutes of higher education were universally recognized as unparalleled in quality and career opportunities.[97] Students took several paths to find their way to the two capitals. Levan Rukhadze recalled sweating out exam results in Yerevan, knowing that only one of thirty-three students would gain admission to a Leningrad radio-technological school in 1969. He expressed frustration that sons of party officials, he was certain, gained favors in the selection process.[98] Oidin Nosirova plotted her studies in late 1970s Tashkent, aware of what disciplines would offer the least competition for spots in Leningrad and Moscow universities; she eventually settled on German philology.[99] Fuad Ojagov selected psychology as a career path, knowing that the discipline was not taught at universities in his hometown of Baku. In such cases, the chances of being sent to Russia, and his preferred destination of Moscow, greatly improved—the Ministry of Higher Education would open spots for professions declared to be "in scarcity" in certain republics.[100]

Nosirova and Ojagov joined swelling numbers of Muslims who arrived in Leningrad and Moscow in the postwar decades. The practice of religion, particularly Islam, emerged as an element that produced confusion and tension among municipal and state authorities. In the 1950s, over ten thousand Muslims gathered on Fridays to worship at Moscow's one functioning mosque.[101] In Leningrad, Tatars and other Muslims struggled to convince city leaders to reopen a mosque that had been closed in the 1930s. Prayers occurred at Leningrad's one Muslim cemetery. Municipal authorities linked requests for a mosque to global Islamic awareness in an age of decolonization. A mosque, they argued, might allow a focus for fanaticism and spread discontent, as it had in British and French imperial holdings. Leningrad's militia sometimes harassed prayer gatherings. The Council of Ministers of the RSFSR, however, ordered the mosque reopened in 1955.[102] It concluded that migrants might engage in antistate activity if they felt cultural needs were unfulfilled. In Moscow, the council worried that the city's one Islamic cemetery was insufficient, given that 90 percent of Soviet Muslims preferred to bury their dead according to religious custom.[103] Moscow's imam, Kamaretdit Salekhov, lauded the state, telling adherents at Eid in 1957 that they should feel fortunate to be under a government that took such care of them and allowed them to practice their religion.[104] By the late 1960s, forty thousand attended services in Moscow's mosque in the officially atheist USSR.[105]

FIGURE 2 Inside a Moscow mosque in 1954. Attribution: Henri Cartier-Bresson / © Magnum Photos

The Cold War rippled in the politics behind Leningrad's mosque reopening. Khrushchev's desire to deploy favored treatment of non-European Soviet peoples as a weapon against the West echoed in the two capitals. Islam played an important role in this strategy, despite the Soviet leader's antipathy to religion. Moscow coordinated policies of the USSR's Muslim Spiritual Board, in part to facilitate state control, and imams played an important role in Soviet propaganda strategies abroad.[106] From the 1950s onward, Moscow's mosque hosted visits from international delegations, including from Syria, Lebanon, and Pakistan, and even a curious West German contingent.[107] The periodical *Muslims of the Soviet East*, published in Arabic, French, English, and Uzbek, portrayed cultural and religious integration into a secular, modern Soviet state. Central Asians emerged as the ideal mediators, with select party members leaving their republican capitals to work in Moscow's foreign policy establishment.[108] N. A. Mukhitidin, an Uzbek candidate member of the Politburo, became known as the Kremlin's "Muslim in residence," escorting foreign delegations on tours of Moscow.[109] Longer itineraries included Leningrad and Tashkent, held up as the Soviet showcase city in Central Asia, a symbol of how the USSR invested in its Asian peripheries whereas the West had abandoned them.[110] Mukhitidin also traveled abroad extensively with Central Asian delegations, including as part of the Soviet Committee for Solidarity with Asia and Africa, founded in 1956. Moscow grew as a stage to project the potential for global equality and non-racism.[111] By the turn of the 1980s, Soviet writers claimed that these decades of interaction offered proof that "no capital has a greater global significance than Moscow, which serves the idea of peace and brotherhood among peoples."[112]

Education became implicated in Moscow's global strategy. Thousands of "Afro-Asians," potential players in the Cold War's struggle for influence, studied across the USSR.[113] In 1960, to formalize and deepen ties with Third World states, the Peoples' Friendship University—renamed the next year the Patrice Lumumba University after the assassinated Congolese leader—opened its doors.[114] Spearheaded by the Soviet Committee for Solidarity with Asia and Africa, the university offered generous stipends to students from the nonaligned world. Even as university leaders union-wide advocated for recruiting Asians and Africans of lower-class backgrounds, who could empathize with the Communist revolutionary cause, places and scholarships were allocated to foreign governments. Cold War imperatives—such as gaining the loyalty of foreign leaders—outweighed loftier and longer-term goals of spreading socialism. Patronage, instead of class background, emerged as the key to prestigious university spots, particularly in Leningrad and Moscow. Efforts to court African leaders extended to invitations to join top Soviet officials atop Lenin's mausoleum to watch Moscow's May Day celebrations.[115] Institutes of higher education proliferated in the two capitals, but could never meet insatiable demands from across the USSR, Communist Eastern Europe, and the Third World. Aryuna Khamagova, a Buryat who failed entrance exams to Leningrad State University, determined that, somehow, someway, she would get an education in Moscow or Leningrad, in her words "the sacred center and subcenter" of the socialist world.[116] By 1979, those with a higher education in Leningrad doubled the all-union average, at 20 percent; in Moscow, the number of students in seventy-five institutes of higher education reached 632,000.[117]

Leningrad and Moscow faced challenges in coping with population growth rates, driven primarily by in-migration. Study and work opportunities provided the foundation for broader dreams. As one migrant from the Russian provinces stated: "Yes, to flee, to flee, to Moscow, to Moscow. . . . Everyone would be more educated, there would be museums, and everything if I were to leave the provinces for the capital of my country."[118] State investment in public housing stock failed to keep pace with a population that, as their education and status improved, demanded better living conditions. Leningrad's and Moscow's ever-growing web of government agencies and enterprises, as in Western global cities chronicled by Sassen, catered to "salaried professionals and managers" through "distinct consumption patterns, lifestyles and high-income gentrification."[119] Even as Soviet practices softened this social differentiation in Leningrad and Moscow, demands for services from an increasingly acquisitive population, as later chapters show, required a broad spectrum of migration to provide the necessary labor. New residents lacking official connections or documentation were renting corners of rooms or living in overcrowded dormitories.[120] Leningrad's and Moscow's pull only increased through the 1970s and beyond. Soviet policies to develop the periphery stalled as the two cities' reputations and opportunities loomed ever larger in the minds of citizens from the most distant reaches of the Soviet Union.

The Soviet Turn from the South

Even as efforts to gain "Afro-Asian" loyalty intensified at the turn of the 1960s, Khrushchev grew wary of continued investment to showcase Central Asia as the epitome of postcolonial success. He complained of squabbling among leaders of the region's republics, which had played a role in scuttling his plan for an All–Central Asian Economic Council.[121] Soviet retrenchment deepened in the Brezhnev era, with capital projects focused increasingly on European Russia and extractive industries in Russia's east. Western analysts at the time noted that this fit with global patterns of reduced engagement between Europe and underdeveloped, former colonial regions, which had amplified global north-south disparities in the 1960s and 1970s. Would Soviet policies now produce, as they had in the

West, substantial movement to the metropole? Would Communist authorities, as had European governments, struggle to contain the growing anger of host societies toward newcomers from former colonies? Even as the USSR maintained distinct social and economic strategies that reduced the scale of migration, it faced challenges in managing mobility as regional inequality deepened.

The Soviet investment that had poured into the Caucasus and, especially, Central Asia in the 1950s and early 1960s did little to advance sustainable regional economies. Soviet planners focused on "showcase" developments, such as the irrigation of the Hungry Steppe (Golodnaia step') in Uzbekistan and the Nurek dam in Tajikistan.[122] Resources and outputs were still tied to an all-union system controlled from Moscow and directed to secondary industries in the European heartland of Russia. Industrial, technical, and administrative leadership remained predominantly Slavic. Even as Central Asians who attended Slavic-dominated, Russian-language technical institutes slowly climbed workplace ladders, Russian engineers and skilled workers flooded these postwar projects to ensure, ostensibly, their success.[123] Artemy Kalinovsky notes that the large, self-contained Slavic presence led Tajik economists to see the Nurek dam as depressing, instead of helping, local employment.[124] Complaints from republican leaderships on the failure to engage Central Asian engineers and skilled labor were met with silence.[125] The effects of these broader policies filtered down to the individual level. Aibek Botoev, who studied in Frunze in the early 1970s, recalled that the dominance of "arrogant" Russians in management and technical positions across Kyrgyzstan prompted him to leave for cosmopolitan Leningrad, where, he hoped, Soviet equality might be realized. His home, he believed, suffered from "colonization, pure and simple."[126]

Reduced investment on the periphery led U.S. Cold War scholars to consider similarities in Soviet and Western models of development. In both cases, industrialized cores were drawing increasing resources from peripheries—either within or beyond state borders—and perpetuating hinterland economies that neither were self-sufficient nor had significantly expanded beyond the extraction of raw materials.[127] As regional disparities increased, growing numbers of Europeans left skilled positions in adopted southern territories for opportunities in the more prosperous—socialist or capitalist—north. In Central Asia's Ferghana Valley, Slavic out-migration lowered the numbers of Russian-language teachers, even as the demand for education in Russian increased. As early as 1967, the Central Committee of the Communist Party of the Kyrgyzstan implored Moscow to dispatch pedagogues to train local instructors who could effectively teach the Russian language, necessary for entrance into prestigious schools even in their own republics.[128] As skilled workers and planners departed, Nancy Lubin noted deteriorating housing stocks and factory maintenance in Central Asia's machine-building, metal, and chemical industries.[129] By 1976, Uzbekistan experienced significant labor shortages in industrial sectors, even as it was one of the least industrialized republics in the USSR.[130] Tajik economists urged Moscow to abandon its strategies of narrow development paths for each republic and advance plans capable of lifting the Soviet south's living standards to all-union levels.[131] Moscow ignored these pleas; Leonid Brezhnev claimed in 1972 that significant problems of regional inequality within the Soviet Union had been resolved.[132]

Patterns of movement by local populations as well as Russians echoed global trends. The 1970 all-union census had revealed that Central Asians were becoming more likely than those in other regions to migrate outside their own republics, with Russia as their primary destination.[133] Far higher birthrates among Central Asians than Slavic populations in the USSR, accompanied by deepening regional inequality, led demographer Robert A. Lewis in 1976 to envisage migration to Russia as a "major influence upon Soviet society" in future decades.[134] Central Asian planners worked to convince Moscow that its young, now well-educated population made it an ideal place to spark Soviet industrial growth, which could also reduce migratory pressures.[135] Despite gaining some sympathy in central planning agencies, the "system ultimately proved too inflexible to balance the social and economic goals of its constituencies."[136]

Kyrgyz, Tajiks, Turkmen, and Uzbeks registered as living in Russia increased from 140,000 to 248,000 from 1970 to 1979.[137] Concentrated among those under thirty years of age, this was important growth to be sure—and, as discussed in later chapters, was accompanied by substantial informal migration. For the moment, Soviet social and economic mechanisms stemmed further movement northward. Moscow's planners allowed collective farm managers to hoard labor, so that ever-increasing numbers of agricultural workers in the Caucasus, and especially Central Asia, retained a level of employment and social support. Wage differentials between the USSR's periphery and core remained far less than those between other former European colonies and once imperial heartlands.[138] Even so, as employment grew 35 percent in Central Asia between 1970 and 1979, the working-age population had grown by 46 percent.[139]

Central Asian leaders and planners, facing declining investment and attention from Moscow, considered narrowed options to develop their republics. Soviet voices and policies characterized local populations as rural in nature and outlook, and channeled them toward agricultural sectors. Central Asians' desires to consider work in Russian-dominated cities or industrial regions, even in their home territory, diminished.[140] Even as official and academic discourse vaunted the advantages of urban life, and as the quality of rural housing declined as investment lessened in the 1970s, some local intellectuals, such as the Kyrgyz writer Tugelbai Sydybekov, argued that the local population should remain in their "natural" homes.[141] In 1982, Bromlei developed arguments that urban, factory life would remain alien to Central Asians unless it was, somehow, made to reflect their traditions.[142] In later research, he claimed, along with Iu. V. Arutiunian, that Uzbeks had the highest rate of any nationality in preferring a "rural life." Early marriages and a high number of children also gravitated against movement away from villages and traditional lifestyles.[143] Cultural differences undergirded stereotypes of the south as a place of excessive corruption, graft, and nepotism. Proposals for economic changes to match and benefit from demographic shifts foundered as "the idea that Central Asians were too different had taken hold too deeply."[144] Soviet leaders saw them as unlikely to work hard in urban or industrial settings—investment monies would be far better spent in the north, where enterprises could be staffed by more advanced populations.

Union-wide disparities between population distribution and economic opportunities became the subject of increased concern in Soviet planning agencies from the late 1970s. Labor shortages intensified in the Far East, home to substantial mineral extraction projects. The Central Statistical Administration affirmed that Central Asian economies, where output and productivity already lagged, lacked the capacity to absorb growing populations, with an average 3.9 children birthrate per family.[145] Collective and state farm practices of employing more workers than needed produced what Soviet scholars now coined "hidden unemployment."[146] The surplus of manual labor led to an underuse of agricultural machinery, the purported vehicles of Soviet modernization in the south.[147] Soviet planners were also skeptical that Central Asians, given their ostensible adherence to "tradition," could be made to move to labor-deficit regions. Efforts to devise natal policies that might discourage Central Asians from having more children, all the while promoting demographic growth among Slavic and Baltic peoples in the USSR, foundered, however, against practical concerns as well as fears of potential accusations of racism. Increased demographic and economic discrepancies appeared inevitable without substantial migration, with unpredictable consequences if young, dynamic populations shifted the Soviet Union's center of gravity to the south.[148]

The State Commission of Labor and Social Problems moved to action as yields of cotton and agricultural goods in Central Asia, dependent on nutrient-killing pesticides and marginal soil, declined over the 1970s. It joined efforts to enroll Central Asians in professional-technical institutes (PTUs) across the USSR to attain skills in service and industrial sectors of the economy.[149] Uptake remained low, despite a public media campaign, which included advertisements in the local press.[150] The state also found challenges in placing graduates where their labor was required, primarily on industrial sites or in new towns, with few amenities or links to home, in Siberia and the Far East.[151]

As these formal efforts stumbled, informal networks built on existing connections to Leningrad and Moscow, which remained the most desirable locations for Central Asians to visit or settle in, short- or long-term. Tourists, students, and others returned from stays recalling the two capitals' quality of life. Moscow was "itinerary number 1" for an overwhelming number of Soviet citizens, who believed "all roads" led to the city.[152] Caucasus peoples also enjoyed well-established connections in the two capitals from the Stalin era, including in food distribution, service, and professional sectors.[153] Informal networks emerged as critical to strategies of social and professional mobility. Even as the regime did not target Caucasus peoples for relocation, their home economic situations worsened in the 1970s and 1980s. The growing attraction of Leningrad and Moscow made them primary destinations for short, seasonal, or long-term movement.

Debates intensified through the 1980s over how to manage the growing populations of southern territories that continued to receive smaller shares of all-union investment. In 1990, Soviet demographer V. I. Perevedentsev agreed with Tajik economists that surplus populations in the Caucasus and Central Asia provided "great demographic potential" for a country that continued to modernize.[154] This potential would be best harnessed by industrializing southern cities, especially in Central Asia, as peoples of still "backward" nations would be less likely to travel far from home. He pointed nonetheless to the continued challenge of European dominance in these sites.[155] Under present conditions, a move to Frunze or Tashkent, much less Leningrad or Moscow, required significant personal desire. The legacies of Russian dominance outlasted Khrushchev's brief campaign to outshine the West in developing once colonial lands within Soviet borders. Inflexibility and inequality set the stage for Caucasus and Central Asian peoples to intertwine strategies of mobility and success in the late USSR.

The Propiska Challenged

Newcomers to Leningrad and Moscow faced the vagaries of the propiska system. Even as it expanded in the 1950s and 1960s to create "archipelagos of privilege" in over one hundred cities, Soviet citizens primarily associated residence documentation with the two capitals, the USSR's most desirable homes.[156] Frustration over the system's confused regulations and selective application paralleled postwar Western tensions over mobility across state borders, when the vast majority of newcomers ended up in major cities.[157] By the 1970s, debates over the propiska's effectiveness became entangled in broader discussions over how to use, or move, the untapped labor pool of Soviet peripheries. Migrants, meanwhile, found ways to use, or bypass, the system, exploiting a state that hesitated to dictate choices to its citizens.

Moscow reported significant declines in birthrate as well as an aging population in the 1970s, just as debates about surplus labor in the Soviet south deepened. By 1975, the city's population annual growth rate, at 1.4 percent, was about half the all-union urban average.[158] From 1971 to 1984, of an annual registered increase of fifty thousand citizens, only fifteen thousand stemmed from "natural" growth, with the rest coming from migration.[159] Leningrad's planners also calculated that 70 percent of urban growth was coming from migration.[160] Natural growth rates placed the two cities below major European and North American capitals. As early as 1971, the Moscow City Executive Committee's (Mosgorispolkom) Office of the Use of Labor Resources affirmed that these demographics were affecting the available workforce, a problem that was exacerbated by the fact that the local population's skills were often an ill fit for available jobs.[161] Soviet demographers argued that the propiska system had become self-defeating. In 1980, Tatiana Fedotovskaia noted that, even if successful, efforts to boost Moscow's birthrate—the preferred choice of municipal bureaucrats—would take decades to have any effect, leaving migration as the sole short- and medium-term solution to fill vacancies in several economic sectors.[162] Perevedentsev reported that areas immediately outside Moscow's propiska zone were growing at twice the rate of those inside. The USSR's planning apparatus, he argued, should be able to eliminate the significant inefficiencies of Western economies, where high living costs drove people from metropolitan centers and resulted in long commutes in what the Soviets called "pendular migration."[163] Municipal authorities' systems of planning—or lack thereof—became a frequent target for criticism.[164] B. S. Khorev claimed that, a decade after the Office of the Use of Labor Resource's conclusion, no strategic studies of how to address Moscow's labor needs, present or future, had been conducted.[165] Discussions, but no action, centered on whether greater attention to "economic regulation"—in Soviet parlance the loosening of the propiska regime to allow a freer flow of labor—would address growing shortages in major cities across the USSR, especially in Leningrad and Moscow.[166]

Soviet planning mechanisms struggled to balance control of not only movement but also citizen behavior more broadly, with economic growth and development. Even as the state trumpeted its ability for rational allocation and distributing workers through the *orgnabor* system, it never prescribed training or workplaces for citizens. Workers had significant freedom to choose their place of employment, channeled by education and skills and conditioned by vacancies. Soviet leaders feared that assigning workers through the plan might lead to dissatisfaction, poor morale, and poor quality of production.[167] Soviet citizens had significant control over their workplace lives. Even as the propiska played a role in limiting movement to "regime zones," it became clear, as David Shearer noted and as seen throughout this book, that "determined people could, with relative ease, bypass passport and residency laws if they chose or needed to do so."[168] Migrant decisions played a determinative role in allowing Leningrad and Moscow to act as the USSR's "showcase cities." "Economic regulation," or the loosening of the propiska system, which Soviet demographers favored, was occurring, even if it remained unofficial and hidden in discourse and statistics. Over the 1970s and 1980s, this "regulation" increasingly featured movement from southern peripheries. Not only demographers were aware of differential birthrates and economic growth as they considered migration's importance to the "two capitals."

Some of these determined people simply showed up in Leningrad and Moscow, seeking whatever opportunity they might find. In the mid-1960s, Narynbek Temirkulov traveled to Moscow a couple of weeks after his army service ended, leaving family and friends in Kyrgyzstan. He slept at a train station before going to see an army buddy, whom he hoped would allow him to stay and help him find work.[169] He saw, as did Western scholar Cecil J. Houston on his visits to 1970s Moscow, numerous poster-board street advertisements for work on gas lines and in construction, electronics, nursing, stenography, and other sectors.[170] Azamat Sanatbaev, as he led his tour groups through 1970s Leningrad and Moscow, recalled job postings on street corners and neighborhood labor exchanges willing to match any worker, regardless of status, with an employer.[171] Certain sectors that suffered a high turnaround of employees—janitors, skilled construction workers, even the militia—recruited through the promise of rapidly granting a propiska to any and all successful applicants. Losing interest in university, Anarbek Zakirov applied to enter the militia in 1981, preferring to stay in Moscow over a return to his Kyrgyz home.[172] He gained the document and dormitory accommodation, with the promise of private lodgings in the future. Soviet employers and managers worked to render the propiska system sufficiently flexible to meet labor needs of rapidly growing cities.

A subcategory of residence documentation specifically designed to meet ever-changing labor needs was the "limited" (*limitnaia*) propiska. This designation, written in to the original propiska legislation, allowed employers to apply for a limited number of supplemental workers over each plan period. These hires would be given time-limited residence permits and be housed most often in enterprise dormitories.[173] Many at the time equated this system, linked to specific employment, to the West German guest worker program.[174] As Leningrad's and Moscow's labor needs grew more acute, this status was increasingly used, with young men who were finishing army service prime targets. In 1973, as Emily Elliott found, the Moscow City Executive Committee concluded that so-called *limitchiki* (those on limited propiski) composed 91 percent of migration-related growth, as enterprise directors worked closely with Moscow's Office of the Use of Labor Resources to issue permits.[175] Victor Zaslavsky believed that *limitchiki* made up 15 percent of Moscow's total labor force, and up to 90 percent in construction, in the 1970s and 1980s.[176] Teachers were also recruited through the offer of limited propiski ("*po limitu*") beginning in the 1980s. An estimated 95 percent of *limitchiki*, who traveled from Russian villages just outside the 100-kilometer zone, and beyond, to the farthest reaches of the USSR, were under the age of thirty, and about half arrived as unskilled labor.[177] Tolkunbek Kudubaev, who was one of the estimated 76 percent of *limitchiki* who arrived independently, rather than being recruited, built installations for new Moscow metro stations after his studies in Osh.[178] His permit was valid for one year and renewable. The potential to be replaced at any time and ejected from Moscow, in his view, proved a strong motivation for performance.[179] Soviet citizens and enterprises alike worked the residence permit system in their favor, even as it remained a barrier to potential migrants lacking the connections or will to arrive in Leningrad or Moscow without the status that granted rights to residence, education, health care, and access to goods.

The Soviet Union's efforts to balance positive representations of, and favoritism toward, its central cities with controlled movement produced all manner of unforeseen, though not always undesirable, consequences. The propiska, as the main Soviet vehicle to control movement within its borders, became entangled in a global debate about how to deal with the human impact of the structural imbalances created through postwar policies that perpetuated, if not deepened, regional and postcolonial inequalities. Missing in the Soviet era was official language or policies that advocated limiting migration specifically from the USSR's south, with its non-white populations. Such movement was encouraged, if only to less-desirable, labor-poor eastern regions of Russia, rather than the republic's major showcase cities of Leningrad and Moscow.

Uzbek migrant Shuhrat Ikramov recalled Leningrad and Moscow, where he studied and worked from 1979 to 1985, as the "centers of [his] part of the world."[180] The two capitals' perch at the top of imperial hierarchies rose in the Soviet period, as knowledge of their privileges spread across the massive state and beyond. Internal and external "Easts" became critical to global Leningrad's and Moscow's status and development. Connections that bound edges and centers strengthened even as, or perhaps because, European powers, including the Soviet Union, focused their attention on Western cores, especially capital cities, in the last decades of the twentieth century. Migration symbolized the agency of those in poorer southern regions and presented dilemmas for host societies as networks and means of travel facilitated movement. To become, or remain, global cities required human energy and capital, something that aging European populations increasingly lacked.

Global cities are marked by paradoxes; even as they sought, and to a degree achieved, control and command functions that stretched across countries and continents, they largely failed to control the movement of people within their own boundaries. Even as, in Stephen Castles and Mark J. Miller's view, "no government ever set out to build an ethnically diverse society through immigration," neither did any government have a coherent plan to prevent one. Global cities became global in terms of demographic makeup, not by intention.[181] In the USSR as in the West, state priorities of labor market flexibility, economic development, and global political power overcame its quest for control over the movement of peoples and subsumed potential resistance from host societies to migrants who looked or sounded different than they did.

Migrant energy surmounted ambivalent state efforts to direct careers and lives. Southern and eastern newcomers were well aware of the Soviet version of "spatially distributed qualities of life" and the spectrum of opportunities, official and unofficial, available in Leningrad and Moscow.[182] They claimed their "right to the city" and brought skills and labor that propelled the growth of the two capitals.[183] Continued Russian dominance in their home territories made Leningrad and Moscow hubs for national as well as personal progress, home for all peoples seeking membership in a modern world.

FRIENDSHIP, FREEDOM, MOBILITY, AND THE ELDER BROTHER

The *druzhba narodov* (friendship of peoples) evokes passion decades after the Soviet Union's collapse. Migrants from Central Asia, the Caucasus, and Asian lands of Russia vividly recall the slogan's effect on their identity and daily lives. Different in appearance and culture from host societies in Slavic-dominated cities, they measured their reception against a mantra that appeared in school textbooks, on large public posters, and in Soviet publications and media for as long as they could remember. The friendship's emotional impact was linked to strategies and opportunities for advancement for those who moved between home regions and Russia's core. Overall sentiments remained complex. Migrants voiced frustration at the privileged station of ethnic Russians in the friendship's hierarchy of peoples, but expressed appreciation for how interethnic relationships evolved. In Leningrad and Moscow, even those unfamiliar with the cities' language or culture felt empathy, or at least equality, in official interactions. Personal, cross-cultural friendships held strong places in their memories. The *druzhba narodov* was recognized as a central Soviet tenet that allowed character and ability to triumph, regardless of national background, in new homes.

The friendship of peoples, devised in the 1930s, praised the contributions each officially recognized nation within the Soviet Union made toward a modern socialist society and a united Soviet people (*sovetskii narod*). Each national territory within the USSR, even as it afforded certain privileges to its "titular" population, was home to all citizens, with minorities enjoying state-sponsored rights and protections. Erik Scott has labeled this policy "domestic internationalism," and it became a guiding precept of the Soviet state.[1] Not all peoples were equal in the friendship, however. Russians emerged as "first among equals" or, when family instead of friendship motifs were used, "the elder brother" (*starshii brat*). Large cities, at once multiethnic and Russian-dominated, became central sites of the friendship. Peoples gathered from across the USSR to seek advancement, for themselves and their state, in lecture halls, offices, and shop floors. They helped each other, in migrant memories, strive for common goals. Mutual enrichment, as well as assistance, was grounded in the idea that each national group possessed a uniqueness, fostered and celebrated by the state. Delegations visited each other's major cities to showcase the USSR's diversity. Leningrad and Moscow topped the urban hierarchy as desired destinations for national festivals as well as seasonal or permanent residence. Leningrad was the USSR's scholarly heart and cultural center. Moscow was "everybody's capital" (*dlia vsekh stolitsa*). Soviet identity was bound to the city. In one typical literary paean, Moscow was a "symbol of a new world, the center for the struggle for peace and friendship among peoples, the center of international connections between actors of science and culture, the meeting place for those seeking social progress, the equality of peoples and happiness for everyone in the world."[2]

Happiness, even love, undergirded the friendship. Its unfurling in words and practice over the decades created what Barbara H. Rosenwein has characterized as an "emotional community," with practical and psychological effects. Emotional communities emerge in political and social environments as "systems of feeling," with common perceptions of what is valuable—in this case, strong cross-cultural relationships and universal progress toward a modern society—and what is harmful—national discord that could threaten social peace or even the foundations of the multinational state.[3] Christine Evans has noted the importance of common emotions in the popularity of Brezhnev-era television. "Emotions," she writes, "not words or social categories, were essential to both revealing and promoting the proper affective relationship to Soviet life."[4] Evans limits her conclusions to Slavic peoples and the Brezhnev era; emotional engagements, this chapter shows, had a broader spread and deep origins. Communities could overlap and clash; Georgians and Armenians, for example, could at times elevate national communities over a Soviet one.

The friendship of peoples, I argue, gained "agentive power."[5] In a society with tight state control of political expression and the media, Alexei Yurchak has argued, the conventions of a speech act can structure lived realities. Soviet citizens nonetheless had complex and differentiated relationships to ideological norms, means, or values, which could be based on individual or community characteristics.[6] They worked to make the friendship their own. Unlike Juliane Fürst, who refers to the "emptied, formulaic nature of the official discourse [which] allows its purely performative practice," the words migrants spoke, the relationships they

FIGURE 3   Representatives of the fifteen constituent republics of the USSR at the 1980 Moscow Olympics. Attribution: RIA Novosti archive / Vladimir Vyatkin / CC-BY-SA 3.0

nurtured, and the rituals they viewed or participated in, draped in friendship, held meaning for individual and state alike.[7]

Emotions overlapped, somewhat unevenly, with the Soviet state's efforts to link citizenship and inclusion to feelings, as a means to prescribe dominant modes of emotional life.[8] The oral histories we collected a decade-plus after the USSR's end demonstrate, as Yurchak writes, a "longing for very real humane values, ethics, friendships and creative possibilities that the reality of socialism afforded."[9] Said Nabiev recalled this longing when interviewed in 2007: "A shared [Soviet] worldview appeared for us, which unfortunately was ripped apart. But to this day, with any older person, I can talk to them about the damage that was done to us."[10] Julie Livingston points to in-person communication in allowing her, as a scholar, to take emotions seriously: "I became frustrated by how distorted my own interviews seemed when they were stripped of their performative and emotional qualities and reduced to texts."[11] Past and present, emotions matter to individuals, especially across the stressful transformation that resulted in the end of the Soviet Union.

Mixing migrant voices and official discourse exposes the layers and complexity of the friendship of peoples and its relationship to Soviet mobility. The state enjoyed the power to set conventions and interactions, but Soviet citizens seized the friendship and perpetuated it decades after the USSR's end. The Second World War, common citizenship, and the place of ethnic Russians emerged as touchstones in the druzhba narodov. Leningrad and Moscow also held special and durable places in this friendship, through festivals that marked their place as homes for all, even if only in a symbolic or temporary sense. The emotional effects of the friendship linked to practical strategies for mobility and psychological states of belonging.

Evolution

The friendship of the peoples emerged from 1930s nationality policies to create and bind citizens, enforce hierarchies that privileged ethnic Russians, and place the state at the center of Soviet life. Equality, uniqueness, and paternalism coexisted, sometimes uneasily, but durably, entwining emotional and practical components. The Second World War provided a legitimizing event and memory that reached to the farthest corners of the Soviet Union and endured through the Brezhnev era. Soviet migrants deployed wartime ideals of unity to emplace themselves as full and equal citizens regardless of ethnic background or location in the vast Soviet Union, even as Leningrad and Moscow retained their privileged status as Russian-dominated cities.

Joseph Stalin laid the groundwork for an ostensible cross-national partnership in the mid-1930s Soviet Union, as part of a suite of policies that included the 1936 constitution. A new statewide alliance could be forged, a generation removed from tsarist imperialism, as ethnic-based civil war resistance to the emergent Soviet regime had finally dissipated. Domestic opposition to Stalin's agenda and the looming Nazi threat also motivated the drive for partnership among Communist Party leaders.[12] Stalin pronounced in 1935: "The friendship of the peoples of the USSR is a great and serious victory. For while this friendship exists, the peoples of the country will be free and unconquerable. While this friendship lives and blossoms, we are afraid of no one, neither internal nor external enemies."[13] Emotional attachment would bind all citizens to protect the USSR; as *Pravda* wrote in 1935, "Soviet patriotism is a burning feeling of boundless love."[14] Nikolai Bukharin wrote in *Izvestiia* that each nationality had its own constituent role as part of a "heroic Soviet people."[15] Stalin's Soviet Union prioritized the creation of an affective community in the face of the challenges of daily life and economic transformation.[16] Trust and camaraderie purportedly abounded among nations, with nationality replacing class as an organizing principle to consolidate the Soviet Union as a body politic.

Citizenship, arriving with the 1936 constitution, provided evidence of the benefits of Soviet rule. All peoples within state boundaries became full citizens as individuals with equal legal rights before the state. A 1938 Citizenship Act made jus sanguinis (citizenship determined through parents' belonging to the state) the sole criterion for inclusion.[17] The act provided numerous paths through which citizenship could be stripped, but none were based on ethnicity. All those who identified with the state, and, especially in the 1930s, its leader, could be classified as good citizens.[18]

Soviet citizenship, as Golfo Alexopoulos notes, evolved around two pillars, both of which played important roles in the expression and reception of the friendship of peoples.[19] The first was action. Citizens were expected to work, to shape their society and move the country toward a socialist modernity. They would participate in political rituals and display loyalty. The second was emotion. In working for the state, the Soviet citizen was expected to be happy and to express this happiness. As Stalin had declared in 1936: "A new emotional life had truly begun."[20] In radiating enthusiasm for life and labor, as standards for the average Soviet person were ostensibly improving, citizens would "arouse envy" among those in the industrialized world, suffering through the Great Depression.[21] Serhy Yekelchyk classified Stalin's efforts as creating "civic emotions," which marked people's inclusion in a political world but did not necessarily reflect personal beliefs.[22] Elizabeth Perry has noted the tie between happiness and labor in other aspiring twentieth-century communist states. Regimes perform "emotion work," looking to direct positive feelings and aspirations toward the creation of an environment that will move states ahead of capitalist counterparts.[23]

The Soviet press performed this emotion work. It used languages of friendship and affection in the 1930s and beyond to highlight the contribution of each Soviet person, and nation, toward the friendship of peoples. Leningrad and Moscow appeared as the centers of emotional life. Moscow, especially, was "the place that every socialist city was supposed to emulate" and "the city that every citizen was supposed to love or cherish more than his or her own birthplace."[24] Figures and delegations from Soviet republics who visited Leningrad and Moscow to present their republic's contribution to the union received featured coverage. The two capitals were praised for their willingness to host individual scholars, cultural figures, or professionals from across the USSR. These contacts allowed Russians, as "first among equals" or "elder brothers," to appreciate and improve the lives of those from various peripheries. Once condemned by Bolsheviks as "Great Russian chauvinism," the discourse that reinvigorated Russian superiority now involved emotions of gratitude, admiration, and selflessness from Soviet peoples.[25] Affection, not exploitation, would guide nations to future equality and development.[26]

The Soviet regime established ground rules of expression within the friendship. Cultural uniqueness was encouraged, but only within the national medium of officially recognized Soviet peoples, and only when devoid of political content.[27] Soviet citizens fortunate enough to receive tickets to visit Leningrad and Moscow in the 1930s received education on proper Soviet messaging to their republics.

Azerbaijan and Central Asia, considered home to "backward" nationalities, were particularly subject to this treatment. Early Uzbek filmmakers studied under the supervision of leading Russian cinematographers.[28] Directors of Kyrgyz theater and concert troupes received education in Western theory and were expected to pay homage to their Leningrad and Moscow counterparts.[29] Efforts to found a Karakalpak national theater were led by Russian poet O. I. Ryzhova, who offered lessons at Moscow's Lunacharskii Theatrical Institute. In subsequent literature, Karakalpak authors lauded Moscow "friends" for "determining the path" of the nation's theater.[30] Such efforts persisted throughout the Soviet era. Said Nabiev, from the mountainous region of Khorog in Tajikistan, gained admission to the Moscow Institute of Cinematography in 1960 at the tender age of sixteen.[31] He joined other youth who were to acquire the foundations of their craft from leading Russian experts, instead of those in their own republics.

The Soviet victory in the Second World War offered concrete evidence of the friendship of peoples and became a foundational memory. Beginning in 1942, Soviet wartime propaganda emphasized the specific contributions of all Soviet nationalities—from Ukrainians to Kyrgyz—in the battles against the Nazi invaders.[32] Friendship and mutual aid, on the battlefield and off, epitomized the common history and destiny of the Soviet Union. Kazakh soldiers gained praise for their role in liberating Leningrad; Uzbek civilians were honored for housing millions of Soviet evacuees in Uzbekistan.[33] Socialism and modernism, as state discourses, took a backseat in press and popular accounts of Soviet suffering and heroism, now the domain of every "patriot nation."[34]

Ideals of pride and sacrifice animated the friendship of peoples, as later migrants to Leningrad and Moscow testified when they considered the war's place in their affection for both their national homeland and the Soviet Union.[35] Farshad Hajiev, a Tajik student who studied in 1980s Moscow, recalled: "My father fought for this country. Hitler overran the entire continent of Europe in months, but there is no way that they could have won against such a multinational state as the Soviet Union. In my family alone we lost eight people: four of my father's brothers and four of my mother's brothers. They didn't fight for Tajikistan. No, they fought for the entire Soviet Union."[36] Jumaboi Esoev, a butcher from the Pamir Mountains who was selected to upgrade his skills in Leningrad in 1983, argued passionately that the "friendship of peoples existed": "It was real. My grandfather fought in the war, together with people from all over the Soviet Union. The entire Soviet Union fought the Nazis together."[37] Fridon Tsereteli saw his experience as a Georgian student in 1980s Moscow as confirmation of the war's enduring impact. It brought Soviet peoples closer, emerging from tragedy to build a great and united country:

It is just the nature of a human being that when everyone is in a bad situation they are able to share their misfortunes and open up their souls to others. In the Soviet Union, everyone was in a difficult situation [as the war ended]. They were closer because of this shared misfortune, because people helped each other out. One person would get a hold of kerosene through connections and share with neighbors, and another would get a hold of some shoes and so on. People of all different nationalities had to depend on each other to get by. Everybody was in the same situation.[38]

Victory and recovery in the Second World War gave a sense of community, durability, and strength based on friendship—one that was, according to Jasur Haydarov, torn asunder by a Gorbachev generation, which, facing far lesser dangers, led the country to ruin.[39]

Mass education, especially after the war, geared itself to perpetuate the friendship of peoples. National intellectuals, many who had trained in 1930s–1940s Leningrad and Moscow, worked in the post-Stalin years to cast the history of each Soviet people within a community that long predated the USSR. Textbooks, lessons, and other educational media stressed timeless unity and amity among now Soviet nations that together resisted, valiantly if not always successfully, outside invaders from the Mongols to the Nazis.[40] Students recalled the emotional effect of the messages they received. In 1950s Samarkand, Marat Tursunbaev remembered: "From childhood and all through my education the idea of internationalism and equality of peoples was instilled in me."[41] Asylbek Albiev recalled from his schooling in Kyrgyzstan: "We believed in the slogan 'all for one and one for all'—Russians, Uzbeks, and Kyrgyz in the school all believed in this idea."[42] As schools became engines of Soviet patriotism, each nation was seen to be bound in a voluntary association based on mutual interests and regard.

Russian superiority remained a touchstone of relations between Soviet peoples. Stalin privileged the Russian people in his renowned toast celebrating victory over Nazi forces in 1945: "I drink, before all, to the health of the Russian people, because in this war they earned general recognition as the leading force of the Soviet Union among all the nationalities of this country."[43] Russian preeminence now transmitted backward to the past. National histories of Caucasus and Central Asian peoples written in the 1950s altered characterizations of tsarist-era conquests. Imperial-era violence and subjugation had already been downgraded—what Soviet writers in the 1920s condemned as the embodiment of tsarist bloodthirstiness and Great Russian chauvinism, had become, a decade later, a "lesser evil" compared to Western colonialism.[44] Now, national historians cast tsarist expansion as a "uniquely progressive phenomenon."[45] Russian settlers to the Caucasus and Central Asia, in their narratives, held proto-socialist ideals, and administrators sought to instill modern economic development. Postwar textbooks endowed Russians a status equal to "all other peoples combined."[46] Ideas of friendship and (big) brotherhood alternated in Soviet discourse, to provide emotive bonds that alternately underlined love, obligation, and voluntary affection over equality.[47]

Russian continued its ascent as the Soviet Union's *lingua franca* in the postwar years. Universal study of Russian became a Soviet mandate in 1938, to prepare recruits for military service.[48] Soldiers from across the USSR learned Russian in the army and brought the language home with them after the Second World War.[49] Russian became the common language of Soviet institutions across the multinational union. The Communist Party saw expanded use of the language as strengthening the friendship of peoples. Debates erupted in the 1950s, as leaders and scholars in non-Russian republics challenged the place of Russian versus titular tongues in national republics.[50] No legislation ever compelled the speaking of Russian, as Communist leaders in Moscow feared provoking a backlash; rather, they, through the media, promoted its common use as a sign of unity and mutual trust. Central authorities maintained a belief that every Soviet student should have the ability to attend a Russian-language school and be able to speak to fellow citizens union-wide.[51] As discussed in chapter 1, such schools rapidly gained recognition as powerful vehicles for social and geographic mobility. The mother of Mirbek Serkebaev, who grew up in the village of Kara-Suu in Kyrgyzstan, sent him to a Russian school in the early 1960s to nurture his "dynamic nature."[52] The school contained Uzbeks, Kyrgyz, Tajiks, Russians, Ukrainians, and others. Its composition symbolized the international aspect of the friendship, even as the exclusive use of one language mirrored and enforced hierarchies among peoples.

Migrants who reflected on growing up in the 1950s and 1960s recalled feelings of unity and friendship within the USSR. Citizenship inspired action and produced positive emotions. Elmira Nasirova remembered, in 1950s Kyrgyzstan: "We very much felt ourselves as Soviet citizens. First, we were involved as 'Little Octobrists' [*oktiabriata*] [an organization for children seven to nine years old], then the Pioneers, and then the Komsomol [Communist Youth League]. They gave us such pride that we were part of the Soviet Union."[53] Arriving in Moscow in 1966, Nasirova assumed the same leading role in a student Komsomol cell as back home. She noted the sameness of rules and regulations and said that she was treated as an equal by Russians and other national groups. Akmal Bobokulov remarked: "It was one country: the Soviet Union. We had the same system, the same rules, the same ideology, so that made it very easy to move around and adapt without any problems."[54] Bakyt Shakiev and others linked a common passport and other features of citizenship to ease of mobility and adaptation: "We felt the same in Bishkek and in Leningrad. That's what the Soviet Union was about. All peoples had the same rights, even as Russians."[55] Sevda Asgarova, recruited from Azerbaijan to study at a Moscow party school in the 1950s, regarded how equal rights and respect spilled over to personal friendships that endured long after she left: "We had friends from various ethnicities: Russians, Kabardians, people of mixed blood. And I associated with every ethnic group. I never noticed anyone considering my ethnicity. Everyone treated me as an individual."[56] Asgarova recalled students organizing evenings devoted to each republic, which sought at once to entertain and educate.

The upholding of Soviet slogans and ideals through practice—in these cases, study, work, or travel—allowed for positive mobility statewide as Soviet citizens adapted to post-Stalin norms.[57] Students noted the continued advantages of a Komsomol membership card (*komsomol'skii bilet*), which triggered emotions of prestige and inclusion, as well as tangible benefits, regardless of national background. Abdul Khalimov recalled from his travels as a student in the late 1970s: "I remember being in Kalinin Oblast one time and I had run out of money. Well I just went to the Komsomol committee and told them who I was, that I was a student of such and such a university, and they gave me money for the trip back home."[58] Citizenship and camaraderie underpinned the friendship of peoples, eliciting emotional responses among Soviet-era migrants for a world of imagined and lived equality, one that foundered at the end of the 1980s and then disappeared. Memories of uniform rights and treatment glimmered in their eyes and words as they considered the absence of these ideals in the postcommunist present.

Common Soviet citizenship, under the friendship of peoples, still allowed for national identification and privileges. Russia's superior place was overwhelmingly understood, if not always accepted. But privileges based on nationality accrued to more than just Russians in the post-Stalin era. Nationality emerged, Terry Martin argues, as a form of "social capital" alongside emotional attachments in the post-Stalin period. Advantages in terms of housing allocation and employment, for example, could accrue to those of "titular" nationalities in their homelands, be they Georgians in Georgia (the Georgian SSR), Russians in Russia (the RSFSR), and so forth. Russian-language ability facilitated, but did not always determine, advantages.[59] As a line on each citizen's passport, nationality became an essential part of one's identity and livelihood. Devotion to the Soviet system, and the ability to procure advantages offered by the "elder brother" or "first among equals," enabled a practical as well as an emotional attachment to the friendship, especially in Leningrad and Moscow, the summits of the multinational Soviet Union.

Leningrad, Moscow, and the Friendship

Soviet citizens recognized Leningrad and Moscow as dual cores of the friendship of peoples. Migrants expected and witnessed a vibrant associational and cultural life that epitomized their sense of being Soviet. The Second World War had endowed Leningrad, the USSR's cultural center, with "hero city" status, and Moscow hosted sites and events that symbolized its home as a multinational and Soviet, as well as global, city. Emotions of satisfaction and gratitude dominated many migrant narratives, as they saw their own contributions, and those of their peoples, recognized and celebrated at the heart and soul of the USSR.

Moscow emerged as an aesthetic ideal as well as a place of happiness in the postwar era. A typical description emerged in a featured 1961 *Pravda* article: "Moscow: It is even more beautiful and joyous on the eve of the New Year. A sea of light washes over its spacious and wide boulevards and squares. Everywhere there is holiday activity. People hurry to houses of culture, clubs, theaters, or friends to celebrate."[60] Emotional discourse in the press, dating from the 1930s, preceded programming that Evans finds on late 1960s and 1970s television, when she notes "a broader shift in Soviet propaganda . . . toward emotional and spiritual qualities as the defining feature of both the new Soviet person and of Soviet socialist civilization as a whole."[61] Soviet citizens, especially from distant regions, felt great pleasure at their nations being recognized in the capital. Moscow hosted top chefs from the republics, as it became the USSR's culinary center. Georgian food spread among Moscow's elites in Stalin's time. Opened in 1940, the Aragvi restaurant featured music and dance ensembles from Georgia and became one of the city's most popular establishments. After the Second World War, the Baku, Ararat, and Uzbekistan restaurants symbolized the cosmopolitan nature of "everyone's capital," which represented the USSR to visitors from across the country and beyond its borders.[62] These establishments allowed tender reminders of home for long-term residents from outside of their republics and also were icons for tourists and others of Moscow's status as a multinational and global, city.

Pride swelled up in migrants and visitors as they considered the multinational and Soviet nature of Moscow's top attractions. Lenin's mausoleum was frequently cited as a place where all citizens could honor the equality of their union and the solidarity that developed under the first leader's rules and philosophy.[63] Moscow's Exhibition of Achievements of the National Economy (VDNKh), opened in 1939, where each union republic had a permanent pavilion, also gained union-wide repute.[64] Haydarov recalled his pleasure at being able to visit a site he had heard about as a schoolboy in the 1960s: "I was very proud to be in Moscow. At VDNKh's entrance was a fountain with statues representing all fifteen republics. We went to the pavilions to see images of each republic with enjoyment, intensifying our pride that we were one country."[65]

Moscow was the USSR's "internationalist city" in Soviet discourse, with streets and districts named after different locales countrywide. In June 1968, *Vechernyi Tashkent* reported on Moscow's new "Tashkent Street," which "cemented an unbreakable friendship" two years after its engineers were among the first to contribute to Tashkent's rebuilding after the horrific 1966 earthquake.[66] Central Soviet media emphasized how Leningrad and Moscow connected to life in distant republics. In one 1980 campaign, collective farms across the Soviet Union named "Leningrad" and "Moscow" gained significant press attention.[67] On 24 February, in an article titled "A Friendly Family," *Pravda* headlined a letter by M. Khodzhaeva, a worker at the Leningrad collective farm in central Uzbekistan. Khodzhaeva praised Leningrad and Moscow engineers, who shared technical advances with farmworkers. Combined with her colleagues' hard work, the farm had increased cotton production from thirteen to seven hundred tons, to the benefit of the entire union.[68] In another article, "Our Richness Is in Friendship," *Pravda* announced that the "brotherly, helping hand [of Moscow educators sent to the Caucasus region]" assisted Abkhazians—they could now hope to emerge victorious in academic "Olympiads" sponsored by the Party Central Committee in various school subjects, including the Russian language, with republican winners advancing to an all-union competition in Leningrad and Moscow.[69] Afterward, top students "attained success in Leningrad, Moscow, and Tbilisi universities."[70]

Emotional language, now ubiquitous in media and daily life, framed Soviet peoples' attachment to "everyone's capital." A 1982 book by that name, designed for a popular audience, stated that "all people have love for Moscow," where "the life of all Soviet republics is expressed."[71] Millions came every day, from all corners of the state, to see and be awed by the heart of the USSR. The book featured selections by prominent cultural or political figures from each republic, who were among the thousands to "start their path" in Moscow.[72] Elmira Kafarova, a member of the Supreme Soviet of the Azerbaijan SSR, wrote: "Azerbaijani schoolchildren, when they think of Moscow, they think of the motherland [*rodina*], they think of a friend."[73] Dzh. Tashibekova, a member of the Kyrgyz SSR Council of Ministers, continued that "for every citizen [Moscow] is a city of dreams of hopes, the most enlightened in the land."[74] Such language was common in media across the Soviet Union. Reporting an Uzbek delegation's arrival to celebrate the Bolshevik revolution's fiftieth anniversary, *Pravda Vostoka*—Tashkent's main newspaper—wrote that links between the Uzbek and Russian peoples were the "closest and longest" and, for Moscow, "you are our love—our house is your house."[75]

Such language echoed in the words and memories of migrants who journeyed to the two capitals at that time. Mirbek Serkebaev grew up in his small Kyrgyz village believing that "Moscow itself united the fifteen republics." "We believed in the friendship of peoples. In the day, that idea was very strong."[76] His arrival in Moscow as a young trader in 1983 confirmed this belief. Aryan Shirinov, a Tajik who enrolled in a Leningrad technical school after army service in 1985, echoed many who praised that city's ubiquitous and affordable cultural events and performances, which drew diverse audiences: "People from all over the union became friends. . . . Over my time in Leningrad, my pride in the Soviet Union increased. I thought 'what a strong and varied state we have.'"[77]

The emotive language behind this friendship elided the practical benefits of a relationship with Leningrad and Moscow. One of the most tangible, admissions to institutes of higher education, whether based on merit, as the *Pravda* article on Abkhazia stressed, or through the quota system discussed in chapter 1, evoked passionate responses from migrants regarding the friendship. Several Caucasus and Central Asian subjects claimed that not only were Leningrad and Moscow technical schools and universities open to them, but they also stood a better chance of admission than at home, where connections counted more than ability. Narynbek Temirkulov recalled: "[The friendship] worked! Yes, yes, yes. Otherwise, I could not have enrolled [at Moscow State University]. I was afraid of not gaining entrance to a Kyrgyz university, so I came to Moscow. That was my dream, and there were no hurdles in front of me."[78]

Days, Weeks, and *Dekady*

The most widely publicized manifestations of the "friendship of peoples" were festivals of national art and culture hosted over the span of a day, a week, or ten days (*dekada*). These festivals proliferated in major Soviet cities, with Moscow welcoming important delegations from each republic on a virtually annual basis. Weeks or *dekady* involved casts of hundreds, including administrators, intellectuals, cultural figures, athletes, and honored workers. On their surface, these events propagated the idea of Moscow as at once an international city and one of "celebration."[79] Serhy Yekelchyk argues that the state saw such rituals as critical in monitoring and channeling good Soviet behavior, given that people's thoughts could not be read.[80] Yuri Slezkine has expressed skepticism toward their effects, as one of "the most visible [and apparently least popular] aspects of Soviet official culture."[81] Organizers and participants, however, took these events extremely seriously. Feelings and material interests intersected. Festivals emerged as emotional performances, and inclusion in them was valuable, if not necessary, for advancement in Soviet hierarchies. Festival participants, at the least, gained the chance to enjoy the privileges of the Soviet capital for a few days.[82]

Days, weeks, and *dekady* emerged at the dawn of the friendship. Kazakh, Uzbek, Georgian, and Ukrainian delegations appeared in 1936–1937 Moscow.[83] Festivals were carefully scripted. Central newspapers offered primers on the republics' culture and historical uniqueness months in advance of scheduled appearances.[84] Ukrainian, Central Asian, Caucasus, and other peoples were portrayed in what Terry Martin has called "highly clichéd, essentializing" representations, developed early in the friendship and enduring as symbolic markers of each nation's place in the union.[85] Dress and performances emphasized "traditional" or folk aspects that makers of Soviet nationality policy considered part of storied pasts.[86] Each peripheral nation was linked to a particular role in advancing the Soviet Union, generally tied to cultural or agricultural production. Kyrgyz festivals revolved around horseback riding, storytelling bards (akyns), and the harvesting of cotton.[87] Isabelle Kaplan notes that these festivals also underlined "national progress," judged by abilities to learn from Leningrad's and Moscow's cultural elites. Azerbaijanis used festivals to showcase their introduction of European polyphonies into traditional folk songs.[88] Festivals enforced clear hierarchies that privileged European and Russian forms and centered on Moscow's urban spaces, but also promoted interethnic friendship.

These events deepened in importance after the Second World War, with decision making rendered at the highest levels. Kyrgyz Communist Party first secretary Turdakun Usubaliev controlled correspondence with the Moscow city central party committee, which acted as host for the capital's *dekady*. He signed off, a year in advance, on documents that selected the festival's delegation and events. One 1957 celebration involved intricate preparations to bring twenty-six puppet troupes, sporting demonstrations involving horses, as well as exhibitions of eagle and falcon hunting to Moscow, despite the minister of sports warning of the large costs involved.[89] Usubaliev expressed "deep thankfulness" to his Moscow hosts for their organizing efforts.[90]

The scale of planning signified the stakes involved. Festivals also designated republican elites and celebrities in respective fields. Kyrgyz bureaucrats sought input on potential figures previously awarded certificates of honor (*pochetnye gramoty*) and others who would be best suited to represent the republic to Moscow. Those selected received significant media attention. *Pravda Vostoka* listed performers for an "Uzbek days" (*dni Uzbekistana*) festival in 1974, claiming that they were "renowned throughout the republic and serve as an example to thousands, even beyond their field of specialization."[91] Workers who accompanied them to receive rewards for labor productivity were "living examples of labor heroism."[92] Delegations experienced the prestige and material wealth of Leningrad and Moscow, attending banquets in top restaurants and touring city sights. One Komsomol member from Kyrgyzstan stayed behind for fifteen days to receive care at Moscow's top hospital.[93] Georgians and others, if they performed the European and the "national" elements of their shows extraordinarily well, could be placed in private trains on tours of the USSR or perform at party congresses.[94] Kaplan notes that for republican leaders, however, this was not a risk-free venture. Great fear existed of putting on a poor show. Concerts or performances that failed to entertain their hosts or demonstrate the proper mix of national uniqueness and Soviet loyalty risked foreclosing career paths, especially of gaining all-union posts in Moscow.[95]

Extensive coverage of these festivals in the 1960s and beyond showcased emotional links between peoples. *Tashkentskaia pravda* heralded "Uzbek days" in Moscow in 1966, noting how "warmly, like dear brothers, Muscovites welcomed the visitors from Soviet Uzbekistan to the USSR's capital."[96] The newspaper expressed pride that the republic was the first selected to appear in a series of festivals leading up to the revolution's fiftieth anniversary. In 1974, *Pravda Vostoka* echoed similar sentiments. A festival to mark Uzbekistan's fiftieth anniversary as a union-republic in Moscow showcased how "messengers from a sunny land, heralds of the dawn of a Soviet family, [were] enveloped by the true hospitality and scale that greet[ed] them in the Soviet capital."[97] Canteens and restaurants alike across Moscow served Uzbek food over the duration of the festival—*plov* and *shashlik* (kebabs), as well as *lagman* and *shorpo* (meat-based soups), *manty* (dumplings), and assorted sweets. Such efforts allowed Uzbek delegations to the capital to insist that "Moscow is the native home [*rodnoi dom*] of each Soviet person."[98]

Internal party reports on these festivals echoed the emotional, celebratory language found in the press. Kyrgyz party leaders received a glowing account of their 1974 *dekada* in Moscow from its organizers. The 800-plus delegation was met with "sincere warmth and cordiality" at Domodedovo Airport. The festival began with the unveiling of a new exhibit at VDNKh, featuring Kyrgyzstan's latest achievements. The report stated, "many visitors, with great interest, familiarized themselves with the accomplishments of Soviet Kirgizstan in all economic, scientific and cultural fields."[99] A press conference to celebrate the fifty-year anniversary of the Central Asian republics was to host 150 Soviet journalists, as well as over 100 from other countries, though the report was silent on how many actually appeared.[100] In subsequent days, delegations laid flowers at Lenin's mausoleum as well as met with Russian counterparts at factories, universities, or concert halls. The glamour event of this and other *dekady* was a celebratory joint concert at the columned hall of the Congress of Unions in central Moscow. The report highlighted strong attendance from Moscow's privileged, educated strata (*obshchestvennosti*), industrial workers, and intellectual and dramatic figures, all of whom received the Kyrgyz performance with, once again, "warmth and cordiality."[101] When the Uzbeks gave their own concert at the columned hall for their fiftieth anniversary of the Central Asian republics, great enthusiasm was expressed at the attendance of honored Soviet cosmonauts, whose presence overshadowed Moscow's first secretary of the Communist Party personally greeting guests at the door.[102]

Weeks and *dekady* were the best publicized of any number of tours and exchanges that promoted the friendship of peoples. Leningrad and Moscow remained top destinations; the Kyrgyz SSR's Communist Party logged dozens of organizational requests for tours to the cities, medical exchanges, student conferences, or party meetings.[103] Smaller fairs elsewhere in the USSR fostered relations immediately across republican borders. A Kazakh day of literature and art was held in Novosibirsk in 1982 to celebrate the 250th anniversary of the "voluntary incorporation" of Kazakhstan into Russia.[104] That same year, the USSR's Union of Writers undertook a statewide tour, the "Festival of Multinational Literature." Literary roundtables with representatives from local and republican branches, along with those from fourteen foreign countries, were held in multiple cities in each republic. Events included writers' visits to meet factory and agricultural workers. In Uzbekistan, the tour wound through the Ferghana Valley, also stopping in Samarkand, where a high-profile literary evening included republican leaders. This tour, as well as multinational film festivals, garnered front-page headlines in the local and all-union press. *Izvestiia* framed the events as "A Word on Our Great Friendship" and "With Feelings of Friendship."[105] Evans notes that such tours received significant television coverage. Networks funded travel and significant research time for journalists to present varied cultures as part of a "late Soviet festive system."[106] Fuad Ojagov, an Azerbaijani psychologist who trained in 1970s–1980s Moscow, noted that for scholars, less likely to be impressed by slogans alone, intellectual exchanges and chances to travel animated the friendship of peoples. "The friendship was an ideological cliché, but it had real effects. . . . We had Days of Armenia in Azerbaijan and vice versa, or Days of Azerbaijan in Georgia.[107] Delegations traveled to meet each other. Psychologists held Transcaucasus-wide conferences. Scientists communicated with each other."[108] These broader contacts lessened a sense of isolation from Western academia. The USSR appeared as its own world, with diverse nationalities and cultures striving toward cultural and scholarly achievement.

Pride and Freedom

Emotional language surrounding these festivals echoed throughout Soviet discursive worlds, from leaders' speeches and top-level correspondence to everyday interactions. By the Brezhnev period, the friendship of peoples had become a hallmark of Soviet life, especially for minorities in multiethnic cities such as Leningrad and Moscow. Monique Scheer has argued that emotions work as a medium of communication, as practical ways to engage the world.[109] The discourse and associated practices of the friendship permeated sites of interethnic contact over the late Soviet decades and provided a sense of inclusion and collegiality, even as many realized, and accepted, that it allowed pride of place to Russians. Emotions of friendship and a shared destiny continue in the post-Soviet era as wistfulness for a more compassionate life, a guiding principle for a kinder world that has been lost.

Leonid Brezhnev employed the language of friendship to support his leadership from 1964 to 1982. Frequent speeches on the "indestructible friendship" between workers and citizens of various republics—often tied to pre-festival promotion—received front-page coverage in central newspapers in the 1970s and early 1980s.[110] Emotive language appeared in private party correspondence, connecting Soviet nations in durable camaraderie. In a flurry of thank-you letters dispatched after the Kyrgyz *dekada* in 1974, First Secretary Usubaliev credited "the Communist Party, the Soviet government and the selfless help of the great Russian people and other brotherly peoples in producing great successes for the Kirgiz SSR."[111] Other correspondence cited the "enormous success of Leninist national politics" in conjuring a union of peoples who work with friendship and unity to recognize mutual interests in the service of a great socialist state.[112]

Mutual respect, pride, and other values expressed in high discourse spilled downward in the Soviet Union. Migrants recognized the friendship's power and potential in their own experiences. Its firmness—symbolized by Leningrad's and Moscow's shining lights to all peoples of the union—allowed a sense of inclusion. Abdul Khalimov recalled that his faith in friendship, in Moscow and the multinational USSR, overwhelmed unfavorable interactions with the state as he grew up in 1970s Tajikistan:

> Back then the media constructed the idea of a united people, the *Homo Sovieticus*. The state constructed this idea and the public accepted it. The friendship of peoples was a reality. That is what we learned from childhood. Even though I knew that the Bolsheviks killed my grandfather . . . and I lived in poverty, and they wouldn't let me study a foreign language at university because of where I came from and because I was not Russian. Despite all of this, if a Soviet athlete or team won an event, we all took pride in that. We would all shout and cheer together. We had a pride that united us all. I think that this pride was a result of strong state politics. We were a united nation [*natsiia*]: a united Soviet people [*narod*].

In fact, when I came to Russia during Soviet times, I would say that we were treated very well, better than in our own republics. It was the politicians [during perestroika] who ruined that.[113]

Aryan Shirinov, a student in 1980s Leningrad, also emphasized the effects of consistent state policies and discourse toward the friendship. "State policies acted on peoples, as everywhere and at all times we saw slogans, and on the radio and television, that we were always one Soviet Union, that we were brothers."[114] Shirinov and others pointed to concrete results of the friendship that endured over the Brezhnev era: "We built everything together. There was a strong ideology, an ideology of internationalism. If there was an earthquake in Tashkent, then the whole of the Soviet Union rebuilt the city."[115] The idea of a common destiny flowed through Meerim Kalilova's words, as she reflected on the friendship alongside her opportunities and experiences as a street trader in early 1980s Moscow:

> The Russians are a friendly people. . . . I think the Soviet Union gave many people from different nationalities a chance to work there, live, and get a better education. This is a very important fact to consider, which also led to strong friendship among the different nationalities.[116]

Emotional connections and everyday exchanges interweave in these narratives, with the friendship of peoples an ideal, or at least idealized, discourse linking sojourners and the host society. In migrant memories, the friendship of peoples was tied to individual friendships made in Leningrad and Moscow. When asked about the friendship of peoples, Jumaboi Esoev conjured a personal example. A Tajik, he befriended a Russian and an Ossetian in his workplace dormitory. They became so close that their coworkers called them the "Three Musketeers."[117] The friendship, for him, symbolized not only equality between peoples but also warmth. Migrants could select their own friends by individuality and personality, as peoples of all backgrounds were already close. Shuhrat Ikramov saw a more calculated side to these multinational friendships in late 1980s Moscow. Dormitory mates sought to enlarge their networks to assist with career prospects unionwide, especially as perestroika's uncertainties appeared.[118]

Emotional reactions in oral histories reflected migrants' belief in the friendship as a core doctrine and a fundamental expression of the Soviet Union's values, as well as an entry point to consider individual identity and relationships. Several of them filtered the friendship through Yurchak's list of basic Soviet ideals: "equality, community, selflessness, altruism, friendship, ethical relations, safety, education, work, creativity, [and] concern for the future."[119] Added to this list, when we listened to these migrants, was a value less generally associated with the USSR: freedom. The friendship was seen to facilitate dreams of societal progress and broad-based personal opportunity, even as some criticized the state for imposing an imperial, and perhaps even totalitarian, vision.

Shuhrat Ikramov considered the friendship of peoples the foundation for migrant success in Leningrad and Moscow. All Soviet citizens were to work together to build a modern society from the inside out. Instead of motivated by capitalist individualism, citizens used their respective talents to assist each other.[120] A feeling of common destiny manifested itself in daily life through personal belonging and safety in cities dominated by ethnic Russians. Azamat Ormonbekov, a Kyrgyz who studied in 1982–1983 Moscow, remained uncertain about the friendship, given inequalities between republics, but recognized its values on the streets: "It was Soviet propaganda, this propaganda for the friendship of peoples. But it's hard to know how else it could be done. Whether this was good or bad we don't know. Unlike now, however, at any time of the day you could walk about Moscow and nothing would happen to you, except perhaps an occasional quarrel."[121] Comparisons with violent xenophobia in post-Soviet St. Petersburg and Moscow coursed through migrant representations of a peaceful Soviet era. Jumaboi Esoev recalled in 1980s Moscow: "I never felt threatened in the Soviet Union. I always felt myself to be safe and free. The Soviet authorities set boundaries. Everyone had the same rights. In general, people were more law-abiding."[122]

Fridon Tsereteli focused on the friendship's practical advantages, as part of the freedoms given to Soviet citizens to travel, at least within their union: "We were all citizens of the same country. You could go wherever you wanted. No one would ask you where you were from or question your right to be somewhere. The fact that the people all associated with each other, all the people of the Soviet Union, was a big plus about the country."[123] For so many former Soviet citizens, their world has become smaller since the collapse. Khalimov recalled:

> Life was easy during Soviet times. I was free. No one even asked me for my passport back then. I was not only in Moscow, however; I also traveled through Russia a lot during the Soviet period. I was in Belarus, Ukraine, and the Baltic states as well for my studies. I never felt any fear back then. . . . Sometimes I think that when we talk about citizens' rights, which are something we talk a lot about these days, . . . if we are being honest, I think that my rights as a citizen were better defended during the Soviet Union than they are today. Back then, I could come from a Tajik village and get into university. No one ever asked me for money for my studies, and I didn't have any connections either.[124]

The idea of the Soviet Union as a state that protected individual safety and nurtured individual freedom within a broader community remains popular. Kalilova, a

Kyrgyz trader, noted: "All of us felt that we were equal with others, because we all were a part of the Soviet Union. We lived in freedom and could work freely with no problems. We also did what we wanted to, in a good sense of course. For example, with no problem anyone could find a job then and walk freely in the streets and nobody would offend you or ask for documents."[125] Being spared indignities of passport, visa, and other document checks, ubiquitous across the former Soviet space, loomed large in the idea of Soviet freedom, even though, as later chapters show, there was no shortage of such practices then. The friendship also underlay Soviet postwar success in becoming a superpower, a point of pride especially for those who studied and worked at its heart. Bolot Oruzbaev mixed pride with freedom in his recollections: "I was proud of the friendship of peoples. The Soviet Union was a very powerful country and provoked fear, even in America. There were so many intellectuals [and there was much] heavy industry, light industry, from across the USSR."[126] Murad Imamaliev, inspired by the Kremlin's walls, waxed enthusiastically on the USSR's global power and its capacity to bind its citizens as "one great empire, like China."[127]

Nation, the Elder Brother, and Being Soviet

Migrants spoke with passion when discussing their own place, and that of their nation, alongside ethnic Russians in the friendship of peoples. Pride in national uniqueness, as well as—in many, but not all, cases—Sovietness, blended with complicated thoughts toward the "elder brother." Thankfulness—for the ostensible sharing of a modern, urban culture—mixed with resentment for continued Russian domination in these urban spaces and its impact on national values. Recollections and experiences filtered through Soviet and post-Soviet lenses. Migrants worked to render the friendship meaningful on their own terms, through their memories and patterns of movement within national and state-based frameworks and categories. Views of Russia's, and Russians', place within the friendship also exposed regional and national differences among migrants, as they considered their own people's place in the USSR.

The Russian nation's place as the "elder brother" or "first among equals," cemented in Stalin's time, endured throughout the Soviet Union. The 1955 *Short Philosophical Dictionary* (*Kratkii filosofskii slovar'*) stated that "all peoples and nations of the USSR see in the great Russian people their best friend and guide, their elder brother, who played a decisive role in the struggle for the victory of the proletarian revolution and triumph of socialism."[128] Such discourse percolated to the individual level, sometimes expressed sincerely, sometimes employed ironically, to hold Russians to account, to remind them of their purported friendly or familial duty to share the fruits of their privileged status. The friendship of peoples might be an imposed creation to bind Soviet nations together, but it was one that resonated with even skeptical migrants given the alternative, realized in the perestroika era and beyond, of national conflict.

Russia's, and Russians', favored place in the cultural sphere deepened post-Stalin, even as language stressing the need to assist "backward" republics softened. In the 1950s, leaders of each national republic's union of composers held annual meetings in Leningrad. Reports and speeches underlined the "unbreakable friendship of peoples" as inspiring their work. The meetings' goal was clear, however; Russian composers were to supervise musical composition, to assure continued literal and figurative harmony. Even notes and chords on "national" instruments were expected to adopt European forms through Russian high culture.[129] Azerbaijanis and Central Asians received the greatest attention. In 1954, the Kyrgyz head of composers pronounced: "[Before the Soviet era] we were backward. We have made great progress but still fail to meet the emotional and lifestyle needs of the laboring masses."[130] Emotions of gratitude corresponded to the challenging position of these composers, needing to show loyalty to Moscow. Successfully executing musical "progress" in festivals and high-profile performances was crucial to their positions, with the state as their only patron.

FIGURE 4   Kyrgyz cultural performers at a Kyrgyzstan culture and arts festival in Moscow, in 1967. Attribution: Sputnik International (former RIA Novosti) / © Alamy Stock Photo

Later Leningrad and Moscow migrants repeated such utterances. They lacked the hyperbole of cultural figures, including one Kyrgyz poet who uttered, "thank you, beloved Russian brother, to whom I owe my life"; at the same time, the idea of debt to a more advanced people proliferated.[131] Shuhrat Ikramov, who claimed, as an Uzbek scientist, to be treated as an inferior in an early 1980s Moscow laboratory, maintained that Russian officials and scholars took seriously their responsibility to educate and train "less developed" peoples, even if their ultimate goal was to return them home.[132] Farshad Hajiev, a Tajik student, noted how the idea of a harmonious and symbiotic, if unequal, friendship filtered to the everyday:

> In Soviet times, they treated us better than their own [*svoikh*]. In Leningrad, they would treat us better. Say we went to a café. They would talk and laugh with us and treat us with respect, because they knew that we were from out of town. But back then there were so many different events. On television everyday they would show how much cotton Tajikistan was producing, how much they were helping, or how much Russia was helping them. When that type of thing is being shown daily, it is bound to have an effect. Even more so than Leningraders, we would participate in holidays and in marches, chanting from morning to night: "Long live the party, long live the Komsomol, long live Soviet youth."[133]

Erkin Bakchiev, who traded household goods in 1980s Moscow, believed in the idea of Russian assistance as he considered the place of Kyrgyz like himself: "The Russians were the strongest in science and academics. We were not able to study like them. We worked, picked cotton, while they studied. For that reason, I felt somewhat below them."[134] In migrant recollections, emotions of gratitude and debt accumulated to both Russians and to the state for expressing friendship and channeling assistance to poorer nations.

Several Caucasus and Central Asian students noted that Russian-language education implanted a sense of its superior culture.[135] Sadig Eldarov, a top student at a Russian-language school in 1960s Baku, recalled: "We all loved Russian culture, and felt very close to it. We grew up with the idea of the 'big brother.'" He believed that this image endured in large part because of Azerbaijani national values: "[In our culture] we always treat the big brother with honor and respect. Even when we were told [during glasnost] that all republics were equal, those were only words, and we remained very fond of Russia."[136] Unstated in Eldarov's interview was his now precarious situation as an intellectual in independent Azerbaijan, where the status of social science education, along with his income and stability, had deteriorated and his Russian-language schooling and training in Moscow no longer provided an advantage. Aryuna Khamagova, educated in a leading Russian-language school in 1960s Ulan-Ude, Buryatia, recalled:

"Intuitively, I ascribed myself to Russians, maybe not in the ethnic sense but culturally through language, literature, and history."[137] As she rose from vegetable trader to scholar in 1960s–1970s Leningrad, the city's cultural attractions—music, theater, opera—confirmed Russianness and Sovietness simultaneously as part of her modern, urban identity. Damira Nogoibaeva, who aspired from an early age to study at Moscow State University, noted: "I felt more Russian than Soviet, and I did not even feel Kyrgyz. I had an attachment to a Russian culture."[138]

Russian leadership remains part of the emotional community of the friendship of peoples, when compared to perceptions of a selfish, rough, and dangerous present in states now distanced from the "big brother." Jasur Haydarov, now a pensioner in Kyrgyzstan, pronounced the most powerful image of Russian benevolence: "I believe in friendship. The Russians fed us. They cherished us and pampered us. When the Russians were in control [of Kyrgyzstan] there was no fraud, no one robbed others."[139] Jyldyz Nuriaeva praised Russia's leadership, even as she admitted it came with costs: "I think that the Russian people and the revolution did a lot of good for the Kyrgyz. This is because some of the best representatives of the Russian intelligentsia came to Kyrgyzia and gave us culture, such as opera. . . . At that time, we hardly understood that there was a process of Russification going on. But this is a natural process. Nowadays we talk about Americanization or globalization."[140] Bakyt Shakiev, an Azerbaijani from Kazakhstan who worked on a dairy farm in 1970s Leningrad, accepted Russia's privileged position without denigrating his own nation: "[Russians] may have been in some way older brothers, but not bosses. This is not the same thing. Everything was controlled from Moscow, and everything flowed through there, so they were older brothers, yes, but not bosses."[141] Metaphors of friendship and family course through the interviews as Shakiev and others maintain emotional attachments to the Soviet era. Soviet Russians appear in their memories, if not as family, as patrons—as opposed to post-Soviet experiences with Russia and Russians, outside powers such as the United States or China, and even their "own" national leaders.

Georgian and Armenian migrants to Leningrad and Moscow largely separated their views on the friendship of peoples from relations with Russia and Russians, as well as a broader Soviet sense of belonging. Those interviewed for this project privileged their own national identities and cultural development; assistance from the "elder brother" was not required, as Georgia and Armenia already belonged to a modern, European world. Maia Asinadze, who viewed the friendship of peoples as easing her entry into Moscow from a small Georgian town, emphasized continued adherence to nation. Asked if close friendships with Russians affected her sense of being Soviet, she stated: "I was born a Georgian, I am a Georgian, and I will die a Georgian. My feelings did not change at all. How could they?"[142] Zurab Iashvili, a student in 1970s Moscow, also recalled being accepted as an equal. He expressed appreciation for the friendship, but placed a strong line between national and state identities: "I have never considered myself as a Soviet citizen! I am Georgian!"[143] Eliso Svanidze, a Georgian who worked at a Moscow supermarket in the late 1970s and early 1980s, and who lauded the multinational friendships she made, nonetheless criticized those who remained emotional about Soviet-era attachments: "Actually, I do not believe in that kind of friendship, when it does not happen naturally and it is kind of compelled or encouraged by some other forces. Friendship should happen naturally. So I think that friendship among nations in the Soviet Union was defined by the ruling power and was not a result of natural feelings."[144] Tamriko Otskheli expressed similar sentiments of the friendship as a pale, imposed force: "This idea was invented by a dictatorial ideology, but the will of particular nations to become independent turned out to be stronger than the will to live as friends within the union."[145] Svanidze, Otskheli, and others recognized nonetheless that official festivals and investment in halls, theaters, libraries, and other sites for cultural expression allowed for distinct national development, albeit within a Soviet medium.

Some migrants considered the friendship's division of citizens into national groups as a certain betrayal of Soviet values, which, in their view, should privilege individual identification with, and work for, the entire collective of the USSR. Khamagova believed that the friendship of peoples was "not just a slogan but an essence of the political being of the state," one that succeeded in curtailing discrimination in multiethnic spaces. At the same time, she argued that "[nationality as a category] meant that society as a whole was segregated."[146] Eldarov saw the friendship as undermining Soviet unity: "I cannot say that the friendship of peoples was perfect. In fact, there were different cultures and behaviors that accompanied sometimes hostile ethnic stereotypes and prejudices." He nonetheless credited the idea with pushing average people away from "chauvinist" and toward "internationalist" behavior when dealing with others.[147] Two traders recalled that national territories and networks presaged the proliferation of ethnically based, albeit unofficial, trading circles in Moscow. In their case, it enforced their identity as Talysh, a people in southern Azerbaijan. Central Asians, who credited Soviet munificence for developing modern national identities within their own territorial units, expressed less concern about partitions between individual, nation, and state. Tolkunbek Kudubaev, who worked in construction for the Moscow metro and was one of the few from the region to express reluctance to embrace, simultaneously, nationality and Sovietness, stated matter-of-factly: "I was never a Soviet person, but above all a Kyrgyz, and therefore a citizen and member of the Soviet state."[148]

Emotions of inferiority, fear, and frustration toward Russians crossed national lines. Bakchiev recalled elementary school days in the 1970s in a small Uzbek village within Kyrgyzstan: "Our teachers told us that if we did not know the Russian language, it was impossible for us to be as strong as the Russians." Such words led Kyrgyz and Uzbeks to be "afraid of Russians, only because they were Russians. . . . Just by the fact that they were born Russian, they were one level higher in the eyes of others. . . . It became implanted in our psychology from school years."[149] Bakchiev took this not as a challenge to improve, as perhaps his teachers intended, or to somehow incorporate elements of the elder brother, as several migrants had done, but as a recognition of his status as a permanent second-class citizen, in his own village as well as in Moscow, where he eventually landed as a trader. Others critiqued the two-tier society that they remembered in large cities in Caucasus and Central Asian republics, where Russians felt a sense of entitlement, with their skin color and ethnic background allowing them better opportunities. Aisulu Baisalbekova recalled her youth in a 1960s Kyrgyz village: "I noticed how [Russian students] dressed, their manners, the way they related with others—they were above us."[150]

Association with Russians through the friendship might damage individual psychologies as well as national values. Dylara Usmanova credited the friendship of peoples for managing potential tensions in childhood homes in both the Caucasus and Central Asia, but resented the inequality inherent in a model that allowed for a "first among equals" or "elder brother": "I sensed in many Russians an ambivalence: on the one hand, they always treated me well, but on the other, they always seemed overly proud of their accomplishments. Although they did not demonstrate it, they lived the myth of the friendship of peoples but somewhere deep down disliked people with a different skin color and religion."[151] Dina Ataniyazova, a scholar in Soviet and post-Soviet Moscow, considered the risks of the Russian-dominated friendship, especially on the periphery: "I never felt that the friendship of the peoples was a reality. It started in my family, which by all accounts was an example of such a friendship [Caucasus, Tatar, Central Asian, and Russian], erasing national characteristics to create a future Soviet man. But what I saw were poisoned relations between my parents and their relatives—a rivalry according to their proximity to the 'elder brother' and contempt for those who resisted mental colonization and a Europeanist paradigm."[152]

Ataniyazova believed that this competition and will to undergo "mental colonization" warped national characters in favor of a European, Russian-led social and economic path. "Representatives of the colonies could only achieve something if they were loyal to the regime. Soviet multiculturalism was nothing other than this. I am convinced that in any 'friendship' between Russian and non-Russian peoples an asymmetry was always present, with Russian 'friends' above the savage, underdeveloped non-Russians. It was the friendship of Robinson [Crusoe] with Friday."[153] Usmanova regretted the impact on her Uzbek people through accepting the elder brother's primacy. "Because of the bad influence of Russian modernization, my people lost their best traits: kindness, honesty, unselfishness, sobriety."[154] An unequal friendship made even such deep cultural and moral changes difficult to resist.

Some migrants sought to turn the tables on personal or national feelings of inferiority. Aibek Botoev, who was from a small Kyrgyz village and attended a Leningrad civil engineering institute, insisted:

> [The Russians] told us that they gave us an alphabet, a literature, that we were illiterate/ignorant [*bezgramotnye*] before they came. This is what we had to learn in school. Colonization started with the tsars. The Russians to this day have a complex with us, because of the Tartar-Mongol rule. When they are in our presence they feel this complex [*pered nami chuvstvuiut etot kompleks*]. Now they are the masters, but they are always trying to forget another side of history, that they were once our colony.[155]

Abdul Khalimov sought to express a personal, if not cultural, superiority to those, including fellow Tajiks, who might limit themselves to a Russian orbit:

> Russification brought a lot of negative feelings with it, but at the same time, it helped to create a Soviet identity. I tell my fellow countrymen that I am a Russian speaker. I read Pushkin and Lermontov. I am proud of that. So it has been a win-win situation for me. I tell my Russian friends that they are the ones who lost out, because they are not able to read our great poets and writers. They are only able to read the works of Russians. For me it was a great opportunity. Although there were many Tajiks who could not read their own language, they only read Russian. This was the case of a professor of mine. I even had to read books to him in our native language. So that was one aspect of the Soviet Union that was very negative. . . . Perhaps we are the *Homo Sovieticus*, because we feel as comfortable associating with Russians as we do with our own countrymen. . . . I had a Soviet upbringing, so I am not afraid of Russians; they are as much my people as Tajiks.[156]

Farshad Hajiev's thoughts rested firmly within a Soviet medium. Circulation of Pushkin and Lermontov were prime examples of Soviet regime efforts to promote Russian literary and cultural heroes as representatives of a modern European civilization, which had roots in a progressive and cultured Russian past that streamed seamlessly into a Soviet future. Hajiev recognized Russian success in implanting their superiority: "Russians [in the Soviet period] didn't feel threatened like they do nowadays. They thought that they would always dominate, so they related to us calmly."[157] Even as some migrants sought to subvert ethnic and societal hierarchies, they found themselves thoroughly enmeshed in them.

Azerbaijani traders, most of whom neither attended Russian-language schools nor strived to join multinational, professional ranks in Leningrad and Moscow, had perhaps the harshest view of Russian primacy and the friendship of peoples. Many considered their experiences in the two capitals as betraying the ideals of friendship they had assimilated, if not always experienced, in their home republics. Elnur Asadov stated: "There was no such thing as the friendship of peoples—it was a myth. I saw how [Russians] treated us. We worked hard [to trade in Moscow] and they treated us badly. To make friends with them was impossible. Of course, they carried themselves like bosses—as I worked on their territory they dictated conditions to me."[158] Even those who experienced significant economic success distanced individual friendships with Russian customers from any perpetuation of, or conversion to, a Soviet identity. As in the case of Georgian respondents, these Azerbaijani traders gave pride of place to nation, against the Soviet Union. They stressed not European historical roots or greatness but the strength of the contemporary, resource-rich Azerbaijani state, now untethered from Russian control. Frustration also linked to a perceived lack of support for Azerbaijan in the conflicts that engulfed the last years of the USSR. Georgians and Azerbaijanis alike perceived Moscow as supporting competitor nations—Abkhazians or Armenians—in conflicts that endured long after the end of the Soviet Union.

Emotions and experiences, then and now, produced powerful, passionate, and personal impressions of Russia's and Russians' role in the friendship of peoples. Over a decade after the USSR's dissolution, the memory of Soviet-era links to the "elder brother" produced fervent, sometimes heated, responses. Intellectuals, traders, and others recognized Russia's and Russians' position as not only privileged but also central, a psychological as well as a social and economic touchstone for their identity as Soviet citizens. "Mental colonization" or not, these now post-Soviet subjects recognized the friendship as a constitutive element of a Soviet community, whose legacies endured more than a decade after the collapse.

Wistfulness

Comparisons between past and present inevitably circulate through oral histories and produce significant emotional reactions. Migrants considered what was lost as the Soviet Union fractured and they contemplated their place in an evolving, uncertain post-Soviet world. Emotional attachment to the friendship of peoples permeates the thoughts of even those who celebrated the USSR's end. Svanidze noted: "I liked life during the Soviet Union. People lived very well, without any fears, and all nations coexisted very peacefully. Of course, I am happy that my country became independent, but I also must admit that I remember the Soviet Union only in positive terms with its good life. But that cannot be more important than freedom and independence."[159] Nuriaeva, who recalled frequent discrimination in early 1980s Moscow, said: "There were some ideological facets of the USSR that remain with us. . . . Some of these were quite positive, like the idea that nationalities should live in accord with each other, that we should live in peace, that all people were the same, with similar opportunities, that no hatred would be tolerated. All of this was part of Soviet propaganda, and all of this was torn away from us and an ideology of hatred imposed."[160] The USSR's "very real humane values" seem forever lost amid harsher post-Soviet societal and economic environments, especially for older citizens.[161]

Emotions that sparked such statements became performative. Subjects pressed to ensure that their interviewers, either North Americans or locals too young to remember the pre-glasnost era, understood what it meant to live in the Soviet Union. Words highlighted the importance of an emotional community, as conceptualized almost two decades later. Hajiev recalled: "We tolerated and respected each other. . . . When you think of what has changed in the last ten years or so it is just terrible. . . . No. Without a doubt [the friendship of peoples] was a reality. In the army, at work, and during my studies I felt this way. We were all equal. We couldn't even think to the contrary. Just as for you, the idea of the friendship of the peoples must sound like a myth, am I right? But I lived through it, I was there and it was real."[162]
Maia Asinadze, even as she asserted her Georgianness and remained skeptical of the friendship of peoples as a concept, considered what was lost to her after the collapse:

> We were all close [in the Soviet era]. We all associated with one another. It was all real. When I think about it now, of course today I live in better conditions, but if you offered me the chance to go back in time and live how we lived then . . . I would do it. I swear. Why, I'm not so sure, but probably for those honest, real human relations. You can't compare that with anything. . . . People were more friendly and helpful. Relationships between people were warmer.[163]

The ideas of individual friendships and human relations, as a microcosm of the actual friendship of peoples, permeate among even those who have enjoyed significant post-Soviet professional success, in their own countries or in the West. The strongest emotion we encountered came from a Kazakh scientist, Aliya

Nurtaeva, now working at a U.S. university, who angrily dismissed any suggestion of differences between peoples in the USSR: "Minorities never existed in the Soviet Union. Everyone was the same with similar ambitions. This is a bad question."[164]

The emotional community that bound so many Soviet citizens endures decades after its collapse. The friendship of peoples emerged quickly in our interview process as a yardstick by which migrants measured their association with other citizens and the Soviet state, past and present. Even for those who considered themselves proud, sometimes anti-Soviet, nationalists, the friendship was generally appreciated for its aspirational or actual qualities of peace, stability, even kindness. It was the symbol of Soviet uniqueness, one without comparison in Western or post-Soviet societies.

Migrants emphasized how they made the friendship their own. It could be employed to deliver benefits on multiple levels. Warm, if not always sincere, relations and mutual respect from individuals of various national groups allowed sojourners a sense of personal inclusion in Russian-dominated capitals. Freedom and security regardless of background eased barriers on travel and worries for physical safety. A regime considered color-blind, if not dedicated to helping "less developed" nationalities, enabled professional mobility for all citizens even under the watchful eye of the "elder brother."[165] Festivals honored non-Russian nationalities just as universities opened their doors to them in Leningrad and Moscow, assuring a visible place in a Soviet family at the heart of the union.

Appreciation for the friendship, and beliefs that its heart lay in the Russian-dominated cities of Leningrad and Moscow, perhaps represented the "Eurocentrism and mental colonization" that, Dina Ataniyazova claimed, prompted "southern" intellectuals to submerge their "own" identities into Russian or pro-Russian ones.[166] Once the idea of a modern, European civilization was accepted as inherently progressive, Russian superiority was virtually sealed. Aibek Botoev considered the state's role in such efforts: "I would say that the 'friendship of peoples' was 50 percent reality and 50 percent myth. They pounded us with the idea of internationalism and at the same time practiced colonization in my homeland. They did everything they could to assimilate us. They made us speak Russian. In the Soviet Union, the state always said one thing and did the opposite."[167] Colonization, in a mental as well as a physical sense, provides a counternarrative in migrant stories to those who still idealize the opportunities they felt from contact with Russian culture as experienced through a Soviet prism.

Soviet-era friendship nonetheless facilitated inclusion in a modern, European, cosmopolitan world, one that seems so remote for so many now. Hajiev, Nurtaeva, and others passionately claimed that not only were they Soviet citizens first and foremost then, but they remained so years after the collapse. The strength of friendship, elided into the broader idea of the "friendship of peoples," emerged throughout migrants' journeys as they connected to networks that facilitated their stays in Leningrad and Moscow. Sociability and social advancement went hand in hand as newcomers from the Caucasus, Central Asia, and the Asian regions of Russia contemplated, planned, and began their movement toward the two capitals.

MAKING A PLACE IN THE TWO CAPITALS

Migrants from the Caucasus, Central Asia, and Asian Russia tested expectations of inclusion and success in initial encounters with the cities and populations of late Soviet Leningrad and Moscow. Aware of the advantages that could be procured at the heart of the Soviet Union, and awash with the language of the friendship of peoples, some travelers nonetheless expressed trepidation or resentment at having to move so far from families and homes. Individual initiative, networks, both official and unofficial, and state policies interwove to set citizens on northern or western paths. First impressions and encounters proved critical for migrant incorporation as well as memories of what it meant to be a successful Soviet person in a space far from home.

Leningrad and Moscow emerged as the USSR's central, multinational contact zones in the late Soviet era. Their growth and opportunities symbolized a dynamic, urbanizing, modernizing state. Sojourners might shop alongside, interact with, even participate in the upper reaches of Soviet society, albeit in spaces that remained overwhelmingly Slavic—even if this might seem familiar to those acquainted with major republican capitals. Distinct categories and perceptions of belonging, and relationships that involved gender and class, as well as ethnicity, challenged migrant mentalities and strategies in the two capitals. Even as Soviet ideals of progress and development shaped their dreams, and state policies had critical influences on their pathways, migrants privileged individual determination and intimate connections as they recounted their passages and adaptation to new cityscapes.

The two capitals presented different faces to each arrival. Uzbek students, Buryat villagers, Azerbaijani traders, Georgian engineers, and others came with distinct imaginaries of their new home. Moves to the USSR's core represented spatial dislocation but also a continuity of personal and Soviet aspirations. To capture the dynamics of incorporation, this chapter uses Akhil Gupta and James Ferguson's concept of place making.[1] Place making focuses on how individual migrants render space meaningful through evolving constructions and experiences of similarities and differences between home and away. It stresses continuous trans-territorial connections, with linkages emerging not only through travel but also through networks, in this case softening contrasts of the peripheries and core of the Soviet state. I also use place making to relate making a place for oneself within a broader Soviet place, in this case its ideal of a multiethnic, cosmopolitan city. Inequalities of power challenged place-making strategies but did not determine avenues of incorporation or success. First encounters highlight everyday personal facets, and consequences, of a broader late twentieth-century movement toward global cities.

Migrant voices underscore the importance of mobility in the relationship between state, society, and the individual across the USSR. The traversing of spatial borders—between village and city, and across republics—social borders—between student and professional, trader and consumer—and cultural borders—between tradition and modernity, masculinity and femininity—exposes the USSR's complex, multifaceted character and the spread of Soviet ideas and practices. Soviet mobility, I argue, allowed substantial space for individual expression and freedom. Victor Zaslavsky has maintained that late Soviet movement, sanctioned or unsanctioned, enforced state dominance. Place became a critical, but controlled, indicator of privilege, with closely surveilled Leningrad and Moscow at its apex. Even as, or because, official controls could be bypassed, the system, Zaslavsky contends, created a docile and fragmented citizenry more interested in turning the status quo to its individual advantage than changing it.[2] His arguments, though capturing an underlying rationale behind the state's ambivalence in enforcing its own policies and laws on mobility, overlook the importance of relationships that connected rather than atomized late Soviet society. The dynamic between control and migrant agency for any modern state that monitors internal as well as external borders remains a complicated one; individual narratives help us understand social vitality and unexpected consequences from urban contact zones behind permeable barriers.

Southern and eastern migrants went through three phases of place making in Leningrad and Moscow, from decisions and pathways, to arrivals and initial encounters, and then settling into new homes, cultures, and networks. Connections between individual determination and societal and state factors reveal themselves through words and written sources that highlight migrant experiences.

Home and Away

Leningrad and Moscow beckoned as spaces of social mobility, economic prosperity, and cultural vitality. Motivations to move thousands of kilometers, to risk failure, to disrupt families were as much varied as the understandings of the privileges that might be accrued at the core were universal. Strategies and opportunities to incorporate the two cities' advantages into life chances began in small villages, large interethnic regional capitals, and all points in between in Asian Russia, the Caucasus, and Central Asia. Some of those on the Soviet Union's edges had dreamed of lives in Leningrad and Moscow since childhood, encouraged by the cities' mythical status in friends', families', and teachers' words. Others came after chance encounters or unexpected circumstances altered life trajectories. Some had studied in Russian schools, with support at home and with family in the two capitals as they considered a transition. Others took challenging, often unorthodox paths to residence. Connections, social status, intellectual ability, and individual determination could ease initial adaptation, but hardly assured the beginnings of a successful trajectory in the heart of the Soviet Union.

Passage to Leningrad and Moscow remained easy and affordable throughout the late Soviet era. By the 1970s, air travel became a common way to visit Moscow especially, as the hub for intra-Soviet flights. Georgians could choose one of nine daily flights between Tbilisi and Moscow, for the relatively low and stable price of thirty-one rubles.[3] Flights from Tashkent were somewhat more expensive, at forty-eight rubles, but still provided a direct connection. Moscow was also the junction for inter-republican and international connections to Eastern Europe and abroad; stopovers allowed time for travelers on varied excursions to visit the city between flights.[4] Rail proved an even more popular, and cheaper, way to see Leningrad and Moscow. Family trips frequently, and tourist rail itineraries inevitably, included a stop in Moscow at least. David Somkishvili, who grew up in 1960s Kutaisi, Georgia, recalled that during his early childhood his father, a train conductor, brought him and his family on frequent, weeklong trips to Moscow and occasionally Leningrad. Still strong in Somkishvili's memory were Moscow's zoo and circus. He recalled the wonder and excitement of the children's toy store, Detskii Mir, whose selection far surpassed shops at home.[5] In the Pioneers as a schoolboy, Mirbek Serkebaev recalled frequent stopovers in Moscow on his way to international youth conferences in Budapest and elsewhere. Komsomol-

FIGURE 5   A Central Asian family on the left-hand side of an Aeroflot IL-62 at Moscow Airport, in 1981. Attribution: RIA Novosti archive / Vladimir Rodionov / CC-BY-SA 3.0

sponsored tours, sometimes taking him to Leningrad, would always await as attendees gathered from across the USSR. Troop leaders guided their charges through the glories of a Russianized Soviet past at Leningrad's Hermitage museum and through an idealized present and future at Moscow's all-union Exhibition of Achievements of the National Economy (VDNKh). Serkebaev saw these tours as the ultimate symbols of privilege for motivated young citizens, regardless of birthplace or parents' status.[6]

Moscow's place as a junction box for the entire Soviet Union, and beyond, dawned gradually on Azamat Sanatbaev during family trips to the city as a youngster in the 1960s and 1970s. He arrived each time at a different airport, bus station, or train station scattered throughout the city. Each transit hub was packed with peoples from across the USSR and the rest of the world, from Cubans to Germans to North Africans. "It was there that I realized the multiethnic richness [of the Soviet Union]."[7] His family participated in the quintessential Soviet ritual of visitors to Moscow: shopping. On city streets, Sanatbaev recalled well-dressed people and grew to understand frequent family conversations about "Moscow things" (*moskovskie veshchi*). His family spent much of its time traveling citywide to locate quality goods within their modest budget to bring home to relatives. Sanatbaev recalled the excitement of a trip to the Indian store Ganga (Ganges), which offered clothing and other goods then in fashion in southern Kyrgyzstan. Other visitors and migrants recalled being struck by international stores, selling goods made in countries from Yugoslavia to China. These added to Moscow's mystique as not just a Soviet-wide destination, but one that brought the world to them. Elmira Nasirova recalled her young teenage eyes opening wide when her family took her to Moscow and the shops of Gorky Street, where she felt herself in "another world."[8]

Many childhood memories, evoked as building anticipation for future stays at the heart of the USSR, involved simple consumer pleasures—particularly centered on food. Serkebaev's mouth watered at the memory of the thirty different types of sausage the family could buy in Moscow, at half the price of those sold in Osh. Eteri Gugushvili remembered the huge variety of ice cream flavors in Moscow and how she dreamed of, and relished, her favorite, "Borodino."[9]

Abdul Khalimov recalled his own initial attraction as a young person to the Soviet capital: "When I came here to Moscow, back in my student days [in the 1970s and 1980s] that is, when I came here on holidays, I felt great. We were young of course and we met girls here in Moscow. In Soviet times it was very easy to meet girls and get to know each other." Khalimov recalled the ideal combination of being away from the watchful eyes of family and village elders in his town of Kishlaki and meeting young women unfettered by stricter cultural codes. "In 1983, we went on a trip to Astrakhan [to assist in a building project]. Not far from us was a department of the Moscow Engineering Institute. We met up with the other students from there and made friends and hung out and talked."[10] He expressed his regret that age and the less certain environment of the late perestroika years, when he moved permanently to Moscow, limited his ability to associate freely with the Russian women of his new home. His gendered narrative corresponded to others that emphasized interethnic and international relationships and solidarity among young people marveling at the scale and openness of Leningrad and Moscow and sharing experiences of their transitions from home republics or different countries. Their stories echoed those of the carefree nature and fun amid the delights of the capital that circulated among students, and in the Soviet press, from Moscow's International Youth Festival of 1957.[11]

Visitor and tourist experiences spread the word of the center's delights, but did not excite a universal desire among Soviet citizens to relocate. By the mid-1960s, state investment and economic progress had touched even distant Central Asian villages. Kindergartens, medical clinics, and cultural centers became commonplace, alongside paved, tree-lined central streets.[12] Entrepreneurial collective farm managers and district heads could use connections to build projects like hospitals and even airports.[13] To be sure, shortages, from household goods to basic building materials, endured. And, as discussed in chapter 1, economic disparities between center and periphery mounted in the 1970s and beyond. Most migrants nonetheless considered their early lives in the Caucasus or Central Asian countryside as sufficient, if somewhat mundane. In major republican cities, from Kutaisi, Georgia, to Dushanbe, Tajikistan, modern housing continually expanded boundaries and allowed for healthy population growth. New residents from the countryside—those who forsook the open air and "simple life"—enjoyed gas heating, indoor plumbing, and sometimes even air conditioners, even if the durability of new structures was questionable.[14] Urban as well as rural lives in the republics could be found wanting in many ways, as discussed below—including, for Khalimov and others, feelings of surveillance—but those considering a move to Leningrad and Moscow generally cited opportunity over desperation when deciding to leave home.

Increased Soviet travel could bring newcomers to Leningrad and Moscow in roundabout fashions. Anarbek Zakirov, content with his home life in Kyrgyzstan's Issyk Kul region in the 1960s, recalled a Soviet vacation altering his life, placing him on a multistage path to the USSR's heart. He met a Belarusian teenager when his family was on vacation at a North Caucasus sanatorium. The connection led to the offer of a visit and then well-paid work on a construction site in Minsk. Zakirov left work to perform his military service, but remembered the better salaries and working conditions in Slavic cities. He worked on his Russian language in the army and used his status as a demobilized soldier to register in Moscow, where he gained entrance to study at the institute of the National Historical Archive in 1969.[15]

Ambition, to dream beyond the bounds of village life, could be implanted. Many migrants recalled their families' role in pointing them toward Leningrad and Moscow. Parents' social progress in the immediate postwar years acted as the first stage in their own social and spatial mobility, followed overwhelmingly through education. Farshad Hajiev, born in a small town in the Pamir Mountains, discussed how his father, a Second World War veteran, ascended to the position of collective farm brigadier, with his mother taking care of the children.[16] They moved to Dushanbe so their children could attend a top-flight, Russian-language school. Aibek Botoev, raised in northern Kyrgyzstan, also had a father who rose through the collective farm ranks, while his mother cared for their ten children. Botoev's father's catchphrase was "Don't dither" (*Ne pogulat'sia*).[17] Focus on schoolwork and plans for a professional future were always demanded. Botoev attended a Russian-language school in the 1960s, before many Russians in his village left.[18] He lauded the quality of education, which served him well as he advanced to republican, and eventually all-union, capitals.

Khalimov was born in southern Tajikistan, to parents who were resettled from the mountains to grow cotton after the Second World War. He stressed how his father, though a "simple worker," had come from a wealthy and learned family, devastated by the purges and the forced migration. His father studied Russian on his own, but used Islam to craft a story of mobility that combined tradition and progress under a Soviet roof: "My father would say to me, if you want to become a person [*stat' chelovekom*], then you need to study. . . . In Islam, there were two necessary things: to get an education and to have a profession."[19] Formative parental influences pushed these village sons to seek the best possible schooling, which all took for granted was in Leningrad and Moscow, as a way to the professional careers that represented the apex of late Soviet life.

Parental intervention could continue into adulthood and produce less orthodox paths to Leningrad and Moscow. Jumaboi Esoev initially failed to fulfill the dreams of his father, who worked as a driver, for educated and professional children. He chose instead employment in a meat factory in Khorog, Tajikistan. Esoev recalled frequent paternal browbeating over his decision, which led him to pursue night courses at technical institutes to prepare him for a managerial career. His bosses noted this initiative as they considered trainees for instruction in new meat-cutting techniques developed in Leningrad in 1983.[20] Shuhrat Kazbekov had great difficulties convincing his mother, determined he become a doctor, that his path lay in another direction. He studied premedical courses in secondary education, but found an escape when his talent in figure skating was recognized and fostered in Tashkent, eventually sending him to a Soviet sports school in Leningrad.[21]

Widespread Soviet training courses, which straddled blue- and white-collar work, as well as included sporting and cultural activities, expanded opportunity for those at the far reaches of the USSR. Blair Ruble notes that Leningrad's municipal authorities poured significant resources into training and vocational programs to maintain its "competitive edge" over other Soviet cities.[22] Personal, family, and official strategies dovetailed in these cases to send students thousands of kilometers northward, and their experiences perpetuated the cycle. As a teenager, Bolot Oruzbaev joined top agriculture students in Kyrgyzstan at a one-year practicum at a dairy farm near Leningrad. He recalled, "after I returned, I talked about Leningrad for a year," inspiring friends and family to repeat his journey.[23]

Sanatbaev, gaining employment as a guide for visitors to the Kyrgyz mountain range, ended up at a Moscow institute for tourism. He spent most of his stay in the outskirts (*prigorod*), where he learned how to guide camping trips, light fires, and save drowning people. Sanatbaev noted that his curiosity with the city and his ability led to him accompanying Kyrgyz and non-Soviet Asian tourists to Moscow during his training. Sanatbaev considered this course, and his expanded duties, a sign of his own importance. His training and connections acted as a springboard toward a more permanent stay at the heart of the USSR.[24]

Higher, university education continued to hold the greatest prestige among Caucasus and Central Asian students and families. Medicine was considered a preferred choice, even as doctors' salaries and benefits remained modest.[25] Medicine represented a feasible career path for Georgians, Uzbeks, and others who saw most technical and scientific positions, even in their own republic, occupied by Russians. A Leningrad or Moscow medical degree could open doors at home and across the Soviet Union, combining opportunity and prestige. Lali Utiashvili, who grew up in Poti, Georgia, in the 1960s, recalled: "My mother was a caretaker at a kindergarten. My father worked at a factory where they made flour. Well, of course my parents had dreams for us all. There were four of us: three brothers and myself. They dreamed that we would all finish and receive a higher education. Truthfully though, my mother wanted me to get an education in medicine. But I decided to go to a different institute to become an economist."[26] Utiashvili's family expressed great joy in seeing their daughter in Moscow; even as she had chosen a different career, her place of study indicated her level of ability and potential access to Soviet privilege.

If educational opportunities evoked uniquely positive visions among those as- piring to life in Leningrad and Moscow, gray-market trading opportunities sparked more complicated emotions. Economic benefits weighed against the ex- hausting and competitive nature of the business, which is detailed in chapter 6. Eljan Jusubov noted that trade was seen as best suited to young men. A teacher in his mid-thirties, he turned to commerce, with the aid of former students, to support a large and struggling family, particularly his parents, in a small Azer- baijani town in the early 1980s. As he explored village connections to maximize the quality of goods he might bring to Moscow, he remembered, "many were against it": "They said by nature you are a sensitive person and lack the flexibility to be involved in the business."[27] The challenges of trade, mainly in apples and pears, daunted him also, but he could not see a way around it given his difficul- ties in supporting his relatives on a teacher's salary. Prices had begun to climb in distant regions of the USSR in the years before perestroika.

Traders and educated migrants alike considered travel to faraway Leningrad and Moscow against the possibilities for advancement in their own republics. In trade, word quickly spread of substantially larger profits in major, northern Russian cities, where salaries of their potential consumers were higher and goods grown in the south were in greater demand. In service and professional sectors, south- ern or eastern rural youth quickly gained awareness of the Soviet policies in their homelands, discussed in chapter 1, which favored ethnic Russians and streamed educated Central Asians, especially, toward agricultural institutes or "softer" fields in the humanities. Botoev surveyed pathways for success as he moved from his village to the Kyrgyz capital for university at the turn of the 1970s. He noted: "In Frunze, the population was about 60 percent Russian . . . [they] were arrogant and always placed in top management positions. We really disliked that."[28] Khalimov recalled that Tajik villagers suffered double isolation on arrival to study or work in Dushanbe. Already feeling that the capital, although less than a 100-kilometer journey, was a "world away," Khalimov noted the nerves that he and new classmates experienced at beginning university: "We felt tension not just between Tajiks and Russians but also between Tajiks from the city and people like myself who came from the village. It was a tension based on social position, which ended up affecting interethnic relations. Urban Tajiks spoke Russian well, and, being from the country, I obviously spoke Russian poorly. In university, when they asked questions, I knew the answer, but because I spoke poorly, my marks were lower. That made me angry."[29]

Central Asian migrants' words echoed Soviet discourse that identified and supported large cities as modern, European, or Russian, a progressive destination for those from villages characterized as backward or Asian. Urban residents, especially those in republican capitals, received stronger Russian-language education and connected well to local networks. Accent, language, dress, and other habits marked village "outsiders," regardless of ethnicity. Hajiev, born in central Dushanbe, recalled this divide from the other side: "I had the mentality of a Russian person. I went to Russian schools, with all Russian teachers and other European students."[30] He and his friends looked down on village "hicks" to emphasize their own place in a modern Soviet Union. Erkin Bakchiev, before economic challenges of the perestroika era pushed him to the capital, also remembered cultural differences based on type and level of education: "I heard, it turns out, there are people from Central Asia who studied in Moscow. I was told about them and even saw a few. And I noticed that they were fashionably dressed, and their manner of communication was different. In this sense, they were above us. If even a little bit, but their culture is higher than ours."[31]

Migrants raised in the Caucasus recalled their cities as home to several ethnic groups, without the stark divide between Russian and non-Russian. Fuad Ojagov expressed nostalgia for multiethnic Soviet Baku. Nationalities, including Russians, worked together to build a capital that was once modern and Azerbaijani: "Russians were very adaptable to our norms and traditions. They fit into our lives. Maybe once they behaved like colonialists, but . . . they enriched our lives."[32] Jews, Greeks, and Caucasus peoples contributed to a rich ethnic mix. Ojagov betrayed his assimilation of Soviet, modern hierarchies with his condemnation of the Azerbaijani villagers who "overran" Baku in the 1990s. They fled Nagorno-Karabakh, and their presence, alongside the deadly Armenian-Azerbaijani conflict and the end of the USSR, which prompted a large exodus of Armenians, Russians, and other minority ethnicities from Baku, destroyed the city's cosmopolitan character.[33] Dina Ataniyazova echoed Ojagov's views of Caucasus Russians: "Russians who have lived long in the colonies in the Caucasus and in Asia are much more sensitive, receptive to foreign cultures and tolerant. They often learn well from local people, from the simplest things, like cuisine and customs, to attitudes toward life and neighbors. In the big cities, perhaps, you could find Russians with a 'conquistador syndrome,' but overall they mixed well with the local population."[34] Whether this divergence between Caucasus and Central Asian subjects represents broader perceptions, or realities, of differing behavior in the Caucasus, where the Russian population had a longer history and the ethnic tableau was more diverse, is unclear. Shuhrat Kazbekov expressed a common sentiment among Central Asians, believing the only positive that Russians brought to Tashkent involved preparing him for the Slavic-dominated cities of Leningrad and Moscow.[35]

Collaboration between urban Kyrgyz and Russian elites in Frunze, Jyldyz Nuriaeva claimed, resulted in widespread corruption in the 1970s. Since childhood, Leningrad and Moscow had appeared to her, someone without connections, as an escape from the crooked practices of her capital. She studied hard and earned top grades to merit a designated spot at the Maurice Thorez Moscow State Pedagogical Institute of Foreign Languages, only to see her place given away at the last minute to the daughter of the Naryn executive committee chair of the Communist Party. The experience enforced her belief of wanting "to get away from Kyrgyzstan": "Kyrgyz seemed all so bad, so dishonest. This was the feeling of a seventeen-year-old with communist ideals. And I thought that such things in our system should not be."[36] Nuriaeva gained a spot at a university in Tver. She set herself to work toward a graduate placement in Leningrad or Moscow, where, she believed, her intellectual prowess would be rewarded.

Diverse paths existed to intertwine social and spatial mobility and to propel Caucasus and Central Asian peoples to the heart of the Soviet Union. Movement to Leningrad and Moscow emerged as part of a broader Soviet story. Childhood vacation tastes of ice cream or sausage, experiences with the opposite sex, stories or pressure from families, excellence in education, and personal connections, among other factors, presaged the mobility that bound the center and the edges of the USSR. Chances for personal and professional advancement signaled a dynamism in the late Soviet Union that these migrants were determined to capture.

Periphery to Core

Talent and determination peppered stories of successful transitions, as migrants gauged the qualities required to make a place in Leningrad and Moscow. Working through or around state policies and practices, they gained invitations or made their own way to the two capitals. Bolot Oruzbaev used success in his studies to increase his chances of mobility. He earned a "red diploma" (*krasnyi diplom*), granted to those who achieved a perfect slate of "fives," the highest grade conferred in the Soviet education system. Soviet citizens recognized the diploma as offering an important leg up in higher education placements or employment, though the range of choices varied depending on subjects studied, schools attended, or other factors.[37] From his village of Kara-Suu in Kyrgyzstan, Oruzbaev received an offer to study at a top Leningrad engineering institute. His view on what precipitated success was simple: "All you needed was to have a will and use your head."[38] Sadig Eldarov recalled his delight at receiving a red diploma. Already in a prestigious high school in central Baku, Eldarov believed the award signified that "all roads in front of me were now open."[39] He gained entry to Moscow State University's psychological faculty in 1976. Nino Kvernadze saw the Soviet system as recognizing her husband's talent. One of the most skilled factory workers in Georgia, she stated, he was selected through the organized recruitment (*orgnabor*) system to a Moscow enterprise in 1978.[40] Kvernadze and her husband initially vacillated, as he already had a good salary and they had a home, close to friends and family. The Moscow factory that selected him promised, and delivered on, a multi-bedroom apartment in a nice neighborhood as well as residence permits for him and his entire family. These newcomers all arrived in Leningrad or Moscow confident in the state's ability to identify, nurture, and properly reward intellectual and workplace ability.

Determination—in some cases to have their talent recognized—occupied important places in narratives of migrants who arrived in Leningrad and Moscow outside of *orgnabor* or higher-education channels. Rasul Asgarov vaunted his own combination of skills and resolve. He set himself to improve his, and his family's, economic situation, not initially considering it might lead him to Moscow. Asgarov planned to use his horticultural expertise to make money in nearby Baku. He had found ways to grow, in good quality and substantial numbers, the always-in-demand "Glory to Peace" (*Slava miru*) strain of rose, designed, apparently, for Stalin. Asgarov grappled with multiple challenges as he pursued his career. He feared being charged with "parasitism," as he was selling flowers not from his own individual collective farm plot but on land allocated to friends and family, a practice local police could verify without much difficulty.[41] He could also be accused of "shirking" for not having accepted "socially useful" employment.[42] Asgarov found work at a compressor factory for a few years until gaining a nightshift job with the Baku metro. He could then sell flowers by day, but found the routine exhausting. In 1982, intermediaries approached him to purchase flowers by the thousands to sell in Russia. He spoke Russian well, from his army service in Siberia, and decided to engage directly in sales to Moscow, where profits were highest. With the "cooperation" of Aeroflot staff, he could take four thousand to five thousand carnations on a single plane trip—the cheap and frequent flights between Baku and Moscow allowed him to get there and back in a single day. Asgarov preferred to take his flowers by train, nonetheless, which he found more relaxing. He sold his flowers to established distribution networks in the Soviet capital, with his involvement increasing as he wanted a greater share of the rewards—a flower that sold for fifteen kopecks in Baku could fetch one ruble in Moscow. Unlike in Baku, no one cared about his activities, and Moscow consumers appreciated his quality product.

News of opportunities to make significant money at the USSR's center spread throughout the Soviet Union. Vazha Gigulashvili went to Moscow with her husband in 1974; friends made during his army service told him of plentiful, well-paying jobs in the city. The move entailed risk, but Gigulashvili simply stated: "We wanted to make more money. We did not know exactly where we would find a job or if we would find one at all."[43] Eteri Gugushvili was one of the rare respondents completely unimpressed with Moscow, finding it "not that different" from her Georgian town of Kutaisi (population 25,000) when she began traveling there in 1973. She and her husband, who had attended Russian schools, nonetheless moved to Moscow in 1980 to improve their economic situation. They, like Gigulashvili and her husband, had no idea of where they would work.[44] Alex Koberidze had harvested cotton since he was a child in southern Kyrgyzstan, following his Caucasus parents, who had arrived a generation before with only elementary educations. He could not conceive of a path to leave his village until an older student at his technical school returned from vacation in Leningrad in 1979.[45] This student recounted various street advertisements he saw for well-paid plumbing and construction jobs. Consumer desires had increased in small Kyrgyz villages as televisions, refrigerators, and other modern goods appeared.[46] Despite not knowing a word of Russian, and only fifteen years old, Koberidze applied, and was accepted, to a Leningrad PTU to specialize in plumbing. At the turn of the 1980s, as discussed in chapter 1, authorities in Central Asian republics sought to move growing numbers of youth outside of their republics. Leningrad welcomed quality students, with ninety thousand Soviet citizens studying in its PTUs as municipal authorities recruited blue-collar workers.[47]

Trajectories to Leningrad and Moscow implicated emotional desires as well as practical goals. Bakyt Shakiev, who brushed aside advice that education was the best way to escape his Kazakh village, nonetheless was determined to make it to the heart of the Soviet Union: "Especially me, since childhood I dreamed to visit these cities. I ended up by reaching that dream [through a trading network]. I was ambitious, always achieved what I wanted. [I remember, as a child,] seeing Lenin's mausoleum on television. I sat, watched, and decided I must go to the Kremlin, the seat of our rulers, and see the beauty of Leningrad."[48] Aisulu Baisalbekova recalled her decision to set herself to Moscow from her Kyrgyz hometown of Naryn: "It was kind of a craving. Because we were in fact provincial, and we hardly ever got to leave. And I was able to set myself up to go."[49]

Desires to move to, or remain in, Leningrad and Moscow were not always fulfilled. Asylbek Albiev's initial encounter with the Soviet capital was coincidental;

he began his army service in the Moscow region as part of a squad of one hundred from Osh in 1976.[50] His initial work involved painting and otherwise maintaining aging industrial complexes and adjacent housing in Odintsovo, far from the city center. His squad commander assigned a Kazakh to help him learn Russian. After three months, the squad moved to the new Rossiia Hotel, where they did painting and carpentry work while staying in unfinished rooms. Albiev said the coupons they received to civilian cafeterias, unlike in the suburbs where they ate army rations together, more than compensated for sleeping, several to a room, on hard floors. Albiev worked with top-quality tiles and marveled at the massive mirrors spread across the hotel. He spent the weekends riding the Moscow metro, enjoying a free pass, and seeing the changing of the guard at the Kremlin. Despite hazing at his next assignment, a military academy back in the Moscow region, he returned home reluctantly. His parents lacked other caregivers, forcing him to abandon thoughts of joining burgeoning workforces in construction.

Personal choice and energy did not obviate the role that connections played in setting migrants toward the two capitals. Boundaries between official and unofficial pathways were blurry. The state provided an umbrella for so many activities, with personal relationships having intended and unintended consequences on policies and practices. Along with family members and schoolmates, army buddies played important roles in setting once distant citizens toward the two capitals. Leningrad and Moscow firms, unable to find sufficient labor supply through *orgnabor*, recruited, often through word of mouth, directly from conscripts as they finished their mandatory service across the USSR. Tolkunbek Kudubaev noted that fresh ex-conscripts would have gained a working knowledge of the Russian language and, through associations with urban members of their cohort, an understanding of the differentials in living standards between village and city, edge and center.[51] Soldiers grew close in the challenging environment of military life and kept each other apprised of new opportunities. Leningrad and Moscow service members were frequently taken up on offers to host now fellow ex-conscripts. Kudubaev was finishing his tour in Siberia in 1987 when a former conscript friend told him about vacancies at Moscow enterprises that worked on construction and equipment for the metro. Never having considered leaving Kyrgyzstan before his service, he weighed the opportunity against the fact that he would live in Moscow on a temporary (*limitnyi*) residence permit tied to this specific employment.[52] The salary, and the chance to explore opportunities in the capital, he felt, could not be missed.

Service connections provided, in some cases, roundabout paths to the two capitals. Farshad Hajiev's initial posting was in Leningrad, where he studied nuclear technology. His talent led him to a "secret" placement at the Semipalatinsk test site in Kazakhstan.[53] Afterward, given his unhappiness with previous study in

Dushanbe, where so many career paths seemed closed to Tajiks, he determined to return to Russia. Several universities offered him post-service scholarships based on his skills in nuclear sciences. He stuck with Leningrad, lured there by a previous connection who offered him a prime laboratory. Hajiev also considered Leningrad the USSR's most intellectual and cultured city. Jumaboi Esoev began his army service immediately following his training program at a Leningrad meat factory. After his conscript tour in the Leningrad region ended in 1985, he volunteered to serve in Afghanistan. He recounted his superiors asking him: "Why would you want to go there? You would just be killing your own people."[54] Instead, noting his good marks and upward trajectory, they placed him in a Leningrad technical institute. He also returned to the meat factory, which was always seeking workers, to earn extra money to send home to family.

Relatives in the two capitals also provided opportunities for movement. Lali Utiashvili evoked the power of connections in her coming to Moscow. Her family's "friends in high places" (vysokopostavlennye liudi) helped her husband, who felt he had reached the peak of his career at home, find a position as director at a Moscow agricultural institute.[55] These friends, in their seventies, Russians and Georgians alike, had implanted themselves in top posts in the party and state hierarchies. They had visited Utiashvili's and her in-laws' homes in Georgia during summer vacations. As Erik Scott notes, Georgians retained significant high-level connections from the Stalin period.[56] Few migrants could rely on quite so high-level networks. Terenti Papashvili's Georgian brother-in-law had moved to Leningrad immediately following the Second World War, where he ascended to head of a construction company. Decades later, he was in position to offer Papashvili a job on a temporary residence permit with dormitory accommodation, which would allow him to send money home to his wife, who would remain in Georgia with their children.[57] Levan Rukhadze, after settling into Moscow in the mid-1970s, considered it a duty to help friends, family, even strangers from his region in Armenia: "I helped in any way I could. I was able to help a lot in one respect. In the Soviet Union there were sometimes problems with airline tickets. I had a lot of connections here and made sure that no one overpaid for anything. I would help with hotel reservations as well. I would help people coming from Georgia. I would even help people that I didn't even know. My brother would give them my number."[58] Tamriko Otskheli's Moscow trajectory began when she visited her sister for the 1980 Olympics. During her stay, she witnessed how high Moscow prices were for goods readily available in Georgia and considered how she might become involved in trade, knowing she had a free place to stay in the Soviet capital.[59]

Chance connections also played a role in pathways toward the two capitals. Rukhadze was only able to write entrance exams to Moscow's Ministry of

Internal Affairs military college following a fortuitous street encounter between his father and an old friend, who had risen through the ministry's ranks in Georgia and wanted to repay an old favor.[60] "Guardian angels" allowed instant networks to form around newcomers. An Armenian singer who arrived in 1949 Leningrad found an "astonishing person" who appreciated her talent, even after she failed her conservatory audition. The man gave her thirty rubles monthly until she became successful, winning a Stalin scholarship.[61] Maia Asinadze, a nineteen-year-old librarian outside of Tbilisi, struck up a conversation with an elder Russian female tourist in 1982. Asinadze recalled: "We had an immediate connection. It was like love at first sight."[62] The connection led to an offer of space in a communal apartment in central Moscow and a chance to study. Even as Asinadze's parents had come from intellectual, albeit rural, strata—her father was a village soviet director and her mother, a nurse—she had not envisioned leaving the republic, having attended only Georgian-language schools. Georgia retained one of the strongest non-Russian language education systems in the USSR, which included, unlike other union republics, higher education in the titular tongue. This connection, and offer, however, "awoke something" in Asinadze's teenaged self. She overcame her parents' doubts and accompanied her "guardian angel," Liudmila Grigorevna, to Moscow in 1982.[63]

Connections facilitated migrants' ability to find a place in Leningrad and Moscow. Easy and cheap travel, and common citizenship, substantially reduced the risks and opportunity costs of seeking improved life chances at the heart of the USSR, even when movement was done beyond state purview. Experiences in their republican capitals, or even in smaller towns where they attended Russian-language schools or, often, had contact with Russian administrators and other personnel, lessened worries of a transition to a Slavic-dominated environment. For young men, army service unfailingly placed them in a multinational medium, with Russian the common language and with comrades of all ethnicities who might have connections to the two capitals. Leningrad and Moscow were considered more modern and cosmopolitan, less likely to be governed by ethnic prejudice or "backwater" clientelism. Measures of success achieved in the Soviet system at home enforced their belief that, with hard work, they could compete successfully at the center of the USSR.

First Impressions and Contacts

Expectations and encounters at moments of departure and arrival had the power to shape the entire migrant experience. Initial discrepancies between imagined and lived places provoke significant tension in place making.[64] First meetings shaped a sense of inclusion or exclusion in cities where migrants expected and largely respected the host nationality's primacy.[65] The friendship of peoples, as well as beliefs that Leningrad and Moscow were color-blind homes to Soviet achievement, fueled expectations that these two central cities were also their own.

Apprehension accompanied a sense of adventure, even for migrants who fully trusted Leningrad and Moscow to fulfill their dreams. Selected to continue her education in Moscow in 1977, Damira Nogoibaeva hoped youthful energy would surmount unease at moving from her Kyrgyz home, thousands of kilometers from any relative.[66] Esoev, when he first arrived in Leningrad in 1983 for training at the city's top slaughterhouse, weighed excitement at witnessing the city's beauty and thoughts of career advancement against the warnings of a village doctor, who, on an earlier exchange, was robbed and beaten by the taxi driver who took him from the airport. For traders, uncertainty reigned as they awaited fruit and vegetables to ripen and flowers to bloom in the southern climates of the Caucasus and Central Asia. If seasonal goods in other regions were ready for transport first, competitors could snap up preferred market stalls or street corners for the entire season, threatening profits even after months of preparations. Hazi Begirov had several refrigerated trucks "borrowed" from nearby collective farms in southern Azerbaijan on standby to take fruits and vegetables northward at the first opportunity.[67]

Newcomers' arrival narratives overwhelmingly emphasized initial acceptance, subsuming worries of being singled out as naive newcomers. Esoev presented his entry to Leningrad as far different from his village doctor's. Armed with but a scrap of paper with his dormitory's address, he animatedly described his first encounter: "We approached one man and asked him to give us directions. I guess this Leningrader saw we were from out of town and instead of just telling us, drove us all the way there—from the airport, through the city, all the way to our dormitory. The whole trip took about an hour. He wouldn't even take the money we offered. He said he just wanted to help. Can you believe it, we just asked for directions and he took us all the way there!"[68]

Random kindness, which Esoev and others credited to a true friendship of peoples, also characterized Begirov's arrival story. One year in the early 1980s he flew, with apprehension, to Moscow to scout market locations for his fruits and vegetables, recalling tensions between Caucasus traders and the local population the previous season.[69] When he entered a taxi, however:

> The driver asked me: "Are you Azerbaijani?" Finding out I was, he continued: "Your Heydar Aliev [an Azerbaijani member of the Politburo] works here. He's very influential. Everyone listens to him and works hard for him."

That made me feel very proud—almost like a trusted Muscovite. Our man was here, in Moscow. . . . I asked the driver: "How do you know so much about Aliev?" He answered: "Every day, these days, I take dozens of you Azerbaijanis from the airport. They started telling me about him. Now we've all become interested."[70]

David Somkishvili also recalled an individual whose kindness transformed his Moscow experience: "It was hard for me to write in Russian when I arrived. I had an exam in one of my first classes and I could not write. My professor knew that I studied well and he saw that I could not write well, so he came to me and helped me to write the exam. But that was not because I knew him before or I paid him something. No, it was just his kind will toward me, and I remember this story until now."[71]

Migrants used these foundational memories to structure their place making, recalling their impact at the time and long afterward. Two migrants, who portrayed their overall incorporation as difficult, stressed initial challenges based on their appearance. Aibek Botoev had great expectations as he boarded the train for Leningrad's Institute of Civil Engineering in 1973, ready to leave behind the rampant inequality he witnessed in Frunze. On a brief stopover in Moscow, a drunkard wielding a bottle attacked him and a friend. To Botoev, "[the attacker saw] we were from out of town, Asians, and probably thought we were defenseless."[72] Even then, he used this memory to establish a sense of inclusion at his destination, where locals assisted him in initial struggles to adapt from his Kyrgyz homeland. Botoev structured this narrative of acceptance to stream into the popular, local stereotype that presented Moscow as an uncouth, overgrown village and Leningrad as the cultural and intellectual soul of Russia and the USSR.[73] Jyldyz Nuriaeva's initial Moscow encounter resonated throughout her stay in Russia. Underlining her dark skin color, Nuriaeva remembered unfriendly stares and comments on a commuter train (*elektrichka*) as she connected to her university placement in Tver in 1974. She excused apparent Russian villagers who had been shopping in Moscow and were "too ignorant to know that such a land as Kyrgyzia existed."[74] Cosmopolitan Muscovites had no excuse for their behavior, however. This account established a background for racism she would confront on beginning studies at Moscow State University in 1978.[75]

Regardless of their welcome, migrants spoke with awe of visiting the attractions they had heard, read, and sometimes dreamed about, whether from friends or family, in schoolbooks, or on television. Interaction with Leningrad's and Moscow's physical spaces marked tangible signs of their own progress and sense of Soviet belonging. Marat Tursunbaev recalled: "I had envisaged everything: the beauty of the city, museums, concerts, a high level of education and culture of those who remained faithful to the spirit of the Russian intelligentsia of St. Petersburg [Leningrad]."[76] Gulnara Alieva's appreciation of Leningrad's modernity was on a smaller scale: "I was shocked that people took a change of shoes to the theater. What culture!"[77]

Migrants highlighted Leningrad's physical beauty and exotic nature, with magically opening bridges and the white nights, and Moscow's central buildings. The metro's bustle and the beauty of its stations in the two capitals offered evidence of the fruits of the Soviet modernity they now enjoyed.[78] For one Georgian, Fridon Tsereteli, exploring central spaces evoked more than mere wonder: "The first time I came to Moscow . . . I stood on Red Square and was overjoyed—the Kremlin, the mausoleum. It was very patriotic for me."[79]

Lenin's mausoleum, and its constant, multinational queues emerged as a nexus for new migrants to connect Moscow to the USSR and to themselves as Soviet citizens. Narynbek Temirkulov, a Kyrgyz who came to Moscow to enter university, stated:

FIGURE 6 Central Asians in queue to visit Lenin's mausoleum, in Moscow's Red Square, 1954. Attribution: Henri Cartier-Bresson / © Magnum Photos

[When I first arrived in Moscow and was met by friends] it was very exciting. . . . People were in a hurry and I did not know where they were going. . . . Then I figured out that they were queuing [at Lenin's mausoleum] for Vladimir Ilyich [Lenin]. People came at 2:00–3:00 a.m. to secure a spot. We also wanted to visit, but I was tired. . . . Soon, however, I got a chance to see that Lenin was a normal man. It was a pleasure to see him in reality.[80]

The mausoleum offered a sense of connectivity for Anarbek Zakirov, the Kyrgyz ex-conscript, who had enrolled in archival studies. Zakirov remembered how he "always ended up meeting fellow Kyrgyz and talking with them. . . . All arrivals to Moscow made an obligatory first stop there."[81] Abdul Khalimov, as a medical student, joked that he was one of the few Central Asians unimpressed with Lenin's mausoleum, as he "had already seen enough corpses."[82] Migrants and tourists alike considered these landmarks as multiethnic spaces that underlined common Soviet dreams, realized through the materialist progress of Leninist, socialist modernization.

Migrants from the Caucasus, Central Asia, and Asian Russia remained acutely aware of their national backgrounds as they placed themselves within Leningrad's and Moscow's ethnoscape. In gauging initial senses of inclusion, they measured themselves alongside other non-Slavs. Several migrants recalled what they considered a significant Jewish presence, which differentiated the two capitals from Russian-dominated cities in their home regions.[83] One Tatar stated, "[only] when I came to Piter [Leningrad, in 1979] did I know for sure who Jews were."[84] Jews' presence signaled a cosmopolitan city that could be home to more than just Russians. Gulnara Alieva preferred to approach educated and "welcoming" Jews for directions, instead of uncouth, often rude Russians.[85] She had no doubt that she could distinguish a Jewish person by sight—just as she could those who were not part of Leningrad's and Moscow's host populations.

Africans' presence conjured a vivid first impression of Moscow. Alongside Jews, Africans, primarily students, marked the distinctive ethnoscapes of major Russian cities, particularly Leningrad and Moscow, from the 1960s. Thousands sprinkled across universities as part of Khrushchev's Cold War policy that sought the alignment and allegiance of the Third World.[86] The largest concentration ended up in the Patrice Lumumba Peoples' Friendship University in Moscow. Elmira Nasirova and other Central Asian sojourners expressed superiority over Africans, whose skin was generally darker, whose clothing was more "exotic," who were not citizens and were only at the outer rung of the friendship of peoples.[87] Newcomers from the Soviet south prized associations with Europeans, considered to be chasing a similar Soviet or communist dream. Saule Iskakova recalled her happiness at gaining inclusion in a circle of Latvian students when she arrived from Kazakhstan. Her first name, common also in Latvia, served to initiate friendship and cemented her belief that "ethnos had no meaning."[88] Diverse reactions to non-Slavic newcomers signaled a desire to be included in spaces considered Soviet but also white and European, with space for select numbers of talented, hardworking citizens from across the USSR.

Russian was accepted as the unique medium of communication in the USSR's central cities. A successful adaptation to this linguistic environment was critical to place making.[89] Russian-language schooling and army service softened the transition for many newcomers; others needed to quickly master a new tongue. The Leningrad PTU that hosted Alex Koberidze offered intensive Russian-language courses during and after school hours, hoping to produce graduates who would stay and work in labor-deficient sectors of the city's economy. Other migrants, like David Somkishvili, who lacked Russian-language skills found initial transitions challenging. One Armenian who arrived in Leningrad in 1966 with a mid-level knowledge of Russian failed three attempts to gain admission to the Academy of Arts of the USSR.[90] Asylbek Albiev claimed: "If you did not speak Russian, you were not even a person."[91] Asinadze vividly recalled her first days in Moscow, when her "guardian angel" was off at work. She had balanced her initial apprehension to explore the city by herself with what she considered intermediate language knowledge, having achieved first place in her class in her school's Russian exams. She nervously but excitedly strolled past central tourist attractions and at her favorite spot, the State Universal Store (GUM) on a corner of Red Square, befriended a Yakut girl who spoke fluent Russian. They spent several days exploring the city together. One afternoon, however:

> Maybe she was already fed up with me, or maybe she just wanted me to take the next step. We were going down the escalator into the metro together. She told me that she needed to go home and that I would have to find my way home by myself. I was surprised and asked her if she was joking. I said I couldn't do it. She told me that she wouldn't walk around with me everywhere anymore. She disappeared and I was left there all alone in the metro. I started crying. No one around would help.[92]

After this incident, Asinadze intensified efforts to learn the language, but always felt a touch self-conscious at retaining a Georgian accent, which marked her as a partial outsider in the city, even as she was easily accepted by those who knew her. Aryuna Khamagova, who grew up in Ulan-Ude, Buryatia, and considered Russian her native language, recalled that a slight accent along with her appearance, fair but not recognized as wholly Slavic, marked her as different when she spoke. Her bitterest memories were of patronizing Leningraders who told her, "your Russian is very good."[93] Rafael Voskanyan expressed great annoyance at the constant corrections locals made to his language, even when it was clear, in his mind, that he was understood perfectly well.[94]

Everyday challenges of transition also involved Leningrad's and Moscow's physical environments. Several recalled their first Russian winter as something to be, at best, endured. Alieva echoed recollections of several southern migrants, recounting "cold, rain, and gray skies." For her, "that was my first impression [of Leningrad]. The city appeared unwelcoming; the weather was always gloomy. I was given to a sad mood."[95] Unpleasant weather, gray buildings, endless apartment complexes, and constantly crowded public transportation provided the greatest opportunity for migrants, especially from smaller cities or villages, to delve into positive memories of their homes and homelands. Many used the chance to remember sun shining over open spaces and bounties of fruits and vegetables, straight from nearby farms, for much of the year. Esoev recalled: "I missed my family most of all. Beside our house [in the Pamir Mountains] there was a large peach tree. In the fall, when we would come home from school, we would walk into the garden and pick a peach right off the tree and eat it. They were so tasty—sweet and juicy. Mama was a really good cook as well. I missed that too."[96] Such memories played important roles as transition strategies. They cushioned challenges of, and bumps in, place making in these two large, Russian cities through understandings that home remained welcoming, a haven to store and extract positive recollections. Esoev balanced the taste of peaches as a boy with the fact that by the time he arrived in Leningrad, he was a man, ready to make decisions and grow in life—and, now and later, in different ways, he would continue to contribute to the development of his homeland.[97]

Women's dress and demeanor in Leningrad and Moscow offered a stark contrast of "cultural scripts" from Georgia and Armenia as well as Soviet Muslim regions.[98] Gender emerged as a central terrain to contemplate place making. A broad spectrum of uncertainty reigned on how to interpret roles and relationships between men and women in Leningrad and Moscow, when, according to Azamat Sanatbaev, "women drove cars, smoked cigarettes, and earned good salaries."[99] Gender relations evoked strong memories, especially among those who had not visited the two capitals beforehand—they were seen to differ significantly even from those in large, Russian-dominated cities in the republics. Eteri Gugushvili, who had dismissed differences between her hometown of Kutaisi and Moscow, recalled: "Russian women are different than Georgians. They drink a lot; they even drank more than their husbands, which was very unusual for us."[100] Aryan Shirinov, who had come from a village in the Pamir Mountains to study at a Leningrad PTU after his army service led him to visualize broader horizons, considered this view in terms of his own incorporation, stating:

> I was shocked when I came here. I couldn't believe it. Women were smok-
> ing and drinking. Here they called it equal rights, but it was shocking to
> me. . . . The way men and women related to each other was also differ-
> ent. They were more open in public than we were at home. But what
> can you expect? This is Europe and back there is the East. . . . For some
> it was more difficult to get used to than for me. You know what they say:
> "One man's trash is another's treasure [*Komu voina, komu mat' rod-
> naia*]." Different cultures mean different social norms.[101]

New migrants measured willingness to adapt to the culture of adopted cities
against these significantly different gender relations. Esoev, also from the
Pamirs, considered men and women openly interacting and kissing as evidence
of the "real freedom" that he could now enjoy between his studies and shifts at
the meat factory.[102]

Other newcomers expressed ambivalence toward this new gender script. Farshad Hajiev's first sight of women smoking and drinking led him to see greater
freedom, but he was reluctant to accept this model of behavior as culturally superior. Russian men, he believed, were more likely than other Soviets to mistreat
women who were so open and lacked community protection.[103] Marat Tursunbaev expressed sterner disapproval of women's drinking than most newcomers,
recalling it as the largest shock of his transition: "I was not prepared for the level
of alcoholism, which I saw even among women cashiers."[104]

Sexual openness emerged as an important component of this narrative of ambivalence, as new arrivals considered their place between home and adopted,
whether Russian, Soviet, or modern, cultures, as well as spaces. Alieva's initial
memories of difference held fast throughout her decade in Moscow: "Girls smoked
and were open about every kind of behavior. They had sex more openly. Even
with five in our dorm room, one Russian brought a guy there and had sex with
him at night."[105] Many male migrants discussed overcoming their initial shock
with women's sexual behavior as the first step in a narrative of incorporation to
a freer, more advanced society. Khalimov recalled: "Back in [the Tajik village of]
Kishlaki if you brushed past the skirt of a girl, you would brag, and the whole town
would talk about it for a week. [In Moscow] until you've kissed a girl it's like you
are a stranger to her." Once he realized that such opportunities might be open to
him, he felt "rather pleasant."[106] Hazi Begirov disliked that Russian women "went
with many men at once" but came to realize the "happiness that they took from
life."[107] Shuhrat Kazbekov, considering if new types of relationships unsettled him,
simply stated: "I was a Soviet person, after all."[108]

Hajiev carefully considered the place of gender in his broader cultural adjustment from the Pamir Mountains:

When I first arrived, I was shocked to find that all of these women smoked. Yes, there was a bit of shock. I also found it surprising that women would drink without really thinking about it. Socializing was different here as well. Here it was much more open, whereas back home it was more closed, especially between men and women. But I really liked how things were so open and free here. People were very open, and they are honest and don't lie. Russians will tell you like it really is, which I respect.

This respect was not unconditional, however:

To be honest, when I first arrived, I didn't like the way people acted, especially the way men acted toward women. When they would get drunk, at a birthday party or something like that, they would start to insult the women. This was what would happen when they got drunk. I would be sitting at the table at a friend's house, and the husband and wife would start fighting with each other. This wouldn't be with the [university] faculty. But I worked at the factory [as an engineer] as well, so I had contact with the working class, and they would often quarrel with each other, men and women. I am maybe just from a different culture. We fight maybe just in a different way. But men and women here would just start arguing in a rude manner and swear at each other. So yes, that was also a shock for me. Even when associating with police officers, they would use that kind of language.[109]

Making a place in the city, Hajiev considered, involved finding ways to at least accept different modes of behavior—while continuing to appreciate how relationships worked in the home he left behind.

Female and male newcomers considered how Leningrad and Moscow altered ideas of femininity and masculinity alike. Irma Balanchivadze noted: "Russian women were dominant over men, which was very unusual for Georgian men—in our families, men play the main role. Even when we go shopping men have the money, but in Russia women hold the money, and they are more important players in families as well."[110] Somkishvili also underlined the idea of women's dominance over men in Russia, as they played "leading roles in families and relationships."[111] He claimed that as he came with his Georgian wife, this never affected him. Somkishvili represented other male migrants content to remark on different gendered roles but reluctant to question their own masculine identities. Women as well as men struggled with adjusting to new gendered scripts. Even as Eliso Svanidze was thrilled to find a job in a supermarket soon on arrival in Moscow, which would enable her to pursue a new, independent life, she expressed disapproval of "open" Russian women. "I was not isolated or differentiated from Soviet citizens, but I never felt myself as a Soviet woman."[112] Svanidze feared that accepting these roles would damage her Georgian identity. One Tajik female respondent condemned Russian women as at once undisciplined—unable to control their own children—and manipulative toward their husbands. Gender relations emerged as a space for new arrivals to consider cultural values in national and Soviet contexts. What did it mean to be Georgian, Tajik, or Soviet? How deeply did, or should, they seek incorporation into a modern, Russian, Soviet world that altered men's and women's places?

Cultural scripts popped up in unexpected, and sometimes potentially embarrassing, instances. Maia Asinadze's initial astonishment at Moscow focused not on gender relationships, but on a belief in the inhabitants' immortality:

> I remember when I first arrived I really loved it here. Why? Well, I thought, how many months I have lived here and no one was dying. No one was wearing black. In Georgia, if relatives or close friends are dying—and even when they are not close friends—people wear black. But here no one was wearing black. I didn't see any funerals or burials. To our people, the burial ceremony is very important. It's a tradition to wear black for forty days, and the funeral may last one week or more, people keep coming to your house. And in Moscow, there is nothing like that.[113]

Asinadze used this story of naïveté as a prelude to a closer relationship with her guardian angel, based on cross-cultural understanding. "So one day, I said this to Liudmila. She laughed and said that people died in Moscow every day, but they just take them to the morgue. I began to understand the differences. From that day on Liudmila started to ask me about what was good in Georgia, what types of traditions and customs we had."[114] Sharing cultural beliefs and practices allowed Asinadze to make a place in a new home by contributing rituals from her part of the Soviet Union. The story also established a transition from a green country youth to a city person, increasingly aware of the rhythms of Moscow life.

Freedom, being away from parents and families, and excitement at being in the heart of the Soviet Union wrestled with initial discomfort in the memories of some students and other younger migrants. Sadig Eldarov, beginning his life in a Moscow university dormitory at age seventeen, remembered: "It was my first time having an independent life—a world of new relationships. On the one hand, this new, unknown world lured me with its novelty and its diversity; on the other, it frightened and disturbed me."[115] From his dormitory mates' lack of attention to study—as opposed to his elite Baku high school experience—to their frequency of sexual liaisons, Eldarov remained cautious with his social circles. Damira

Nogoibaeva, who came to study at Moscow State University, characterized "a completely different life," one full of temptations but also of uncertainties, if not dangers.[116] More common, however, were declarations made by those like Aryan Shirinov, who underlined personal agency and determination. "I was young and the boss of my own life."[117] For Lali Utiashvili, even as she held to her Georgian identity and eventually, never fully incorporating to Moscow, built a second home in Georgia: "I arrived here and immediately understood that I needed to accept things the way they were."[118]

Migrants considered the benefits of moving within one Soviet space, under control of a single state. Akmal Bobokulov, who witnessed many fellow Uzbek villagers move back and forth during his service in the Baltic Fleet, saw one USSR as overcoming important differences between the distant rural peripheries and core: "Very little was similar between my birthplace and Leningrad. The climate is different. The culture is different. The way of life is different. But it was also one country: the Soviet Union. We had the same system, the same rules, the same ideology, so that made it very easy to move around the country and adapt without any problems."[119]

Nostalgia for Soviet unity echoes in several narratives of transition. Bobokulov and others discussed how the similar socioeconomic level of the great majority of Soviet citizens acted as a homogenizing force. Even with their showcase status, Leningrad and Moscow retained a somewhat familiar urban landscape to republican capitals across the USSR, in terms of basic housing patterns and services. As Steven E. Harris has noted, the shift to single-family apartments as the preferred model of Soviet housing occurred union-wide, affecting 140 million citizens from 1953 to 1970.[120] The dull sameness of Soviet apartment blocks was commemorated in the popular 1976 movie *The Irony of Fate, or Enjoy Your Bath!* (*Ironiia sud'by, ili S legkim parom!*). Clothing and consumer habits did not differ substantially, even if availability of goods did, between the urban, significantly Russian, populations of republican capitals from Tallinn, Estonia, to Tashkent, Uzbekistan. Soviet citizens could read similar newspapers and watch the same television shows. The same slogans celebrated Lenin and the Communist Party, and many of the same holidays were feted.

Economics student Saule Iskakova and butcher Jumaboi Esoev, from the moment of their arrival, considered Leningrad and Moscow as the physical embodiment of a collective Soviet striving for a better life, on the one hand, and individual social mobility, on the other. This sense of becoming part of a quintessentially Soviet place finds common ground with a Sovietized idea of joining a modern, Western, European world, which necessitated leaving features of former homes and identities behind. Said Nabiev, who came from Khorog to study cinematography in Leningrad in 1960, insisted: "Even though I was born in

Tajikistan, I think it would have been much more difficult to get used to living in a place like Mongolia or Japan. For me, Europe has always been closer. Well, maybe here is not completely Europe, at least not in the political sense, but the style of life is European."[121] Nabiev's account mirrors others that shape Soviet and Western evolutionary discourse toward personal ambitions. Even many traders, whose lack of Russian language skills and education limited their options in Leningrad and Moscow, could imagine, as they walked the streets for the first time, their children enjoying success there, assisted by the money gained from their hard work and state-provided education. Making a place in Leningrad and Moscow signified inclusion in a way of life as much as in a concrete, physical space.

New Homes

Initial housing played a critical role in adaptation to Leningrad and Moscow life. Soviet postwar leaders sought to integrate work and accommodation with an overall socialist culture.[122] Educational institutions, ministries, factories, and other local hosts played important roles not only in building or locating housing but also in offering amenities, from libraries to gymnasiums.[123] In the crowded centers of the two capitals, those on study and work assignments generally received shared dormitory accommodation.[124] Newcomers saw this ubiquitous style of housing for new arrivals—which generally included free or subsidized meals—as leveling opportunities for those across the Soviet Union. Sharing rooms and facilities promoted connections that could be based on ethnicity, friendship, and mutual need.[125] The variety of associations engendered in these sites—despite their exterior gray sameness—highlights Doreen Massey's argument that places do not have single, essential identities. Constellations of encounters in dormitory and other accommodations conditioned initial incorporation and a sense of community in the two capitals.[126] Migrants could test associations and relationships that would best assist them with psychological and practical transitions.[127]

Dormitories' shared sleeping quarters, kitchens, and bathroom facilities emerged as vital initial sites of interaction in migrant narratives. Russians from outside Leningrad and Moscow joined citizens from across the USSR; university residences frequently included students from the wider Communist world and nonaligned countries. Scattered across the two capitals, this Soviet system of housing prevented the residential clustering or isolation that affected former colonial migrants—students or workers—in Great Britain or France, as discussed in chapter 1, and even African Americans who moved to northern industrial U.S. cities following the Second World War.[128] Nancy Foner and others consider residential segregation as severely restricting to incorporation into modern industrial cities.[129]

Moscow State University's towering spires awed newcomers who would be studying and sleeping there. The building appeared as a symbol of opportunity and a reward for their accomplishments. "What a university! What a capital!" exclaimed Iskakova.[130] In Leningrad, university housing conditions changed over time. A few informants who emphasized their village roots considered sharing rooms with up to four other students and bathroom facilities with dozens far from ideal. Alieva was crammed into an aging dormitory in Leningrad's center with her four roommates. Cold, crowded, and dingy residences were replaced by new buildings in the 1970s, albeit farther from the center, as city authorities struggled to match demands for single-family apartments for locals as well as host a rapidly growing population. Overall, dormitory accommodation of even less renowned institutes of higher education in both cities was greeted with satisfaction. Narynbek Temirkulov praised his room's orderliness, with bedding tidily stacked in the corner, as a symbol of the respect given to new arrivals. Hajiev's monthly stipend in early 1980s Leningrad allowed occasional restaurant dinners or theater tickets, given that canteen food was heavily subsidized and the university offered free cultural performances. For many graduate students, the dormitories compared favorably to those in home republics. Shirinov expressed the most common sentiment: "I was young and did not need anything more."[131]

The dormitory emerged in migrant stories as the embodiment of the friendship of peoples—both for its multinational character and for the sense of common striving toward a Soviet goal of personal and societal progress. Wonder and nostalgia highlighted memories:

> Russians, Ukrainians, Uzbeks, Turkmen, Kazakhs, Kyrgyz, Azerbaijanis, Armenians, Georgians, Chechens, Dagestanis, Belorussians, Tajiks, Buryats from the Lake Baikal region, Tatars, Birobidzhanis, and so on; maybe I am forgetting others.[132]
>
> My neighbors were from all over the world. There was one brother from Turkmenia, from Moldavia, from Poland, from Nigeria, from Afghanistan, yes three from Afghanistan, a girl from Peru, from Yemen, and two girls from Palestine.[133]

Student solidarity tightened interethnic bonds in these stories. Zakirov recalled being impressed with his Russian and Caucasus dormitory mates' knowledge of Chingiz Aitmatov, the renowned Soviet Kyrgyz author, which eased his comfort level in faraway Moscow.[134] Advanced students took newcomers on city tours and to dinner at graduates' flats. Occasional arguments, blamed on alcohol, personal disagreements, or, most frequently in the memories of both male and female migrants, "girls," did not threaten communal harmony.[135] One dissenting voice emerged from our Soviet respondents, and it was a strong one: Dina Ataniyazova chose to rent a flat as part of her graduate studies in the 1980s, as "dormitories were always considered to be a hotbed of all kinds of evil in Moscow's universities—from debauchery to drugs and drunkenness, and, besides, they were a place where ethno-minorities were melted in a smoldering Moscow boiler."[136]

Overall memories of dormitory life among students from Soviet peripheries clash with accounts and recollections of Africans. As Maxim Matusevich writes, African student letters home and memoirs emphasized crowded conditions, bad food, poor sanitary facilities, and the overall drabness of dormitory life. Unsatisfactory housing generally preceded complaints from Africans of "no cars, no cafés, no clothes, no good food" or "[nowhere] a trace of the civilized pleasures of Paris, or even Dakar."[137] African students, often elite members of their own society, had grown up in Western colonial environments and were not conditioned to Soviet lifestyles or life paths. Constantin Katsakioris notes that African students complained of isolation. Either Soviet students ignored them or they were made aware of their inferior status in the eyes of authorities—Moscow State University divided foreign students into three tiers: first, Europeans and Latin Americans; second, Asians and Arabs; and, third, Africans.[138]

Solidarity persisted in migrant memories of dormitories assigned to Leningrad's and Moscow's temporary labor force, despite conditions. A 1975 Moscow district study revealed that temporary worker housing was in a deplorable state.[139] Cockroach infestations and a lack of functioning basic utilities were commonplace. A decade later, Tolkunbek Kudubaev recalled that ramshackle worker dormitories were at least one step below those assigned to students in terms of quality. Still, on his floor, he noted that Russian dorm *komendanty* (leaders) "acted without pretension toward non-Russians."[140] He considered poor heating, lighting, and plumbing as placing residents in the same boat, quelling possible tensions. Terenti Papashvili, who arrived in Leningrad in 1985 as a temporary construction worker, found the lack of privacy in dormitories challenging, even as he believed them suitable for temporary stays and compensated for by good working conditions and salary.[141] Above all, lodging was free, and included many meals, allowing him and others to send as much money home as possible. On weekends, for relaxation, he could stay with his brother-in-law in a private apartment.[142]

Student or worker dormitories provided "unofficial" spaces for family members, friends, or villagers who visited the two capitals to sightsee, to shop, or perhaps to investigate their own potential pathway to Leningrad and Moscow. Mirbek Serkebaev noted that he would sometimes bribe his floor monitors to allow guests to sleep on the floor of his room, a practice commonplace throughout the cities. New arrivals, even as they placed pressure on kitchen and washroom facilities, recalled being easily accepted, even when there for months at a time. Dormitory space existed, in migrants' minds or at least their memories, for anyone who had the will and energy to seek opportunity in Leningrad or Moscow. Visitors brought fresh stories of home and enlivened connections with room- and floor mates through cooking and celebrating local holidays. Bolot Oruzbaev noted the delight of those who found that the wide availability of meat and other food-stuffs in Leningrad and Moscow allowed for the better cooking there, even of "national" dishes, than in their homelands. Narynbek Temirkulov believed dormitory life made the transition to alienating cities "not difficult": "I grew up in a collective, and did not require special conditions. In [my first] dormitory I lived in a collective, as I did in a children's house."[143] Bonds allowed a cushion, even a place of refuge, for those who sought to become "city people" as they gauged Leningrad and Moscow life, without forgetting their homelands.[144]

Making a place in Leningrad and Moscow involved gaining comfort and security within physical spaces, new networks and homes, as well as envisioning pathways to improve life chances. Broader ideas and initial efforts to join "Europe" reverberated in student and professional memories. Traders and blue-collar workers with short- or long-term visions of stays in the two capitals also found new aspiration and inspiration in modern Soviet ideas of progress as they joined multiethnic communities. Leningrad and Moscow's faces generally met, if not exceeded, the initial expectations of those who arrived from thousands of kilometers away, with all varieties of backgrounds and hopes. Once they found their feet, they sought to navigate these complex and dynamic worlds, with different cultural traditions and practices. Relationships forged even before they came to the two capitals, as well as those formed on arrival, proved critical as the place-making process shifted to one of everyday life in the classroom and at work. Leningrad's and Moscow's versions of Soviet hierarchies, with which these newcomers already had degrees of familiarity, became the next major test for incorporation.

RACE AND RACISM

Racist epithets and behavior accompanied the welcoming words and acts that darker-skinned or darker-haired Soviet newcomers experienced in Leningrad and Moscow. Migrants from the Caucasus, Central Asia, and Asian Russia heard calls of "blacks" (*chernye*), "black snouts" (*chernomazye*), or "black asses" (*chernozhopy*). "Black"-themed insults extended to fair-skinned Caucasus traders, though were not applied, as elsewhere in the industrialized world, to South Asians, African Americans, or Africans; the last were characterized as "*negry*," a moniker that became racialized but lacked the bite of the terms hurled at fellow Soviet citizens. Blackness became a discourse and a category to articulate anxieties of some white, or European, Russians toward growing migration from former colonial peripheries.

Epithets and other discriminatory acts in Leningrad and Moscow underscored a dimension to everyday interethnic interactions that the regime sought to conceal. The friendship of peoples denied prejudice within the USSR's borders while condemning it elsewhere in the world. State practices generally recognized equality among citizens. Even as newcomers reported numerous pathways to integrate into Leningrad and Moscow, however, so-called black migrants faced unique challenges. As movement to the USSR's "showcase cities" grew and evolved, race emerged as a category of inclusion and exclusion in Leningrad's and Moscow's streets and workplaces. Nationalist groups sought to capture this tension, claiming southern migration as a threat to Russia's dominance, and perhaps its existence.

Increased late twentieth-century migration from once colonial peripheries connected Leningrad and Moscow to global patterns of south-north mobility.[1]

On the streets of London, Paris, and elsewhere, the appearance of former colonial subjects triggered significant, though not ubiquitous, intolerance.[2] Sporadic racial violence in the West was mirrored in attacks on African students in 1960s Moscow. Soviet citizens appeared to avoid deadly racial confrontations; those interviewed for this project remained proud of their common citizenship—one state, one passport, one set of laws—that distinguished them from postcolonial migrants in the West as well as non-Soviets in Leningrad and Moscow.[3] They lauded the freedom and dynamism of the late Soviet era, symbolized by the two capitals. Racist epithets and actions, however, had a particular affective resonance that could constrain life hopes and plans. In a system with limited opportunities for collective mobilization, personal agency and everyday relationships played critical roles in determining newcomers' paths, as, sometimes, "blacks," at the centers of the Soviet world.

Racial ideas in late twentieth-century Europe evolved, David Theo Goldberg has argued, largely within this specific dynamic of migration—the "empire c[oming] home to the metropole."[4] Efforts to guard white, European privilege at the hearts of former empires led features such as skin color and hair texture as well as certain behaviors to become identified at the everyday as well as the scholarly level as racial, with the understanding that these differences were rooted in biology and transmitted through culture.[5] As Barbara J. Fields and Karen E. Fields note, racism as a practice emerged seamlessly from race as an idea: inborn traits, which at once separate groups, inevitably place one above another.[6] Identifying specifically racial differences remains a "moving target"—as Rogers Brubaker has argued, categories of ethnicity and, what was most common in Soviet parlance, nationality operated alongside race as an "integrated family of forms of cultural understanding, social organization, and political contestation."[7] Blackness offered another tool—alongside Soviet national hierarchies—to elevate Russians. It was also mobilized to suppress differences and undermine positive, albeit essentialized, representations of former colonial subjects that circulated through the friendship of peoples. In the USSR, "black" subsumed varied Caucasus and Central Asian nationalities, just as in Great Britain, "black" united South Asians, West Indians, and Africans.[8] In both cases, blackness related not simply to phenotype but also to popular images of migrants whose presence ostensibly threatened European host societies' socioeconomic hierarchies and ways of life.[9]

Ethnic, national, and racial categories interacted with other Soviet hierarchies as differential opportunities catalyzed migration. As in other industrial states, narratives that trumpeted urban, Western cultural superiority percolated to newcomers themselves, reshaped toward an idea that individual ability and desire would allow the abandonment of "Asia" to join "Europe."[10] Those who claimed to possess the appropriate social or intellectual background, talent, or energy to

belong in large urban centers, particularly the USSR's two capitals, placed themselves above those from the hinterland.[11] Ideas of culture, civilization, and class
could mix with labels of ethnicity, nation, and race to challenge as well as establish hierarchies and to allow space for victims of racism to meet goals in their new
homes.[12]

The discrimination encountered by Soviet "blacks" on Leningrad's and
Moscow's streets can be examined within a global south-north migration pattern
as well as within a dynamic USSR. Prejudice, shaped by state policies, street-level
discourse, and perceptions of appropriate hierarchies, narrowed paths of incorporation. Migrants shaped and interpreted everyday encounters within an individual and a Soviet context, balancing inclusion and humiliation. The alternate
hierarchies they designed challenged ethnic Russian domination in Leningrad and
Moscow society and linked Soviet migrant goals and actions to those across the
postcolonial world.[13]

The Spectrum of Intolerance

Intolerance against Soviet migrants from the Caucasus, Central Asia, and Asian
Russia ran the spectrum from stares to epithets, from slights to violence. Skin or
hair color, facial features, clothing, cultural expressions, and language mixed with
other aspects of identity in marking boundaries. Incidents were discrete; migrants
agreed overwhelmingly, though not unanimously, that discrimination was neither
pervasive nor universal and that the Soviet state enforced peace on Leningrad's
and Moscow's streets. Several discussed intolerance in broad strokes; instead of
highlighting specific incidents, they spoke of common but "subtle," "ironic,"
or "concealed" discrimination. David Mellor and his colleagues have noted
this phenomenon in Western countries: "Subtle racism occurs in the context of
everyday routines, such as shopping, using public transport, and eating in restaurants; it has a major negative impact on those who experience it in their daily
lives."[14] Soviet migrants noted unfriendly, penetrating stares. Questions, however intended, such as "where do you come from?," signified otherness if not
rejection.[15] Sojourners from southern and eastern regions became an undiffer-
entiated category of visitors, who nonetheless held varied opinions on the effect
of the host society's reactions on their life chances.[16]

Shouted on the streets, in restaurants, or in queues, racist epithets became a
feature of daily life for many subject to their sting. Uzbek student Marat Tursunbaev heard constant cries of "black" in the 1970s.[17] Black-related insults reached
the ears of most of the Soviet migrants we interviewed over their time in late
Soviet Leningrad and Moscow, from the 1950s to the end of the USSR. African

students recalled a different set of epithets: "Black monkey," at times, alongside the more frequent "*negry*," as well as formulations such as "go wash your body."[18] Aryuna Khamagova, of mixed Buryat and Russian heritage, who considered her fair appearance as saving her from such attacks, recalled other terms that reverberated with several migrants. "Aggressive Leningrad dwellers [in the 1970s] offended my non-Russian classmates with words like 'non-Russian,' '*chukchi*,' or '*churkoi*.'"[19] Another term she and others recalled from that time was "*ponaekhali*." Author Anya Ulinich captures its meaning: "The single word *ponayehali* means 'they arrived over a period of time, in large enough masses as to become an annoyance. . . . Here abuse is compact and efficient; two prefixes do the job of a sentence."[20] Caucasus, Central Asian, and eastern Russian migrants considered it singularly demeaning, signaling outsiderness and emphasizing that their "own" Soviet centers of power, the wealthiest two cities in the union, were not for them.

Outsiderness struck Khamagova most deeply when in line at a Leningrad theater in the mid-1970s. A male Russian companion, invited by her Buryat friend, heard someone yell to him: "Shame on you for walking with such a monkey. You should find a Russian girl for making love."[21] Tensions over interracial dating, well known in London and Paris, had migrated to the USSR, though generally applied to relationships between outsider men and local women.[22] African students accompanying Russian women recalled verbal and physical abuse from the arrival of the first contingents in Moscow at the beginning of the 1960s.[23] Just after a 1958 attack by young whites on a mixed-race couple escalated into an all-out battle with hundreds of participants, involving knives and petrol bombs, in London's Nottingham and Notting Hill neighborhoods, Russian vigilante squads formed to police interracial contact in their capital.[24] A declaration of Russian nationalism written for a Moscow Komsomol leader in 1965, titled "A Code of Morals," called for the "sterilization of women who give themselves to foreigners."[25] Russian nationalist intellectuals grew alarmed at the divergence in birthrates between their nation and those in the Caucasus and Central Asia in the 1970 census. Alexander Solzhenitsyn wrote in 1974 that "the fate of Russians concerns me above all."[26] The theme of protecting the nation occurred in samizdat literature and certain sections of the Communist Party, even as it never rose to the level of official doctrine in the 1970s and 1980s.[27] Russian superiority in the USSR required demographic as well as political dominance; the growing presence of dark-skinned or dark-haired Soviet migrants in Russia's most important cities—symbolized through the epithet "*ponaekhali*"—bore witness to statistical evidence that this dominance was slipping.

Waits in Leningrad's and Moscow's ubiquitous queues—where competition for scarce goods stoked all types of friction—produced multiple stories of racialized encounters and epithets. After an hour in line waiting for meat in early 1980s

Moscow, Emin Gazyumov heard the clerk announce that no more good cuts remained. Another shipment was in transit, but those who wanted fattier portions could approach. Doing so, he heard from an aggressive crowd cries of "*Ponaekhali!*," "*Chernozhopie!*," which made him aware of the consequences of his dark skin.[28] Aibek Botoev recalled how cries of "*chernye*" and "*churkoi*" in queues and on the streets made him and his friends "rabid with anger" and unsure how to respond.[29] Tatars found most offensive other epithets, including "pork snout" (*svinoe rylo*) and "donkey ears" (*oslinoe ukho*), spoken even in children's play areas.[30] Everyday encounters did not require epithets to carry a sting of intolerance. Jyldyz Nuriaeva, a doctoral student, recalled constant stares on Moscow's buses, shops, and streets, which she credited to her particularly dark skin. Gulnara Alieva, like Nuriaeva a Kyrgyz, recalled numerous incidents, from comments on the bus when she was wearing a headscarf—"you see, Asia is everywhere"—to having the receptionist at her dental office continually asking her, "You are here again?"[31]

Several migrants downplayed intolerance to highlight their own incorporation into Leningrad and Moscow. Anarbek Zakirov recalled how easily he joined Moscow's main police force, or militia, as part of the Administration of Internal Affairs in the 1970s, rising quickly to the level of sergeant. He only made this move, however, after a professor's "hidden chauvinism" toward his Kyrgyz background affected his studies at the National Historical Archive Institute of Moscow State University. On the streets in his new employment, even as Zakirov professed not to be bothered by constant questions of "where are you from?," he spoke about conflicts "on the level of daily life" (*na bytovom urovne*) and about people who "tried to bring him down."[32] He was only willing to elaborate on positive memories, primarily how his fellow militia and everyday Muscovites appreciated his work and how easily he made friends. Tacking between memories of inclusion and exclusion, Zakirov's ambivalence over how to interpret discrimination highlights the complicated, individual nature of reactions toward prejudice. How these incidents became activated, in his and others' cases, depended on personal psychology as well as broader structural and ideological contexts that situated darker, postcolonial migrants as particular aliens in, if not threats to, European cities.

Dina Ataniyazova labeled host Russians' subtle efforts to distance darker-skinned "blacks" as "ironic chauvinism," given their ostensible obligation under the friendship of peoples to help Soviet citizens from less-developed regions. She appreciated that the doctrine of friendship allowed her to interact in a relatively "normal" way in official life, as her colleagues were careful to avoid outright discriminatory language or acts. Ataniyazova, from the North Caucasus, recalled nonetheless, as did many others, isolation when Russian colleagues or neighbors would exclude her from social activities or professional networks. This was intensely frustrating given her position as a doctoral student in the Oriental Studies Faculty at Moscow State University, where the goal was to understand "the East" but where Russian colleagues considered themselves superior interpreters of foreign cultures and denigrated her "local" knowledge.[33]

Fuad Ojagov and other, predominantly professional, migrants from the Caucasus considered their fair appearance as saving them from street-level prejudice and allowing them to pass for Russians or Slavs in educational institutes or workplaces.[34] Physical features increasingly replaced other markers of inclusion and exclusion. Nikolai Mitrokhin's study of Russian nationalism noted that in the postwar decades, the idea of a common Christian heritage, which once bound Georgians and Armenians to Russians, waned.[35] Kyrgyz Mirbek Serkebaev offered his own explanation for the purported easier integration of Georgians and Armenians. Parroting early representations of Soviet national hierarchies, he argued that the two Caucasus nations "reached civilization earlier than us [Central Asians]."[36] In addition to demonstrating the resiliency of state-generated national discourse, Serkebaev gave a concrete example: in Moscow, Russians far more often frequented Georgian and Armenian restaurants than Azerbaijani or Central Asian ones. Phenotype, nationality, and ideas of modern culture mixed as markers of insiderness and outsiderness.[37] Charles Quist-Adade, a Ghanaian student in 1980s Moscow, noted that among Africans, skin tone mattered. North Africans who, he thought, could pass for Central Asians, were less subject to discrimination. Other aspects, including their country's loyalty to the communist cause, might also factor into relations with the host society.[38]

Personal names could also activate discrimination. Tatars who were sufficiently light-skinned, Oksana Karpenko writes, adopted Russian names on arrival to Leningrad or Moscow—Kamil would become Nikolai, or Kolya.[39] Migrants who had children in Moscow sometimes gave them Russian names and worked, generally through bribery, to have them declared ethnically Russian on their passport even if that was not the nationality of either parent.[40] This was a risky strategy. One Tatar informant whose teacher discovered his background ridiculed his Russian name, humiliating him in front of students. Ataniyazova noted the derision Russians expressed when it was "discovered" that a colleague with a Russian name or passport nationality had a non-Russian ethnic background.[41] Ojagov considered his education, coming from a top Russian-language Baku school, as well as his light skin color as allowing him to pass quite often for Russian. But he recalled faces darken when he told Muscovites that he was an Azerbaijani.[42] Efforts to transgress the friendship of peoples' establishment of distinct nationalities, and to challenge the popular notion that appearance was a "biogenetic" marker of nationality, led to insults and isolation, for children and adults alike.[43]

Institutes of higher education could be a shelter from insults, but also a site of discrimination. Resentment of the quota system, which guaranteed students from non-Russian republics spots in Leningrad and Moscow universities, was widespread.[44] Gulnara Alieva recalled professors constantly complaining that Central Asians had a lower level of education but refusing them extra assistance, in her mind in the hopes that poor marks would force them home.[45] Azay Husynov recalled one professor openly stating that she had given him a lower grade because she did not like peoples from the Caucasus.[46] A Jewish professor himself recalled in an interview after emigrating from the Soviet Union: "One may hear many anecdotes about the illiterate scripts received by Central Asian graduates."[47] Shuhrat Ikramov, an Uzbek science postdoctoral student, believed he was not given the same level of training as Slavic colleagues.[48] Antipathy toward the quota system also emerged in the street-level cries that Khamagova heard of "our children cannot get a higher education because of you."[49] Ikramov, Nogoibaeva, and others, as they recalled the superior resources of Leningrad's and Moscow's universities and generally good relations with Russian students, echoed Goldberg's findings of Asian and African migrants in Europe often being reminded: "Your sojourn is temporary, so do not get too comfortable."[50] Soviet officials and media publicized student, intellectual, or professional exchanges that brought Uzbeks, Georgians, and others to enjoy the benefits of the two capitals. Their goal, however, if not always realized, was to deploy newly trained and educated graduates back to their places of origin. Knowledge and skills acquired through contact with the elder brother would be deployed to elevate the USSR's peripheries.

Attacks against darker-skinned Soviet citizens occurred on Leningrad's and Moscow's streets, though there is no evidence that they reached the seriousness of those toward African students in the early 1960s. With or without Russian women, Africans reported to their embassies that they were subject to frequent physical violence in public parks and other spaces, with police choosing not to intervene.[51] The death of Ghanaian Edmund Assare-Addo, found beaten along a roadside in suburban Moscow, prompted an unsanctioned protest in Red Square by several hundred African students against racism in 1963.[52] Adverse worldwide publicity led to a burst of activity in universities and among officials to address racial tensions in the city that claimed to be the center of a global antiracist movement.[53] Mitrokhin, examining Soviet-era criminal records, and Quist-Adade, focusing his own research on African media and interviews with African students, both discuss later attacks as sporadic and random, even though they could be quite violent.[54] Among student and professional migrants interviewed for this project, only Aibek Botoev recalled violence against his person, attributing his "Asian" appearance to a drunkard's attack on him and a friend at a Moscow train station in 1973.[55]

Caucasus or Central Asian traders emerged as targets for physical violence in the oral histories we collected. Trade evoked sharply negative imagery in the socialist state. Victor Shnirelman has connected trade to the term "black," used by Russians to refer to speculation and criminal activities undertaken largely by minority populations.[56] Intertwined images of nation, race, and commerce precede the USSR. Early twentieth-century tsarist-era Russians saw business as alien to their nation, a demeaning activity to be undertaken by others.[57] Ethnic riots, often triggered by food shortages blamed on petty merchants, targeted Germans and Jews as well as Caucasus and Central Asian peoples, whose activities were considered "dark" (*temnye*) or "black."[58] The connection between the racialization and socioeconomic foundation of Russian/Soviet "blackness" finds parallels in London's conceptions of "dirty labor" and the racialized underclass that Malcolm Cross and Michael Keith see as characteristic of Western industrial capitals.[59] In imperial Russia and the USSR, these dark or black peoples were seen as potential exploiters of vulnerable white locals, as well as symbols of backwardness.

As their numbers grew in 1970s–1980s Leningrad and Moscow, Caucasus and Central Asian peoples came to dominate overlapping images of traders and aliens. Street-level tensions developed even as many merchants emphasized the appreciation they encountered from the host population for providing quality, affordable goods in markets and at bus and metro stops. Samizdat and other pamphlets linked Caucasus and Jewish peoples, through their business practices, as exploiters of the Russian nation. This marked a change from the Stalin era, when Caucasians—primarily Georgians—were seen primarily as political exploiters.[60] Emil Draitser notes that Georgians became the initial target of ethnic humor as numbers of Caucasus traders increased.[61] The back rooms of the main Georgian restaurant, the Aragvi, gained a citywide reputation as the engine of Moscow's unofficial economy.[62] "Dark-haired men with mustaches" selling goods across Leningrad, Moscow, and other major Russian cities became recognized by the 1980s as not just Georgians, however, but "individuals of Caucasian nationality" (*litsa kavkazskoi natsional'nosti*, or *LKN*), a term that itself became racialized. Azerbaijanis gained a reputation as the most aggressive salesmen.[63] Jokes sought to make light of the common assumption that these southerners were exploiting host Russian societies.[64] Azerbaijani trader Elnur Asadov and others interviewed for this project remembered catcalls such as "the blacks have come to take our money" alongside the usual epithets. The idea of the "blacks want to take over everywhere" circulated among everyday Russians.[65] Sporadic fistfights and brawls, usually sparked by accusations of cheating, are detailed in chapter 6. Eljan Jusubov believed that so-called black traders served as a scapegoat for locals' everyday troubles, intensifying as perestroika roiled the country at the turn of the 1990s.

Caucasus traders' greatest frustration involved the actions of local police. Asadov remembered officers frequently robbing him, even after he paid bribes to trade on specific street corners.[66] Gazyumov, though not a trader himself, recalled his anger at markets when the militia took the word of Russians who blamed Caucasus merchants in any conflict, regardless of whether they had witnessed it or not.[67] Jusubov noted the "moral suffering" of constantly being stopped and asked for identification. He hated this more than dealing with occasional angry and violent customers, who were at least balanced by Muscovites who treated him with kindness.[68]

Discrimination in Leningrad and Moscow affected newcomers from the Soviet south and east on the street, in universities, in workplaces. Whether experienced directly or related by a friend or colleague, racial or ethnic epithets and actions emphasized distance from the local population. They challenged integration into cities considered the height of Soviet achievement. At the same time, these migrants overwhelmingly considered prejudicial incidents as sporadic rather than systemic, not posing impregnable barriers to the realization of their own goals. The act of understanding and interpreting, as well as recalling, discrimination emerged as at least as important as the act of experiencing it.

Responses to Intolerance

Understanding and responding to racism and related forms of discrimination, as they flow from political or (post)colonial positions, socioeconomic inequalities, or perceptions of difference, is an intensely personal exercise. Migrants offered varied interpretations of and explanations for intolerance in their new environments. Those labeled as Soviet blacks overwhelmingly isolated the responsibility for racism to discrete sections of the host society as they sought inclusion in Leningrad and Moscow. Their words and memories show discrimination as a relationship between individuals and groups who benefit from racial privilege and those who are victimized by its language and actions, shaped by societal patterns of behavior and implicating multiple hierarchies ranging from culture to class.[69] Each newcomer employed strategies, unique or tied to collective discourses and practices, to cope with minority status. The rarity of physical violence in late Soviet Leningrad and Moscow eased efforts to strive for professional or economic opportunities unavailable in home republics. Migrants reshaped the two capitals to portray themselves as insiders even when recalling the resentment that accompanied reminders of their inferior status as non-white, non-Slavic minorities.

Newcomer efforts to shape new homes employed the advantages offered by the Soviet system, including citizenship and the symbolism as well as the policies behind the friendship of peoples. Documents and everyday official speech referred to newcomers to Leningrad and Moscow by their nationality, rather than as migrants or aliens, even though non-Russians' accepted home was in their "own" union republics.[70] Unlike in late twentieth-century Western Europe, where migrants coalesced around social or political organizations to fight inequality, claiming legal and constitutional protections, the Soviet environment offered no opportunities for mobilization outside the officially color-blind state, heightening the importance of unofficial networks for collective action.

Dina Ataniyazova, in her studies of ethnic relations in Moscow and experiences as a Caucasus resident there, argued that broader understandings of issues such as power and colonialism are needed to interpret prejudice. Ataniyazova echoed Philomena Essed, whose work on everyday racism in the Netherlands stresses the importance of possessing both "general knowledge" of patterns of prejudice and "situational knowledge" of acceptable behavior in particular circumstances; otherwise, as one Netherlands migrant remarked, "you notice something [a manifestation of intolerance], but do not dwell on it."[71] "General knowledge," however, needs to be understood as recognizing the ambivalence as well as the foundations of street-level prejudice. Soviet migrants had general knowledge of the socioeconomic differentiation that placed Leningrad and Moscow far above their home cities, as well as of their minority status. They were also aware of pathways to overcome, or use, their ethnic identity in Leningrad and Moscow. Potential opportunities, implanted in the minds of postcolonial migrants, made Leningrad and Moscow, as they did Paris, in Dominic Thomas's words, "doubly universal, by virtue both of the belief in its universality and the real effects this belief produced."[72] In European and Soviet cases, the desire to access privilege shaped responses to prejudice. Recognizing, labeling, and interpreting intolerance were complicated exercises.

Seeking to underline their own incorporation into the host society, several student and professional migrants considered intolerance as emanating primarily from lower social strata in Leningrad and Moscow. Dea Kochladze, who ascended to the position of practitioner and teacher of neurology, recalled of mid-1970s Moscow: "You could easily go out into the street or around the metro or a market, where there were people from a different level of society, people without an education, and there you might hear people freely telling you off, telling you to go back home from where you came."[73] Rafael Voskanyan echoed these sentiments: "Of course in the street I was not accepted as equal, because some native habitants would not like other nationalities, were ignorant and emphasize that you differ."[74] Narynbek Temirkulov, a Central Asian student, recalled being in Moscow when Caucasus traders first began to arrive in significant numbers, in the 1970s. He blamed the Russian working class for subsuming all eastern and southern migrants in the same category of these more visible newcomers. Once at ease on city streets, he began to hear cries of "these Caucasians, they want to be here in Moscow? Let them go home—there is nothing for them here!"[75]

Other migrants who worked in factories, or, in some cases, as traders, defended the "simple people" (*prostoi narod*). Shuhrat Kazbekov, the Uzbek figure skater who also worked in a Leningrad film studio, recalled: "I never had any problems because of my ethnicity. The working class was everywhere. They are a simple people, and accept everyone as they are, and for who they are."[76] Farshad Hajiev, echoing these sentiments, argued: "The working class actually treated each other better than academics, because they are just simple people. I worked with them at a factory. These people were open and honest, and there was a real sense of solidarity and friendship."[77] Jusubov emphasized strong relationships with "simple" Russian customers who appreciated his quality goods.[78] Others argued that glasnost and subsequent national tensions, created by politicians for their own benefit, spoiled bonds between average citizens and increased tensions that continued after the Soviet collapse, precipitating the violent racism of the 2000s.[79]

Such narratives flowed to a degree from an internalization of the Soviet lionization of the working class. More fundamentally, however, worker, trader, and professional migrants used similar strategies: to distance prejudice from their more immediate environments. After condemning street-level discrimination, Kochladze offered a rejoinder common to respondents: "The people I associated with would never say anything like that."[80] Newcomers sought to contain potential harm to efforts at inclusion, privileging relationships that might advance goals of social and professional mobility or economic advancement as they sought to make Leningrad's or Moscow's spaces their own. Many respondents highlighted the Soviet work collective, which is detailed in chapter 5, as limiting the potential for discrimination. Kyrgyz Bolot Oruzbaev glorified the multiethnic solidarity of his Moscow glass factory; later in the interview, when he remembered racist epithets tossed around on the shop floor, he isolated them to "older workers" who were soon to be pensioners.[81] Joanna Herbert and her colleagues, in their work with Ghanaians in London, noted how they brushed aside street-level prejudice, focusing instead on relationships with colleagues and managers.[82] Lena Sawyer has argued that dark-skinned migrants in the West considered strategies to surmount racist encounters as individual, underpinned by personal strength or desire.[83]

Such approaches gain even more currency in the Soviet case, where collective organization outside the state was substantially limited before perestroika.[84] Migrant narratives stressed personal efforts and an ability to belong. Racism, as seen through interviews with Zakirov and many others, was a difficult subject to discuss. Subjects were hesitant to volunteer stories that prompted anger and humiliation, as Kenneth J. Bindas found in his study of African Americans and Janis Wilton experienced in her work with Chinese Australians.[85] Migrants often began to talk about encounters with prejudice through examples that implicated others, such as Khamagova's story of her Buryat friend and Russian boyfriend. Emotions, as they recounted these incidents, could become quite vivid. Oksana Karpenko's study of Leningrad Tatars found one mother poignantly recalling an older Russian woman chasing her daughter out of a sandbox at a housing complex in 1973, and how she had to explain the concept of prejudice to someone so young, especially her child.[86] Maia Asinadze, like several other migrants, distanced intolerance from her own experience during her interview, stating: "I heard of people having problems, but I never did."[87]

So many respondents' portrayals of post-Soviet life as a dystopia, rife with economic uncertainty and racism, especially from 2007–2011 when these interviews were conducted, complicate understandings of the two capitals. The Soviet era emerged in migrant retellings as one when youthful energy allowed boundaries—national, ethnic, or social—to be easily surmounted. The USSR's perceived dynamism, alongside nostalgia for social harmony, allowed migrants, reflecting over a decade after the collapse, to brush aside many incidents of Soviet-era discrimination. As Temirkulov observed, everyday prejudice rose in the 1970s and 1980s alongside the incentives to migrate given growing opportunities at the center.[88] Newcomers cited individual determination as a crucial ingredient for a successful transition as state, and indeed global, economic trends propelled mass south-north movement.

Migrant determination, alongside state policies, promoted a narrative that at once recognized and isolated intolerance to "native" Leningraders and Muscovites. Central Asian, Caucasus, and Asian Russian migrants saw themselves alongside Russians from outside the two capitals, Ukrainians, and other Soviet citizens, all striving for success at the USSR's core.[89] The residence permit system—all these nonlocals were subject to the same requirements—shaped the discourse of prejudice emerging from privileged and self-important natives. Student dormitories often excluded Leningraders and Muscovites, who, it was believed, preferred to live with "their own."[90] Damira Nogoibaeva recalled Leningrader and Muscovite racism as part of a localist, anti-migrant sentiment: "If there were a number of Caucasus or Central Asian peoples in queues, we would hear: 'We are forced to bear the black snouts [*Vot ponaekhali chernomazye*] when we have hardly any food supplies. They live on our dime.' When there were only Russians, however, the anger would turn to insults of villagers: 'Look at these hicks from [the Russian town of] Riazan, dragging our sausages in their backpacks.'"[91]

Verbiage, tracing back to the tsarist period, that linked "dirty" lower-class Russians to colonized, non-white nationalities had lessened in the late Soviet

Union.[92] Russian peasants might have been considered backward but were seen as victims of growing unofficial 1970s–1980s trade, with Caucasus and Central Asian entrepreneurs muscling in on produce and other sales. Emergent nationalist groups considered the health, and fertility, of rural Russians critical to the revitalization of the nation, which had spread itself too thin in leading the multiethnic USSR.[93] Average Leningraders and Muscovites, however, might also view village Russians alongside "blacks" as lacking the proper cultural background as well as the status to contribute to the lives of the two capitals.[94]

Social, regional, ethnic, racial, and urban hierarchies interacted in complicated ways across late twentieth-century Europe. Claire Alexander has argued that British postwar racism tempered long-held class differences among the English population. A broader belief in white superiority developed with the arrival of migrant waves from the West Indies, Africa, and Asia.[95] In Moscow, even as so-called blacks remained identifiable strangers to isolate—Gazyumov believed that "Muscovites had bad relationships with all eastern peoples"—Leningraders' and Muscovites' privileges prompted multiple strains of intolerance. Late Soviet modernization discourse that favored urban spaces, particularly strong (*krupnyi*) cities, as the engines of the USSR, bolstered a sense of difference among citizens, even as they were to serve as shining lights for all of them.[96] Several migrants believed that ostensibly worldly Leningraders and Muscovites were failing in their obligations to welcome, educate, and train willing but less advanced Soviet citizens. Khamagova, as she recalled Leningraders resenting Caucasus and Central Asian students, discussed comforting her friends. Prejudice, she told them, arose from the *skobari*, a term she used to refer to those who arrived only following the Nazi blockade, and not "true Leningraders" who had established the city as the USSR's cultural and intellectual capital in the 1920s and 1930s and sought to transmit its modernity.

Jyldyz Nuriaeva balanced exclusion with inclusion as she recounted a racist incident at her Moscow State University dormitory, years after suffering hostile stares on her first *elektrichka* ride in the city. "One day [in 1980] my husband and a friend came to visit. . . . My [Russian] roommate was washing the floor and muttering to herself. We listened, and it turned out that she was swearing at us: 'These black snouts, we work for them, and they live on our dime.'"[97] Nuriaeva reported the incident to university authorities, who transferred the roommate, threatening her with expulsion unless she apologized. Nuriaeva considered this an appropriate statement of Moscow's hierarchies: "My mom was a theater director, my father an engineer, and my husband and his friend from intellectual strata. Of course, it was unbearable that some girl from the Russian woods could insult us, only because the color of her skin and cut of her eyes was different from ours."[98] For her, culture and status determined inclusion in Moscow's upwardly mobile world.

Nuriaeva's characterization of this incident stressed Moscow's cosmopolitan character. Migrants from across the Soviet Union claimed their rightful place not only in the capital but also in a "Europe" that they considered fundamentally different from their "Asian" homes. In so doing, they sought to upset racial, cultural, and spatial binaries. Aryan Shirinov, a Tajik, believed that his constant striving for self-improvement placed him in Europe, rather than "back there, in the East."[99] Oruzbaev declared that his knowledge of European poetry placed him above most Muscovites. Meenakshi Thapan has noted that Asian and African migrants continue to view Europe as a land of great cultural history as well as economic opportunity.[100] Considering oneself European, or at home in Europe, linked Soviet newcomers to those from the edges of other former empires who aspired, in many cases from childhood, to participate in the richness and prestige of the hubs of their worlds. Spread by family members or others who traveled or worked there, stories of success in European capitals redounded worldwide. Repositioning Europe away from ethnic or racial exclusivism allowed a mental pathway to integration against intolerance from the host population.

Claiming oneself as an insider, or a European, meant finding outsiders or non-Europeans.[101] Russians, be they Leningraders, Muscovites, or villagers, could be considered outsiders for their ignorance and intolerance, which betrayed the modern and Soviet values associated with Leningrad and Moscow. Eastern or southern residents or newcomers to the two capitals also singled out "their own" or other southern minorities. Several student and professional migrants opposed themselves to Caucasus and Central Asian traders, who flouted appropriate European culture, from calm behavior and appropriate dress to the use of the Russian language.[102] Many Tatars believed that the presence of Caucasus and Central Asian traders threatened their own hard-earned status as insiders, based on their long-standing history with Leningrad's and Moscow's social and economic rhythms.[103] In the late 1970s and 1980s, for the first time, these Tatars heard calls of "*chernye*" and "*nemestnye*" (nonlocal, alien) directed at them, which they attributed to their similar phenotype and religion as now ubiquitous southern street traders.[104] Fuad Ojagov condemned his "own," rural Azerbaijani traders for their tight ethnicized circles and overaggressive solicitation of customers. Such behavior, he believed, laid the groundwork for Russian racism, which broke loose in the last years of perestroika and after the end of the USSR.[105] Central Asians also criticized Azerbaijanis, but not their own, who were involved in trade. Oruzbaev considered Azerbaijanis "more temperamental" than Central Asians, quick to argue with locals over the quality and price of goods.[106] Azamat Sanatbaev stated: "Where there are Caucasians, there is corruption."[107] Soviet jokes, for him, had a basis in fact and sullied Central Asians who were lumped together with Caucasus peoples as "blacks." Stereotypes that emerged in migrant narratives mixed social and cultural composites and divisions with ethnic and racial ones.[108] Images of the rude and pushy, though wily and economically successful, Caucasian and the modest, passive Central Asian had developed in the late nineteenth century and provided the basis for Soviet ethnic characterizations, even in a modern, Russian-led industrial, socialist society.[109]

African students provided the most direct contrast of dark-skinned outsiders on Leningrad's and Moscow's streets. Sanatbaev and others had absorbed, through children's cartoons and racist caricatures, stereotypes of Africans as undeveloped jungle-dwellers, ignorant and incomprehensible.[110] Quist-Adade and fellow Ghanaians who studied across the Soviet Union heard calls, even from children, such as "go back to the jungle."[111] Central Asian and Caucasus students packaged these prejudices within a narrative that positioned themselves as "Eastern" leaders of the friendship of peoples, bringing Africans along to European values. Farshad Hajiev, as he discussed mentoring efforts in 1980s Moscow student dormitories, noted also that university authorities carefully policed interactions between Soviet students and the "guests" whose presence signaled success in the Cold War. One night at a dance: "We had a misunderstanding [with an African student] and I hit him. There was a disciplinary meeting and they almost threw me out of the Komsomol. . . . They asked how I could hit a guest student in front of everyone."[112] Such an official reaction was far from universal. Even after efforts to calm racial tensions in the mid-1960s, "aggressive" Africans often received blame in violent incidents with Soviet—mostly Russian—students.[113]

Caucasus and Central Asian students—themselves the target of local anger over admission quotas to institutes of higher education—shared broader Leningrader and Muscovite frustration over African student privileges. Africans received higher stipends—as much as ninety rubles monthly as opposed to the standard thirty rubles given most Soviet students—as well as whatever funding might be given by their home governments.[114] As African governments selected candidates to study in the USSR, those who came to the most desirable destinations of Leningrad and Moscow could be the children—mostly the sons—of elite families. These students also enjoyed unheard-of travel privileges. Twice-yearly trips to Western Europe allowed African students to purchase and resell in-demand goods, from electronics to blue jeans.[115] Ojagov recalled his annoyance at the "haughty" attitude displayed by African students.[116] Distance from, as well as leadership of, these Africans allowed for a sense of inclusion for Caucasus and Central Asian students through adherence to Soviet values, from the demonization of trade in foreign goods to anti-elitism.

Jews also played a role in Central Asian and Caucasian narratives of inclusion. Kazbekov recalled that in Tashkent and Leningrad he often heard the fifth line in a Soviet passport, with the space for one's nationality, referred to as the "Jewish line."[117] Hajiev believed that Jews were the principal targets of discrimination in Leningrad and Moscow, especially after emigration to Israel became commonly known in the 1970s.[118] Mitrokhin's study of the Soviet-era Russian Right indeed concludes that Jews were primary victims of ethnically motivated crimes in major Russian cities.[119] Kazbekov appreciated the fact that Jews absorbed prejudice in Leningrad and Moscow, even as he complained about the relative absence of Central Asian and Caucasus peoples in the politics, administration, and media in two cities presented as all-white. Aibek Botoev also noted relief, with a guilty tone, of Jews being the principal target of prejudice in his intellectual circles; others recalled Jewish jokes as being the most pronounced after those referring to the northern Chukchi people.[120] Interviews of Caucasus residents of Moscow in the 1990s showed that those who had resided there from the Soviet era joined ethnic Russians in considering Jews as the richest, most dominant ethnic group in the city at the time.[121]

Anti-Semitism presented a common Soviet discourse that could include Caucasians and Central Asians, although it was employed only indirectly in two of our interviews, both with students. Irina L. Isaakyan notes that academia became a hotbed of anti-Semitism in the late Soviet period.[122] Admission quotas disfavored Jews, who had no recognized national homeland. Firings of Jewish academics proliferated. Gulnara Alieva, in her interview, paused on the one professor at Moscow State University who did not like her and looked down on her for her Central Asian background. She thought about it and then stated: "I recall now that he was a Jew."[123] Sadig Eldarov bitterly recounted the story of a Jewish professor who tried to hinder him with low marks and whose treatment made him lose his self-confidence.[124] Neither implicated ethnicity as a direct factor in their professors' behavior, but the critique dovetailed with broader, unfocused Soviet suspicions of Jews in higher education.

Newcomers to Leningrad and Moscow focused on inclusion as they reacted to racist words and acts. Individuals carefully considered their own place in new student, work, or street worlds and sought to understand and interpret prejudice within their life goals at the centers of the Soviet Union. Policies and practices that offered them status and protection as Soviet citizens, and their own sense of belonging vis-à-vis other outsider groups, softened the extent and depth of discrimination.

The State, (In)tolerance, and Home

The Soviet state received credit for invigilating over everyday inclusion of minorities. Positive representations of the state accompanied pride, and yearning, for the days when migrants, regardless of background, were citizens of a global power and could achieve personal success at the heart of a modern society. Sanatbaev and Bakyt Shakiev recalled that, during their military service, any racist remark or behavior could be punished with a fifteen-day detention. Hazing or other practices that divided conscripts and soldiers along ethnic lines, they insisted, resulted from individuals who abused their position to cement power or indulge racist beliefs. Given the ubiquity of violent hazing practices in the Soviet military, such narratives reveal efforts to absolve a state that could assist integration, even given, at best, inaction toward some racist practices.[125]

Several respondents who attended Leningrad or Moscow universities followed Hajiev in underlining the Komsomol's role in encouraging, sometimes enforcing, harmony. Alexei Yurchak has noted the organization's importance at conditioning students to accept state policies and practices.[126] Every Soviet citizen had the right to Komsomol membership, just as every Soviet citizen had a right to equal treatment, regardless of ethnicity, through the constitution. Elmira Nasirova believed that the ability of any student to join in itself prevented discrimination.[127] Non-Russian students ascended to leadership posts at Komsomol university branches. Komsomol membership also allowed challenges to institutional as well as ethnic hierarchies. Nurlanbek Satilganov recalled success in confronting a chauvinist professor: "I talked about my encounters with him at a Komsomol meeting and defended the honor of the Kyrgyz. And then people were severely punished. I, a third-rate student, could oppose the teacher! [The state] tried to carefully take of us, create a coziness."[128] Damira Nogoibaeva led student efforts to deal with what they considered an abusive classroom environment. Their agitation prompted personnel changes. "Imagine," she wondered, "as a student I had power over my professors."[129]

Policing equality was not unique to the postwar USSR; Western industrial states increasingly adopted legal and social protections for minorities who faced ethnic prejudice or racism.[130] Race relations acts passed in Great Britain "prohibited incitement to racial hatred and discrimination" in public places and were extended in 1968 to housing and employment.[131] François Mitterrand developed the concept of a "plural France," with significant social spending for the integration of primarily North African migrants, including in housing and education, following acute racial tensions in the 1970s.[132] In these and other European cases, migrant mobilization in protests, and links with community and political groups, drove change. Efforts to integrate dark-skinned postcolonial immigrants nonetheless confronted partisan politics. Western European parties that sought support on the right, including British conservatives, catered to purported white anxieties by favoring the narrowing of socioeconomic opportunities and benefits for former imperial subjects, among other migrants from Third World countries. Mitterrand's

FIGURE 7   The Nineteenth Komsomol Congress in Moscow,
May 1982. Attribution: RIA Novosti archive / Boris Kaufman /
CC-BY-SA 3.0

idea of a "plural France" faded as public opinion swung toward anti-immigrant politicians, who gained power in the 1980s and 1990s.[133]

Immune to electoral pressures, the Soviet government affected a consistent anti-racial discourse—whether it responded to popular feelings or not—as well as assumed a greater role in important aspects of everyday life for all residents, including in the press and publishing, housing, and employment.[134] Even as the state perpetuated images of Central Asian and Caucasus peoples as villagers beholden to traditional cultures and responsible for delivering raw materials to the center, it did so under the umbrella of the friendship of peoples and did not limit rights for citizens on the basis of nationality.[135] Said Nabiev argued that a strong state presence, as well as common citizenship, was necessary given Russian propensity toward racism.[136] Maia Asinadze said simply that the state would never condone racist behavior.[137] Aliya Nurtaeva, a Kazakh scientist, believed that the state had managed to eradicate prejudice altogether: "Racism was unacceptable in the Soviet Union. It never existed at all. I was accepted as a Soviet citizen like everybody else."[138]

The state's ability to police, if not eradicate, racism emerged in continued narratives of freedom in the Soviet Union.[139] Esoev believed that a strong militia presence allowed minorities to feel "free" wandering Leningrad or Moscow, day or night.[140] No respondent complained about, or even noted, the lack of dedicated schools, media, associations, or spaces for ethnic minorities, features that became key organizing mechanisms in the West and emerged in glasnost-era Leningrad and Moscow.[141] Informal linkages, based on family, ethnicity, or work, and state-based associations and oversight provided a level of comfort in an environment where discrimination was still far from ubiquitous.

Common citizenship did not guarantee equal status in the eyes of all Soviet legislation, and among all officials, however. The confused application and irregular enforcement of residence requirements, as discussed in chapter 1, allowed for potential abuse. The militia, it was widely accepted, was more likely to examine papers of non-Slavs with darker features, who might lack proper documentation to live in Leningrad and Moscow. Central Asian, Caucasus, or eastern Russian migrants reported markedly varied experiences in the two capitals. Some claimed to have lived for years without a residence permit (propiska), or at least never having had theirs checked. Others stated that they faced constant police demands for documents. Bribes might be required, even if papers were in order, to avoid further questioning and potential removal from Leningrad's and Moscow's "regime zone." Traders reported the greatest challenges with militia; otherwise, memories of interactions tended to correlate with the degree to which individual migrant narratives highlighted overall positive or negative experiences in Leningrad or Moscow.

Street-level surveillance increased at the turn of the 1980s, as numbers of southern street traders grew and as preparations for Moscow's Olympics intensified. One Western observer noted police forcibly removing Caucasus street traders operating in central Moscow in early 1980.[142] Those affected by this pre-Olympics campaign were "taken to the 101st kilometer;" that is, dumped outside the propiska zone around the Soviet capital.[143] Azerbaijanis considered it more difficult to gain registration documents for Leningrad and Moscow in the 1980s and increasingly resorted to bribes. Lower-level militia and administrators selectively enforced or undermined state policies, themselves ambivalent toward migration's role in their showcase cities.

Migrants balanced criticism of particular practices involving the state, or state representatives, with an overall appreciation of its role in opening doors to opportunities for citizens of distant Soviet republics. Marat Tursunbaev recalled his frustration that all business at university Komsomol meetings was conducted in Russian. No accommodations were made for Muslim practices or holidays.[144] To succeed in the Komsomol and, subsequently, party or state organs, Uzbeks and Kazakhs needed to become, in Tursunbaev's tongue-in-cheek words, "holier than the pope," abandoning their culture despite the rhetoric of the friendship of peoples.[145] Humiliation retained a place in accounts of Soviet migrants who still praised, to varying degrees, the state for allowing them to trade, study, or work in the two most privileged cities in the USSR. Elnur Asadov stressed that his success as a trader only partially atoned for the "moral suffering" that came as he was subject to racist epithets on a daily basis in officially approved markets of early

1980s Moscow, as militia stood idly by.[146] Fridon Tsereteli, who credited the state with opening avenues to a top Moscow university and then a position as an all-union administrator, nonetheless bitterly recalled ubiquitous "Georgian jokes," even in state offices: "Why do they have to joke about us like that? Let it be on their conscience. Why is it funny to laugh at someone because they have an accent? It doesn't matter who the person is, it is not acceptable to make a joke about someone's ethnicity."[147] Even as most migrants stated that they generally viewed humor against Georgians or other nationalities as harmless, Dea Kochladze, whose fair appearance led her Leningrad colleagues to believe that she was Russian instead of Georgian, expressed shame at not speaking against frequent, demeaning workplace humor.[148]

Expressions of personal suffering generally came later in interviews, after migrants related overcoming obstacles to meet personal goals. Khamagova, who had initially stated that her fair appearance immunized her from racist encounters, later said: "When I was young I deeply suffered because of manifestations of intolerance."[149] Having praised the friendship of peoples, she continued: "I was not so silly not to see that in everyday life this friendship hardly existed. I explained such things to myself as problems of life that made people angry; really, life was very hard."[150] Here, Khamagova filters intolerance through broader challenges that united Soviet citizens—a rare, albeit vague, mention in our interviews of difficulties of everyday life in the Brezhnev era—as she continues to balance inclusion and exclusion.

Other Soviets identified as black placed prejudice in a broader human context. Only a few made connections to Western racism, which the Soviet media had portrayed as constituent of the capitalist, colonialist world and targeted mainly at Africans or African Americans in the United States who suffered from segregationist laws and were frequently beaten or murdered. The Soviet case seemed to them something different.[151] Recalling racist catcalls in 1980s Moscow, Gulnara Alieva stated: "I understood then that people need enemies. The easiest thing to do is to single out someone who does not look like you, in terms of the measure of their eyes or the color of their skin. . . . This is human nature."[152] Dina Ataniyazova expressed a "deep personal torment" inflicted over decades, from her Moscow arrival in 1970. She blamed a "blanket hatred of Russians toward Caucasus and Central Asian peoples."[153] Ataniyazova, who continued to work in post-Soviet Moscow, conflated, as did other migrants, racist experiences before and after 1990–1991—when racism emerged openly in Leningrad and Moscow.[154] She was unusual, however, in minimizing differences before and after the state's collapse. Most recollections contrasted 1980s equality and dynamism against a post-Soviet era marked by xenophobia and lack of opportunity.

Comparing accounts of those who spent significant time in Soviet Leningrad and Moscow and recalled neither facing nor hearing ethnic or racial prejudice to those—of the same ethnic background, with similar physical appearance and social status—who asserted it was an integral part of their daily lives is an extremely challenging task. Responses filter through divergent experiences and perceptions of their time in Soviet Leningrad and Moscow as well as during the post-Soviet transformation. Personal encounters, and memories of them, become especially important for understanding the Soviet case, where the media dissimulated the challenges of interethnic relations and independent public organization was highly restricted. Individual thoughts and experiences remain crucial to an understanding of racial and societal integration in not just the Soviet Union. Thapan notes that North African migrants to Italy framed broader images of their migrant lives based on specific, personal relationships in their place of destination as well as emotional reactions and ties to their adopted and existing homes.[155]

Certain narrative strategies became clear—the tone of respondents' descriptions of discrete experiences most often correlated to how they perceived state and society as promoting or forestalling future personal success, then and at the time of the interview.[156] Botoev recalled his time in Leningrad with fondness, providing the education and skills that led to lucrative and satisfying work there and, after the USSR's end, on his return to Kyrgyzstan. He pushed aside his initial memory of being attacked by a Russian drunkard and stories of uncouth Muscovites. He realized nonetheless the difficulty in stretching memories: "Maybe there were problems, but I just don't remember. They were good times."[157]

Nostalgia alone is insufficient to explain exclusively positive memories. Abdul Khalimov vividly recalled his sense of confidence: "In Moscow I felt really comfortable. No one made rude gestures toward me. I was free."[158] Migrants, barring some traders, consistently recalled personal safety and security under Soviet rule. Safety was not the only issue in terms of "freedom," however. Several Central Asian villagers considered the anonymity of the modern city a respite from prying family eyes—another trope that unites them with migrants from across the postcolonial world who arrived from tighter social units.[159] Ataniyazova recalled: "I wanted to escape from the Caucasus, from the influence of family and others, who often resented or showed excessive interest in me. I was attracted to the anonymity of the big city, where nobody knew you and nobody would be saying things behind your back."[160] Others—professionals and traders, lighter- and darker-skinned alike—spoke of intense friendships formed with native Leningraders and Muscovites. Hazi Begirov stated: "We invited many Russians to our house for social occasions, and they did the same with us. We didn't have any conflicts. We treasured our friendships. Overall, I think that they liked Azerbaijanis."[161]

For those who recalled the two capitals as sites of equality, the main issue was a belief that these cities could never be home. Even those with several Russian friends found that they felt like guests rather than accepted Leningraders or Muscovites. Shuhrat Ikramov stated that all plum laboratory assignments went to ethnic Russians, because they were expected to stay in Moscow: "It was well known by my professors, who considered me a temporary person."[162] Students, professionals, traders, and others from the Caucasus, Central Asia, and Asian Russia cycled continuously through Leningrad and Moscow, seeking training, knowledge, or money, all of which might significantly improve life chances, and life, in their home republics. As economic difficulties in southern peripheries increased, Leningrad and Moscow retained their advantages and allure. Ever-growing migrant numbers were present during perestroika, when open racism burst into the Soviet media as well as on the streets.[163]

The arrival of tens of thousands of darker-haired or darker-skinned migrants to Leningrad and Moscow in the 1970s and 1980s added a racial element to forms of intolerance and division between the host society and newcomers. "Black"-themed epithets gained currency on city streets, and migrants remained conscious of their skin color and appearance as well as ethnic background. Degrees of prejudice varied; while many sojourners from the Caucasus, Central Asia, and Asian Russia recalled the humiliation of street-level insults or differential treatment and threats at the workplace, the state policed potential social division and many local Russians appreciated the services provided by "southerners" (*iuzhnye*).

Even as broader structural disparities catalyzed movement and prejudice, racism and related forms of intolerance emerged as relationships between perpetrators and victims, shaped by the perceptions and reactions of those potentially subject to their sting. Migrants worked to overcome distance from the host population and adapt to cities that presented opportunities far superior to those in their home republics. Personal abilities to maneuver emerged as increasingly important as migrant numbers and the subsequent reaction to "blacks" grew. Newcomers worked to reshape their adopted cities away from the domain of fair-skinned Europeans and Russians toward places of accomplishment.

We need to consider a Soviet context for racism, alongside and often intersecting with ethnic, social, and other forms of prejudice, within a broader world of postcolonial movement. Even as interview subjects rarely used "race" or "racism" as terms, they frequently discussed intolerance based on skin or hair color, the shape of one's eyes or face, and other characteristics deemed at once biogenetic and linked to culture. Antiracist discourse, the friendship of peoples, and common laws and citizenship under a strong, socially vigilant state did shelter, at least somewhat, Soviet migrants from discrimination. Epithets and efforts to debase darker newcomers in Leningrad and Moscow nonetheless echoed those in the West, where racial violence emerged in relation to south-north movements of primarily less-privileged former colonial subjects.[164] Soviet migrants lacked the tools to understand the sweep of discrimination or to mobilize formally against it until the last years of the USSR.

Some mysteries remain in the development of Soviet racism. How and where did the idea of and term "black" (*chemyi*) originate and evolve, and how did it become applied to late Soviet Caucasus and Central Asian migrants? How do we relate prejudice against so-called blacks to prejudice against rural Russians, whose phenotype and common national background removed barriers to integration but who could also be denigrated by the host population? The Soviet urban-rural hierarchy, enforced by the practice of propiski, hardened internal boundaries, ethnic and nonethnic, alike.

Many Soviet arrivals from southern and eastern regions offered words and examples that placed them above host Leningraders and Muscovites as well as ethnic Russian newcomers, defying binaries as the host society attempted to establish them. Class and social standing interacted with ethnicity and race in complicated ways in alternate visions of Soviet hierarchies. Migrants alternately demonized or lionized "simple people" as well as professionals from the host society in order to highlight their own incorporation into Leningrad or Moscow society. Belonging was gauged largely on the extent to which those in the two capitals acquired or displayed color-blind traits considered alternately as "European," "modern," "urban," or "Soviet": dynamic, city-wise, economically successful, well educated, and having the desire to work hard. Such tropes linked to migrants in London, Paris, and other major Western cities, who used discourses of equality that coursed through enlightenment-inspired laws and constitutions as well as societies to seek inclusion.[165] As the USSR wobbled and evaporated, southern and eastern migrants confronted a new political order with exacerbated socioeconomic and center-periphery inequalities. The tumult of the 1990s played heavily on their minds and memories as they considered a lighter past against a darker, violent present.

BECOMING SVOI: BELONGING IN THE TWO CAPITALS

It was the best time of my life when I was a student, a young person who conducted a carefree life, filled with studying, friendship, love, my relations, grandiose cultural impressions, and not less grandiose plans for the future.

—Aryuna Khamagova

Aryuna Khamagova downplayed occasional racism she witnessed as she recounted her adaptation to, and life in, 1970s Leningrad. Her journey through migrant and student worlds highlights how ethnicity, social background, relationships, networks, and ambition mixed in the quest for inclusion in dynamic centers of Soviet life. Born in Ulan-Ude, Khamagova identified as Buryat due to her father's heritage. Her Russian mother's birthplace of Leningrad, however, led her to grow up listening to family members recount the city's cultural and intellectual achievements. Relatives who endured the Second World War imbued her with stories of heroism and the tragedy of the siege. Daughter of a professor, Khamagova studied in the most prestigious school in Ulan-Ude, surrounded by the children of the "red bourgeoisie"—party members, intellectuals, and other well-connected citizens.[1] Her victories in school olympiads in English, literature, and history, she thought, would prepare her well for study at the "sacred subcenter" of the Soviet Union.

In 1972, Khamagova, then seventeen, embarked to take her entrance exams at Leningrad State University. Her enthusiasm evaporated when she failed. Determined to make her way in a city she had fallen in love with, and not wanting to return home as a letdown to her intellectual parents, she found employment as a temporary worker (*limitchik*) at a Leningrad vegetable depot.[2] The position came with dormitory accommodation. Her roommates, who had also failed university entrance exams, became her first friends and network—a Russian girl from a Siberian town, who claimed that she was punished after refusing to sleep with the examiner, and a Korean from Kazakhstan, who was convinced that ethnic discrimination was involved. No one in her dormitory, she found, believed their failure was due to their own shortcomings. The three, along with others, supported mutual efforts to study in noisy rooms for the next round of admissions and comforted one another at being so far from families. "We were all in good relations, feeling our commonness."[3]

Dreams of success in Leningrad fueled them. Despite cramped accommodations, without bathing facilities, they considered themselves fortunate. Each worked on a different market team—one potatoes and onions, another apples, a third cabbages and carrots—and they each brought home some of their goods as "trophies" for dinner. Khamagova also recalled the filling five-kopeck lunches they received at their workplace. For "a special woman [in the dormitory] responsible for [their] cultural growth," Khamagova stressed her great appreciation: "She distributed tickets to the Opera House, drama, theaters—you can't understand how difficult it was to 'get' tickets to the ballet or Tovstonogov's theater [the Bolshoi Drama Theater in Leningrad], and we had them, sometimes absolutely free—as well as to museums and exhibitions."[4] This "special woman" was their *vospitatel'*—a republic-wide position created in worker dormitories to "cultivate Soviet socialist values" among youth new to large Russian cities and oversee their cultural, physical, and educational development.[5] Twice weekly, Khamagova and her friends mixed with the cream of Leningrad society.

Such practices and networks allowed Khamagova to integrate into Leningrad's cityscape. Her focus remained on university entrance, and she brushed aside any challenges adjusting to her new environment: "I did not pay attention to the external side of life—I can easily adapt to bad weather and poor facilities. As for other people, I don't communicate with those I dislike."[6] Khamagova passed exams the following year and secured admission to the Institute of Oriental Studies of Leningrad State University. She was thrilled to gain her first choice of study and to follow in the footsteps of her father, a leading scholar. Khamagova was a "victim" of Leningrad's heavy demand for new housing in the 1970s, however. As construction strained to accommodate the state's shift from communal living to single-family apartments, she was assigned a dormitory in Petrodvorets, about thirty kilometers outside the city center.[7] The commute—crowded, unpleasant, and well over an hour each way—challenged her ability to succeed in the program, as she was expected to quickly master three Oriental languages. Her vociferous complaints at needing to awaken at 5:30 for morning classes wore down university officials, who transferred her to a closer residence building on Vasilevskii Ostrov. This success confirmed Khamagova's belief in the Soviet system's responsiveness and understanding of the need to nurture dynamic citizens. Students in Oriental studies, with their language skills and knowledge of foreign cultures, were "very special," with contacts and travel opportunities beyond the USSR's borders.[8]

Khamagova watched as students, who initially associated with their own coethnics, made friendships of all sorts in dormitories. She recalled leading a spontaneous all-Soviet protest against some East Germans who, drunk in their rooms, began yelling "Zeig Heil." Success provoked "national and patriotic" common feelings, blending republican and Soviet patriotism that flowed from common memories and family experiences in the Second World War.[9] As residence life normalized, Khamagova became witness to another housing challenge in Leningrad. A family network that included one of her Buryat aunts still resided in a communal apartment (*kommunalka*). Khamagova occasionally assisted her aunt in the challenges of living in a sixth-floor flat without a lift, but her main purpose involved dealing with a "neighbor alcoholic and hooligan." Khamagova struggled alongside her aunt to "keep this man within the frames of nearly normal behavior."[10] State authorities in this case provided no assistance. Other communal apartment residents, who preferred not to intervene, instead patronized Khamagova. Comments about her Russian, which she considered her native language, being "very good" made Khamagova "feel offended," she said, "as if they accused me of inferiority."[11] Her ability to restrain this "hooligan," however, through gaining eventual support of other commune residents, secured her sense of becoming a local.

Khamagova's life changed again in 1975 when she met a Polish student, whom she would eventually marry. A legal quirk prevented Soviet citizens like her who wed foreigners from different faculties within the university to claim city housing together. After fruitless battles with Leningrad's administrators, Khamagova left for educational training in Delhi. On return, her frustration was quelled as her husband, "the best student in Leningrad," was now receiving a monthly 100-ruble stipend, as well as grants from the Polish embassy. Together with her own grant of 46 rubles, they rented an apartment in the prestigious Kupchino district in 1977. The couple "conducted a life incomparable to many classmates," enjoying meals at restaurants across the city and hosting parties well supplied with food and drink. "Most of all," she related, "I loved it when people mistook me for a Leningrader."[12]

Khamagova began to aid relatives of family acquaintances coming from Ulan-Ude, fielding phone calls in the late 1970s from worried parents who asked her "not to drop their daughter" in the big city. She comforted Buryat friends who experienced racist taunts from Russian Leningraders. Khamagova believed all roads were open to her and her charges, who could select any number of educational paths toward a vibrant professional career. In a decision tinged with regret, however, she followed her husband to Poland in the early 1980s. Khamagova left a place that offered "every opportunity to realize one's personality" and that she now considered her home, even as she recognized that she lacked the links to party, state, or KGB (State Security Committee) officials who could fast-track her career, as she saw with others in the Academy of Sciences. She recalled "kitchen discussions" that stoked frustration at uncompetitive Soviet goods and the dangers of a resource-based economy. These longer-term worries, however, presented no barriers to the state assuring her and her colleagues good, comfortable personal and professional lives. She imagined herself—if not a scholar—a teacher, translator, international tourist agent, or foreign affairs officer, as she considered the paths her friends pursued.

Aryuna Khamagova's story encapsulates the social mobility aspired to and, in many cases, achieved by new migrants to Leningrad and Moscow. Her move from vegetable seller to student to resident of one of the city's most renowned neighborhoods encapsulates a broader Soviet dream. This chapter focuses on the next stage of life in Leningrad and Moscow, after new arrivals had undergone the initial phase of place making and as they understood or confronted, in some cases, intolerance from the host population. These migrants weighed to what extent they would seek, or attain, the status of "*svoi*"—"belonging" or "one of us." Was a lasting identification with, as well as stay in, these cityscapes a desirable or necessary part of a Soviet dream? I argue that this dream extends beyond the one ably conceptualized by Donald J. Raleigh, who invoked professional accomplishment, measured through quality of life as well as material goods.[13] Migrants from Central Asia, the Caucasus, and eastern areas of Russia also sought to stabilize and improve their own and their family economies as well as prove their worth, to themselves, each other, and the state, through friendship—as a microcosm of the friendship of peoples—and hard work. Work would hasten their identification as *svoi* in the two capitals, considered as sites of merit and accomplishment.[14] Alexandra Oberländer contends that the amount of time Soviet citizens worked was "immense," if we look beyond Western conceptualizations of employer-centered labor and include less formal endeavors, often inspired by friend or family links.[15] Oksana Karpenko argues that non-Russian migrants in the Soviet and post-Soviet eras sought *svoi* on three levels: among kin networks and other migrants, with locals, and as part of the state itself.[16] Newcomers also equated becoming *svoi* with what Alexei Yurchak calls the ability to lead "normal" lives. Each sought recognition as one among millions striving for social advancement in the two capitals.[17]

Migrants' efforts to incorporate into Leningrad and Moscow, and the quest to become *svoi*, continued to highlight power inequities between host societies and newcomers within shifting, multiple hierarchies. Beyond those of ethnicity and background, education, class, status, skill, and drive played critical roles. Once again, migrants' words privileged personal determination in finding success in the two capitals. As their incorporation deepened, so did their linkages, providing everything from cultural support to career mobility. Leningrad and Moscow, to quote Doreen Massey on her conception of world cities, were "not so much bounded areas as open and porous networks of social relations."[18] Alena Ledeneva has detailed the scope of informal networks in Soviet cities as critical components of *svoi*, but the fashion of individual migrant integration remains untold.[19] Place of birth, accommodation, profession, and friendship were only some of the factors that offered connections to migrants once they settled into Leningrad and Moscow.[20] Host Russians played critical roles in ideas of place and belonging. Native Leningraders or Muscovites could exhibit social power through isolating newcomers by various means even as their friendship reduced psychological as well as social tensions in private and public life.[21] Many networks intertwined society with the Soviet state.

Interactions across state and society, simultaneously constraining and privileging migrant agency, are captured by Anthony Giddens's concept of "structuration." Existing power structures, overwhelmingly state-based in the USSR, condition movement and fields of opportunity. Certainly, as they made choices of temporary or permanent homes, Soviet southern and eastern migrants were aware of state decisions to decrease flows of investment to the periphery and its involvement in conditioning, if not dictating, their choices and places of study, employment, and livelihood paths. Yurchak argues that the Soviet system allowed for independent thought, but not binary opposition, and its control over education, media, and social organizations conditioned conformity to state norms.[22] Structuration highlights nonetheless a range of options open to individuals and the possibility for everyday actors to bypass structures or initiate large-scale change.[23] Jon Goss and Bruce Lindquist emphasize the individual as a social actor, knowledgeable of opportunities and constraints presented through structures.[24] These actors, I argue, are the foundation of the dynamic nature of the Brezhnev era. Individual migrant actions then and, as chapter 7 shows, in the Gorbachev era operated within official ambivalence toward laws and policies aimed at newcomers, especially when enforcement threatened the privileged status of Leningrad and Moscow, which relied so heavily on their energy.

Networks and Belonging

Bonds of family, locality, ethnicity, and friendship with other new or established migrants provided important early linkages in Leningrad and Moscow and retained their saliency for years or decades. Nancy Foner notes the continued role of initial minority migrant networks in her studies of North America and Western Europe. Arrivals continually reevaluated their own identities and incorporation within and alongside their first contacts, often members of the same ethnic or geographic background.[25] Connections within migrant groups could forestall integration into Leningrad's and Moscow's host societies, especially in the years surrounding the Second World War. Newly arrived Tatars, who worked primarily in small-scale trade or menial professions, revealed a first generation's quest to maintain their homeland's rhythm of everyday life in 1930s and immediate postwar Leningrad. Seniors and housewives, Oksana Karpenko noted, remained sheltered, charged with safeguarding cultural and religious values. Families provided mutual assistance in finding jobs, educational placements, deficit goods, even spouses.[26] Soviet state-assigned housing prevented families from forming their own enclaves; in response, one Tatar recalled: "We rented [neighboring] dachas for more than 30 or 40 years. . . . [A]ll summer we were together."[27]

Armenian Leningrad cobblers studied by Olga Brednikova and Elena Chikadze, arriving in the 1930s and the first postwar decade, strove to create "micro-Yerevans" or re-create cuisine and traditions from their regional homes. Tightly knit social circles reflected long-held connections before their movement north.[28] As in the case of Tatar communities, patriarchy—the "cult of the father," as one Armenian so raised in recalled—and gender roles assumed important places in Armenian cultural continuity.[29] One exception involved the Russian language, used at home; as one Armenian informant stated, "My father, though generally quite a simple [prostoi] person, understood that to grow up speaking with an accent would have made life very difficult."[30] These cobblers saw their children as future Leningraders.

Other Armenians, who arrived later and often independently, forsook micro-Yerevans to integrate into Leningrad's or Moscow's multiethnic population. One singer limited contacts with coethnics to annual restaurant gatherings in 1960s Leningrad to commemorate the 1915 Armenian genocide, an event that had become increasingly important to national identity surrounding its fiftieth anniversary.[31] Bonds loosened as sons and daughters of the first postwar generation considered Russian their first language and intermarried with Russians or more recent arrivals from Armenian cities. Village Armenians coming to Leningrad and Moscow were seen as "hicks." Even so, encounters proved important to a sense of identity; the Armenian singer recalled the broad circles who came to genocide commemoration events: "[They] seemed like another world, that I had been torn away from. It felt like I was not alone."[32]

Bonds loosened among the Leningrad Tatar community, even as the importance of coethnic, or perhaps coreligious, ties continued. The city's mosque, reopened in 1955, provided a central place for gatherings among recent arrivals and established Tatars alike, especially at holidays. Food from home was cooked and shared on festive evenings.[33] The Council of Religious Affairs watched the mosque closely as a potential "center of national feeling."[34] "National" seemed appropriate given Tatar dominance among Leningrad's varied Muslim populations at religious ceremonies. Ninety percent of Tatars whose loved ones died in the city sought Muslim burials through the mosque. Broader connections within the community did not foreclose external ones, as many younger members considered Russian their first language, breached cultural and religious norms, primarily the consumption of pork, and became involved in interethnic relationships and marriages. This generation of the 1950s to 1970s continued to see practical as well as psychological value in "national" networks, even as they felt increasingly at ease as Leningraders.

Later arrivals from the Caucasus lacked the pressure or desire to isolate themselves from Leningrad's and Moscow's rhythms of life. They still blended smaller-scale, more intimate networks with broader identities and connections to anchor their place in ever-larger, ever more dynamic cities. Tamriko Otskheli recalled how her own networks spread from family: "On arriving [to Moscow, in 1980] I joined [my sister and husband]. Later my first child was also born there. . . . We and other Georgians were together very often. I had many friends and relatives among those Georgians who lived in Moscow, and there were many Armenian and Azerbaijani people as well. We were good friends and often invited each other home and helped one another a lot." Otskheli praised this Caucasus community given Moscow's anonymity, which, for her, remained challenging. Unlike in Georgia, she never felt she could bother a neighbor with a request or problem.[35] Terenti Papashvili considered his own arrival to Leningrad in 1985 important for maintaining the Georgian identities of relatives, who had been away from home for years or decades: "I met my relatives in my free time. I tried to have more contacts with them and advise them not to forget the Georgian language, to buy Georgian books and attend services at Georgian churches. We celebrated holidays together with great pleasure, with traditional Georgian food."[36]

Those who arrived without established family or community ties found choices of networks critical in maintaining balances between home and away, between safety, stability, and ambition. Almost all migrants interviewed for this project discussed *zemliak* links as their first sense of *svoi* in the two capitals. *Zemliaki*, a term coined in the nineteenth century to designate circles of fellow villagers in industrializing Russian cities, now referred to coethnics among migrants to Leningrad, Moscow, and other major Soviet, multinational cities.[37] *Zemliaki* remained crucial in shaping migrant integration experiences, especially given ubiquitous frustration with native Leningraders' and Muscovites' "aura of privilege."[38] Fuad Ojagov remembered how Muscovites in his university classrooms smugly displayed their scientific preparation gained from elite schools and looked down on outsiders in social interactions, when they deigned to participate. Azamat Sanat-baev called Muscovites a "capricious people" who took great offense at anything not to their liking and who never considered him an equal throughout his many years in the capital.[39] Saule Iskakova remembered being excited at receiving a din-ner invitation from her professor, a native Leningrader, but then being berated by him and friends at the table for the fact that "non-Russians were undermining the Russian economy" in the early 1980s, with the ostensible subsidization of pe-ripheral regions holding back the center.[40]

Even the small numbers of "native" Leningraders and Muscovites who stayed in university dormitories generally avoided association with outsiders, accord-ing to migrant narratives. The sense of superiority extended to university person-nel. Jyldyz Nuriaeva recalled humiliations from local staff when she arrived at Moscow State University in 1983. After Nuriaeva asked to see the rector who as-signed housing, a secretary shouted: "You mountain people are full of yourselves, thinking you can see the rector without permission!"[41] Encounters with hostile dining staff followed. Nuriaeva related a story of a sweeper approaching her and some international students, striking their legs with her broom, and ranting about "non-Christians." Russian students from outside the city, familiar with such be-havior from conceited Muscovites, Nuriaeva claimed, expressed apologies that they had to undergo such insults.

Educational quota systems facilitated *zemliaki* through placing significant numbers of students from each republic at institutes and universities across Len-ingrad and Moscow.[42] Aryan Shirinov, when he began studies at a Leningrad PTU, met a fellow Tajik from the Pamirs, who remained his closest friend throughout his time in the city; in his words, "*zemliaki* were different: they were always closer."[43] Also beginning life as a student, Gulnara Alieva recalled: "[When] I came to the dormitory, I met other Kyrgyz girls. These *zemliaki* helped me immensely. They were older than me and had studied already for a while." She quickly returned the favor to her new, or "green [*zelenye*]" coethnics, especially those from small villages who lacked her big-city experience, as she had grown up in Frunze.[44]

Migrants presented dormitory *zemliak* links as providing comfort, friendship, and security in their quest to broaden networks. Ojagov appreciated that his *zemliaki*—from top Russian schools in Baku—accompanied him to monthly lunches at the Azerbaijan SSR's legation in Moscow. He sheepishly admitted that these events were reserved for those with connections to Communist circles of power. Alex Koberidze found a more quotidian gathering, taking a few dormitory mates to a Caucasus and Azerbaijani circle that met regularly at the Oktiabrskaia Hotel, which evolved into his main social group.[45] Alieva, like most migrants, recalled *zemliaki* existing alongside multiethnic dormitory associations. She recalled befriending Russians, Koreans, Estonians, and Uzbeks on "trips" arranged by her faculty to help pick potatoes outside of the city during harvest season. Alieva eventually distanced herself from her university *zemliak* circles, or *zemliachestvo*: "Everybody drank a lot, and the Kyrgyz fellows constantly flirted with me. They followed me to my dorm, but I wanted nothing to do with them."[46]

Ethnic ties did not guarantee common bonds. Kazakh *zemliachestva* in Moscow State University dorms rejected Iskakova for being raised in Kyrgyzstan. Soured by this experience, she sought other Soviet and East European students with similar interests as well as "fellow" Kyrgyz. Khamagova—who had always considered Buryats one, close people—remembered her own surprise on realizing that ethnic linkages were not all they seemed. A *zemliak* at her first dormitory related to her that there were two subethnic groups—western Buryats, who occupied the best positions in government and the Communist Party, and eastern Buryats, whose paths to social mobility were limited to science, education, and the arts. *Zemliaki*, Khamagova considered, could be a double-edged sword. Every grouping, which fostered a connection to home and allowed comfort in large Russian-dominated cities, created outsiders. Regional as well as subethnic differences abounded: she recalled her neighbors from Dagestan disparaging each other's backgrounds with comments such as "She's canny because she is a Lezgin" or "She is as stupid as all Laks."[47] Such pettiness made it easier for her to leave university dormitory life to care for her aunt. *Zemliaki* provided a first stop for almost all migrants, but evolved according to individual experiences in efforts to incorporate into Leningrad and Moscow.

Limitchik dormitories, tied to particular enterprises, lacked the critical mass that allowed coethnic ties to form for Caucasus, Central Asian, and Asian Russian arrivals. Newcomers needed to work their way into different social circles, to find their own, first sense of *svoi*. Tolkunbek Kudubaev, at his dormitory for workers of the Moscow metro, recalled, in the mid-1980s, a similar interethnic collegiality to the one described by Khamagova at her first Leningrad residence. Facility with the Russian language—a given among university students but not among construction, service, and other *limitchik* workers—emerged as critical for incorporation among Caucasus and Central Asian peoples. Kudubaev credited his determination to learn Russian during army service with his ability to communicate and befriend his work and dormitory mates. Common interests as well as personality matches determined associations in *limitchik* dorms, as residents sought to fashion their own *zemliaki*. Kudubaev stated: "I hung out with my brigade. We were multinational: our brigadier was Ukrainian, and workers Moldavian, Tatar, Russian, Kyrgyz. [We] observed birthdays . . . [and] went to theaters and museums."[48] His circle continued group trips to cultural institutions even without a *vospitatel'*. Emily J. Elliott has found that these positions faded from the late 1970s onward as state authorities and dormitory captains privileged policing—against drunkenness, "hooliganism," and other disorders—over cultural development.[49] Against such uncultured behavior, ostensibly usually practiced by village Russians, Kudubaev's friends encouraged one another to exhibit comportment necessary for strong recommendations for permanent employment: punctuality and sobriety on the job, obeying orders, and returning to dormitories by 10:00 p.m. Aspiration guided associations and behavior. *Limitchiki* as well as students carefully considered intertwined personal and professional associations to fit future goals.

Maia Asinadze highlighted the personal and emotional side of connections with close associates, which cushioned the none-too-easy goal to succeed at the USSR's heart. She recalled the difficult conditions of her Moscow communal apartment, where she stayed with her "guardian angel," Liudmila, until the mid-1980s. But living challenges, as well as closeness, had their advantages.

> In Moscow we didn't have hot water. The conditions were not great. We were cramped, but [my *kommunalka* mates] were kind souls. You knew people were waiting for you at home and would open the door for you on arrival. There was warmth, real warmth that covered up everything else. . . . When I went home after my studies, people would ask me what happened. Today nobody would care. Your neighbors wouldn't sit down

FIGURE 8 Roommates from across the Soviet Union sharing a meal in a multinational dormitory room in 1960s Moscow. Attribution: Thomas T. Hammond / CC-BY-SA 4.0

and ask you about your problems. . . . I would tell [my flatmates] about how I didn't pass my exams and they would comfort and encourage me. They would tell me that I would pass it the next time.[50]

Warmth, kindness, and friendship highlight a key aspect of the "Soviet dream." Common understandings and mutual affection softened what migrants viewed as the unfettered individualism of the West then, and the post-Soviet world now, on the path toward success and prosperity. Liudmila exemplified the efforts of Asinadze's new circle of friends to not only integrate Asinadze into Moscow but also incorporate her own Georgian background into "everyone's capital." Years after Asinadze's arrival and astonishment that no one in Moscow wore black on the death of friends or relatives, Liudmila accompanied her home to her father's funeral back in Georgia.[51]

> She came along and dressed in black with a black headscarf. My people were surprised but very pleased. It was a great sign of respect. When we came back to Moscow she continued to dress in black. She wore it the whole forty days. Neighbors would ask her what happened. Why was she wearing only black? She told them that my father had died and that she respected this tradition. She asked me later to remember her in this way when she passed on.[52]

Asinadze and Kudubaev created their own friends and networks, untethered from regional identities but providing the mutual support that so many other migrants identified as crucial components of *zemliak* links. Common ties forged in early encounters remained critical throughout their time in Leningrad and Moscow.

Status and the Cities

Numerous avenues existed to gain documentation that allowed for legal, long-term stays in Leningrad and Moscow, even as migrants disagreed on the necessity of appropriate paperwork. By far the most common stamp of approval was the propiska (residence permit), discussed in chapters 1 and 4. Students and professionals recruited to the two capitals received propiski as a matter of course, and demobilized soldiers serving in the region, as a potential skilled blue-collar workforce, also appeared to gain one virtually on request.[53] Other newcomers—those who came of their own volition, without a sponsoring organization—had to decide how to handle their undocumented status if they were to consider longer stays. Seasonal traders and construction, factory, and service-sector workers, among others, made individual decisions regarding residence status. Connections and comfort levels affected degrees of worry about possessing a valid propiska. The application of residence status was unclear and enforcement sporadic, but a lack of status could hinder the practicalities and psychology of incorporation and belonging.

The teenaged Aryuna Khamagova and Tolkunbek Kudubaev started their odysseys in the two capitals through obtaining a limited residence permit. This status placed them in a "gray zone" among Leningrad's and Moscow's millions.[54] Offered by their employer and including accommodation, these permits had to be renewed annually and were tied to their specific job. The Soviet regime kept the numbers, and for the most part even the existence, of the limited residence permit unpublicized, even as, from 1976 to 1978 in Moscow alone, factories and enterprises received and issued registrations for 178,000 workers.[55] At the turn of the 1980s, Moscow's Office of the Use of Labor Resources viewed *limitchiki* no longer as a solution to chronic labor shortages, but as an added stress on resources, particularly housing. Greater efficiency, not more workers, emerged as a preferred strategy. Whether this shift was due to decreased numbers of available young workers from Slavic regions, and increased numbers of Caucasus and Central Asian peoples simply showing up in Moscow, is unclear.[56] Limited workers retained agency, however; as Elliott showed, they petitioned, often successfully, Moscow's Supreme Soviet for redress of poor housing and other issues.[57] Even as their status tied them to a place of employment, differences in wages and living conditions between *limitchiki* and more permanent employees in Leningrad and Moscow were not sufficiently extreme to lead the former to express grievances at the conditions that allowed stays at the heart of the Soviet Union.

Locating pathways to permanent status preoccupied Khamagova, who had always dreamed of life in Leningrad, and Kudubaev, who realized shortly after his arrival in Moscow the opportunities the Soviet capital presented, from high salaries to cultural life. Between trips to museums and birthday parties, Kudubaev and his friends plotted avenues to a full propiska. Admission to an institute of higher education, as with Khamagova a decade earlier, emerged as the clearest route. They debated, but dismissed from a lack of confidence, another common strategy: finding a Muscovite to marry.[58] Only on his eventual return to Osh in 1989, choosing, with regret, family over higher education, did Kudubaev recall being informed that Caucasus peoples obtained residence documents, with relative ease, through bribery. Georgians, Armenians, and Azerbaijanis had established connections in Leningrad's and Moscow's district Soviet offices. Georgians, according to Erik Scott, had substantial passport-forging operations able to accommodate those seeking to move anywhere in the USSR.[59] Terenti Papashvili, before coming to Leningrad from Kutaisi, Georgia, was aware of clandestine practices: "I heard that when people wanted residence permits, there was corruption.

Officials asked for a certain amount of money to issue residence permits."[60] Papashvili never tested this personally. He arrived with *limitchik* status arranged through his wife's brother, who headed a Leningrad construction company, and could renew the status at will.

Such operations and networks may explain why other Georgians outside of student and professional circles interviewed for this project recalled no issues with status. Vazha Gigulashvili, who arrived in Moscow in 1974 specifically to find a job that would earn her and her husband more than they could at home, recalled, without discussing specifics: "We had all the legal documents needed for living in Moscow, and we did not have any problems. Then it was very easy to get a residence permit, so we also had it."[61] Eliso Svanidze breezily addressed her status as she arrived in Leningrad to work at a supermarket, a job arranged by her sister in 1975: "I had a residence permit, because without it I would not have been able to work. My friends helped me to get it, and I received it without any problems."[62] Alternately, Irma Balanchivadze, who came to Moscow in 1980 with her husband to work, first at a vegetable market, but then ended up taking care of their two children full-time, simply stated, "no one ever asked us for a permit," so they never ended up getting one.[63] Newcomers from Central Asia and the Caucasus alike noted the ease of renting flats from the local population throughout the late Soviet period without the need for any documentation. By the 1980s, "agencies" existed for this purpose. Like Balanchivadze, many assumed—or hoped—that the lack of a propiska would not affect their stays, of uncertain duration, in the two capitals.

The ease of gaining, or lack of worrying, over residence status was not universal among Caucasus peoples. Erkin Abdullaev, an Azerbaijani who sold fruits and vegetables and lacked the network to obtain any kind of permit, constantly fretted. He hired Russian women to staff his market stalls, where he sold apples and pears from Baku, taking diminished profits instead of risking any encounter with officials or militia that might expose his lack of status.[64] Some traders had their own form of documentation that allowed temporary stays in Leningrad and Moscow: a *spravka* (certificate), issued from their collective farm director, which stated that the goods being sold were their own, from designated private plots, and therefore legal. Rasul Asgarov's *spravka* testified that the flowers he sold in Moscow were grown on his designated land of about one hectare, on a collective farm not far from Baku. The village soviet would issue the document after local militia made a visual inspection to verify that flowers were grown on his plot. Once the *spravka* was issued, he could sell any type of flower anywhere in the Soviet Union.[65] Like the limited residence permit, the *spravka* nonetheless placed these traders in a gray zone. Many hoped it would act as a shield for more extensive commercial activity in Leningrad and Moscow. Others noted that the *spravka*, whether being employed "properly" or not, failed to absolve them from confrontations with Leningrad's and Moscow's militias.[66] As with the limited residence permit, efforts to move from the *spravka* to a more permanent, secure status signaled a desire to find a degree of stability and inclusion as a regular denizen of Leningrad or Moscow.

Even a full propiska might offer a halting integration. Sectors deemed "labor deficit," as discussed in chapter 1, could use the promise of unlimited residence status to attract personnel. Anarbek Zakirov gained a full propiska after being hired through a recruitment drive of the 107th Division of Moscow's militia in 1971. His former position as an army sergeant allowed for a smooth workplace transition, as he guarded museum exhibitions and investigated robberies.[67] Zakirov found that even being fast-tracked through Moscow's housing hierarchy provided challenges. He began in a militia dormitory on the city outskirts, near Luzhniki Stadium, which acted as a waystation for single officers and young families. After a year, he received space in a relatively uncrowded communal apartment on the old Arbat, shared with a Russian pensioner couple and a Jewish family. He was just about to receive his own apartment, with his Kyrgyz wife, when he decided to return to Frunze and pursue a life in academics. Zakirov regretted the timing, but he waited four years for the state to offer him permanent, single-family accommodation. Housing stock in Leningrad and Moscow alike struggled to keep up with population growth. The situation worsened in the 1980s, especially for unconnected youth, which contributed to efforts to restrict *limitchiki* in favor of increasing productivity.[68] Unofficial networks emerged as progressively vital to newcomers seeking accommodation at the USSR's heart.

Only one of the subjects we interviewed detailed the option to permanent status, with ready-made accommodation, debated by Kudubaev's circle: marriage to a native Leningrader or Muscovite. Such a strategy was infamous with Soviet citizens. Stories filled the literature of the time (and since). Academics recognized the phenomenon through the term "marriage migration" (*brachnaia migratsiia*). Could significant outside marriage numbers, demographers wondered, compensate for city populations struggling to attract youth?[69] As married couples shared living space, such "recruitment" might be a desirable way to offset housing challenges, while meeting demographic needs. Fuad Ojagov, who heard of such strategies at his monthly meetings with other invitees of the Azerbaijani legation to Moscow, recounted:

> Some Azerbaijanis married Russians. I had friends who were married to Russian women. They married very quickly. Sometimes then they divorced or separated but continued to live in the same flat. Many had this idea when they first arrived: go to Moscow, marry a Russian woman,

stay in Moscow. Get a residence permit, an apartment, a career. I had a
friend who married a general's daughter. True, he later took to drink and
died. Moscow certainly had a lot of chances for a career.[70]

Certainly, few marriages in Moscow led to such severe consequences, but the
divorce rate was about twice that of elsewhere in the country. The effect of marriage migration on this, however, remained anecdotal. "Marriage migrants" might,
as Ojagov believed, use a first marriage simply as a stepping stone to a more
permanent life in Moscow, which could include a search for a more suitable
partner. An in-depth study of marriage data undertaken in the glasnost era concluded that "marriage migrants" in Moscow produced a stable influx of between
thirty-five thousand and sixty-five thousand new residents annually. Non-Russian
Muscovites were more likely than Russians to marry "outsiders" from their
own ethnic group, often someone in their home republic. This tendency was especially marked among Armenians, who were 10.6 times more likely than the
general population to marry non-Muscovite coethnics.[71] Overall, however, the
most significant number of marriage migrants came from elsewhere in Russia,
with the main common point being a high level of education (likely couples who
met as students). The study admitted it could offer no insight into how many
marriages were "fictitious."

The propiska retained an important social and symbolic role, whether required
or not in everyday life. It eased access to medical care, placed children in school,
and allowed placement on waiting lists—however long—for housing and other
basic services.[72] It perpetuated the reputation, as well as the reality, of Leningrad,
Moscow, and other major urban centers as places where quality goods were not
only more plentiful but also more affordable and where the quality of culture and
other aspects of daily life was higher.[73] Louise Shelley has noted that cities under
the "regime system" had lower crime rates. First-time offenders, stripped of or
unable to gain propiski, were generally sent to live far from key urban areas.[74]
The prestige of living with a full propiska enforced degrees of otherness—Dietrich
André Loeber notes that in late Soviet Moscow "*limitchik*" was pronounced with
a tone of sympathy or contempt, but signaled one whose place was not permanently in the capital.[75]

Multiple paths, official or surreptitious, existed to offer the stamp of regular
or long-term status in Leningrad and Moscow. Ambition, talent, cunning, or
connections—along with, potentially, a significant amount of work—allowed permeable boundaries to be breached and the USSR's civilizational centers to be
joined.[76] Leningrad and Moscow embodied a Soviet dream as conceptualized by
citizens at least as much as the state—one where individual will and labor within

and beyond one's own networks facilitated ascension to personal and collective success.

Work and Achievement

Official efforts to manage migration to Leningrad and Moscow broadened as much as narrowed opportunities for Soviet migrants from the faraway Caucasus, Central Asia, and Asian Russia. As the resident populations of the two capitals declined and aged, growing urban economies required ever more human capital.[77] Research institutes, government departments, and enterprises continually sought new employees, and consumers sought services. With propiska requirements slowing migration from nearby regions, employers privileged newcomers who entered on union-wide official work or study programs, as well as those with the boldness to simply show up in Leningrad and Moscow to offer, or be willing to acquire, the broad spectrum of skills and work needed in these global cities.[78] Zakirov believed in the necessity of desire to survive and prosper in these chaotic but rewarding worlds. His time as a militia sergeant investigating crimes in 1970s Moscow, and, after a short stint at home in Frunze, as a graduate student in 1980s Leningrad, convinced him that a growing gap existed between those citizens who thrived in the two capitals and those ground down by competition, crowds, and commotion, who lived in increasingly poor conditions.[79] Those from distant republics, like himself, willing to game the residence system and work hard enough, could vault themselves above not only the millions of Russians who remained in surrounding, less privileged villages, towns, and cities but even native Leningraders and Muscovites.

Hard work emerged in so many migrant narratives as a route to inclusion that, even if unrecognized, drove success in Leningrad and Moscow. The connection between work and incorporation links Soviet migrants from the Caucasus, Central Asia, and eastern regions of Russia to postcolonial migrants in Europe and African Americans who moved to northern U.S. cities in the late twentieth century. In all cases, work exists as a concept and ideal, to overturn popular and pseudo-scientific myths of dark-skinned peoples' laziness and to highlight their ability to integrate into Western industrial societies as productive citizens. Kenneth J. Bindas notes that respondents in his oral histories of black American migrants pivoted from discussions of discrimination to their own hard work, minimizing the pain of intolerance and stressing an ability to overcome obstacles.[80] Soviet southern and eastern migrants frequently pointed to cultural characteristics or connections that allowed them not only to work alongside but also to outwork the local population.

Leningrad's and Moscow's educational institutions provided the ideal space to employ values of hard work and advance quickly in the Soviet system. Compared to their home republics, migrants unanimously noted that the two capitals' university libraries were "fresher," laboratory and other resources were greater, and their colleagues' quality was higher. Oidin Nosirova found the "fathers" of Russian linguistics in front of her and expressed awe at how they would render regular assistance even outside the classroom.[81] Marat Tursunbaev vividly recalled the level of freedom at Moscow universities, where students could say what they thought. He was shocked to realize, even in the late 1970s, that he no longer needed to memorize party leaders' writings to be successful in his studies.[82] Bakyt Shakiev noted the continued intellectual richness and challenges that Leningrad offered. He gained inspiration to ever-greater heights of scholarly achievement, knowing that he would constantly be competing against the best brains in the Soviet Union.[83] Admission and advancement to Leningrad's and Moscow's institutes of higher education were not just rewards for talent or work but an acknowledgment of loyalty to modern Soviet values, from scientific achievement to the friendship of peoples, ones that allowed a privileged space of communication and interaction for Soviet citizens regardless of background.

Outside the university environment, Maia Asinadze believed that her friends' and networks' support released her individual talent and facilitated her success. Once she found her feet in Moscow, in 1982, even before she felt fully comfortable in Russian, Asinadze entered a pharmacological institute. The study of economics, chemistry, biology, and anatomy alongside better-prepared students was, she

FIGURE 9   Patron at the V. I. Lenin State Library, Moscow, January 1980. Attribution: RIA Novosti archive / Fred Grinberg / CC-BY-SA 3.0

recalled, "incredibly difficult . . . I used to cry a lot."[84] Professors chided her for poor grades on her first set of exams. Her flatmates' reassurances inspired her to study ever harder, and by the end of her first year she had raised her grades from "twos" to "fours." Teachers took notice and began to help her. Asinadze expressed pride in catching up and keeping up with some of the top students in her field from across the Soviet Union.

Success in her studies propelled Asinadze to work terms at Moscow pharmacies and a permanent position on graduation. She felt immediately accepted by her colleagues, in a multinational staff that included a Tatar, another Georgian, and a Tajik, as well as Russians. "All that was really important," she noted, "was how you performed your work." Staff enjoyed their jobs and one another, with the attitude of "you are with us."[85] Patients appreciated her knowledge of pharmaceuticals, which allowed her to prescribe different medicines than those ordered by doctors. Patients appreciated her efforts and the results: "I received so many 'thank-yous' from people. 'You cured me,' they would say. When it was my day to work, there would be a line of people waiting for consultations with me."[86] She underlined the importance of her Georgian background in this narrative of accomplishment. Once Asinadze overcame language difficulties, her connections to home enhanced her value. She consulted her grandmother on folk cures and different herbs to prescribe alongside her array of medications. On retirement, "I am telling you the truth, [customers] cried."[87] Her migrant story came full circle, from a young woman struggling to adapt to the USSR's alien capital to one using her ethnic background and networks to improve the lives of its citizens.

Soviet migrants found a sense of *svoi* in "informal microgroups" or "microworlds" as they adapted to the scale of the two capitals.[88] Asinadze's microworlds—from *kommunalka* to institute to workplace—contained a mix of nationalities, privileged inclusion through friendship, and recognized talent through work. Such worlds materialized across social classes and professions in Leningrad and Moscow. Even as migrants made these worlds their own, they were often defined by state policies and practices. Skills developed in Soviet schools channeled citizens into educational or professional enclaves, with top tiers gaining positions in Leningrad and Moscow.[89] In professional and industrial work, migrants privileged inclusion through their work collective (*kollektiv*). Sarah Ashwin has demonstrated the importance of such groupings, designated by the state to play roles in the provision of food, housing, medical care, and social opportunities, including leisure.[90] Collectives—and individuals within collectives—worked to gain vouchers for cars or washing machines, better or longer excursions, vacations or dormitory rooms.[91] These opportunities and mutual obligations led members to feel "genuine attachment" toward collectives.[92] In interviews, collectives evoked a far more emotional and detailed response than unions (*profsoiuzy*), which gained one positive mention for approving maternity leave.[93] Work collectives facilitated satisfying interpersonal relations and translated from work into personal lives and friendships.[94]

Collectives could provide a space of equality with Leningraders and Muscovites and a springboard to personal success.[95] Newly arrived professionals praised initial workplace encounters. Lali Utiashvili recalled coworkers greeting her as a new friend when she arrived with minimal Russian at a Moscow agricultural institute in 1979. She received her position as a spousal hire to accompany her husband, an accomplished scientist, to the capital.[96] Some Georgian and Armenian respondents attributed such a welcome, and eventual professional success, to national reputations for intellectual achievement, stemming from, according to one, a Christian background. The extent to which their treatment differed from Soviet Muslims remains unclear; Central Asians praised collectives in similar terms and never noted religion as a distinguishing factor. As Levan Rukhadze stated, differences in multiethnic workplaces were irrelevant if coworkers considered members "necessary to us, our workplace, our collective."[97] Azamat Sanatbaev said his tourist agency collective reminded him of his small Kyrgyz village, as members looked out for one another. He recalled a time when he had to go home to visit an ill family member and colleagues in his collective all pitched in money to help him go.[98]

Collective solidarity extended to microworlds beyond professional spheres as migrants considered their place as *svoi*. Shuhrat Kazbekov's unusual path had led him from the world of figure skating to a career at Leningrad Film Studios (Lenfilm). His talent opened doors as he moved between top sports schools to Leningrad. Due to his creativity on the ice, Kazbekov recalled, "I was so respected. People would give me bouquets of flowers at competitions. [Leningraders] loved me."[99] He noted that he carried positive feelings to his more menial position as a driver, dismissing a question on difficulties as one of the only non-Russians at the studio. "What does it mean to be difficult? I just went to work. . . . It just depends on the type of person you are. For me, it was all easy." Of the conscious decision he made to adapt—he already spoke Russian well and worked carefully to follow local and workplace customs—he stated: "You don't go into another's monastery with your own rules [*V chuzhoi monastyr' so svoim ustavom ne khodi*]."[100] Kazbekov used social and professional skills to "create" a position as stuntman. As driver or stuntman, he cited nothing but warm feelings from colleagues. "We all helped each other. Here in Leningrad, I feel like *svoi*, but if I returned to Uzbekistan, I would feel like a stranger." His energy and dignity, which he credited to the importance Uzbeks placed on watching out for families, gained him great appreciation. He delighted in recounting one story about how his fellow workers admired him for defending the honor of a female actress by throwing a lecherous Russian through a stage window.

Individual talent and social skills meshed in narratives of these collectives and microworlds. Vazha Gigulashvili recalled that her husband's hard work, ability, and leadership at a Kutaisi factory led to his recruitment to Moscow through *orgnabor* in 1974.[101] His value was judged highly enough that he received the rare offer of a private apartment for his family immediately on arrival. She soon joined him with a full propiska and choice of her line of work, either independently or with state assistance. She discarded the potentially lucrative avenue of trading for its long hours on Moscow's streets, instead taking positions in a pharmacy and, later, a supermarket. "Courageous and sociable," she changed jobs frequently when offered higher salaries, noting that in Moscow "if you were willing to work hard," it was easy to climb the employment ladder.[102] Friendships enabled workplace solidarity and comfort. Gigulashvili, as did Asinadze, kept in touch with Russian and Ukrainian coworkers from their collective years after leaving their positions. Jumaboi Esoev also made several friends at the meat factory as he sought higher salaries and social mobility. He greatly appreciated the fact that he did not have to change employers: factory managers and union leaders collaborated, he recalled, to place workers in the best position to succeed. Significant horizontal mobility—allowing the acquisition of a variety of skills—accompanied vertical mobility to higher positions such as shift foreman, with accompanying status and salary.[103] Kudubaev had similar recollections; even as a *limitchik*, his employer offered training at various positions, widening avenues to inclusion in Moscow.

Leisure activities linked to collectives played a large role in narratives of belonging. Gigulashvili and many others recalled the subsidized, or free, vacations that work collectives received. These extended from day trips at nearby dachas to two-week vacations at sanatoriums in Crimea or across the Soviet Union.[104] Irma Balanchivadze, who worked at a Leningrad vegetable depot a decade after Khamagova, recalled vacation tickets being distributed to every worker. Alex Koberidze's repair and construction institute in 1980s Leningrad had a "tourist base" (*turbaz*) at Zelenogorsk, on the coast of the Gulf of Finland. He, his colleagues, and managers all socialized on the weekends, swimming, sailing, and roasting kebabs in the summer and cross-country skiing in the winter. He did not partake in the regular drinking rituals, however, wanting to show himself a disciplined worker.

Stories of outperforming the host society became an almost obligatory part of migrant narratives, as outsiders sought to prove—to colleagues and others then and to interviewers now—their place as *svoi* in Leningrad's or Moscow's cityscapes. Narratives and stereotypes lowered Russians' place in cities that these migrants deemed not home to one ethnic group but the pinnacle of Soviet success. In her agricultural institute, Utiashvili mirrored Asinadze's and others' tropes of hard work leading to recognition from within the collective and beyond. In Moscow, unlike in Georgia, Utiashvili stated: "Most important was a person's drive." She claimed her effectiveness prompted rapid promotions. "I was always in first place. I received many awards and recognitions. I received bonuses and always fulfilled my plans."[105] Saule Iskakova, who worked for a Leningrad economics institute simply recalled: "I was very respected because of my intellect."[106] This overcame worries she had about cultural adaptation. The equating of intelligence and respect abounded in migrant narratives, supplementing the ideal of work, as summed up by Bakyt Nizomov: "If you are capable enough, you will have no problems at all."[107]

Migrants evoked talent and hard work to legitimize their success and to characterize the Soviet Union as a meritocracy. Farshad Hajiev broadened the Marxist conception of work in his thoughts on the USSR to a virtually universal one: "It was all fair, a completely fair world. Marx was a genius. All the people were equal. It didn't depend on nationality. Marx's writings reflect the equality found in the Bible or Quran. Work dictated how much you achieved."[108] Dea Kochladze, however, highlighted the challenges of rising in a Russian city, where hard work was the ultimate judge. Even though she had come to Moscow at age ten and attended some of its best schools, Kochladze recalled constant stress and the need to outperform host Russians to gain entrance to a medical school and eventually a career in neurology, which included a teaching position at a top medical institute. "To be successful in Moscow you have to work a lot. There are lots of people willing to work and few spaces, so you have to work so that no one else can do it as well as you."[109]

Bolot Oruzbaev discussed hard work less as a matter of inclusion and more as a necessity for one who sought to support his family in Kyrgyzstan. Never considering becoming *svoi* in the Soviet capital, he sought cash in 1980s Moscow. His skills as an agronomist led to a position at the "Luch kommunizma" farm in Moscow's outskirts. Even his "Lenin stipend," however, proved insufficient to allow significant remittances home. He scanned Moscow's ubiquitous message boards for a second job. He first worked as an evening chauffeur-secretary for an enterprise manager and then became a night security guard. The ease of finding relatively lucrative, unofficial employment lured his wife, whose family was the one in financial need. She found work during the day at a glass factory and at night mopping floors. The attraction of Moscow's professional opportunities nonetheless beckoned. Oruzbaev's wife carved time between her two jobs to study, gaining admission to an accounting program at a Moscow institute of higher education. Even Oruzbaev, though not claiming a desire to incorporate, sought to highlight his superiority to Muscovites in terms of high culture, stating that his continued thirst for Farsi poetry, as well as his knowledge of Russian masters of verse and literature, gave him access to knowledge enjoyed by few in the city.[110]

Levan Rukhadze offered the most direct statement of ostensible advantages possessed by Caucasus and Central Asian newcomers in a city where work was everything. In discussing his rapid advancement from aviation engineer to lead on his team, and then to head of his institute, he stated:

> May I be a little bit immodest? I was hardworking, didn't drink, and those two qualities set me apart. This is one of the negative qualities of the Russian people. After work, they must relax "well," and by this I mean drink. Well, of course, not only Russians like to relax and unwind after work, but you have to know your limits. It's one thing to have a mug of beer after work and go home; it's another to get so drunk you don't know how to get home. Unfortunately, this type of behavior was frequent with Russians. I also never complained about anything at work. If they gave me extra work, I didn't say anything, I always did it.[111]

Rukhadze joined Koberidze and others in highlighting their refusal to join "Russian" drinking culture. Caucasus and Central Asian migrants used sobriety as a cultural value that signaled they were a better fit for the achievement-driven two capitals than the host population. Papashvili noted the dangers that Russians' drinking posed at construction sites, where break-time rituals placed the entire team, not to mention anyone nearby, in danger. Hajiev believed that Russian drinking betrayed the myth of the "big brother." "Something that really bothered me about living [in 1970s Moscow] was how people here would drink, smoke, and then sit around doing nothing [*bezdel'nichit'*]." He expounded on the difference in work ethic between Russians and his fellow Tajiks: "In the East, when things are tough, say you have a family to support, we will do anything, any kind of work, to make sure that our family lives better. Or if a man is feeling down on himself, he will go out and find something to do with himself, he will go out and work, just to take things off his mind. But here it's the opposite. If a man is doing badly, he will just go out and drink, and then continue to drink. It is not like that back home."[112]

Hajiev recalled fatal drinking parties in early 1980s Moscow. These activities had already drawn official attention, with *druzhinniki*, volunteers who policed resident behavior, including drunkenness, superseding the *vospitateli* in worker dormitories.[113] These pervasive alcohol-driven narratives equate to migrant accounts in the West. Newcomers underline superior cultural as well as individual qualities that facilitate their contributions to, and success in, modern cities. Insider and outsider status shifted when Leningrad and Moscow were portrayed as places of accomplishment rather than homes to a particular ethnicity.[114]

Azamat Sanatbaev simply believed that Muscovites expected work to be handed to them and did not like physical labor.[115] An Armenian interviewed by Iohannes Angermiuller believed that Russians were "idlers," as opposed to the Armenian value of making use of God's gifts by working hard.[116] Oruzbaev, akin to Kazbekov and others, considered that certain cultural values—including respect for elders, manifested in allowing Russian senior citizens to take seats on mass transport and assisting them when necessary—allowed Central Asians to gain great appreciation in major Russian cities.[117] Russians themselves recognized and, to a degree, accepted this narrative. Emil Draitser noted that Soviet ethnic humor combined indignation and envy at the ability of southern minorities—primarily Georgians—to succeed in large Russian cities.[118] A capacity to work within as well as around the system appeared to escape the host population.

Svoi and Sex

Male migrants from the Caucasus and Central Asia used their ability to attract local women as means to express inclusion and ascendancy. Sexual exploits provided strong evidence that they not only belonged but also thrived at the heart of the Soviet Union. Sex and relationships contained multiple discourses. Women could be a "distraction" from the hard work needed to succeed in the two capitals, and some saw interethnic relationships as threats to "traditional" Caucasus or Central Asian values. Other male and female migrants considered their cultural values and beliefs on gender, as well as family, more compatible with a modern society than those held by the host population.

Russian women, just like employers, purportedly noticed the advantages of sober citizens. Shuhrat Kazbekov gained a reputation as a reliable escort to take women home from Lenfilm and from after-work parties. His kind manner persisted even after his Russian colleagues had descended into various states of alcohol-driven stupor. Emin Gazyumov believed that Russian women quickly realized the advantages of sober and hardworking partners and the greater likelihood of finding one among Azerbaijanis: "They would trade three of their own for one of us."[119] Elnur Asadov proudly proclaimed that "success" with Russian women allowed him to overcome frustrations over the discrimination faced by Azerbaijani traders. "The locals saw how we came and went out with their women. . . . This provoked great unhappiness. Russian women went out with us, went to restaurants with us."[120] Dina Ataniyazova offered a female perspective on such relationships, believing that they significantly increased newcomers' status within their own networks as well as allowed a sense of superiority over host Russians.

Soviet ethnic humor reflected such tropes of interethnic relationships. Southern men were endowed with sexual and economic prowess, distributing their
"gifts" to Russian women. Some jokes were tinged with resentment, portraying,
for example, Georgians as uncivilized and bestial as well as hypersexed.[121] Migrants
interviewed for this project brushed off such jokes as simple jealousy; Asadov
noted that as much as Russians disliked seeing "their" women go out with Azerbaijanis, they were consistently too drunk to take even their own dates home.
Zakirov noted that Central Asians' reputation for sobriety allowed him to gain
the approval of his Moscow fiancée's parents for marriage, though the relationship later collapsed.

Other migrants critiqued Russian women's ostensible promiscuity, believing
it less suited to a modern, hardworking city than their more humble culture. Bakyt
Shakiev claimed that women could not resist the male conscripts who were serving in his company outside of Moscow in 1976. They would yell from outside the
windows and climb drainpipes to "visit" with soldiers. Shakiev noted proudly
that he resisted such advances, which harmed company productivity. He believed that skewed demographics, with few men in the area, might have played a
role along with Russian cultural values in aggressive female behavior. Shadulla
Agaev's story awkwardly mixed censure of women with his own personal pleasure. Dating opportunities arose for him almost immediately after his arrival to
trade in Moscow in 1982. Agaev claimed that Russian women went with "several men at once."[122] He professed to reject advances, citing a sense of honor and
respect, a desire to privilege work, and knowledge that he could never marry a
Russian, which would be considered a "sin" in his home village—a barrier that
Central Asians also considered in their relationships with women. Agaev's effort
to balance attachment to home and aspirations to incorporate in the new, big
city prompted contradictions even within the interview. He later told a story of
being beguiled by a pretty Russian woman who passed by his trading stall. What
began as offerings of free tomatoes ended with them living together.

Fuad Ojagov believed that the temptation of Russian women ensnared many
migrants and could endanger a successful professional career. Ojagov combined
his personal narrative of sexual observation, and eventual participation, with
one that counterposed his preferred city—professional, disciplined Moscow—to
Leningrad:

> Relationships between men and women at the time were very different
> in Moscow from [those in] Baku. Then, relations in Moscow and in
> Russia were freer. There were loose morals. When a man from the Cau-
> casus comes to Russia or Ukraine, he feels freer. I saw especially loose
> morals in Leningrad. I went there five times as a student. Leningrad was

a depraved city. I remember the bar in Leningrad—it was called for some reason "Ulster." When we got there, we were just blown away by the debauchery [*razvrat*] that reigned there. For example, I was not a ladies' man [*lovelasom*]. But thanks to the freedom I could gain experience, which was not available in Baku. Azerbaijanis saw going with Russian girls as sport.[123]

Ojagov, like Agaev, mixed a narrative of disapproval with one that trumpeted his own success, showing him as *svoi* on multiple levels: as a hard worker, someone who could attract a Russian woman, a Muscovite, and someone who could participate in a "sport" with his network.

Central Asian women expressed superiority over Russian women, seen as poor wives and mothers. Tajik wives who came after their husbands considered Russian women as frequently drunk and manipulative, liable to waste money or cheat on their husbands. This, in their view, was the cause of much of the alcoholism around Russian men. Such actions destroyed the family unit as well as careers and paths to prosperity. Children were also raised without values of discipline and sacrifice that so many migrants saw as critical in determining Soviet paths toward upward mobility. Eliso Svanidze, once she settled into Moscow from Georgia, expressed sadness at how Russian women's behavior—which she saw as tied to their relationships with men—differed from that of the ideal Soviet woman, strong and well educated, that she had grown up seeking to emulate.[124] Caucasus and Central Asian women as well as men used gender roles to enforce, or perhaps question, their sense of belonging in Leningrad and Moscow.

Svoi and the State

The state conditioned forms and relationships of belonging. Residence status, policies and practices on placements to universities and workplaces, the formation and roles of work collectives, models of gender relations: all held critical places in determining the social and ethnic composition of, as well as the values seen to symbolize, major cities. Migrants nonetheless overlooked the state's centrality, preferring to privilege personal initiative and networks. These newcomers recognized their own ability to turn institutions and procedures to their advantage. *Zemliaki* and collectives emerged as organic institutions, used to enable personal strategies of advancement. Cultural characteristics were untethered from ones promoted by the friendship of peoples and seen to conform to personal and family values and ideals of achievement. The consistency of its structures, across time and space, also accounts for the state's backgrounded presence in migrant narratives. Institutions remained stable from the Khrushchev to the late perestroika years. Stalinist-era intervention and urbanization conditioned what Morgan Liu has called a "modern populace."[125] Ideals of a progressive socialist civilizing mission and the reality of Soviet bureaucracy radiated outward, reaching to distant eastern and southern villages. Migrants recalled encounters with the state in Leningrad and Moscow primarily when complicated issues needed to be resolved. In these cases, they considered official institutions and administrators pliable. Success in dealing with the state provided another level of *svoi* to Caucasus, Central Asian, and Asian Russian migrants and verified their own belief in late Soviet dynamism emanating from below.

Maia Asinadze echoed Aryuna Khamagova's view of tenaciousness wearing down, and eventually overwhelming, bureaucrats. This included battles over scarce resources, such as housing:

> At the time [in 1982], we were relocated from our old apartment building [in the center of Moscow]. There were many people registered [*propisany*] in our apartment: Liudmila, her two sons, me, and others, and they were obliged to give each one of us new lodgings. At first they didn't want to give me, as a newcomer, anything. But I said that I am registered in Moscow, at this apartment, and that I have every right to a new apartment. I had every right because it was the Soviet Union. It was the Soviet Union. Well, they listened to me, they filed my claim, and they gave me an apartment on Prospekt Mira. Later on [in 1985], I exchanged that apartment for the one I live in today. Also in the center of Moscow, thank you very much. In those times, they just couldn't deny me what I had a right to. At first, they wanted to give me an apartment on the outskirts of Moscow, but I refused. I had always lived in the center and I would not accept this type of exchange. I went back a second time and they agreed to give me what I wanted: an apartment on Prospekt Mira in the center of Moscow.[126]

"It was the Soviet Union" echoes through migrant narratives and highlights how migrants gained a sense of *svoi* through connections to their state. Abdul Khalimov believed that bureaucrats were afraid of citizens at the time.[127] The will to assert social rights as citizens, even as distant migrants in Leningrad and Moscow, facilitated inclusion and mobility. Tamriko Otskheli opened her own shop after ruling out applying to university. She considered dealings with officials as proving her value to Moscow:

> Nobody interfered in my small business, but it was very hard work to deal with everything. I worked alone in the shop; sometimes my family members helped me. . . . I had to deal with the city officials once, when I was opening my shop there [in 1980]. Everything was settled very soon without any problems. Also, when my daughter was born, the mayor of the city helped my family. For the first six months, they gave us food for the kid for free and this was really a great help for us.[128]

Persistent complaints did not guarantee success. Levan Rukhadze, despite his position as director of an aeronautical engineering institute, received only a small apartment for himself and his family in one of Moscow's distant suburbs in the early 1970s. He was told to expect a ten-year wait to receive something close to the city center. Migrants had the option of the informal housing market, though that came with its own risks. Dina Ataniyazova, who refused to live in a "debauched" student dormitory, had to find a place on her own. Her first experience was harrowing. "I had to live a few months in a communal apartment, renting a room, and there was a second resident—a Russian alcoholic with a wife from the Moscow region, who stole food and alcohol from my refrigerator, soaked his trousers in a common bathroom for days, ran with a knife while drinking, and so on. As soon as I found an opportunity, I rented a separate apartment."[129] Absent in this narrative was any blame placed toward, or even any mention of, the state. Ataniyazova privileged her own ability to work around official housing practices to get, eventually, what she wanted. This persistence embedded her own sense of belonging as a capable and hardworking citizen, against, in this story, a drunk and pernicious Russian, one from outside Moscow, who lacked the desire or sobriety to succeed. Everyday life issues were problems for Soviet citizens to solve, in the first instance, on their own, before taking their chances with the bureaucracy.

The Komsomol emerged as a site not just of equality and privilege, as discussed in chapters 2 and 4, but where personal skills and new networks could be constructed as one rose through the ranks. Kochladze, one of the few migrants we interviewed who spent her secondary school years in Moscow, remembered its importance in facilitating her success in the capital's hypercompetitive environment:

> I was very active in the Komsomol back in Soviet times. I was a secretary in my school. In fact, my sister was the secretary of the Komsomol at her school too. They were in different areas of Moscow. She is older than me, so she was in the Komsomol before I was. We both have the same last name though, so when I came to the headquarters and they asked me for my last name, they already knew who I was. They said,

"Another Kochladze!" So our family was quite active. It was an important organization really. It helped to keep young people busy. It united us in an ideological sense. We believed in our bright future and it kept us united. It took up most of our free time and kept us out of trouble. I am really thankful to the organization because I learned a lot about leadership and planning. Now at work, I don't have any problems with organizing myself and making the most of my time. It's easy for me to lead a group or teach a class at the institute. Not only did I not feel like a minority in the Komsomol, I was a leader.[130]

In university cells, students shared information about career paths and contacts, and leaders worked to widen opportunities. Anarbek Zakirov, whose cell was headed by a Tatar, noted that his fellow members felt bound by their past in the Octobrists and Young Pioneers before the Komsomol, regardless of where they were raised.

Communist Party membership emerged as a more carefully considered choice, one that could build careers but might also lead to distance with friends and within networks. Aibek Botoev recalled: "I was in a union, and of course everyone was in the Komsomol. I never felt any different than anyone else. I never joined the party though. That was just a career move. People would join just to move higher up the ladder. The party was not for me; in academia I didn't really find it necessary. It was easy to join through the army. They offered me this opportunity, but I declined. I was not willing to stay in the army just to get into the party."[131] Fuad Ojagov deliberated carefully on this choice, knowing from his family's privileged background in Baku the advantages and connections that flowed from membership. In Leningrad and Moscow, it could allow him to become *svoi* among the "refined society of young, intellectual elites."[132] At the same time, he did not want to signal agreement with party policies or view himself as a state agent. As we see later, in chapter 7, he would regret his eventual decision to join the Communist Party in the perestroika years.

Corruption—or more accurately, navigating corruption—could lead to a sense of belonging and leadership, as well as frustration. Oruzbaev expressed pride in his ability to deduce corruption at the Soviet state airline, Aeroflot, and assist fellow coethnic travelers. "Without bribes, you could often not get tickets, even when planes flew half full. If you gave your passport and asked for a ticket to Osh, they would say, 'There are no tickets left.' If the ticket cost sixty [rubles], and you put ten extra in your passport, so the tip shows, . . . without any problems they immediately wrote a ticket."[133] Oruzbaev, as he demonstrated to the interviewer his aptitude in slipping this extra money to staff, appeared happy in his incorrect belief that post-Soviet Aeroflot had gone bankrupt, which he saw as justification for a state that allowed such behavior across the USSR.

City Life and Loyalty

Leningrad's and Moscow's cityscapes beckoned for migrants, who, when not engaged in work, sought inclusion within crowded streets and cultural life. Levan Rukhadze, even far from the center, marveled at the attractions he could access. One suburban train ride could bring him and his children to any number of theaters or events designed for young people. He could always find a friend or relative to take them for the evening while he and his wife attended a ballet at the Bolshoi Theater. Gulnara Alieva found herself becoming a Leningrader simply by walking along Nevsky Prospect—either in the early morning, when the quiet allowed her to imbibe the architecture, or in the middle of the day, where the bustling crowds surrounded her. She marveled how she could be a part of one of the most beautiful cities in the world. Proud Leningrader-migrants continued to express inclusion by denigrating rival Moscow. Sanatbaev claimed Muscovites were always in a hurry and preferred pushiness and uncultured pleasures over Leningrad's regard for basic human relations and the arts. Ojagov's portrayal of a "depraved" Leningrad showed these stereotypes worked both ways.

Mirbek Serkebaev's sense of *svoi* in Moscow came from its ever-increasing multicultural palette, allowing him to merge home and away. Whenever he felt lonely, Serkebaev would stroll central streets, where he would never fail to see "one of his own" from the Ferghana Valley, recognizable by their *tiubeteika* (cap).[134] Farshad Hajiev loved attending the various *dekady* and other festivals held by each republic on Moscow's streets and in cultural halls.[135] Abdul Khalimov appreciated at once Moscow's multinational character, but even more that, unlike Western cities he saw portrayed on Soviet television, it lacked ethnic "ghettos." All peoples, he believed, lived together, walked together, and worked together in relative equality and harmony.

Religion could be practiced in Leningrad and Moscow, regardless of faith, but with care. Only a handful of our interviewees considered observing their beliefs in adopted cities. Most professed to prefer a secular or an atheistic lifestyle or to consider their spirituality an internal, individual matter. Maia Asinadze reported visiting several Orthodox congregations before settling on one that had a significant Georgian presence. Lali Utiashvili did the same, praying at a cathedral on holy days, coloring eggs, and lighting candles. She kept her attendance hidden from colleagues, however. "[For a] person in my position," Utiashvili stated about moving up the ladder at her agricultural institute, "if someone found out about this, they could have me fired."[136] Farshad Hajiev's initial disquiet at attending Leningrad mosque services stemmed from the dominance of Tatars in the congregation, but he reported fitting in easily—even as a nuclear scientist, he expressed no concerns regarding potential danger to his position.

Outside of traders, whose experiences are the focus of the next chapter, migrants overwhelmingly reported a sense of safety on Leningrad's and Moscow's streets. Street crime was considered extremely rare, if it existed at all. Serkebaev believed that Moscow's police were far more lenient than those in his hometown of Osh. Even after getting drunk in a train station one night and being picked up by police, he only received a verbal warning—less than he thought he deserved.[137]

Anarbek Zakirov recalled his pathway to feeling himself a Muscovite (*moskvich*) over his first tour in the city. His transformation came first from what he and other students felt as the "freedom in our hearts," with access to international academic material and the ability to discuss any academic—though not political—viewpoint. His appreciation for culture mounted during his time in the militia. He received postings to guard valuable art exhibits and gained a love for French impressionism as well as Russian art. He felt himself at once part of the city and a global community. He befriended local Muscovites and integrated into urban culture, especially as his relationship with a local woman grew serious. For him, "being Muscovite includes everything: speech, clothing, the way of thinking, the style of living."[138] Much of this, for him and others in Leningrad or Moscow, included visiting cafés and bookstores and attending cultural performances, where low prices allowed them to mix, in a sense, with the city's elite.

Contrary to the myth of the cold urban landscape, Claude S. Fischer has argued that cities are dense with potential networks for newcomers.[139] Ostensibly restricted through the propiska regime, postwar Leningrad and Moscow emerged as centers of union-wide strategies for advancement. Geographic and social mobility became intimately linked, prompting frustration for some who unwillingly uprooted but satisfaction for others—unskilled, semiskilled, or skilled, traders, workers, or engineers—who turned Soviet spatial hierarchies to their advantage, whether they remained in the two capitals or returned home. Individual ambition and skill mixed with connections and microworlds in their achievement of a Soviet dream.

Migrant networks, developed before and throughout their stays in Leningrad and Moscow, had lasting impacts not only workwise but also on identities and quality of life.[140] Professional, trader, and other linkages, stretching to the USSR's eastern and southern tips, transformed the everyday lives of millions of Soviet citizens. Leningraders and Muscovites encountered Georgians, Uzbeks, and others in universities, multinational work collectives, and trading stalls. Encounters stimulated professional and personal relationships. Established migrants assisted newcomers and family members at home as they looked for avenues to become *svoi* within the two capitals. Underpinning a late Soviet dynamism was the ambiguous nature and sporadic enforcement of state policies toward internal movement. Its actions structured migrant mobility and networks, but the Soviet state emerged as far from controlling its citizens' lives. Broad spaces opened for personal talent and initiative, which then stimulated official recognition and rewards.

Background, social status, and other Soviet categories, alongside individual plans, conditioned stays for Caucasus, Central Asian, and eastern Russian migrants, even as they envisioned multiple avenues to inclusion in modern, European, wealthy, upwardly mobile worlds. As Sara Ahmed and her colleagues have found in incorporation efforts elsewhere, these migrants underlined their blend of local, national—as well as, in this case, Soviet—and universal values as allowing them to outperform the host society. Their work and accomplishments, sexually, professionally, or otherwise would be recognized by fellow migrants, the host society, or the state, making these cities their own.[141]

Limits as well as possibilities of the late Soviet era emerge in these narratives. The hierarchy of residence permits complicated the lives of those who lacked affiliations to educational institutions or official workplaces. The system kept out more timid, if far closer in distance, citizens and privileged those with the will to live in the "gray zone" of unofficial status. Living situations could become dangerous. Corruption festered. Migrants overall sought to meet challenges and prove their ability and adaptability to cities they sought to storm. Belonging might entail trials, but friendships and relationships, networks and collectivities, official and unofficial, allowed avenues to security and advancement at the USSR's core. Stories of incorporation grew less rosy, however, among 1980s traders and during perestroika.

LIFE ON THE MARGINS

"When will you come back?" asked Aijamal Aitmatova's children as she boarded a train in southern Kyrgyzstan in 1986. Another long ride and monthlong stay selling headscarves in Moscow awaited their mother. Fears that she could no longer provide for her children pushed Aitmatova to join the hundreds of thousands who traded in Soviet Russia's streets and markets, particularly in the capital. Elnur Asadov's fears had involved ailing parents, and an ailing economy, in Baku. He joined a well-established flower-selling network in 1982. That same year Jasur Haydarov turned to selling fruit to support his sister, whom he had brought to Moscow from his small Uzbek town to seek expert medical care. Meerim Kalilova forsook her Kyrgyz village, turning to trade only after failing in her goal to pursue higher education. All knew well, or grew to know, Moscow's unparalleled privileges and resources. Aitmatova, Asadov, Haydarov, and Kalilova joined the rapidly growing numbers on the margins of the Soviet capital's metropolitan society, as divergences grew between the Russian core and southern peripheries.

Moscow's bounties attracted millions of visitors annually, from weekend shoppers who brought their prizes home to nearby cities and districts on what became known in the 1970s as "sausage trains" to buyers and sellers from distant republics.[1] Consumer trade outside of official channels increased substantially in the 1980s.[2] Postwar Leningrad, Moscow, and other major cities had established collective farm markets for peasants to sell household production legally. The provenance of goods that ended up there, and the ability of merchants to sell them, depended, however, more on networks and relations, intimate and long distance,

than on administrative regulations. Street trade expanded in the last Soviet decade to busy street corners and bus and metro stations, regardless of municipal
sanctions.[3] James Millar coined the "little deal" to designate a tacit agreement between the Brezhnev-era state and an increasingly privileged, acquisitive urban
society. In exchange for political quiescence, Leningraders, Muscovites, and others
could go beyond the official sector to the USSR's "second economy" to satisfy demands for goods and services.[4] Natalya Chernyshova questions whether burgeoning consumer trade was as much the product of a deal as it was the state's
inability to stem the ever-increasing flow of goods bought and sold union-wide,
with its epicenter in Moscow.[5]

"Urban informalities," as Oren Yiftachel has labeled them, are not unique to
the Soviet Union.[6] Informal economies, powered by newcomers such as Aitmatova, Asadov, Haydarov, and Kalilova, underpin the continued growth of major
modern urban spaces, whose residents demand ever-better standards of living.
Migrants who arrive to these cities without necessary documentation for long-
term stays provide creative and economic energies at low short- and long-term
costs. Yiftachel connects late twentieth-century informalities to the new "urban
colonial." Once imperial powers, as they neglect former possessions, see population flows, formerly dominated by European settlers moving outward, reverse.[7]
Saskia Sassen-Koob labels this phenomenon "the peripheralization at the core."[8]
In the Soviet Union, the most desired destination was the center of Moscow, ever
more occupied by Central Asian and Caucasus traders. The Soviet state, its agents,
and the host population greeted street merchants and their so-called deficit (de-
fitsitnye) goods with a mix of welcome, tolerance, and repugnance, complicating
integration into Moscow's cityscape.

The late USSR's expanding informal economy remains understudied, examined until now primarily from a viewpoint of state capacity.[9] This chapter reveals
its manifold effects in linking the USSR's center and edges, influencing household
economies, consumer behavior, and everyday relations union-wide. Individual
stories show how agency from below shaped the contours of the late Soviet economy and reveal challenges as well as opportunities of participating in informal
exchange. In practices that at once undermined and sustained the system, these
traders worked through the arteries of migrant networks. Michael Kearney
characterizes these networks as "vascular system[s] through which flow persons,
information, goods, services, and economic value"; such systems, however, depended on intimate, personal, and sometimes chance and contingent links.[10]
Traders and networks undergirded vibrancy in the southern republics as they reacted to a changing core-periphery relationship. This dynamism then shaped
consumer and street life in Moscow and Leningrad and across the USSR in the
1980s.

These four traders' stories highlight fraught, in some cases wrenching, decisions to separate from friends and family. Each emphasized his or her ability to overcome distance as well as the strange faces, cramped spaces, and gray buildings and skies that represented Moscow's alien environment. Individual deftness and determination, as well as a common Soviet culture, they believed, assisted them in fitting into Moscow's Slavic-dominated but diverse ethnoscape.[11] Trading networks formed largely along ethnic lines—Aitmatova, Asadov, Haydarov, and Kalilova suit Min Zhou's portrayal of transnational ethnic entrepreneurs in modern Western cities. "Bounded solidarity" facilitates the ability to identify and fill lucrative opportunities unrecognized by the host society. Solidarity also combats social and cultural isolation and potential discrimination.[12] In Moscow, ethnic difference, as has been discussed in earlier chapters, endowed Caucasus and Central Asian migrants with a particular status. As Asadov recalled significant racism, the other three traders hewed more closely to the discourse of the friendship of peoples. They contended that, despite social isolation, Moscow became a "second home," though perhaps not a first one, to Russians and non-Russians alike.[13]

Continued attachment to home and families, combined with official and societal ambivalence to their presence, confused issues of identity for these traders. Except for, possibly, Kalilova, they did not seek, like migrants in the previous chapter, to become *svoi*. Concurrent but separate attachments predominated, with ideas of success linked to Moscow and ideals of family and nation connected to home. Ethnicity and family became "soils of significance" in the words of Sara Ahmed and her colleagues; that is, as "fragments which are imagined to be traces of an equally imagined homely whole."[14] Migrants employed conceptions of a bounded Soviet community with a single "mythico-history" as well as a "mobile and processual" sense of identity.[15] Distance and isolation remained, even as these traders' words emphasized degrees of inclusion into Moscow's social life and recognition of the attractiveness of modern ideals, including gender equality and higher education. Self-identification as success stories at the pinnacle of Soviet power sublimated, if not fully compensated for, day-to-day remoteness.

Soviet discourses emerge in these stories as powerful shapers of identity, then and now. All four traders, a generation after the end of the Soviet Union, framed their memories within state-sponsored tropes of home and away, backwardness and progress. Their movement enforced an affiliation to official categories of nationality, which they saw as governing their networks. Their experiences deepen the contemporary findings of Iu. V. Arutiunian, who argued that contrary to many Soviet sociologists' and planners' hopes, migration would not catalyze a post-national "new Soviet person." Migrants to late Soviet cities continued to regard ethnic attachments as central dimensions of their identities.[16]

These four interviews were chosen for their richness and variety of perspectives. They follow two female and two male migrants with a range of ages: Kalilova was seventeen when arriving in Moscow, while Haydarov was forty-one; of ethnicities: Asadov an Azerbaijani, Haydarov Uzbek, and Kalilova and Aitmatova Kyrgyz; and of different motivations and life situations. Their stories illustrate though do not necessarily represent the untold thousands involved in trading networks from southern regions to the Soviet capital's streets.

This chapter follows these migrants to Moscow and back. A section on their initial journeys precedes another on their settlement and work life in the Soviet capital. I then shift to relations with, and perceptions of, the host society. Interethnic interactions emerge as one element that enforced or altered these migrants' sense of self as each balanced ethnic, Soviet, social, gender, and individual identities. The impact of trade and migration on their home communities in the Caucasus and Central Asia reveals the extent and permeability of borders between core and periphery, global city and former colony, and their effects on individuals and families in the late Soviet Union.

The Journey

Personal and family decisions, sometimes painful, marked these migrants' turn away from their homes. They each considered their villages, cities, and republics as lacking the capacity to satisfy economic, professional, or, in the case of Haydarov, health-related goals. Geographical movement had emerged as one of a narrowing range of options on the late Soviet periphery to seek improved social opportunities or standards of living.[17] Connections or chance encounters drove the four to Moscow. Informal associations created an infrastructure for movement differing from, but parallel to, the official one that greeted students and professionals invited to live, study, and work in the Soviet capital. Networks and connections intertwined sanctioned and unsanctioned mobility, just as they intertwined first and second economies.

Stories of Moscow's renown reached the USSR's southern regions through schools, media, and returning visitors. These four traders recognized, to varying degrees, the Soviet capital's preeminence in the natural order of things. Growing up on a collective farm near Osh, Jasur Haydarov recalled listening only halfheartedly to teachers proclaim the glory of Moscow, never imagining his path would lead him so far afield. He expressed pride, however, when, in 1973, his elderly father traveled to the capital as part of a Kyrgyz delegation to be honored for his accomplishments in picking cotton. Aijamal Aitmatova, who, like Haydarov, left school after the ninth grade, also recalled losing interest when talk turned to

Moscow. She had started a family by eighteen and expected to spend her life on a state farm in southern Kyrgyzstan. Elnur Asadov never imagined leaving his family and home, returning to an Azerbaijani-language education after Russian kindergarten and forsaking Russian friends. Meerim Kalilova was the only one of the four who paid rapt attention to teachers and villagers who had traveled to the capital. From an early age, she dreamed of studying in the shadow of Red Square, testing herself among the best and brightest in the Soviet Union. She lamented her lack of Russian language skills—like Aitmatova, Kalilova recalled her teachers, largely descendants of earlier Russian migrants who had come to build socialism, leaving the Central Asian countryside in the late 1960s and 1970s.[18] Aitmatova, for her part, lost hope of entering a Russian-language high school or university in her home republic, which would have allowed her to compete for the coveted spaces allotted to her republic at Moscow's institutes of higher education.

Unexpected circumstances or encounters combined with revived or new connections to spark these migrants' journeys. In 1981, doctors in Osh discovered a serious heart defect in Jasur Haydarov's sister. At forty-one, with only the most rudimentary knowledge of Russian, Haydarov decided to travel to Moscow to seek the best medical care. He cast back to his teenage years to tap one of the USSR's main motors of network building: the Soviet army.[19] A buddy from his conscript days, Vasilii Didenko, invited Haydarov to share his Moscow flat. After the city's top medical institutes refused to admit his sister, Didenko also helped him scour hospitals. Haydarov recalled weeks of agony—first, when the city ground to a halt following Brezhnev's death, with no one available to talk to him; second, when he met hostile staff. He recalled one cardiologist berating him: "You did wrong, bringing your sister here. You'll need a whole lot of money"; he finished with, "you have to understand, this is Moscow, there is no place for you here."[20] Haydarov attributed the remark to Muscovite arrogance, believing that as a Soviet citizen he was entitled to care in the capital, though legal rights for a non-city resident in this case were unclear. Didenko and Haydarov finally found a hospital to admit his sister, with the provision that Haydarov cover costs for the operation as well as pre- and postoperative care, forcing him to procure resources far beyond the means of a cotton picker.

Elnur Asadov's trip to Moscow was sparked by his father's death. Like Haydarov, Asadov assumed charge of his family, particularly his ailing mother. He considered rising prices and lowered state hiring in early 1980s Baku as an "economic crisis," squelching opportunities to replace his father's income.[21] A friend from his family's home village of Shuvelian told him of a network that sold flowers in Moscow over the winter holiday season, from the Great October Revolution's anniversary to International Women's Day in March. Moscow's city council permitted the sale of flowers, as well as fruits and vegetables, from southern regions with longer growing seasons, to improve the mood and well-being of its residents and enforce the capital's status as a privileged consumer destination. Flowers emerged as a virtual necessity in Moscow life. In 1966, Soviet authorities imported foreign flowers when a domestic shortage appeared rather than face an angry public unable to fulfill social obligations.[22] Flower traders could conduct business directly on city streets, and flowers fetched six to ten times the price of those in Baku. The lure of an established trading network and a clear plan for financial gain overcame Asadov's hesitation to travel to a Russian city, and he left for Moscow in the autumn of 1982.

Aijamal Aitmatova's concerns for her five children and the state of her marriage preoccupied her in the early 1980s. Jobs beyond seasonal cotton-picking were scarce, and costs of clothing and other necessities were rising.[23] A chance meeting with a former classmate in the village bazaar planted the idea of Moscow. The classmate had worked in the capital with her husband, returning home at her parents' insistence once she became pregnant. The conversation "stirred" something in Aitmatova, but her husband's scorn at the idea that a village girl with almost no Russian could go to Moscow deflated her.[24] Two years later, as she struggled to supply her children for school, the idea returned. She sought out her friend, whose Moscow income had allowed financial stability and apparent happiness. Over her husband's threats of divorce and taking all the children, Aitmatova said: "Do whatever you want, but I cannot live this life any more with daily quarrels over money."[25] She sold her family's horses, and on the "worst day of [her] life," without any clear idea what she would do, she waved good-bye to her children and boarded a train to Moscow.

Enthusiasm predominated for Meerim Kalilova as she left the same village in 1983. Her motivations differed from Aitmatova's, whose profile mirrors what Erin Trouth Hofmann and Cynthia Buckley consider a "constrained choice" of female periphery-core migrants who undertake and construct their journey within family and larger social networks.[26] Kalilova set off on her own, with parental support, to pursue her dream of higher education in the capital. She found a friend of a friend to establish her in Moscow. But though Kalilova's goal was clear, her path was not. After only a few days, she realized that her poor Russian skills would make starting university impossible. Ashamed, Kalilova refused to return home to be branded a failure. A chance encounter with a fellow Kyrgyz studying at a Moscow polytechnic institute led to an offer to share a dormitory room and the opportunity to join a small circle of fruit traders in the city's markets.

These four would-be traders saw hope in geographic mobility, to exploit the "uneven spatiality" characteristic of modern Western societies, as well as the unique status of the USSR's second economy.[27] Moscow remained the center of what Diane Koenker calls a "mature consumer culture" during the last years of the Soviet Union.[28] Disposable income continued to grow in central urban spaces, and socialism's success had become ever more tied to improved standards of living centered on consumption.[29] Shortages in Moscow's grocery stores in the late 1970s and 1980s constituted a primary citizen complaint, worrying authorities.[30] Calls regularly circulated from Moscow's city council to Party Central Committees of other union republics to supply deficit goods—one in 1976 demanded Kyrgyzstan immediately ship its onions to the capital.[31] After Yuri Andropov's ascension to Communist Party general secretary in 1982, the KGB commenced a mass operation against Moscow's Fruit and Vegetable Office. The inquiry found that nearly half of the supplies that reached Moscow's Sheremetevo Airport never arrived in grocery stores.[32] Communist Party officials diverted food supplies for their own receptions and private use, and some found their way to collective farm markets, where they could be sold at two to three times the price of state stores.[33] Corruption and other manners of state incapacity highlighted the intertwining of formal and informal economies in the USSR, with people, goods, and money circulating to fill gaps in official production and distribution.

Rural regions in Russia as well as the USSR's southern peripheries faced growing shortages of basic consumer goods at the turn of the 1980s, without the compensating markets and unofficial trade ongoing at the center.[34] For these four migrants, the hope or anticipation of reaping the benefit of uneven Soviet spatiality was tempered by frustration that basic goals—to provide for the health and well-being of families, to gain a top-flight education—could not be accomplished at home. Emotions and hardheaded practical calculations combined as the four worked to adapt to significant cultural and geographic distances.

Adaptation

All four migrants, even as they framed their time in Moscow as success stories, took pains to emphasize initial challenges in their assumption of trading life. Elnur Asadov, alone among the four with a command of the Russian language and an established network, still recognized his marginalization as a minority, unofficial resident, and participant in the informal economy.[35] The Central Asian traders joined varying types of ethnic networks on arrival, gaining access to "multi-stranded social relations" that eased displacement between home and away.[36] In addition to the role such linkages played for migrants discussed in previous chapters, these ones drove economic relationships as well as acted as proxies for state services. The stories of Aitmatova, Kalilova, Haydarov, and Asadov expose these networks' contingent nature, reliant on individual initiative and relationships. Each trader needed to calculate for himself or herself the thin balance between support and constraints, profit and loss, achieved through respective connections in a flourishing but unstable consumer market. The rougher edges of the informal economy exposed specific dangers as well as prospects for long-distance traders.

New connections settled Aijamal Aitmatova and Meerim Kalilova into Moscow's vast network of dormitories. Aitmatova's ex-schoolmate's husband, Talant, who worked in a Moscow restaurant kitchen, offered her a bed in a room he shared with a Kyrgyz couple. She found adjusting to four people sharing one room, with one kitchen and bathroom for every ten rooms, difficult, as "Kyrgyz people are used to . . . no limit of space."[37] Kalilova expressed only excitement at being able to live with students who were following her own, albeit indefinitely postponed, dream. Both of their sponsors found them temporary (*limitnye*) residence permits, tapping school or workplace connections even as Aitmatova and Kalilova lacked the formal employment necessary for registration.[38] Kalilova recalled occasional militia passport checks in her dormitory, but the gray market documents papered over unofficial status.

Haydarov and Asadov rented private apartments, neither considering the need for a residence permit. An elderly Russian supporting her parents let Hayadrov a room with full board and, importantly for the Uzbek migrant, allowed him a sense of family life. Asadov's trading network rented a series of flats in Moscow. Each housed four or five Azerbaijanis who worked as well as lived together. New arrivals, according to Asadov, gratefully followed advice and assistance from more seasoned colleagues and enjoyed celebrations of national holidays. Yet the closeness soon became stifling. Traders, always with an eye on profit margins, sought to upgrade accommodation through dating and eventually moving in, rent-free, with Russian women.[39] The instability and unofficial nature of their living situations complicated efforts to incorporate into Moscow's society.[40]

Asadov was immediately introduced to the traders' world. He outlined a complex, national-level network that highlighted the scale and importance of informal trade for the republic. Azerbaijan appeared to follow Georgia, where republican and local authorities turned a blind eye to this aspect of the informal economy.[41] Baku-based "elders" assigned Azerbaijanis from particular regions each a quadrant of Moscow. Asadov's group worked the Cheremushkii district, on Moscow's outskirts. Work group members rotated tasks, from arranging plane, train, or truck transport for flowers from Azerbaijan to dealing with storage and accommodation. Profits from sales came only after paying credits owed to farmers and intermediaries. This system, Asadov noted, placed substantial pressure on those dealing in these perishable goods: "You could never rest or take a break. We sold flowers everywhere we could: at the bazaars, on the streets, or around metro or bus stations. You had to be creative. The task was simple: sell as many as you could as fast as you could."[42] The local militia demanded significant bribes for turning a

blind eye to street trade. Asadov recounted these bitterly, but noted a broader accord between Azerbaijani traders and police: the former could sell across the city in
exchange for payments if they refrained from "criminal" activities.[43]

Selling in winter, inside or outside of Moscow's markets, Asadov reported the
most difficult conditions of all the traders. He vividly recalled January in Moscow: "You get out there and it's frozen—twenty degrees below zero. And you have
to sit at the bazaar and sell flowers. . . . And so we went forth—we drank a lot of
vodka, to keep warm and not get sick. Otherwise, there was no way we could stand
on our feet from morning to midnight."[44] Profits depended on satisfying demand,
which was insatiable during the holiday season. Tempers flared when "unauthor-
ized" sellers, Azerbaijanis or those from other republics, muscled in on certain
neighborhoods, disrupting contingent agreements made in Baku. In such cases,
mutual assistance proved critical. According to Asadov: "You had to have guaranteed
connections and could do nothing by yourself. . . . You could at any moment be
'gobbled up'—as there could be stiff competition even among 'your own.' If you
became afraid, your competitors would eat you alive. You needed mutual support and honesty, so your colleagues knew to trust you."[45]

The three Central Asian traders found their paths only after arriving in Moscow. Haydarov began on his own. To pay his sister's hospital expenses, he went
home and returned by train with one hundred kilograms of pomegranates and
grapes to sell in "Leningrad" bazaar, one of Moscow's largest markets. There he
met other ethnic Uzbeks from across the USSR who provided support and advice, conversing and sipping tea between sales. Kalilova's patron-student, whom
she called "*eje*" (older sister), managed a network of six Kyrgyz traders. Each periodically traveled back to Andijon, in Uzbekistan, where *eje* had contacts among
growers. They returned with specifically assigned goods: one would sell cherries,
the other nuts, the third dried fruit. By avoiding intra-network competition, Kalilova noted, the system maximized mutual support. Aitmatova's approach was
unique. After several weeks unsuccessfully hunting for opportunities, she seized
on a comment by her Moscow patron, Talant, that "foreigners" at the local bazaar
were looking for material to make headscarves. She recalled thinking to herself:
"There you go—a good idea of what to do."[46] Returning to her village, Aitmatova
used contacts to buy velour and other material produced in Japan. Like Haydarov, she set up shop by herself in a market. Russian women occupied all the
neighboring stalls; communicating through hand gestures, she gained their trust.
Contrary to Asadov, the three Central Asian traders reported positive interactions with the authorities.[47] Within city-run markets, they dealt primarily with
special market security rather than the regular militia. Haydarov praised Leningrad
bazaar's "sanitary state" and only recalled guards at the market verifying scales
and the quality of goods.[48] Kalilova was sometimes invited to join security

patrols. Of the three, only Kalilova complained of working conditions—Moscow's rains and grayness and the need to stand all day. Narrating her adjustment in national terms, she claimed that her Kyrgyz background, spending summers pasturing animals, had given her a healthy constitution and the ability to spend long days in the elements.

All four traders framed their narratives around hard work. Discussions of work betrayed less a desire to express superiority over the host population and highlight incorporation into a modern Soviet world, as among professional migrants discussed in the previous chapter, and more a necessity to fulfill economic goals. This connects them to varied service strata of postcolonial migrants worldwide. Shinder S. Thandi argues that a consciousness of hard work among Asians in Great Britain underscored their existence on urban margins, as they were pushed to fields, such as petty entrepreneurship, with long hours and slim profits.[49] Nina Glick Schiller, Linda Basch, and Cristina Szanton Blanc have noted migrants' tendency in global cities to develop "enclave economies"; for Soviet citizens from the Caucasus and Central Asia most visibly in trade. Close networks encouraged the hard collective work needed to meet economic objectives and minimized discrimination.[50] Asadov claimed from the beginning of the interview: "I had a concrete goal: not to enjoy myself [guliat'] in Moscow, but make money."[51] One day off, or even one off day of poor sales, could destroy margins.

Careful planning was crucial to profit making in long-distance trade. Haydarov recalled calibrating the amount of fruit to transport each trip, considering time to spoilage against his experience that individual purchases amounted to only one-quarter to one-half a kilogram. He settled on 100–150 kilograms. This amount required a longer journey by train, with the risk of fruit rotting balanced against the energy and cost of taking smaller amounts by plane. Aitmatova recalled the monthly strain of long train rides, traveling with large amounts of cash on the trip from Moscow, and the sadness of saying good-bye to her children when she departed again for the city. Every day she was on the train or at the bazaar. Thoughts of home spurred her to work: "Family would always occupy my thoughts and mind. So I had no strong desire to go out and have fun."[52] Of the four, only Kalilova, young and without a family to support, linked work and leisure. Whereas Haydarov and Aitmatova recalled being struck by Moscow's cityscape and enjoying the occasional stroll or outing, Kalilova talked of frequent "vacations" to central shopping arcades, river cruises, parks, and concerts, as well as evenings hanging around the Arbat, enjoying the company of other young Muscovites.[53]

Ethnic bonds and individual initiative laid the foundation for intricate networks that provided support and profits to traders and in-demand food and consumer goods to a dynamic Moscow market. Haydarov, Kalilova, Asadov, and Aitmatova, along with other traders interviewed for this project, found significant

FIGURE 10   Multinational construction workers on the job site of Molodezhnaia Hotel along Moscow's Dmitrovskoe Highway, in 1979. Attribution: ITAR-TASS News Agency / © Alamy Stock Photo

comparative advantages in the USSR's spatialized informal economy. Consumers in the capital would pay substantially higher prices for their quality goods than would those at home.[54] The state supplied cheap travel, by plane or train, even with large shipments of goods, from these southern destinations with long growing seasons, and provided clean bazaars, all to uphold Moscow's preeminence as a consumer destination. The capital's bounties attracted one million out-of-town shoppers on any given day, many from surrounding rural regions starved of either affordable or quality goods.[55] Boundaries between core and periphery were not wholly permeable, however; the traders' unsanctioned existence and difficult working conditions perpetuated a distance from a host society and city into which none believed they could fully integrate.

The Host Society: Perceptions and Encounters

Ethnic networks, combined with varied language skills, limited these traders' encounters with the host population. In the workplace, nonetheless, relations with Russian customers, or, in Aitmatova's case, fellow Russian sellers, were critical to success. Personal interethnic contact emerged as an important component of migration narratives. Each trader formed strong though divergent images of Moscow's primarily Russian population. All four explicitly compared their own Soviet experience to the far darker period immediately preceding their 2009 interviews, when racial violence was widespread.[56] Asadov sought to display the 1980s roots of post-Soviet ethnic violence. The Azerbaijani trader's story attests to the Soviet melding of ethnic and occupational identities, as host Russians conflated southerners, so-called blacks, and particularly Caucasus peoples, with those who engaged in gray- or black-market trade.[57] The three Central Asians expressed nostalgia for the USSR. They mixed a consciousness of difference from and admiration for the host population, as well as a Soviet awareness, as minorities, that they should not challenge the host national group's primacy in their "own" space.[58] Stereotypes and perceptions mixed with encounters to shape views of their Russian hosts, whose ostensible characteristics helped to define migrants' own identities.

Elnur Asadov recalled significant tension between his fellow Azerbaijani traders and their Russian customers, as well as with officials. He reported frequent insults in the bazaars. The ones that most bothered him—a trader from necessity, not choice—mocked his economic activity rather than ethnic background, including calls of "*torgash*" (petty trader) and mothers who would tell their children, "Look who we have here now: speculators."[59] Asadov credited his relatively light skin for making Russians more comfortable in dealing with him, increasing his profits. Scuffles between Azerbaijani merchants and Russians erupted over sales disputes or ethnic insults. Traders sought to ignore racist taunts, as any fracas would bring official attention. The militia always favored host Russians and frequently robbed or imprisoned Azerbaijani merchants.

Markets, even officially sanctioned ones, could emerge as places of significant danger. A harrowing account of deadly conflict at the turn of the 1980s in Moscow's Zhdanov (now Liublin) district comes from a Russian scholar's mother:

> One day, shortly after our arrival from the Urals to visit my grandmother, my mom went to get some [of the] delicious milk we always looked forward to. When she reached the destination, she found that the central entrance of the main building was closed and so were the side gates leading to small shops and numerous pavilions around the main trade area.
>
> She was puzzled because it was not a market off-day or a "sanitary closure," which many Soviet markets usually had on the very last day of each month. Nobody was there and the whole view seemed very suspicious—some windows were broken, and so on. Then she saw a janitor, sweeping the pavement near the entrance, and asked her what on

earth was going on. And the janitor told her that the day before there was a huge fight—so fierce that the regular market guards were not able to cope and the militia had to be called.

The apparent cause of the conflict was that one of the Caucasus traders killed (unintentionally or not) a customer, who was buying fruits or strawberries. The customer believed he was being skimmed and started to express his disagreement very loudly. There was a quarrel, and the screaming and mutual cursing became heated; the two men started to push each other, and in one moment the trader grabbed one of his lead weights and hit the other guy in the head. The blow was fatal, and the poor guy died before anyone could help him. His family was there, seeing all this horror with their own eyes. That was enough for the rest of the customers (regular Muscovites) to turn into a lynch mob. They started to crush the counters and boxes all around, trying to take the murderer out of his stall and to kill him for revenge, looting the shops of other Caucasus traders. In the mess and turmoil, the looters missed the moment when the director of the market, from the Caucasus himself (as it was told), took the killer, bleeding and injured almost to death, and locked him in his office—saving his life, basically.

Then a couple of police cars arrived [along] with a squad of mounted policemen on horses, which dispersed the angry crowd. People were pushed out of the building and the whole market territory locked down and sealed. I have no idea of the consequences of this incident—if there were any fatal victims or trials, or how many people suffered. The guy who fatally injured the customer could have been of any Caucasus nationality. [Azerbaijanis were present at the market and the narrator recalled Georgians selling flowers—beautiful roses and carnations—as well as mandarin oranges.] It was around then when the notion "*litso kavkazskoi natsional'nosti*" [individual of Caucasian nationality] became very popular, as for average ("white") customers they all could look the same. However, sometimes people identified them by their hats—for example, Georgians wore very big caps known as "*aerodroms*."[60]

Rasul Asgarov, who sold flowers in the same district as Asadov, recalled a police raid looking for illegal documents in 1982. From the time of the Moscow Olympics, which initiated campaigns to remove southern street traders but failed to stem growing numbers, municipal authorities sought to exert more control over markets. Here surprise more than violence was the main issue:

I remember one raid on the Cheremushkii market in Moscow. I'm standing there at 6:00 a.m., preparing to offload my goods [flowers, to his retail sellers], and suddenly a rumor spread through the bazaar that a police raid is occurring. The bazaar was cordoned off and everyone was checked. I frantically dropped my goods and somehow, I don't even know how, I climbed a drainpipe to the roof of a neighboring house. Then I wondered why I was running, as I had all my documents on hand. But I could not go down, as I would be caught looking like I had something to hide. And only then, after crossing the roofs of other houses, I returned to the market, to my goods. I showed my papers and I was allowed to unload the goods. If it were now, the militia would insult me and take everything away. But then, as I paid officially for a place in the market, I could sell my goods.[61]

Outside of the workplace, Asadov recalled insults aimed at him and his colleagues such as "the blacks have come to take our money." He credited his circle's ability to "exploit Russians" as partially compensating for his grief at being on the receiving end of frequent prejudice.[62] Asadov's group hired Russians for transportation or distribution work or to sell surplus flowers, and they charged Moscow's Russians far higher prices for flowers than they might in Baku. He enjoyed hearing and mimicking Russian stereotypes of wealthy southerners.[63] Handing a few rubles to those he characterized as "drunken Russian beggars," who appeared on Moscow street corners in the early 1980s, provided him special satisfaction.[64]

None of the Central Asian traders claimed to witness discrimination, though our broader interview set presented no clear link between Caucasus or Central Asian traders' regional or national backgrounds and perceptions of, or experiences with, ethnic prejudice.[65] Aijamal Aitmatova sought to avoid contact with local Russians almost completely the first month, given her lack of knowledge of the language and culture. She nonetheless recalled in great detail immediate heartfelt relations with the Russian women who sold textiles alongside her. They became her only circle outside of her Kyrgyz flatmates. These new friends helped her with Russian, kindly correcting mistakes and buying her a Russian-Kyrgyz dictionary for her birthday. They also learned Kyrgyz phrases to showcase their common status as Soviet citizens. This warmth did not extend to every aspect of Aitmatova's experience, however. She simultaneously discounted and validated thoughts of limits on her incorporation into Moscow: "Every day it was the same story: I went to the bazaar and then back home. Every day you see and communicate with the same people. At home I would talk to Talant, Jamal, and Janysh [her Kyrgyz flatmates]. At work I would talk to three to four Russian women, and that is it. So maybe this was the reason why I did not feel any isolation from the community."[66] Later she allowed that any isolation from Muscovites paled compared to the loneliness she felt in being torn from her own family. She did not mind being alone in Moscow, with her favorite place the restaurant where her friends worked, which she described as "the only place where I could feel free from everything and I would just sit and think for a long time."[67]

The three Central Asian traders contended that the value they brought to Moscow suppressed any ethnic prejudice.[68] Natalya Chernyshova has characterized the Soviet consumer as a "dynamic and skillful social operator."[69] Moscow's consumers understood the quality and availability of products supplied at relatively affordable prices in the city's markets and, increasingly in the 1980s, on its streets. They generally recognized the advantages of maintaining a positive relationship with sellers, who controlled prices and might offer better-quality goods to favorites. Haydarov noted: "You sold to [customers], made general conversation, and asked about each other's health."[70] The occasional Russian mocked his limited language skills. Among positive memories of interactions, Kalilova recalled one incident where a Russian insulted her friend as a "Chukchi." What upset her friend, however, was the ethnic misidentification, linking her to the national group from the Soviet north widely derided as quasi-primitive.[71] Haydarov, Kalilova, and Aitmatova believed that accepting their place in a Russian society and fitting in to a "Russian way of living" in terms of clothing, behavior, and values was crucial to ethnic harmony. After improving his Russian, Haydarov came to befriend customers. A request by the rector of a medical institute to obtain mumie (moomiyo or shilajit), a plant compound found in Central Asia that the Soviets regarded as having significant anabolic and tonic effects, led to a lasting friendship, with Haydarov sometimes staying at his host's apartment on shorter trips.[72]

Asadov and the others folded discussions about the host society into narratives that emphasized the extent, more than the limits, of their adaptation to Moscow, given their narrower goals. Each considered himself or herself as providing an important societal service, exploiting agricultural conditions and connections in their southern homelands to bring in-demand goods to the capital. Nikolai Mitrokhin notes that Russians recognized, if not always happily, the health benefits of fresh fruits and vegetables, considered to possess needed vitamins for those in northern climates.[73] Competition led to traders needing to sell goods of the highest quality. Rather than questioning the Soviet system, the Central Asian merchants expressed appreciation for a state and a host society that offered them the opportunity to escape limited futures in their homelands. They considered minor racial incidents an inevitable, if not desirable, trade-off. All four migrants used their memories to sculpt a sense of identity as a post-Soviet citizen. Direct comparisons to early twenty-first-century racism in Moscow abounded, even if the four shifted blame for the phenomenon among post-Soviet governments,

post-Soviet Russians, and a new, ostensibly less willing to acculturate, generation of southern migrants.

Movement and Identity

Engulfed by work, concerns of daily life, and worries about their families, these
four traders nonetheless perceived important shifts in self-identities. Emotions
and a sense of place in the present and future evolved alongside changing relationships and activities.[74] Asadov, Aitmatova, Haydarov, and Kalilova alternated
between a sense of embeddedness with and displacement from their southern
homes as well as the capital. Efforts to make or hold places in both show the difficulty in applying, as have Liisa Malkki and others, rootless and cosmopolitan
models of identity for those on the move.[75] At the same time, the significant cultural and geographical distances traversed by these migrants endowed them with
a sense of uniqueness, as they measured personal transformations against origin
and settlement societies alike. Their migration experiences, often expressed
through a gendered lens, prompted significant reevaluations not only of person-
hood and place within and between societies but also of links to broader structures,
including nation and state. Degrees of emplacement within Moscow's community
offered a sense of power and possibility, allowing them to imagine themselves,
even if fleetingly, as part of a modern Soviet world.

Elnur Asadov's time in Moscow "made [him] feel like a man." He reminisced
about how, after scraping by with his family in Baku, "[i]n Moscow, money,
women, and drink suddenly appeared for me." After discussing how work dominated his life, Asadov shifted to a narrative that highlighted his ability to spread
cash around at eating and drinking establishments. Even after recounting stories
of "going home" with Russian women while "their" men continued to drink, however, he claimed never to have had romantic relations, even as his colleagues fell
prey to temptation. His desire to emphasize a moral as well as a national superiority to the host Russians culminated with his exclamation that it was his desire
not to "live an amoral lifestyle" that led him to return to Azerbaijan in 1984 to
find a wife.[76]

Aitmatova stressed her personal evolution in terms that epitomized the dreams
of the Central Asian and Russian feminists who had sought to modernize ostensibly backward or oppressed women, and then cultures and societies, through encounters with the city from the 1920s.[77] Aitmatova expressed an initial romantic
view of her childhood in a small village, surrounded by her family and nature. "I
thought that this is what it meant to live—I could not even think of living a better life."[78] As a young bride, however, Aitmatova soon confronted limited village

opportunities and a domineering husband. Her migration had a rapid and pro-found effect: "Once I arrived in Moscow and saw how people lived, I understood that I was not living before, but only existing."[79] Just as Asadov felt himself a man, Aitmatova felt her ability to earn money made her a new person. Her narrative offers a poignant, if formulaic, transition from submissive village bride to inde-pendent, modern woman—though Soviet feminists would not have imagined this transition realized through private entrepreneurship. On arrival in Moscow, Ait-matova professed: "[A]s Kyrgyz girls, we were taught to obey our husbands and have deep respect for men, never to argue with them. But I was shocked to see how Russian women saw themselves equal to men in all ways." This discovery, inspired, as official Soviet discourse might dictate, by the Russian "elder brother" (or in this case, elder sister),[80] "changed my view about my own life," she said. "I became more independent." This assertiveness and financial success gained her respect at home: "My husband also saw changes in me, but he would not say a word, as I was earning money for the family. I knew that I should also change the lives of my children and make them feel independent, despite what other Kyrgyz might say."[81] Self-confidence, gained among the inspiring towers of the capital, made Aitmatova fall in love with the city she felt nonetheless she could never call home.

Jasur Haydarov's migration narrative also fit a Sovietized version of evolution-ary development. He recalled early naïveté, of being scared when the plane bumped down at Sheremetevo Airport. Like Aitmatova, he described how he was initially like a "puppy," seeing the capital simultaneously with fear and delight. Haydarov compared the "advanced" and beautiful Moscow to his home city of Osh. His walks past Red Square made him feel that this city was a "home town" (*rodnoi gorod*) as well as a capital. He regretted that advanced age prevented him from considering student or professional life in Moscow. Meerim Kalilova be-lieved that the capital would allow her the ability to advance professionally with-out losing her Kyrgyz identity. As she adapted to Moscow's public life, she cooked Kyrgyz dishes and celebrated birthdays, holidays, and weddings with her network in "national" style. She equivocated over dating Russian men, noting family pres-sure, but wondered what she might have done had she been more confident in her language skills. Aitmatova's attitude toward dating also showed an attachment, albeit unconsummated, to her temporary home: "Maybe if I was younger I would have tried to meet some guy and have fun outside of work, but I was married."[82] All three of the younger traders invoked marriage as a point where it would have been especially difficult to balance local identities with more cosmopolitan, So-viet ones.

Memories and nostalgia extended somewhat unpredictably as traders discussed Soviet-era relationships and considered their individual place within ethnic networks and cultures, then and now. Asadov spoke fondly of good Azerbaijani restaurants where his migrant friends came together after hard days. His memories of street life, however, soured him on not only Russians but also his own national group. Incidents of internecine theft and fights led him to conclude that "Azerbaijanis were an assorted bunch: some were good, others treated you badly."[83] Haydarov's fond memories extended more to his Muscovite customers than his Uzbek friends. He reverted to a precolonial and subsequently Sovietized discourse of the dishonest Uzbek, or "Sart," trader, who cheated not just naive Kyrgyz and Turkmen nomads, as they had in the nineteenth century, but now also Russian customers.[84] Haydarov recalled warmly meeting a fellow Uzbek at the Exhibition of Achievements of the National Economy (VDNKh). When, over dinner, this new friend revealed his dislike for Moscow, Haydarov cast him aside and sought Russian friends. He still, like Asadov, expressed strong attachments to ethnic cuisine, in this case Moscow's "Uzbekistan" restaurant.[85] Aitmatova and Kalilova retained a fonder view of their coethnics. They maintained that their Soviet migration experiences revealed levels of mutual trust and support among all Kyrgyz that extended beyond republican borders, a situation that, in their view, no longer existed in Moscow or even in their home republic.

Only Asadov challenged the Soviet concept of the friendship of peoples, alongside Soviet mobility patterns. Even as he claimed not to think much about broader political questions, in his own experience the Azerbaijani trader recalled: "I never felt equal with Russians. I felt sometimes above them, and sometimes below them."[86] Russians, he claimed, acted as "bosses," ensuring that the best opportunities for mobility and enrichment remained in Moscow. Showing a sensitivity toward core-periphery systems, he decried the necessity of people like himself being forced to leave for Russian territory, where their masters could "dictate the conditions" of their lives.[87] Kalilova lauded Soviet Moscow as a place where all citizens could realize their dreams. In an emotional response, she stated: "I think the Soviet Union gave different nationalities a chance to realize their futures [in Moscow]. This is a very important fact to consider and led to a strong friendship among nations. . . . It gave opportunities for immigrants such as us to live, work, and study there. Which country would do that? Only the Soviet Union. And Russian people would not pretend that they are the leaders or something in this sense. They are friendly people." She recalled her pride at first seeing Lenin, the father of a multinational state where people were "brought up as they should be—patriots of their own homelands."[88] Aitmatova saw Moscow as proof of the USSR as "the center of a[n equal] relationship between different nationalities."[89]

Haydarov's nostalgia reflected his Stalin-era childhood. He fondly recalled VDNKh as one of his favorite spots. "At the entrance," Haydarov noted, "was a fountain and photographs of women from each of the sixteen [*sic*] republics. We looked at the photographs with delight and pride, that we were all one country."[90] "All of this," he continued, "was thanks to Stalin. He was the one who brought us all together. . . . Stalin found his place in the heart of each people."[91] Stalin defeated the scourge of Nazism, whereas Gorbachev folded before the far less dangerous United States, losing the Cold War and the country. Haydarov blamed the last Communist leader for the late 1980s to early 1990s exodus of Russians from Central Asia, which deepened its economic crisis.

Considerations of, and nostalgia for, the Soviet Union blended with recollections of, and longing for, youth. Thinking through their lives, Asadov, Kalilova, Aitmatova, and Haydarov linked migrant experiences to transformative moments, alternately allowing a family to surmount debilitating economic difficulties, a family member to get well, a young woman to find her eventual path to higher education, and another to gain a self-confidence she never dreamed possible. Each talked of the comfort that memories of home provided through networks, family, culture, even ethnic food, itself a significant component in official Soviet conceptions of nationality.[92] Each of the four, in different ways, manifested a contemporary identity as one who succeeded in the center of their part of the world, even if this success had uncertain results after their return.

Links to Home

From temporary residences in Moscow, the activities of ever-greater numbers of southern migrants had important effects thousands of kilometers away. The impact of Soviet-era periphery-core movement on southern, sending societies remains far from clear, though these four narratives show mobility driving all manner of transformations.[93] Webs of trading networks, whether family-based or large, regional enterprises, stretched into and across the far southern reaches of the USSR, involving Soviet citizens by the thousands, at least. Migrants' families received remittances in cash or in kind. Experiences away altered life trajectories at home for individuals, families, and communities, as traders realized the limits of incorporation into their "second home" and contemplated reintegration.

Asadov's involvement in a republic-wide network to supply winter flowers was one of many that brought goods from tea to spices to fruits and vegetables to Moscow through intertwined first and second economies. Erik Scott's work might overstate Georgian "dominance" in tea, tobacco, and citrus, but he highlights how state planners in that southern republic privileged crops that would provide proper nutrition for the Russian core and how land devoted to "export" goods continually increased.[94] Other traders interviewed for this study noted how they used state property, from land to trucks, with or without permission, for unofficial trade.[95] Asadov's enterprise began with growers in the Shuvelian, Mardakian, and Nardaran regions providing flowers on credit. Each trading circle would calculate how many flowers to order to supply their quadrant of Moscow. Designated members shuttled the flowers to Moscow and balanced payments against credit back. Asadov noted that his decision to undertake trade to buttress a family economy placed him in a minority; younger Azerbaijanis were more interested in bringing money home to improve their status or find a good marriage partner, as well as enjoy themselves in Moscow. The difficult nature of the trade led to a high turnover. New recruits were always available, however, given the lack of opportunities in the formal economy in 1980s Azerbaijan.[96]

Central Asian students in 1960s–1970s Moscow provided the starting points for trading networks. *Eje*, Kalilova's patron, came to Moscow for the first time in 1972 to visit a friend at university, sleeping on her dormitory floor. As markets— with stalls then mainly staffed by Russians from nearby agricultural districts— had mushroomed across Moscow, she realized, along with Kyrgyz students, the potential to make significant profits simply by hauling fruits and vegetables north by train or plane during holidays or vacations. Word of mouth in home villages broadened trading networks as underemployment increased. Trade increased beyond foodstuffs and beyond the USSR's borders, as Aitmatova's experience showed—with her market aimed at fellow Muslims in Moscow. As networks operated on ethnic lines, republican borders appeared irrelevant. Haydarov associated with Uzbeks from all republics and worked with suppliers in his home village in Kyrgyzstan; the Kyrgyz traders linked to Kalilova worked with sellers in the Uzbek city of Andijon. Even though less formal and smaller in scale than Asadov's Azerbaijani one, Kalilova's network demonstrated a clear hierarchy. Less structured networks led each trader to make frequent trips south to bring back goods. Aitmatova emphasized the stress of long, tiring monthly journeys by train, eating up precious earning time, even as they allowed her a chance to see her children; Kalilova, however, looked forward to trips home. Although working in a profession she found undesirable, the prestige of the capital rubbed off on her. Village Kyrgyz and Uzbek girls, seeing her clothes, whispered behind her: "Oh, she came from Moscow, she is so cool."[97]

Each trader sought to deliver financial gains home. Asadov helped his family survive increasing living costs in Baku. Haydarov initially supported his sister as she underwent heart surgery and a six-week recovery period at a Moscow-area sanatorium. Once she returned to health and home, his earnings went, in his words, for "gifts" for his seven siblings and nine children. On trips to Osh, he would find out which goods were in short supply and purchase them in Moscow—

linens and children's clothing being two of the most common. His age, Hayda-rov said, caught up to him; returning home for his fiftieth birthday, he never went back to Moscow. His dream to maintain links to the city—both as a physical and an aspirational space—through his children went unfulfilled: "I thought to teach my children well, so that they would come to Moscow and study. . . . But none of them succeeded in the scholarly field. They became carpenters, mechan-ics. I could never get them to that level, where they dreamed big dreams. I wanted to study [in Moscow] myself, but I lacked the strength and could not speak Russian well enough."[98] Although never explicitly connected, these profound regrets framed Haydarov's frustration toward the end of the USSR and the post-Soviet transition.

Aitmatova faced acute financial needs, leading her to resist pressure to come home for four years. All her spare earnings went to immediate and extended family. Her benchmark for return also revolved around a longer-term goal. She wanted to save sufficient funds to move her family to a larger town near Jalal-Abad, where she could transmit values learned in Moscow, "changing," she said, "the life of my family to a better side."[99] In this endeavor she joined women migrants worldwide in a heightened consideration of how lives abroad can transform home environments, especially for children and family.[100] Aitmatova recalled her pride when her husband's family, who had searched for a new wife for him, now acquiesced to this decision. Her defiance of her mother-in-law in going to Mos-cow, she felt, had been a watershed moment in her life. Of the four traders, only Meerim Kalilova, without dependents at home, credibly envisaged a long-term future in Moscow. She realized her university dream, eventually being accepted to Kuibyshev University in Tomsk. She married a fellow Kyrgyz student, and they returned to Moscow for a brief period, until the uncertainty of the late per-estroika years led them, with regrets, to return home to raise their family.

Reflecting on their lives, Aitmatova, Asadov, Haydarov, and Kalilova recognized the unprecedented opportunities that awaited them at the center of the USSR, the product of Soviet spatial and political geographies that paralleled global south-north divergences. Their individual and collective migration strategies paid off, even as they were forced away from their families and remained on the margins of society for important periods of their lives. The nostalgia for the Soviet Union that coursed through the interviews was based not only on ethereal perceptions, such as a sense of trust and community, but also on lived experiences, from a lack of internal borders to cheap travel, and the ability to profit from center-edge and urban-rural inequalities. On an individual level, these migrants elided aspects of the USSR that they viewed positively—professionalization, modernization, urbanization—with their own personal aspirations and development. Even as their ventures remained on the borders of accepted practices and limited their ability or desire to incorporate into Moscow society and culture, their words and actions bear witness to the centrality of the second economy to the late Soviet Union. Only Asadov criticized the very elements of the system that had allowed their success: the concentration, and often the diversion, of social services and economic resources from the Caucasus and Central Asian peripheries to the USSR's center, culminating in the showcase city of Moscow. The informal economy highlighted and enforced the power imbalances between central, northern urban spaces and an increasingly neglected south even as it was shaped by dynamic forces from below.

Ethnically bound networks, extending from family and community links, cushioned the transition for these migrants. They could see their journeys more as ones of fluid movement than shocking displacement, even as they struggled to balance the distance between native and adopted homes. Self-awareness of their marginal status appeared most clearly when these migrants discussed their lives in a longer-term perspective. Dreams to take full advantage of the cultural, social, and intellectual opportunities of the capital were deferred in Kalilova's case and denied, even a generation later, in Haydarov's. Moscow, for all but Asadov, became, paradoxically, a home city where none of them could stay. The Soviet capital remained a space unwelcoming to long-term guests who did not fit certain geographic, ethnic, or social profiles. As Kalilova discovered, the challenges of living in Moscow mounted at the end of the 1980s. Many migrants highlighted the last two years of perestroika, more than the end of the Soviet Union itself, as a turning point in the intersection between their own trajectories and the changing nature of social and national relations in Leningrad, Moscow, and across the union.

PERESTROIKA

As economic conditions worsened and goods disappeared from his village's store shelves in spring 1987, Erkin Bakchiev set off for Moscow with a suitcase full of rubles. He aspired to purchase goods in short supply at home in southern Kyrgyzstan and resell them at the main bazaar in nearby Osh. Between obligatory visits to Lenin's mausoleum and the Kremlin, Bakchiev perused various stores and found overstocked shirts branded "Mercury," in sizes too small for most Muscovites but suitable, he thought, for Central Asian men.[1] A small bribe to counter staff at the First of May department store procured him these shirts at below-retail prices. His sojourn also led him to believe he could sell loofah, cheap in his village, as dishwashing sponges in Moscow. Bakchiev found a Russian grandmother willing to let him a room in her flat whenever he came to the capital. His search for deals also took him to Leningrad, where he stayed with an army buddy. Bakchiev visited the Hermitage, noting with satisfaction that former soldiers could bypass the queue and regretting that he had only one afternoon to see a museum that it would take a month to properly appreciate. Back to business in Riga, Latvia, he encountered his first hard-currency traders and decided to buy some U.S. dollars as a hedge against potential money problems in the rapidly changing Soviet Union.

As Moscow's economy worsened in 1990, with rising prices and sporadic shortages, Bakchiev turned to trading food. He sold apricots and melons "wholesale" to a group of Tajiks, whom he had met on one of his long train rides to Moscow. Bakchiev sought to avoid at all costs trading on Moscow's streets. Increased numbers of merchants from across the USSR produced cutthroat competition. Document checks proliferated. Even as life grew harder, new luxuries reminded Bakchiev of the stark differences between his own village and the USSR's two capitals. He recalled a trip to Leningrad, where he used a pay toilet in a fancy hotel that was "so clean," all in marble, "that you could have drunk coffee inside."[2]

Bakchiev worried that Mikhail Gorbachev was proving unable to balance this luxury with even stable living standards for the general population, especially in faraway villages like his own. The Soviet leader, he thought, was turning his homeland "into a foreign country," with extremes between rich and poor.[3] By 1991, as inflation surged, average Muscovites, hawking their own household goods, joined traders on the street. Suddenly, life in his own Central Asian village, where they could grow food and control their own livestock, appeared better than at the heart of the Soviet Union. Bakchiev tempered pride in his own success and his village's ability to survive perestroika with a realization that a collapse of the state, suddenly distinctly possible, would threaten his livelihood and alter his and his family's life paths.

Abdul Khalimov also balanced his positive trajectory during the perestroika years with the growing tension that would eventually end the USSR. At Sheremetevo Airport in 1985, on his first trip home to Dushanbe from Moscow State University, where he was enrolled as a medical student, he scoffed at an old man who, seeing him reading a book of Farsi poetry, yelled: "Why are you reading that here? They could arrest you for that!"[4] He recalled the thirst for knowledge, among Tajiks and Russians alike, as more and broader literature appeared daily in markets and bookstores—it seemed by late 1987 that no topic was off-limits, that all literature could not only be read but also be openly discussed.

Khalimov discovered that perestroika's freedoms had a darker side. On a visit to Vilnius, Lithuania, in 1988, shopkeepers ignored him when he spoke Russian. He soon discovered the best way to communicate was to speak Tajik—once he made clear he was not a native Russian speaker, then a conversation could be held in Russian without a problem. Outside he "felt [interethnic] tension on the streets."[5] Like Bakchiev, he recalled a turn in 1990. Living standards in Moscow declined, and heat that winter was cut off to many flats. Amid "cold and hunger," some Muscovites grew receptive to nationalist figures who shouted: "Let's forget about the republics and feed our own people for once."[6] This rhetoric echoed what he heard from Tajik nationalists on his trips home to Dushanbe, where antigovernment riots in February 1990 turned into an attack on the Russian population. Hundreds of injuries and several deaths occurred.[7] Noting violence in Tbilisi, Georgia, and across Armenia and Azerbaijan from 1989 onward, as well as tension in the Baltics, Khalimov always found himself relieved to return to Hospital No. 50 in Moscow, where he served a practicum in the last years of perestroika.

Amid mounting ethnic and political tensions, Khalimov recalled a lighter moment to highlight the everyday penetration of nationalist ideas over the perestroika years. In 1990, he accompanied a friend to Kharkov for a weekend. This friend, from western Ukraine, recently began to insist that he be called "Volodimir" instead of "Vladimir." He brought Khalimov along for help in meeting local women. Khalimov spotted two pretty girls outside Kharkov's central department store and struck up a conversation. Volodimir followed, speaking in Ukrainian. When the young women answered in Russian, he chastised them for not speaking Ukrainian, as they were in Ukraine. "[The] girls told us to get out of there in not so many words." Khalimov upbraided Volodimir for asking him to meet girls, then destroying his chances. What did it matter, he asked, what language a pretty girl spoke?[8] What had made ordinary citizens turn away from the friendship of peoples?

This story allowed Khalimov to catch his breath as his narrative turned darker. He finished his practicum and returned to Tajikistan in 1991, just in time to see the country engulfed in a civil war. He fled the bloody violence in 1992 and found himself a virtual refugee in a small Russian town in the southern Urals. His attachment to Moscow endured, and his skills as a surgeon allowed him to return, as well as to gain Russian citizenship in a new, post-Soviet world. He found life in Moscow far worse for his Tajik compatriots, many of whom had also fled the war and lacked an education or established trading network. He opened a diaspora organization to familiarize them with the city's and the Russian Federation's laws and to shelter them from growing prejudice by ethnic Russians, no longer constrained by the friendship of peoples or the existence of a multiethnic Soviet Union.

Perestroika had evolving and profound outcomes for the hundreds of thousands on the move in the USSR's last years.[9] Brezhnev-era societal dynamism infused itself upward, to the Communist Party, by the mid-1980s. Freedom to read, to express oneself, and to form public associations now accompanied the ability to relocate and to exploit educational or entrepreneurial prospects, as Bakchiev and Khalimov had done, through intertwined official and unofficial sectors. Freedoms also exposed tensions and inequalities between the Soviet core and its peripheries. The friendship of peoples, which had solidified ethnic identities and connected citizens to individual opportunities, buckled as economic uncertainty intensified and maneuvers for political power increased union-wide. Ties between the USSR's center and edges, nurtured by decades-long mobility and networks, deepened even as linkages that bound the union frayed at the turn of the 1990s.

Perestroika evolved unpredictably over its six years, assuming different and changing forms and meaning to individuals and regions alike.[10] Migrants recalled the early period as holding great potential. It was for Khalimov the "best time of his life," one that rewarded and recognized an increasingly vibrant society. At the same time, Stephen Kotkin overstates his case when he claims that "[i]n the 1980s, Soviet society was fully employed and the regime stable."[11] Divergence between a privileged core and distant, underfunded regions with growing underemployment typified Soviet political and economic behavior and drove ever-increasing human movement over the pre-perestroika decade. Perestroika's attempted reforms exacerbated discrepancies long apparent to Communist leaders and planners alike and provided a backdrop for national tension.[12]

Nationalism and racism fomented at the center also, precipitated by the same patterns of south-north and east-west mobility. Street-level racial tensions apparent in Leningrad's and Moscow's markets and elsewhere over the 1980s drew the attention of nascent right-wing organizations, which progressively targeted "southerners" (*iuzhnye*) or "individuals of Caucasian nationality" (*litsa kavkazskoi natsional'nosti*, or *LKN*). These now popular monikers, added to "blacks" (*chernye*), increased in intensity alongside economic insecurity at the turn of the 1990s. They evolved with another dominant stereotype—the Jew who was manipulating the move to a market economy. As confusion spiraled into crisis, Caucasus and Central Asian migrants entered into the crosshairs of the two capitals' citizens and politicians. These unwelcome newcomers were reputed to be taking over Leningrad's and Moscow's streets, bringing dangers that ranged from miscegenation to AIDS. "Southerners" were now considered a threat to the health and life of the Russian nation.

Perestroika's combination of tension and freedoms shone a light on Caucasus, Central Asian, and other burgeoning ethnic minority communities in Leningrad and Moscow. Informal networks transformed into broader, recognized organizations, holding public events, assisting newcomers fleeing natural or man-made disasters, and working directly with local government. Southern minorities gained the attention of Soviet scholars, including growing numbers of "ethnosociologists," who had previously limited examinations to better-established communities in the two capitals. Alongside racist screeds in a burgeoning right-wing press came thoughtful discussions in the glasnost-era media, including survey material on a multiethnic Moscow and its meanings for minorities and the host population alike.

In perestroika's early years, hope, uncertainty, and economic challenges mixed. In 1990–1991, the Soviet armed intervention in Baku, a sharp and sustained rise in prices, political maneuvering, and other factors shook and then ended the Soviet Union. Perestroika ignored or exacerbated interconnected and already-existing tensions in the center and on the periphery, which continue to this day. Through the eyes of migrants, new and established, interviewed for this project, as well as archival and press material gathered on the USSR's edges and in Leningrad and Moscow, are displayed the complex social, economic, national, and political ramifications of the period and the personal impact of the state's downfall.

Early Perestroika

Perestroika entered the vocabulary and lives of Central Asian and Caucasus migrants in varied fashions, from increased freedoms and national feelings to, the hope at least, of state-led economic invigoration. Paths of development remained uncertain. Optimism reigned that Communist Party leaders had realized the need to connect themselves to societal dynamism. Early nationalist incidents, from the everyday to the extraordinary, nonetheless displayed the potential to challenge the ethnic accommodations that had proved critical to Soviet ideals and practices of citizenship and mobility in past decades.

Many southern migrants counted new liberties as their first realization of changes from above. The confidence to read openly, to wave away those who warned of consequences, as in Abdul Khalimov's case, provided satisfaction in cosmopolitan Leningrad and Moscow. Georgian intellectuals in the Soviet capital, as Erik Scott has shown, had long sought greater freedom in creative expression, research, and international travel.[13] Taboo topics, from religion to suicide, appeared in the Soviet central media in the months and years surrounding Gorbachev's stated policy of glasnost in 1987.[14] Aibek Botoev, a civil engineer who had been in Leningrad and Moscow since the early 1970s, remembered: "During perestroika and glasnost you felt a sense of freedom, like you were able to breathe. We said what we thought, which was something that we never could have done before, when we always used to censor what we said."[15] Togrul Mammadov, a trader from outside Baku who had been back and forth to Moscow since 1980, heralded the era as one where "true democracy" could now be built. Literature and media, once behind closed doors, only for the elites, could now be accessed by the entire population.[16] Dea Kochladze, entering university, saw the economic potential of such openness. A more open, rational, intensive utilization of resources and labor, along the lines of Gorbachev's early desire for "acceleration" (*uskorenie*) would build on the USSR's already impressive achievements. "We thought there would be changes for the better, the tempo of work would increase, supporting the economy, helping everyone."[17]

The freedoms of early perestroika, though, still had their limits. National rights and collective grievances were treated with care by Soviet newspapers and television, which feared sparking potential conflict, especially in multiethnic regions like Ukraine and Central Asia.[18] Rafael Voskanyan, a self-proclaimed Armenian nationalist from the time of his 1982 arrival in Leningrad, was the only one interviewed to claim he understood from the beginning that glasnost would release the energies and frustrations of what he considered subject nationalities, eventually giving them independence.[19] More often migrants remembered from those early years discrete incidents that highlighted the growth of national feelings, along the lines of Khalimov's ill-fated flirtation in Kharkov. And most often, as with Khalimov, these involved encounters with "western" national groups, Ukrainians and Baltic peoples, whose nationalist feelings had grown over the Brezhnev years.[20] David Somkishvili, an architecture student, recalled his "initiation" into glasnost in his Moscow dormitory through western Ukrainians who would refuse to speak Russian with other Slavic students.[21] Shuhrat Kazbekov echoed Khalimov's experience in the Baltic republics. Kazbekov visited Riga in 1986 with several of his Russian friends. Stony silence, his group discovered, greeted any request for service in Russian. In desperation, he asked a vendor for theater tickets in Uzbek. The woman smiled and helped him in perfect Russian. The Uzbek, he noted with irony, became in effect a translator for his Russian friends in Latvia. His tactic seemed the only way to get seated at a restaurant, ask for goods in stores, or attend cultural events.[22] Kochladze, who had come from Tbilisi with her parents at the age of ten, heard "rumors" of ethnic tensions at her former Moscow high school in the mid-1980s. She remained confident that, as long as she associated with caring people, she would never experience problems.[23]

Gulnara Alieva's initial encounter with perestroika hinted at its bleaker side, however, and illustrated how tensions on the periphery moved to the center. Unrest in Kazakhstan's capital of Alma-Ata followed Gorbachev's decision in December 1986 to replace its Communist Party first secretary, Dinmukhamed Kunaev, who had served since 1964, with an ethnic Russian, Gennady Kolbin, new to the region. Crowds of students and others protesting the regime's decision, and in some cases Russian control over Kazakhstan, met violent suppression. Even as the regime minimized the event's scale, later evidence showed that more than one hundred Kazakhs were killed.[24] The violence reverberated in Alieva's dormitory at the Kirov Textile Institute in Leningrad in 1987. Three women in her program were expelled early that year, accused of sheltering a Kazakh man who had stabbed a Russian in anger over the attacks in another section of the dormitory. At the time, Alieva recalled, no one considered either the Alma-Ata unrest or the dormitory violence to be a harbinger of ethnic tensions; rather, they were seen as isolated incidents that did not affect strong friendships between Kazakh and Russian students.

The Periphery Neglected

Perestroika sought to restructure an economy that a new generation of Soviet leaders considered ailing, but it never addressed the union's fundamental imbalance. Growing populations and lessened job opportunities in southern republics had gained the attention of Soviet planners at the turn of the 1980s.[25] Tajikistan had grown more rural, not less, over the decade as nominal investment in light industry proved insufficient to spark growth.[26] Reforms under Gorbachev and his Russian-dominated leadership exacerbated inequalities in economic development between Russia and the USSR's south. Caucasus and Central Asian citizens, who had been leaving their republics in mounting numbers over the decade preceding perestroika, found these disparities apparent on bare store shelves, in rising prices, and in lack of jobs. This downturn, alongside the unpredictable trajectory of the late 1980s, increased the number who now factored long-distance mobility into life decisions. As the state's efforts to match people with work placements in isolated regions thousands of kilometers away fizzled, the informal economy provided the most direct path to, if not prosperity, stability in family economies in uncertain times.

Central planning agencies worked behind the scenes to manage these discrepancies. How could the growing pools of young labor in southern republics be effectively mobilized to contribute to perestroika? A fluid labor market might compensate for the continued, if not intensified, investment in Russia's core and energy-rich districts.[27] In early 1986, Moscow charged southern autonomous and union republics with developing a plan for "socially useful work for the unoccupied portion of the working-capable population of union and autonomous republics in Central Asia, Transcaucasia and the North Caucasus."[28] The Central Committee of the Kyrgyz SSR's Communist Party responded in April, presenting the republic's stark economic challenges, especially in the south. Employment in Kyrgyzstan stood at 84 percent, compared to 89.6 percent nationwide. That did not include 147,000 citizens deemed "excess labor," mainly on collective farms, for whom the republic was unable to find "socially useful work."[29] As a result, growing numbers of Kyrgyz citizens were engaging in "speculation," many outside the republic. The document used the nineteenth-century term *otkhodnichestvo*, designated to refer to the practice of doing mostly seasonal work outside villages to supplement meager lifestyles, to relate to current "uncontrolled migration," much of which went to Leningrad and Moscow. A vicious circle had developed: as the quality of village schools declined—a phenomenon that began with the out-migration of Russian teachers in the 1960s—fewer students attended, leaving a smaller pool to be selected by professional-technical institutes (PTUs) or institutes of higher education and used as "success stories."[30] A lack of human examples rendered it difficult to counter what was seen as Central Asians' natural tendency to remain with family and village life.

Tajik leaders promoted official pathways to employment outside their republic. Communist Party first secretary Kakhor Makhkamov stated to his party congress in 1986 that the party should "support and promote among youth in every possible way the desire and readiness to work wherever the interests of our multinational motherland demand, where large-scale macroeconomic objectives are being met, and [where] energy and territorial production complexes significant for the growth of our country are being developed."[31] A renewed union-wide campaign to encourage southern youth to study in PTUs in Ukraine and Russia, as a first step in such an enterprise of labor mobility, had high initial hopes. Komsomol activists scoured villages in southern republics to drum up recruits. The first results, however, were less than promising. In 1986, of 1,000 spots designated for ethnic Kyrgyz in Kyrgyzstan, only 706 were filled, a failure blamed on ineffective Komsomol activity and lack of coordination between state labor agencies.[32] This significantly weakened authorities in their battle against speculation. The Kyrgyz Central Committee appealed to the Komsomol as well as local party and state organs in the south to find ways to increase employment at home. It asked Moscow for funds to build and run nurseries and day cares, to accommodate the republic's high birthrate, and to provide work for village men and women alike. Even amid these warning signs, the campaign to persuade Central Asian youth to take up "socially useful" employment in Russia, particularly the Far East, accelerated.[33] The Komsomol organized work tours (*komandirovki*) for students to gain exposure to the mineral-rich regions of Russia, from Tyumen to Irkutsk. Their seeing firsthand the opportunities for employment and the ability to make a life elsewhere in the USSR would, it was hoped, inspire chain movement.[34] Efforts were made to confront the declining numbers of villagers learning Russian.[35]

Economic and demographic problems emerged in public view through the glasnost press. In May 1987, Tashkent's *Pravda Vostoka* struck an encouraging tone on out-migration in its reporting on a congress of Uzbekistan's teachers. Meeting the challenge of engaging and employing "youth, especially of the local nationality," the newspaper reported these teachers helped 140,000 Uzbeks travel outside the republic to assist in work projects, including for the Baikal–Amur Mainline (BAM) railway and in resource-rich areas of western Siberia. Three thousand now attended PTUs in Russia, Ukraine, and Belarus.[36] Later in the year, the reporting turned grim.[37] A *Pravda Vostoka* reporter's meeting with a member of the Ferghana district branch of the Communist Party began by stating that "there is no shortage of problems" in the Ferghana Valley.[38] A "demographic explosion" resulted, in which for every 25 workers in the region, only 18 were truly needed. The rest were performing "home labor," a luxury that the USSR could not afford in a time of intensification. And another 150,000 were excess labor. Organized recruitment campaigns had taken only a small number of these—3,400 had traveled to industrial and cultural centers, from Moscow to the fishing towns of Sakhalinsk. The newspaper sought to portray a positive future for these outmigrants, who were earning high salaries and enjoying an independent life, whereas those who remained heard "rumors" that unemployment would still grow.

Gorbachev, meanwhile, reduced subsidies to southern republics, which were already significantly disadvantaged by a Soviet tax system that undervalued primary goods. In the mid-1980s, direct funds from Moscow constituted 10–15 percent of republican budgets.[39] The Soviet leader chose to allocate funds elsewhere in a reform process that was rocky from the start, hurt by falling oil prices that reduced the budgetary room for maneuver, and creating what Stephen Kotkin characterized as an "economic halfway house" between a command and a market economy.[40] Archie Brown mischaracterizes one factor challenging perestroika, however; that it faced a conservative society.[41] Soviet citizens who contributed their voices to this work demonstrated their creativity in adapting the Soviet system to their own needs and desires; they worked within, and around, what they knew. Ashraf Bayramov, from his village on the border with Iran, concluded by 1987 that difficulties on the USSR's periphery would increase vis-à-vis the center.[42] He called a friend, a Jewish lawyer from Leningrad he had met several years before at a soccer match in southern Azerbaijan, for help to move to the city. Leningrad at the time was experiencing shortfalls in the service sector. The city was paring back *limitchiki* and sought to develop more intensive industries that would rely on fewer workers given the city's low birthrate.[43] This contact found him work as a cook, with a tiny room in the back of one of Leningrad's "cooperative" restaurants.[44] He recalled the tight, dark living space increasing his pain at being far away from his family. Bayramov stayed throughout the perestroika years, however; as the economic situation worsened in his hometown, he saw his continued absence as the only way to feed, clothe, and educate his children.[45]

Kemal Jafarov confronted a difficult decision when his southern Azerbaijan state farm, starved of funds, abruptly ceased operations in early 1988. Two hundred employees now had uncertain futures. Perestroika remained a mystery to them, and no one stepped forward to renovate the farm to fit with market-style reforms. Jafarov turned to contacts from his army days, when he served in Leningrad, and mobilized a network to take fruits and vegetables from the former state enterprise northward. His Leningrad friends connected him to retail traders at the "Sofia" food warehouse, one of two major wholesale distribution nodes in the city.[46] Azamat Sanatbaev traveled frequently between Moscow and his southern Kyrgyz home as a tour group operator. He noted that with each late

1980s visit he witnessed inflation, declines in quality of education, and increased worries in his village intensifying over the unofficial northward movement that the Kyrgyz Communist Party decried.[47]

David Somkishvili recalled the early years of perestroika with deep disappointment. He had to withdraw from his degree program at Moscow State University when, in 1987, his parents could no longer afford to send him money from Georgia. Even the small rise in prices that year in Moscow made life unaffordable without family help. His days, he lamented, of going to discos, playing billiards, and camping in the forest in between his studies at one of the USSR's top schools were over. He left Moscow for Kiev to live with his brother, working in restaurants and sometimes as a courier. But life there also grew more difficult, with food becoming alternately scarce and more expensive by the winter of 1989–1990. He returned home to Georgia, where he could be assured of life's basics even as he forewent dreams of a professional career.[48] Economic erosion was seeping slowly but steadily from the southern peripheries, through the national republics, as it approached the USSR's core.

Change to Crisis

Established and new migrants alike worked to turn perestroika's freedoms to their advantage and manage its growing uncertainties in Leningrad and Moscow. Food insecurity presented opportunities and challenges alike for the traders and others who had traveled the hundreds, or thousands, of kilometers north and west. National mobilization emerged from a blend of glasnost's liberties and economic anxieties and built on reactions to growing differences on the basis of appearance and culture in the decade preceding Gorbachev's rise to power. Among certain of Leningrad's and Moscow's minorities, awareness of a broader diaspora consciousness heightened alongside destruction and violence in home republics, while the host population became ever more conscious of the cities' multiethnic character.

Caucasus and Central Asian peoples headed to Leningrad and Moscow at an unprecedented rate in the perestroika years, though the imprecisions of registration and other data render impossible precise determinations. Richard H. Rowland estimated numbers of migrants, excluding Russians, to the "northern USSR" in the 1980s at 382,488 from the South Caucasus and 105,102 from Central Asia, though it is unclear whether that would include seasonal traders who were increasingly the face of south-north movement.[49] L. V. Ostapenko and I. A. Subbotina noted that Soviet census figures did not capture traders or short-term workers.[50] V. I. Moiseenko wrote that migration from the "Asian USSR" accounted for 95 percent of Moscow's growth by the end of the Soviet era, as opposed to 40 percent a decade earlier; Ostapenko and Subbotina calculated that rates of migration from the Caucasus to Moscow quadrupled in the 1980s.[51] The propiska remained an imagined barrier for those in rural Russia who might otherwise be tempted to leave villages also suffering economically, whereas Caucasus and Central Asian people increasingly ignored the ostensible required documentation for residence in the two capitals.[52]

Gulnara Alieva recalled Moscow's streets transformed during perestroika. Groups of motorcyclists, gangs dressed in military fatigues, and punk rockers asserted their presence alongside "normal" city residents in 1986–1987.[53] Sanatbaev recalled the novelty of street demonstrations protesting one or another local or state policy. Donna Bahry has argued that perestroika-era youth, especially those who were more educated, placed dwindling amounts of trust in the state and challenged Gorbachev's desire to dictate the pace of reform.[54] Eteri Gugushvili, along with other new arrivals, noted an intensifying Westernization of culture in Moscow, from fashion and other consumer goods to cars, culminating in the opening of McDonald's in Pushkin Square, and its hours-long queues, in 1990.

Perestroika's evolving economic situation dominated most memories. Gorbachev's rise and policies came at a tender time in Moscow, amid hundreds of arrests focused on trading organizations, particularly in the food sector.[55] Soviet bureaucrats stood accused of siphoning supplies destined for grocery stores in the capital and other northern cities to party leaders, wealthy patrons, and street markets, where they sold for a much higher price. Defendants claimed that their behavior presaged the market economy envisioned by perestroika; remaining bureaucrats and Moscow's party leaders expressed discomfort at new bosses brought in from the provinces.[56] In August 1986, as grocery store shelves remained almost bare, the Central Committee of the All-Union Communist Party sent a declaration to its Kyrgyz counterpart to improve means to supply the populations of Leningrad and Moscow with fruits, vegetables, and potatoes "in the shortest time possible."[57] The Kyrgyz committee ordered available fertilizer and machinery diverted to farms that were supplying the two cities. It pledged to raise procurement prices and to have trucks standing by to take goods northward. Trains with food for Leningrad and Moscow were to receive priority on the rail network. Kyrgyz leaders perhaps hoped that resolving such a crisis might produce greater attention to the republic's own needs.

Mirlan Musabekov noted that higher purchase prices confirmed for those in his southern Kyrgyz village the chance to make significant profits by selling foodstuffs privately in Moscow. He and two others from his collective farm began to take anywhere from ten to one hundred tons of foodstuffs at a time northward to sell at major produce depots. Musabekov also surveyed the market to begin growing "boutique" goods that would fetch higher returns. Muscovites found the radishes grown on his farm to be particularly appealing, as they were "good for the liver."[58] Musabekov decided to stay in Moscow from time to time between his farm's shipments, selling honey. He only found melon sales disappointing. Their quality fetched high prices, but Musabekov grew annoyed at the customers who would ask to buy just one slice at a time, a request which would be considered insulting in Central Asia. Center and periphery, formal and still-informal economies combined to enforce Leningrad's and Moscow's privileges, but in a way that provided concrete benefit to select citizens in southern republics.

Omnipresent market and street sales, concentrated on food, constituted Dina Ataniyazova's dominant memory of perestroika. She knew from new students in her dormitories and from her family in the North Caucasus that life options on the periphery were narrowing from 1987 onward. Musabekov noted growing tensions in depots and marketplaces between newcomers like himself and other Caucasus and Central Asian traders who had occupied prime trading spaces from the late 1970s and early 1980s. New opportunities arose with a series of decrees in 1986–1988, which sanctioned individual retail sales to state enterprises.[59] Erkin Bakchiev was among many new entrepreneurs who concluded deals either to sell Caucasus or Central Asian goods in Leningrad or Moscow stores or to buy surplus products in bulk and ship them southward. Many Muscovites appreciated shops in the mid-perestroika years being stocked with fresh fruits, vegetables, and meats along with canned, often foreign, goods, but at two to three times the price they paid at state-run stores.[60] Trading activities broadened to include apartments, which could be, in this case still unofficially, bought and sold.[61] Azerbaijanis gained a foothold in Moscow's Izmailovsky Market. According to Arif Yunusov, they also dealt in automobiles and narcotics, using the Aragvi and Uzbekistan restaurants as bases.[62] The image of the uncouth Azerbaijani trader grew to a dark and dangerous figure. Shuhrat Kazbekov, the Uzbek figure skater, noted: "There have always been conflicts with Azerbaijanis. They are not polite. They are not particularly cultured either. . . . They came here and took over the markets [during perestroika], [and their] associations with Russians, and with other nationalities as well, became even worse. They behave poorly and act like they own everything."[63]

National mobilization, accompanying economic problems as a dominant characteristic of the perestroika period, altered Leningrad's and Moscow's mood and composition, even as the cities were spared the bloody outbursts that erupted on the USSR's periphery. The stabbing Alieva recalled proved indeed to be an isolated incident in the capital. Rafael Voskanyan praised how glasnost allowed national groups to explore their backgrounds and culture beyond Soviet limits. In 1987, the Tatar organization Nur appeared in Moscow, and the Tatar Cultural

Center opened in Leningrad in 1989; ethnic communities in both cities could now hold "national" events in state-run cultural centers.[64] Openness to religion, a central feature of glasnost, showed in the significantly higher number of Muslims who worshipped at Moscow's mosque, leading its imam to petition the city administration for greater staffing.[65]

Soviet media debated the varied implications and consequences of national identification in glasnost's increasingly open environment. The newspaper *Argumenty i fakty*, with a circulation of thirty million in the late 1980s, undertook a telephone poll in 1988 to query Muscovites about whether to keep the "fifth line," denoting nationality, in Soviet passports.[66] Did the line, absent on passports elsewhere in Europe, distance the USSR from the West and divide Soviet citizens? Most respondents, 60.4 percent, favored keeping the line, versus 26.7 percent opposed. Some argued that the loss of the fifth line endangered nationality's practical advantages (primarily for those of the "titular" nationality in their republics). Pride, and a sense of belonging to a national community, however, was the largest barrier to any proposed change. Soviet citizens wanted to be seen as equals, but not the same. A removed line would create confusion in daily encounters with militia and bureaucrats in a society where nationality was a critical organizing principle. A minority, however, cited the line's "aggressively chauvinistic and openly unfriendly" character.[67]

The newspaper also surveyed broader questions of national identification and relationships. Few respondents—only 9 percent—claimed to see nationality as determining a person's character, and 67 percent said that nationality played no role in their relations with others. Even so, national tensions existed on Moscow's streets: 19 percent of respondents "came across unfriendly relationships with those of other nationalities" "often," and 39 percent "rarely, or sometimes." Of those under twenty-six years of age, either newer migrants or younger Russians, "often" jumped to 43 percent. Respondents considered Jews as most likely to suffer prejudice, followed by Caucasus and Central Asian peoples. Discrimination was most liable to occur in markets or stores, on the streets, or, with Jews, in higher education. Authors L. Babaeva and E. Nazarchuk ended the article by expressing hope that elucidating the roots of nationalism and chauvinism, now possible under glasnost, might help to confront it in Moscow, especially given worsening tensions among youth.

Nationalism and chauvinism had become implanted in Leningrad and Moscow, as it spread through the USSR. Dina Rome Spechler found Russian nationalism over the perestroika era "provoked widespread sympathy among Russian masses, particularly urban youth."[68] Jumaboi Esoev remembered how quickly some of his own, younger friends in Leningrad spoke less of Soviet citizens and more about "all of us Russians."[69] Russian nationalist authors, whose work had circulated previously in samizdat, gained broader forums. Jews and citizens from the Caucasus and Central Asia emerged as main targets, with their images as speculators gaining now sinister resonance. Viktor Astaf'ev's 1986 story *The Catching of Gudgeons in Georgia* included passages such as this one: "Otar [a Georgian trader] sticks out like a sore thumb, turning up in all the Russian town markets, up to Murmansk and Norilsk, scornfully robbing trusting Northerners blind when selling them rotten fruits or crumpled half-dead flowers. Greedy, illiterate . . . everywhere, without restraint, throwing his money about, taking it from overstuffed pockets."[70] Later that year, the Leningrad journal *Chasy* published historian Natan Eidelman's criticism of such xenophobic stereotypes, as well as Astaf'ev's response that the criticism "was filled with overboiled pus of Jewish high intellectual arrogance."[71] Even as the periphery suffered from reduced subsidies, Russians—led by renowned figures such as Alexander Solzhenitsyn—felt that they had "borne disproportionate burdens" in "helping" underdeveloped peoples and republics.[72] Such calls applied also to Africa. Now public appeals to reduce involvement on that continent and end policies that gave African students privileged status and funding in the Soviet Union gained widespread sympathy.[73]

Nationalism and anti-Semitism found a home in Pamiat, mobilized before glasnost as a society to preserve Russian culture. Pamiat's representatives used the glasnost media to spread a nationalist message in television appearances, including on one of the most popular news shows of the time, *Vzglyad*.[74] Calls included those to prevent the "mongrelization" of the races, given the increased Caucasus and Central Asian presence in Leningrad, Moscow, and other Russian cities.[75] Tolkunbek Kudubaev, traveling between his dormitory and factory, recalled hearing increasing chants of "Russia for the Russians" between 1987 and 1989. He and others noted the presence at the end of the decade of neo-Nazi groups, including the Black Hundreds, named after a tsarist-era organization that unleashed pogroms on Jewish populations.[76]

In 1988, new waves from the south joined traders and others looking to escape economic difficulties. These arrivals fled disasters, man-made or natural. The first of these internally displaced peoples arrived from Armenia. On 20 February, Armenian deputies of the parliament of Nagorno-Karabakh, an autonomous, majority-Armenian region surrounded by, and a part of, the Azerbaijan SSR, voted in favor of unity with the Armenian SSR.[77] The move ruptured relations between Armenians and Azerbaijanis, who lived side by side in towns and cities in Nagorno-Karabakh and across the Caucasus. One week later, bloody clashes in the Azerbaijani town of Sumgait resulted in the deaths of dozens of Armenians.[78] Thousands of remaining Armenians fled Sumgait and nearby cities, with over five thousand arriving in Moscow alone.[79] On 7 December 1988, an earthquake devastated northern Armenia, leaving twenty-five thousand dead and over one hundred thousand homeless.[80] As assistance from the central government came haltingly and nowhere near addressed the scale of devastation, tens of thousands of Armenians dispersed across the USSR, with thousands arriving in Leningrad and Moscow. The poor Soviet response to the earthquake diminished Moscow's authority in Armenians' eyes, heightening anger and frustration over the perceived lack of support for Nagorno-Karabakh's claims. Once the center of the friendship of peoples, Moscow was now perhaps a refuge, but also a disobliging entity that had failed the republic in its time of need.

The most pronounced effect of these waves occurred within Leningrad's and Moscow's Armenian communities. Olga Brednikova and Elena Chikadze's study of Leningrad Armenians noted how these newcomers, who tended to be rural and did not speak Russian, struggled to adapt. Leningrad Armenians expressed surprise that new arrivals, who considered themselves Caucasus peoples more broadly, lacked a sense of the nation's "historical fate."[81] This included unawareness of the 1915 Armenian genocide, which had gained symbolic currency in uniting Leningrad and Moscow Armenians.[82] Iu. V. Arutiunian, who was studying Moscow's Armenians when these newcomers arrived, also remarked on newcomers' stark differences with the established compatriots who agreed to support them. Most second-generation Moscow Armenians spoke Russian at home and displayed only "subtle" differences in behavior from the host population.[83] They enjoyed overall higher salaries than Russians of equivalent education levels and possessed larger flats, even if they complained more about the capital's tight living space. Over half of Armenian marriages were mixed, 60 percent of these with Russians. Eighty-eight percent of Armenians in these marriages, however, expressed a strong attachment to their ethnicity. Even arrivals to Moscow in the early to middle 1980s came from larger cities in the Soviet Union, so they were already acculturated to a Russian-speaking environment and had little understanding of these newly displaced ruralites.[84] Newcomers' group solidarity centered around the Armenian language, which many in Leningrad or Moscow were not comfortable speaking.

Despite these differences, Leningrad and Moscow both saw significant numbers of Armenians mobilizing to fulfill what they saw as a patriotic duty. S. S. Grigor'ev, a member of the Academy of Sciences, formed a Moscow-Armenian organization in 1988 to assist with incorporation.[85] In Leningrad, the Sumgait violence, the earthquake, and increased tensions over Nagorno-Karabakh heightened Armenians' sense of identity. Religion provided common ground. Armenians vaunted that their nation was first in the lands of the now Soviet Union to adopt Christianity. The opening of Armenian churches offered a focal point for renewed national feelings—the conflict with Azerbaijan sharpened the Christian component of Armenian identity.[86] Stewardship over displaced coethnics gave form to an Armenian community in each of the two capitals, where the Soviet idiom had forestalled a diaspora identity.

Violence in Georgia also mobilized Leningrad and Moscow communities, Russians as well as Georgians. Eteri Gugushvili recalled the impact of the violent suppression against demonstrations in Tbilisi on 9 April 1989. Over 1988 and early 1989, Georgians had grown angry over support that they perceived Moscow giving to Abkhazia, an autonomous region whose leaders sought to leave the Georgian SSR, either for the RSFSR or to have their own status as a union republic. Many called for Georgia's independence. Amid cries of "Down with Russian imperialism," Soviet Interior Ministry troops attacked and gassed the crowd of thousands. Twenty demonstrators died, with hundreds wounded. The attack sent shock waves across the USSR. Gugushvili recalled:

> I was in Moscow for my diploma then, and there were many people in Red Square displaying their condolences to Georgians. They exhibited pictures of the riot, and local people were coming and bringing flowers and letters and so on. They knew quite well what happened in Georgia, and they were very friendly toward the Georgian nation and toward Georgian citizens of course. . . . Our [Russian] housewife [landlord] was very close to us. She was coming, and we had dinner together; she was a very easygoing person, and she was saying: "Every country is my country."[87]

Amid this violence, Georgian intellectuals mobilized to take advantage of new associational opportunities. The Georgian *zemliachestvo*, a Moscow society, opened in 1989 alongside other efforts to engage the city's national community, including through language lessons and cultural performances. State cultural houses or Pioneer facilities hosted events organized by varied ethnic networks formed in the Brezhnev era.[88] Some sought to unify all coethnics; others had a regional or professional basis. Officials or professors at Moscow State University assumed leadership of many growing organizations. They hoped to establish publications or assist with cultural development, rather than supporting any particular political agenda as new, often anti-regime, movements sprouted union-wide.[89] Early associations remain difficult to trace, as they were subsumed by larger bodies in the aftermath of the USSR's end.

By late 1989, these organizations' presence, alongside increased numbers of non-Slavic peoples on the streets, led commentators to speak of Moscow as a "multinational city." The journal *Arkhitektura i Stroitel'stva* sought to map the city's ethnic communities.[90] An article noted the vibrancy of cultural centers and nascent initiatives, which included efforts to form museums of national histories of Moscow. Even as "such a situation demands careful attention . . . [and] the need to regulate national relations," diversity gave the city a cosmopolitan feel.[91] Stores and TV shows on national lines proliferated in late 1980s Moscow. The authors believed, however, that truly multiethnic spaces remained rare. Ones cited as important by our interview subjects, such as Red Square and VDNKh, were not considered. They called for a "friendship of peoples" park and lamented the dispersal of ethnic communities, aside from an Armenian pocket on Chernyshevsky Street and Georgians who lived on Georgia Street, where a deteriorating Georgian Orthodox church still stood. Tatars gathered at Moscow's mosque and with other Muslims in Izmailovsky Park for summertime religious ceremonies. In time, hopefully, the authors wrote, each union republic's titular nationality would have a dedicated cultural center and store, to show off the capital's international nature. In 1989, the USSR still appeared as a durable state, one that had survived far worse than perestroika.

Said Nabiev arrived in Moscow in 1989 with great expectations for a renewed Soviet Union. He joined a wave of political newcomers through Gorbachev's gambit to renew the state through multicandidate elections for what was designated as the USSR's new, supreme legislative assembly.[92] These elections for the Congress of People's Deputies, which included Nabiev as an Academy of Sciences representative from Tajikistan, sought to end "democratic centralism" and conservative Communist Party resistance to economic and political reforms. Nabiev's first memories of Moscow involved film, given he was a leader in the USSR's union of cinematographers. He watched with great pleasure the variety of Western and Soviet movies shown throughout the city and their handling of delicate, once taboo, social issues. He remembered in the 1970s being questioned by the KGB for approaching sensitive topics in his works, some of which were banned. He also recalled the freedom he experienced at the congress: "I was so equal that one day when I disagreed with the chair [of the Congress of People's Deputies], I kicked in his office door with my foot. Let him try to forbid me to do something! He would never forbid me directly, just tell me not to do something—to take a trip to Israel, for instance—and I would go just to get his goat."[93] The congress affirmed his belief in equal Soviet citizenship, which had triumphed over a repressive—albeit lightly repressive—state.

Intensifying hardship and violence on the USSR's southern peripheries nibbled at Leningrad and Moscow through the end of the 1980s. More than ever, the two capitals provided opportunity—associational and political life blossomed, higher education acted as a refuge, and traders charged ever-higher prices for goods, even as they had to face increased competition. Leningraders and Muscovites balanced inflation and the appearance of ostensibly exploitative southerners against increased freedoms of speech, media, and association and availability of goods from across the USSR and worldwide. Discrimination appeared dangerous in words and on paper, but hope remained that this might be a transitory phase until market reforms were established. Soviet interconnections provided help for citizens on the move; however, they also forecast that troubles on the periphery would arrive in the two capitals.

The Center Does Not Hold, 1990–1991

Dina Ataniyazova believed at the time that the Tbilisi violence reflected the "fraying of the Russian imperial idea, which had severe consequences both on the periphery and in the center."[94] Caucasus and Central Asian professionals, students, and traders saw 1990 as a major turning point, as perestroika's hopes evaporated amid economic crisis and national tensions. The economic halfway house was crumbling faster than it could be built, as Soviet citizens, to the extent they ever had it, lost faith that liberalization could stem joblessness and growing shortages of needed goods.[95] Open nationalism and racism replaced the friendship of peoples in Leningrad and Moscow. Caucasus and Central Asian citizens could no longer laud the safety and freedom of city streets. Even as municipal authorities devoted attention and resources to nationalities issues, increasing numbers of migrants began to debate whether to remain in cities that no longer appeared equally open to all Soviet citizens.

Another violent Soviet intervention, in Baku in January 1990, underlined Moscow's apparent impotence to control events in union republics, where nationalist leaders were demanding autonomy, if not outright independence. Unlike the Tbilisi violence, which occurred on local orders, this incident could be traced directly to Gorbachev, who commanded Soviet forces to the Azerbaijani capital, where anti-Armenian pogroms had resulted in several deaths. A nationalist political alliance, the Popular Front, had proved an effective challenger to the Communist Party. Over twenty-six thousand troops gathered to enforce a state of emergency. Soldiers opened fire on civilians in battles that raged over three days; anywhere from one hundred to three hundred were killed.[96]

The 20 January attack ended Fuad Ojagov's short Communist Party career. He had joined only a year earlier, overcoming political misgivings, hopeful that glasnost and open elections of the Congress of People's Deputies signaled a turn toward a freer union. Ojagov admitted that career advancement was his primary motive; he had just gained a position in the Faculty of Psychology and Law at Russia's Academy of Sciences, a prime Moscow post but an "ideological" unit, where party membership played an important role in promotions. Ojagov nonetheless could not countenance an attack ordered by the Soviet leader on his Baku hometown and determined to find ways to seek a post-Soviet order.[97]

The January violence in Baku marked the latest turn toward what quickly became a downward, union-wide spiral. Another wave of Armenian refugees headed northward, totaling 180,000; like Ojagov, Azerbaijanis also lost hope in their republic's future under a Soviet government.[98] Tajik economists had already openly condemned "the strict regulation of regional development from a single center, which infringes on local and regional interests, [and] suppresses initiative and enterprise from the population."[99] As perestroika's reforms failed to deliver improvements to the Soviet economy, Gorbachev ping-ponged between conservative and radical politicians and policies to ensure political survival as well as a sense of economic headway. Inflation mounted and then skyrocketed, to 10 percent in 1990 and 140 percent in 1991. A sense of crisis gripped the Soviet press and public as mass street demonstrations in Eastern Europe precipitated the loss of the Communist bloc and violence intensified in Nagorno-Karabakh. Nationalist movements attracted mass followings, especially in the Baltic republics. Associational life spilled over glasnost's bounds of "socialist pluralism" to those calling for the USSR's end, on the periphery and at the center.[100] Economic difficulties and national tensions drove increasing numbers of Soviet citizens to seek refuge in Leningrad and Moscow, sleeping in train stations, public buildings, or apartment corridors. Soviet homelessness became visible. The glasnost press openly discussed "*bomzhi*" (those without a determined place of residence), confirming what established residents saw in their cities.[101]

Some migrants expressed their frustration toward Gorbachev and leading politicians for losing their way after the initial promise of perestroika. The extremes of wealth and poverty, with Western cars and restaurants, on the one hand, and homelessness and old women selling their household goods on the street, on the other, startled established residents of Leningrad and Moscow, including minorities. Bakchiev's worries that Gorbachev wanted to make the USSR into a "foreign country," where human and republican bonds were ruptured, resonated. Kazbekov recalled: "Life became far worse during perestroika. All our wealth was stolen from us. Everything we had worked our whole lives for was gone. I lost all my savings [due to inflation]. We became nothing overnight. They robbed us blind [*Obokrali nas*]!"[102]

Aibek Botoev, somewhat isolated from economic difficulties by his privileged position as a leading civil engineer, nonetheless sensed trouble following the Tbilisi and Baku attacks, combined with perestroika's economic failures. "When the machine known as the Soviet state stopped working, when it stopped churning out the idea of internationalism, there were bound to be problems. And we began to see a crisis for Russians [*Russkie*]: a crisis of self-worth."[103] The myth of the "elder brother" had been shattered. Heading a superpower induced pride; but what was the value, for Russians, in leading a state in crisis, threatening to come apart at the seams? Why continue to give subsidies, as the glasnost press had them believe, to poor regions? Eastern Europe was already gone, and the state seemed less and less able to support its elder brothers, the first among equals.

Blame for perestroika's failures landed at the feet not only of the regime, according to Russian nationalists, but also of those who would exploit the nation. Timothy Colton noted that even as Russians themselves grew to loathe the bureaucracy around the propiska at the turn of the 1990s, fears persisted that its elimination would turn Leningrad or Moscow not into "a New York or London . . . but into a Russian Calcutta or Mexico City, with brushfire growth, shantytowns, and bruising competition between migrants and indigenes."[104] The idea of the Soviet Union becoming another country expanded, even if future images were vague. Nationalist groups began a movement of "going to the people" in 1989–1990 as "unmotivated Russian youth" sought a scapegoat for deepening unemployment and shortages.[105]

A burgeoning, albeit fragmented, nationalist press was unleashed by Gorbachev's June 1990 law on press freedom.[106] Periodicals appeared and disappeared at a time when general circulation was falling, given economic difficulties. Antigovernment forces sought readership through blatant racist and nationalist appeals, portraying Gorbachev's reforms as favoring ethnic minorities. As the prospect of the USSR's massive transformation, or end, loomed, an ethnically pure homeland became a priority. Jews played a central role in images of otherness and exploitation, underlining popular conceptions that they were the wealthiest ethnic group in Moscow and stood to gain the most from market reforms.[107] Pamiat and other organs presented Jews in league with reform-minded Soviet politicians. Together, they, using Kazbekov's words, were robbing the average (in this case Russian) citizen blind. A united front of Russians, Ukrainians, and Belarusians needed to coalesce to save the Slavic nation from Jewish-led disaster.[108] At the beginning of 1991, the nationalist newspaper *Russkie vedomosti* connected anti-Semitism to a possible post-Soviet future in an article titled "Russia for the Russians."[109] Its author echoed a common complaint that Russians were a people without a state—the RSFSR, alone among the union republics, did not have its own institutions. Russians were adrift in the Soviet Union. The author compared Russia's plight to Palestine; both were lands where Jews had been able to exploit a stateless people. Radical measures were required to reverse the Jewish domination that had consolidated with perestroika. Jews could be shipped as a people to peripheral areas of Ukraine, presumably re-creating the tsarist-era Pale of Settlement and allowing Russians, unfettered, to rule a post-Soviet state, a distinct possibility in 1991.[110]

"Southerners," as the nationalist press labeled them, joined and threatened to surpass Jews as a threat to the Russian nation at the turn of the 1990s. Publication of the 1989 census, combined with the increased numbers of traders on the streets of Leningrad, Moscow, and other Russian cities, set off alarm bells. Right-wing commentators seized on census figures showing Russians clinging to majority status in the USSR, at 50.8 percent, and losing ground demographically even in Russia.[111] Fertility and mortality rates ensured that majority status would soon be lost, if it had not been already.[112] Leningrad's *Russkoe delo* in early 1991 published the tract "Caucasus Syndrome" by the head of the Fatherland (Otechestvo) foundation, a nationalist, antigovernment association that included several Afghan war veterans, among them Alexander Rutskoi.[113] The author abhorred decade long efforts of Caucasus peoples to seek their fortune in St. Petersburg, as he referred to the city, often illegally.[114] In the last year, their control of central markets had grown ever more galling to city residents, now forced to rely on the private sector as the state distribution system collapsed. Criminal gangs from across the Caucasus had tightened their grip on market areas and expanded activity citywide. Well armed, their networks indiscriminately robbed and murdered host Russians.[115]

Southerners now became linked to a "genocide" (*genotsid*) of the Russian nation. By 1990, they had replaced Africans, in popular and press discourse, as the largest threat to bring AIDS to the two capitals. The disease had ignited panic across the Russian glasnost media, especially among conservative nationalists. AIDS symbolized the dangers of opening to the world. *Narodnoe delo*, another Leningrad newspaper, tied the AIDS threat in 1991 to its campaign against miscegenation, which it considered the Russian nation's main peril. Pure white people, it claimed, were immune to AIDS, which struck mulattos or dark-skinned peoples. Jews, as a unique hybrid of black and white, might or might not be immune depending on their specific blood components.[116]

Golos Rossii, the organ of the National Republican Party of Russia, saw an independent nation as a necessity to preserve the Russian people. It blamed the nation's ills on Russians themselves, as much as minorities. Self-determination would resolve economic problems, as Russia would no longer cover the budget deficits of poor Caucasus and Central Asian nations. It possessed sufficient raw as well as finished materials to supply its people and remain a global power. More fundamentally, however, independence could allow a nation to heal, to understand and right the causes of its failing health. Communism had "denationalized" Russians. Broken families had resulted in low fertility rates. Alcoholism and other factors rendered them vulnerable to exploitation by southerners and others. Census figures showed that Muslims would soon dominate the USSR.[117]

Nashe vremia complained of growing numbers of Tajiks across Russia. Their presence had expanded from urban markets, across cities, and to the Russian countryside. The author claimed that these people had no idea of how to live in a civilized manner. The USSR was becoming like the United States, where dark-skinned southerners freely, and in great numbers, moved to what once were white, northern spaces.[118] Independence—this author had subtitled his article "The Soviet Union's Undeclared War on Russia"—was not a cure-all, however. In its first postindependence issue, *Russkaia gazeta* noted that the new country's ethnic, social, and demographic problems remained acute, especially in Moscow.[119] Refugees from the Armenia-Azerbaijan war continued to flood the city, joined by new waves of migrants from China and Vietnam. Census figures showed that between 1979 and 1989 the number of Tajiks in Russia had grown 45 percent, Uzbeks 34 percent, and Kyrgyz and Azerbaijanis 24 percent, while the Russian population had increased only 5 percent. Politicians, even under a new nation, had limited power to alter societal patterns. The author exhorted every Russian to be a patriot and "defend the homeland," although how that would be done was unclear. *Golos Rossii* continued to warn of the Russian nation's downfall. An article titled "Russians and Turks" published shortly after the end of the USSR argued that as long as Russians committed demographic suicide, Turkish nationalities such as Tatars within the new Russian Federation would assume ever-growing roles. Little could stop them from inviting their "brethren" from the southern republics, and the new country from assuming a "Turkic-Muslim" ethos, effectively killing Russia.[120]

Nationalist and racist language in the Russian press reflected and drove street-level tension. Tamriko Otskheli, who left in 1989, recalled Muscovites considering her a "naughty Caucasian."[121] Prejudice remained then at the level of "not very good attitudes." She increasingly kept her family home, however, that year; the USSR's fraying, following the Tbilisi events, could have unpredictable consequences that might lead to street-level violence. Social tensions increased as shortages in basic goods appeared later in 1989. Moscow's city council debated a rationing plan to address mounting frustrations that Russians from neighboring regions were taking food away from the capital to feed their own smaller cities and villages.[122] The council began to purchase goods directly and stock stores in Moscow's densely populated neighborhoods, often through foodstuffs supplied at depots by Caucasus and Central Asian traders. As social disaffection mounted, municipal leaders introduced rationing for staples such as bread and sugar in May 1990.[123]

Living near Red Square, Eteri Gugushvili recalled the evolution of street markets from her window. In early 1990, elderly Russians, either Muscovites or from the countryside, sold household goods, watches, shoes, individual cigarettes— whatever they could to increase their incomes against inflation. They might then buy food from neighboring Caucasus or Central Asian merchants. Efforts to prevent food leaving Moscow prompted conflict with nearby cities and districts whose residents also relied on these markets. Gugushvili recalled a compromise reached in winter 1990–1991, whereby state stores would sell rationed goods on Sundays to those without a propiska. As a result, market activity virtually ceased on Sundays, replaced by massive queues at stores offering staples at far cheaper prices.[124] Gugushvili appreciated the "relief" of an off day from what she considered market chaos, where she could not walk a few steps from her flat without someone offering to sell her something.[125]

Market tensions struck fear into Terenti Papashvili in 1990–1991. Robberies, at his shop or even waiting in line at one of Moscow's ever-growing queues, had become commonplace. Abdul Khalimov recalled the heightened anxieties over the winter: "There was no bread or groceries to be had. Well, I guess that is when it started: interethnic tensions. There wasn't anything that happened to me directly, it was just a feeling. It wasn't like I was afraid to go out in public or anything like that, but I could feel it on the streets. People were cold and hungry."[126] Eljan Jusubov expressed "great appreciation" for his ability to work in Moscow at that time, as food from southern Azerbaijan fetched extremely high prices, more than enough to keep pace with inflation. At the same time: "After work, we were very tired. We came home and ate—we did not go anywhere, because it was dangerous. We cooked for ourselves, watched television, and went to bed. At 7:00 a.m. we had to be at the workplace. We did not go to cafés and restaurants, because it was expensive and dangerous. . . . It was dangerous to leave the house in the evenings. Attacks could happen anywhere, and did to my friends."[127]

Attacks also occurred against Africans: four Nigerian students were severely beaten in 1990.[128] Ataniyazova did not worry about food, as universities remained well supplied. But the economic tensions "sparked all kinds of smoldering ethnic conflicts. People blamed each other for their troubles, and this was expressed in skirmishes in the markets, in stores, on the metro."[129] Bakchiev recalled with irony that, after his whole life envying or enjoying the capital's riches, he would be better-off back in rural Tajikistan, where he could, he thought at the time, be safe, grow food, and raise livestock. He wistfully replayed the moment when the Soviet Union, for him, no longer existed.[130]

Azamat Sanatbaev recalled less the street-level tension in Moscow than a marked change in attitude from his Russian friends, whom he always considered tolerant. They began to ask, of Caucasus and Central Asian traders as well as Russians from outside Moscow: "Why are they coming here? They should stay home and make opportunities for themselves there."[131] Moscow's city council's moves to restrict rights of non-propiska holders, as well as the vitriol of the Russian nationalist press, offered easy arguments for how to start to cure the city's ills, even if fundamental social and economic problems ran much deeper. Sanatbaev, for his part, in a patronizing tone, argued that the USSR could have held out longer if Russians had learned Caucasus and Central Asian traders' work ethic.

Tension grew in a parallel fashion in Leningrad / St. Petersburg. Kemal Jafarov recalled heightened conflicts validated his decision not to undertake street trade, but instead to sell wholesale at one of the city's large depots. "We lived close to where we worked. I did not trade in the bazaars. If one of our own [Azerbaijanis] hung or laid out even one spoiled tomato, a potential buyer could incite a disturbance."[132] Russians, he claimed, believed that Nagorno-Karabakh's "mountain refugees," playing on sympathies from the host population and established traders, had vaulted themselves to a standard of living higher than the rest of the city's population, which suffered from shortages and inflation.[133] In St. Petersburg, in contrast to portrayals in Moscow, Jafarov recalled tolerance between Armenian and Azerbaijani traders. Fear of robberies, assaults, or police held them and others together in mutual assistance. Azerbaijanis and Armenians were bound by the now common pejorative of *LKN*.

Stay or Go?

As tensions increased across the USSR, students and shuttle traders, professionals and service workers alike entered complicated decision-making processes about where best to weather what would become the last two years of perestroika: in the two capitals or in their southern home republics. Work opportunities beyond market trade were rapidly contracting in Leningrad and Moscow. Moscow's municipal soviet nonetheless floated the idea of selling propiski to raise desperately needed funds for social assistance.[134] The growing dangers of ethnic violence meant that neither the center nor the periphery was assuredly safe. Which networks and support systems, in this climate, could best uphold personal and family livelihoods? As the USSR appeared on its last legs, in particular following the failed August 1991 putsch, what would become of St. Petersburg and Moscow?

Eteri Gugushvili sought refuge in study, continuing in Moscow for a graduate degree in archival science in 1991. Like Dina Ataniyazova, she recalled university, with its always stocked canteens, as a sanctuary from the shortages and inflation sweeping the city and country. Gugushvili encountered a virtual revolution at Moscow State University, as mandatory courses on the history of the Communist Party disappeared, and Marx and Lenin were barely mentioned. Professors no longer assigned textbooks, claiming that no truths could be found in existing literature. She and her colleagues prepared for classes by reading newspapers and journals, the main source material for new oral examinations, which had replaced written tests. The experience was disorienting, but she still envisioned a positive future within a reformed Soviet Union. Sanatbaev echoed a far more common sentiment—with the benefit of hindsight, however. By 1991, given the economic failures and unrest across the Soviet Union, people were "exhausted" (*nadoelo*) with democracy, dooming Gorbachev's reforms.[135] What remained now was steering oneself and one's family through an unpredictable present and an unknowable future.

Returns home failed to provide comfort to migrants from republics that were themselves engulfed in conflict. Abdul Khalimov recalled the impact of February 1990 rioting in Dushanbe, as related to him by relatives during a trip home that spring. Soviet troops had killed unarmed protesters, and Tajik nationalist forces threatened the Communist Party's hold on power. All-union, republican, regional, and network loyalties eroded. "In Tajikistan," he recalled, "politicians pitted the people against the Russians, and in Russia, the politicians pitted the people against everyone but the Russians."[136] He remained in Moscow, but followed with great sadness Vladimir Zhirinovsky's campaign in open elections for the new post of president of the RSFSR in June 1991. Running on a nationalist and racist platform, Zhirinovsky received over six million votes. Later in the year, his rhetoric grew even more extreme, tracking the right-wing press. His pronouncements included: "I have a solution for all these Asians: pack them off to their native lands. . . . Russia is for us, Russians. After that, we'll build a second Great Wall, like the Chinese did—they were clever boys, you know. Let the Muslims bring their goods to the gaps in this wall. From then on, our own merchants will carry them into our lands. In this way we will prevent their demographic explosion from undermining Russia."[137]

Maia Asinadze considered a return to Georgia during the economic and political chaos of 1991. After a 31 March referendum, Georgia declared independence from the Soviet Union on 9 April, to commemorate the second anniversary of the Tbilisi violence. Discussions among her friends who had formed her Moscow work collective grew strained when the future of the USSR was debated. Torn between her adopted home and her family now in another country, Asinadze only decided to stay when her ex-colleagues told her: "Well, let them break away from us. Let them leave us. But you will stay with us."[138] Jumaboi Esoev found his own desire to return home to Tajikistan foreclosed. His late perestroika story began with fondness: he had succeeded in marrying the girl of his dreams in 1990 Leningrad. He had admired her from afar, but only gained the courage to start a conversation after accidentally hitting her on the head with a volleyball during a university game. As life worsened month by month, they planned to leave for his home republic. How his Russian wife might be received, however, gave them pause. They stuck out life until shortages and inflation became unbearable in 1992, but by then "the civil war had already begun in Tajikistan." "It was horrible. People were starving to death from blockades. People were eating animal feed just to stay alive. Back home was complete chaos, so I decided to stay in Leningrad."[139]

Some migrants remained in the two capitals after the USSR's end to assist co-ethnics, using associational freedoms to carve new places for themselves. Akmal Bobokulov, who had lived in Leningrad / St. Petersburg since 1972, contemplated his future as Islam Karimov declared Uzbekistan's independence from the USSR on 31 August 1991. He decided that St. Petersburg was home and threw himself into helping fellow Uzbeks, who would now be foreigners in the city. An Uzbek "friendship society," formed in 1990, provided a vehicle—Bobokulov recalled how he and others, inspired by glasnost, initiated circles to read "national" literature and planned cultural performances.[140] He turned himself into an amateur lawyer, trying to understand the words and effects of new legislation, especially after the USSR ended. Bobokulov and his colleagues registered the organization with St. Petersburg's authorities in a new Russian state, and he continued to work there through the 2000s. Aryan Shirinov's associational ethos also shifted. In 1991, he formed an association of Eastern martial arts in Leningrad. His gym quickly became a gathering place for Tajik friends. "We used to meet, but unofficially of course. . . . We supported each other. We spoke in our mother tongue together."[141] Discussion increasingly turned to the economic challenges and violence faced by fellow Tajiks, established and new. As Tajikistan split from the USSR and became engulfed in conflict, he opened his own diaspora organization to assist coethnics in a new "gray zone": in possession of Soviet Union passports but with an unclear status in the new Russian Federation.

Moscow's city council sought to manage nationality issues, before being engulfed by 1991's political and economic chaos. It registered ethnically based organizations like Bobokulov's and noted growing tension on city streets. Continued waves of refugees from conflict zones in the Caucasus and Central Asia, requiring significant assistance, joined the tens of thousands of traders and others who left an economically depressed periphery. Newspapers were reporting—without evidence—that refugee waves had swelled Moscow's Azerbaijani and Armenian populations to over one million each, in what seemed an effort to stoke racial tension.[142] A board to study the national question formed in 1990 became the Moscow International Commission (Moskovskoe mezhnatsional'noe soveshchanie), with seventy members who claimed to represent thirty-eight ethnic groups.[143] Beyond promising help to those fleeing active wars, however, the commission remained an organization more on paper than an active feature of Moscow's multiethnic life at the end of the USSR.

Shifting feelings toward ethnic minorities in St. Petersburg and Moscow over the late perestroika period and the first years of an independent Russian Federation received confirmation in post-Soviet survey data. Moscow State University's Center for the Study of Social Opinion interviewed 447 Moscow residents of over one dozen nationalities to understand their identities and relationships in 1992, in the hope of considering the future of "Moscow's multinational world." The survey's authors stated that this self-selected group could not be considered representative—indeed, most appeared to be highly educated—and warned of the challenges of assigning "national" identification to those who self-identified as "Muslim," "Caucasian," "native [*vykhodtsy*] from Central Asia," or even "non-Russian." The survey highlighted a strong degree of integration of established minorities through mixed marriages, overwhelmingly with host Russians: 90 percent for Georgians, 60 percent for Uzbeks, and 50 percent for Azerbaijanis.[144] Only 5 percent of those in these marriages claimed their children as "mixed" ethnicity, however, hewing to the Soviet practice of assigning them one identity. Most (presumably male) respondents assigned their own ethnicity, though others said that they were waiting until their children turned sixteen, when they would make a final determination, based on phenotype, language, and the practical advantages of declaring a "passport" nationality. Caucasus and Central Asian nationalities remained far more likely than western ones to recall being reared in the "spirit of national traditions": Georgians responded most positively, at 88 percent, followed by Uzbeks and Azerbaijanis at 80 percent. These minorities' privileged status (60 percent had a postsecondary education) is reflected in their most frequently naming Russians (28 percent) as the poorest nationality in Moscow, while Jews (17 percent) appeared as the wealthiest. Such stereotypes indicate the success of nationalist groups in inciting a sense of crisis for the Russian people, dominated by other ethnic groups, Jews in particular.[145] Questions on national relations produced a mixed picture: 74 percent of respondents reported that no national group caused them problems, leaving a quarter who agreed. Tatars, not Russians, expressed the greatest negative feelings, in their case toward "Caucasians." As discussed above, this frustration could well spring from the consequences of ethnic (mis)identification, with Tatars increasingly grouped as "*LKN*" or "black." Overall happiness with life in Moscow, during the chaos of perestroika, was below 50 percent for all groups, including Russians. Thirty percent of Russians, more than double any other nationality, stated that they would prefer a monoethnic work environment.[146]

A subsequent, unscientific fall 1992 survey in the populist newspaper *Moskovskii komsomolets* showed a much greater willingness to express hostility toward "southerners." The article, "The Chechen Problem as Seen by Muscovites," ranked interviewed Russians' views toward national groups. Here, only 8 percent of respondents claimed negative attitudes toward Jews, paling in comparison to those from the Caucasus and Central Asia: 33 percent expressed negative feelings toward Georgians; 34 percent toward Armenians; 40 percent toward Chechens; with Azerbaijanis, at 46 percent, emerging as the most "problematic" nationality. Assigning significance to this unscientific data is difficult, but interviews and reading of the right-wing press at the end of perestroika display hardening attitudes against Central Asians and Caucasus peoples, built over a decade as traders' presence increased and sharpened by the economic and political uncertainty. Dangers in St. Petersburg and Moscow, straddling the line between everyday discrimination and violence, still paled for many in comparison to the open warfare in certain home countries or the uncertainty of living in a periphery now untethered from its core.

Given the chaos of 1990–1991, was the USSR's collapse inevitable, or desirable? Past and present filtered through a variety of migrant responses. Eteri Gugushvili, sheltered in higher education, recalled: "Even in the last couple of years no one could imagine that the Soviet Union would collapse. It was very difficult for us to predict this. No one felt that 'look, here are Moldavians, or Azerbaijani people, or Georgians.' There were no differences or such kinds of relations. We were all citizens of the Soviet Union."[147] Her links with Moscow remained strong after 1991 as she improved her educational qualifications to advance in the National Library of Georgia. She insisted that the USSR allowed all its citizens to hold national, transnational, and all-union identities—that every nation was "ours," even as minutes earlier she recalled the depth of Muscovite anger at being "robbed by Asians" in the last months of the Soviet Union. Terenti Papashvili, having retired as Gugushvili did in the Georgian city of Kutaisi, lived the perestroika years in Moscow as a *limitchik* in a construction company. He appreciated his better salary in Moscow but not the fact that he had to go there to get it. As Georgia struggled, the 1989 violence only confirmed that Russia was "a governor, not a neighbor."[148] Once the USSR showed its stripes as an empire, it was bound to fail.

Erkin Bakchiev, whose narrative began this chapter, remained loyal to the idea of the USSR. Kyrgyzstan retained perhaps the friendliest relations with Russia of all Central Asian republics, and Kyrgyz and Tajiks, the most dependent on twenty-first-century Russian assistance, repeated many of the tropes of the USSR's collapse that predominate among (now) older Russians. For Bakchiev, "Gorbachev made a mistake. Over his rule people began to think only about themselves. If Gorbachev had ruled more strictly, then people would have been equal. It became much more difficult for people to live. Nothing remained in the stores. I saw with my own eyes how the stores did not have sausages or other products. There was nothing left. Putin corrected the country."[149] The idea of a strong leader who could allow a broad field for mobility but at the same time police inequality resonated with several Central Asian migrants. Efforts to model strong, durable, wise leadership emerged with Nursultan Nazarbaev in Kazakhstan and Islam Karimov in Uzbekistan, among others regionally, but the worlds they governed were much smaller and post-Soviet dreams proved harder to envision, much less realize. The USSR shone as a world where movement, accessible to all in their own fashion, rather than money, could produce a better life for citizens and their children.

Perestroika's challenges and crises emerged from economic imbalances and practices that preceded Gorbachev and were most visible in the USSR's southern republics. Unofficial networks, mobility, and remittances had forestalled a reckoning for policies that were at once imperial in style and saw fit to leave an ever-growing service sector in gray, informal spaces. Migrant dynamism broadened and strengthened as Soviet leaders grappled to reform a system already with a robust market economy, albeit an unofficial one; with strong ethnic identities, only partially harnessed by the friendship of peoples; and with an economy that disfavored peripheral regions and, by the end of perestroika, vastly broadened gaps between rich and poor in the two capitals and union-wide. Archie Brown has argued that perestroika "was not so much a case of crisis producing reform as of reform precipitating crisis."[150] Perhaps—we do not see an imminent crisis in the early 1980s, but neither do we see the effects, as well as the policies, of perestroika spring from nowhere. Its path was indeterminate even to mid-1991, but perestroika reflected ultimately failed efforts to manage and handle a Soviet Union whose vigor existed largely underneath socialism's hood from Brezhnev to Gorbachev. Intensified linkages between center and periphery in the USSR's last years could not save the country, instead showing its frayed edges. Economic crises provided the fodder for conflicts that quickly gained a national character and spun out of the control of the regime, when Brezhnev-era dynamism that hummed through below-the-surface networks transformed into desires for a wholesale takeover of political institutions of a weak state.

RED OR BLACK?

The late Soviet Union was a society on the move. Millions of citizens from across the USSR flooded Leningrad's and Moscow's train and bus stations and airports, then proceeded to markets or stores, tourist attractions or cultural performances, technical schools or universities, worksites or offices, dormitories or apartments. This mobility, ironically, produced the images of immobility that came to be associated with ostensible stagnation (*zastoi*) under Brezhnev. Soviet citizens waited in seemingly endless queues for Leningrad's and Moscow's consumer goods, tickets to popular performances, even simply to catch a glimpse of the country's first leader. Education and urbanization had broadened the horizons of so many young Soviet citizens, who understood the privileges of their modern state were best realized in large cities, culminating at the two capitals. Even a short stay in Leningrad or Moscow, to gain knowledge, to make money, to join networks, could alter individual and family life plans.

Soviet migrants' stories, in their own voices, illustrate the choices they had, and the decisions they made, to fashion their lives in the last decades of the Soviet Union. Opportunities for mobility operated within a framework of deepening divergences between the Caucasus, Central Asian, and Asian Russian peripheries and European Russia's urban core. Ethnic stereotypes and racist behavior toward the Soviet Union's "blacks" counterbalanced equal citizenship and the friendship of peoples. Ambition, determination, and work emerged as central attributes as migrants considered their journeys to, and time in, Leningrad and Moscow. They created or joined networks that epitomized late Soviet dynamism. Individual, family, village, or ethnic connections inspired capillary systems that linked center and margins, formal and informal economies. Networks underlay the prosperity and happiness essential to late Soviet dreams in the two capitals, in faraway villages, and across the late socialist state.

Movement proved a crucial ingredient in fulfilling state and societal aspirations for progress. The Soviet government set a field of play that stimulated unofficial as well as official sojourns, short- and long-term, to its privileged urban spaces. Personal will, alongside family and network support, drove this pattern of postwar mobility. Late Soviet scholars acknowledged that the energy of everyday Soviet citizens was vital in ensuring youthful and dynamic cities and advancing the USSR's modernization. Those who arrived from distant towns or republics envisioned the two capitals as "spaces of possibility," limited not to native Leningraders and Muscovites, or ethnic Russians, but open to all who could contribute to the prosperity and development of the Soviet Union.[1] Migrants might do this by offering residents fresh fruits and vegetables; learning workplace skills in training programs; providing pharmaceutical advice that blended practices from home republics; completing a university program to open career paths, at the center or in home republics; or heading aeronautical or other institutes. Individuals fused personal and collective stories of success, emulating the discourse of their Soviet upbringing. This fusion provides a fascinating window on the Soviet experience then and how it is remembered now as post-Soviet states abandoned socialism for a range of policies and practices that substantially altered the relationship between individual, collective, and state.

Long-distance migrants represented a unique slice of Soviet society, but their words and experiences revealed pathways open to all citizens in the USSR's last decades. Dynamism and opportunity percolated under the hood of a regime characterized as sclerotic and then, at the turn of the 1990s, almost anarchic. Education, training, infrastructure, and ambition powered the postwar Soviet Union. Spatial and social mobility worked in parallel. To acknowledge this is not to overlook systemic flaws in the regime that would precipitate its dissolution. Its ambivalences in policies and practices toward movement proved indicative of a state challenged to govern a modern society through a conservative bureaucracy. Investment and distribution plans neglected a growing service sector and produced ineffectual solutions to changing demographic patterns. Informal networks, some of which penetrated the state, undertook ever-larger roles in a modern, dynamic economy. Andropov's and Gorbachev's efforts to streamline administration and bring the economy under greater control failed to overcome the power of unofficial connections. Inequalities between center and periphery, underpinning so many migrant narratives, produced a union that crumbled from the outside in. Related, and increasing, national identification and racial discrimination had a fatal effect on the USSR at the turn of the 1990s. Migrants' time in, and memories of, Leningrad and Moscow also shows their place as "canaries in a coal mine" for Russian xenophobia. Far larger post-Soviet migrant waves from the Caucasus and Central Asia crossed now international borders in efforts to overcome continued, and in many ways deepened, south-north inequalities. Several Soviet-era migrants saw in the growing racism on the streets of 1980s–1990s Leningrad and Moscow a harbinger for the deadly violence that erupted in the first decade of the 2000s.

Closeness and distance, familiarity and strangeness operated as critical dualities in the thoughts of Soviet migrants from Central Asia, the Caucasus, and Asian Russia, as they did with those who left once imperial margins worldwide. Weakened connections between distant centers and seemingly isolated peripheries animated thoughts and discussions of movement. Stuart Hall recalled how the imminent British decolonization of Jamaica prompted his decision to get on the "banana boat and set sail for the hub of the world."[2] Soviet citizens, as did British subjects in the second half of the twentieth century—the so-called Windrush generation—exploited their abilities to move to and, with some effort, reside at the centers of their parts of the world.[3] These newcomers claimed their right to work, study, and live in the cities where the benefits of integrated imperial and postimperial economies, which included their regions, were realized. Ambivalence marked reactions to their presence. States that saw the appearance of subjects or citizens of different ethnicities under their control as markers of regional or global power also maintained their major cities as European-dominated. Migrants brought needed goods, labor, and creativity to aging urban spaces but, especially in the Soviet case, remained isolated from corridors of local or societal power.[4] White European residents might appreciate these newcomers' contributions, and even enjoy friendships and personal relations with them, but also might demean or discriminate on the basis of appearance, behavior, or language. Among European postcolonial states, the Soviet Union's distinct models of residential integration, national relationships, and citizenship helped Central Asian, Caucasus, and Asian Russia's residents consider themselves insiders in large Russian cities, even as, in poignant memories, they grappled with thoughts of home and away.

Ideas of home implicated and intertwined place, time, and feelings. Questions on the topic burrowed to the roots of migrant identities as Soviet citizens and members of a post-Soviet world. Vazha Gigulashvili, interviewed in Kutaisi, Georgia, in 2011, evoked poignant mixtures of past and present in considering home and away. She retained overwhelmingly positive memories of her degree program at Moscow State University in the perestroika years. Gigulashvili remained in the city in a lucrative position as a professional before returning home in the 2000s. To her:

I never felt that Moscow was my home, I always thought of Georgia as my home country and Kutaisi as my home. I always knew that I would go back to Georgia and Moscow was just a temporary living place for me and my family. When I think of those years that I lived in Moscow, I was very happy. All the good things in my life happened at that time. My two kids, one girl and one boy, were born there. We got a new flat, bought a new car, so everything good and important in my life is connected to that time. How can I not like it?[5]

Personal success and family life were not quite enough for Gigulashvili to abandon her conception of Georgia as home, across the Soviet/post-Soviet divide. Whereas Gigulashvili privileged home as a place, Irma Balanchivadze evoked home in time:

I felt at home in the Soviet Union because there were many jobs and almost everybody was working. Now it is very hard to live and there are no more jobs. Our government in Georgia is trying to make the country look prettier, but they do not create any job possibilities for young people. My son died after the breakup of the Soviet Union. Before that he always had a job. But then it was hard for him to get a job; he was married and had a child, so he needed money and was very nervous about it. He died of a heart attack; if he had had a job, he would not have died. Also, when I look at these young boys, they do not have anything to do and spend most of their time outside.[6]

Anarbek Zakirov, as he pondered ideas of home after spending different stages of his life in Frunze/Bishkek and Moscow, believed that the USSR's success in implanting nationality as a core identifying and organizing principle complicated migrant efforts to consider themselves at home outside of their "own" republics.[7] The Soviet Union, however, could be a home—in terms of mentality, space, and, after 1991, time.

Ideas of a discrete Soviet time, marked by everyday behavior, beliefs, and opportunities as much as by the existence of a state, framed the views of Central Asian, Caucasus, and Asian Russian migrants then toward those in St. Petersburg, Moscow, and other Russian cities now. Even as he considered Georgia his home, and expressed pride in an independent Georgian state, David Somkishvili echoed the thoughts of many migrants who felt more at home in an ostensibly more compassionate and ordered time:

I always knew and remembered where I was from. Maybe it is because I felt good [in Soviet Moscow] and I did not feel any threat to my identity. I had more friends among Russians, Ukrainians, and Armenians

than Georgians there. . . . Even when I lived in Moscow [where he returned and purchased a flat in the mid-1990s], I still could not think of
Russia as my home. But I would add that I do not like how Georgians
live now in Russia. They come and do not know how to behave, do not
like to obey any rules. They often shout at night when everybody is sleeping. They try to use others, and Georgians as well, to have some benefit
out of particular relationships. I have experienced this myself a couple
of times. So now I just try to be friends more with Armenians and Russians, or Azerbaijanis and Belarusians, than Georgians.[8]

Fuad Ojagov criticized Azerbaijanis in 2000s St. Petersburg and Moscow in similar terms—their unkempt appearance, crude behavior, and lack of Russian language enabled xenophobia. I was surprised that our informants used questions
about contemporary Russian racism more often to draw a line between their
Soviet migrant generation and a later one—particularly, of their own national
group—than to express sympathy for victims of almost commonplace employer
abuse, official harassment, and extortion, as well as brutal attacks and murders.[9]
Farshad Hajiev, who remained in Leningrad/St. Petersburg and formed a diaspora organization, offered the strongest defense of his coethnics:

These guest workers [*gastarbaitery*] who come from Tajikistan now, they
work seventeen hours a day. They come here and they have one mission:
to work, to make money for their families back home. They work day
and night for years, and although they are paid almost nothing, they work
so much that they make something of themselves. And say, after several
years, they have saved enough money to open a store here in St. Petersburg. Well, all it takes is for one of these [racists] to come by and set this
store on fire and all those years of hard work amount to nothing. It all
goes up in flames. Do they think about how much work these people have
done to achieve this, to open a store here? I can't imagine that happening to a Russian, to work that hard and see it all destroyed. It happened
not to just Tajiks, but to Azerbaijanis, and Georgians, and Armenians.
To see what has happened to our society, it is just sad. Many of the
academics I worked with at the university just couldn't stand what was
happening to us, and they left, they emigrated.[10]

St. Petersburg, Moscow, and the Russian Federation now deal with the same tensions as the Soviet Union, balancing the needed energy and labor of new migrant
waves sparked by core-periphery inequality with efforts to manage, now, international movement and relations with the host society. As in the USSR, migrant

determination is propelling efforts to claim a right to Russian cities, forcing state reactions in now multiethnic St. Petersburg and Moscow.[11]

Hajiev framed the positive narrative of his post-Soviet coethnics around hard work, much as many Soviet-era citizens did when characterizing their own migration stories. In the USSR, hard work, these migrants maintained, almost always equated to success. I would argue that the prevalent discourse of Soviet freedom among these migrants derives from the combination of easy travel (albeit within state borders), personal safety, and the belief in a meritocracy. Skill, savvy, and determination allowed migrants to realize personal family and family goals, which appeared unattainable in the post-Soviet period, when the lines between rich and poor, have and have-not, white and black appeared unbridgeable. The Soviet dream that grew more challenging to access through the 1980s and evaporated in 1990 retained a hold on these migrants as they relived their youth and revisited their life chances and plans.

ORAL HISTORIES: PLACES, PEOPLE, RELATIONSHIPS

Oral histories define this study. I encountered the migrants who would become such central actors in my research on my first trip to Russia in 1992—I just missed visiting the Soviet Union. Instead of being surrounded by the dour bureaucrats and stern babushkas, crafty hockey players and talented ballerinas—ethnic Russians, all—who occupied my imagination growing up in Cold War Canada, I found St. Petersburg and Moscow replete with Central Asian and Caucasus peoples of all ages, as well as Africans, East Asians, and others. They were selling, shopping, talking, and strolling, making the city their own. I originally considered studying Leningrad / St. Petersburg and Moscow as postcolonial, multiethnic cities, motivated by finding comparisons to my Trinidadian father's stories of 1950s London. How much difference, I wondered, would the Soviet context make to late twentieth-century cities that hosted their former empires, and the world? In published sources, I sought largely in vain for accounts of the multiethnic everyday in Leningrad and Moscow, the colors and flavors of human struggles, accomplishments (beyond state-sponsored awards), and relationships (outside of formulaic declarations of the friendship of peoples). To find out how peoples from Asian regions of the USSR, my long-standing research interest, experienced the two capitals, I would have to talk to them.

I had always been intrigued by the possibilities of exposing new historical actors through oral histories. I had often wondered what I would ask the nineteenth-century residents of Tashkent, the subject of my first book, if I had a chance.[1] With oral histories, I could locate subjects of all backgrounds and professions; control lines of inquiry; follow up on initial responses to gain layers of detail

TABLE 1   Interview subjects

MIGRANT NAME (PSEUDONYM)	INTERVIEW DATE	MIGRANT ORIGIN	MIGRANT DESTINATION	MIGRATION DATES	MIGRANT OCCUPATION
Abdullaev, Erkin	26 Jun 2009	Lenkoran, Azerbaijan	Moscow	1982–1989	Trader
Agaev, Shadulla	16 Jun 2009	Baku, Azerbaijan	Moscow	1982–1984	Trader
Aitmatova, Aijamal	20 Jul 2009	Tash-Komur, Kyrgyzstan	Moscow	1986–1989	Trader
Akhmedov, Shuhrat	27 May 2007	Ferghana, Uzbekistan	Leningrad, Moscow	1979–1985	Student
Albiev, Asylbek	8 Jul 2009	Andijon, Uzbekistan	Moscow	1976	Soldier
Alieva, Gulnara	5 May 2007	Frunze, Kyrgyzstan	Moscow	1977–1987	Student
Asadov, Elnur	5 Jun 2009	Baku, Azerbaijan	Moscow	1982–1984	Trader
Asgarov, Rasul	12 Jun 2009	Baku, Azerbaijan	Moscow	1982–1983	Trader
Asgarova, Sevda	14 Jul 2009	Baku, Azerbaijan	Moscow	1951–1954	Student, party worker
Asinadze, Maia	29 Nov 2007	Mtskheta, Georgia	Moscow	1982–	Student, pharmacist
Ataniyazova, Dina	6 Dec 2008	North Caucasus	Moscow	1970–	Student, professor
Baisalbekova, Aisulu	26 Aug 2009	Toktogul, Kyrgyzstan	Leningrad, Moscow	1972–1988	Trader
Bakchiev, Erkin	9 Aug 2009	Kara-Suu, Kyrgyzstan	Leningrad, Moscow	1987–	Trader
Balanchivadze, Irma	23 Jul 2011	Kutaisi, Georgia	Moscow	1973, 1980–	Food depot, market
Bayramov, Ashraf	25 Jun 2009	Lenkoran, Azerbaijan	Leningrad	1987–	Cook
Begirov, Hazi	25 Jun 2009	Lenkoran, Azerbaijan	Leningrad, Moscow	1981–	Trader
Bobokulov, Akmal	13 Nov 2007	Andijon, Uzbekistan	Leningrad	1972–	Naval officer
Botoev, Aibek	8 Dec 2007	Sokuluk, Kyrgyzstan	Leningrad Moscow	1973–1975 1978–	Student Engineer
Eldarov, Sadig	15 Jul 2009	Baku, Azerbaijan	Moscow	1976–	Student, psychiatry
Esoev, Jumaboi	17 Nov 2007	Khorog, Tajikistan	Leningrad	1983–	Factory worker, student
Gazyumov, Emin	19 Mar 2009	Baku, Azerbaijan	Moscow	1983–1987	Student
Gigulashvili, Vazha	23 Jul 2011	Kutaisi, Georgia	Moscow	1974–	Factory worker, trader

(continued)

TABLE 1 (continued)

MIGRANT NAME (PSEUDONYM)	INTERVIEW DATE	MIGRANT ORIGIN	MIGRANT DESTINATION	MIGRATION DATES	MIGRANT OCCUPATION
Gugushvili, Eteri	26 Jul 2011	Tbilisi, Georgia	Moscow	1987–1991	Student
Hajiev, Farshad	11 Nov 2007	Pamir Mountains, Tajikistan	Leningrad	1980–	Student, conscript, nuclear engineer
Haydarov, Jasur	23 Jul 2009	Osh, Kyrgyzstan	Moscow	1981–1984	Trader
Husynov, Azay	28 Jun 2009	Baku, Azerbaijan	Leningrad	1982–1987	Trader
Iashvili, Zurab	23 Jan 2007	Tbilisi, Georgia	Moscow	1972–1977	Student
Ikramov, Shuhrat	18 Sep 2007	Tashkent, Uzbekistan	Moscow	1985–1989	Student
Imamaliev, Murad	8 Feb 2007	Baku, Azerbaijan	Moscow	1971–1976	Student
Iskakova, Saule	10 Jul 2007	Frunze, Kyrgyzstan	Moscow	1973–1976	Student
Jafarov, Kemal	25 Jun 2009	Lenkoran, Azerbaijan	Leningrad	1988–	Trader
Jusubov, Eljan	5 Jun 2009	Baku, Azerbaijan	Moscow	1988–	Trader
Kalilova, Meerim	17 Jul 2009	Tash-Komur, Kyrgyzstan	Moscow	1983–	Trader
Kazbekov, Shuhrat	13 Nov 2007	Tashkent, Uzbekistan	Leningrad	1983–	Figure skater, stuntman
Khalimov, Abdul	30 Nov 2007	Kishlaki, Tajikistan	Moscow	1984–	Medical student, doctor
Khamagova, Aryuna	12 Feb 2007	Ulan-Ude, Russia	Leningrad	1972–1982	Food depot worker, Student
Koberidze, Alex	2 Apr 2009	Osh, Kyrgyzstan	Leningrad	1980–1990	Plumber
Kochladze, Dea	26 Nov 2007	Poti, Georgia	Moscow	1975–	Student, neurologist
Kudubaev, Tolkunbek	15 Nov 2008	Osh, Kyrgyzstan	Moscow	1987–1989	Construction
Kvernadze, Nino	23 Jul 2011	Kutaisi, Georgia	Moscow	1978–1987	Homemaker
Mammadov, Togrul	6 Jun 2009	Hajigabul Raion, Azerbaijan	Moscow	1980–	Trader
Musabekov, Mirlan	10 Aug 2009	Osh, Kyrgyzstan	Moscow	1986–	Trader
Nabiev, Said	28 Nov 2007	Khorog, Tajikistan	Moscow	1960–1965, 1989–	Cinematographer student

(continued)

TABLE 1 (continued)

MIGRANT NAME (PSEUDONYM)	INTERVIEW DATE	MIGRANT ORIGIN	MIGRANT DESTINATION	MIGRATION DATES	MIGRANT OCCUPATION
Nasirova, Elmira	11 Jul 2007	Frunze, Kyrgyzstan	Leningrad	1963–1965, 1979–1980	Student
Nizomov, Bakyt	27 May 2007	Tashkent, Uzbekistan	Leningrad, Moscow	1979–1985	Student
Nogoibaeva, Damira	6 Aug 2008	Frunze, Kyrgyzstan	Moscow	1977–1987	Student, professor
Nosirova, Oidin	28 May 2007	Tashkent, Uzbekistan	Moscow	1979–1981	Student
Nuriaeva, Jyldyz	9 Jul 2007	Frunze, Kyrgyzstan	Moscow	1978–1984	Student
Nurtaeva, Aliya	25 Oct 2006	Alma-Ata, Kazakhstan	Moscow	1969–1978	Student
Ojagov, Fuad	25 Jun 2009	Baku, Azerbaijan	Moscow	1974–	Student, psychologist
Ormonbekov, Azamat	16 Jul 2007	Frunze, Kyrgyzstan	Moscow	1982–1983	Student
Oruzbaev, Bolot	8 Jul 2009	Kara-Suu, Kyrgyzstan	Moscow	1984–	Student, engineer
Otskheli, Tamriko	27 Jul 2011	Tbilisi, Georgia	Moscow	1980–1989	Shopkeeper
Papashvili, Terenti	25 Jul 2011	Kutaisi, Georgia	Leningrad	1985–1990	Construction worker
Rukhadze, Levan	25 Nov 2007	Yerevan, Armenia	Leningrad	1969–	Engineer
Sanatbaev, Azamat	14 Jul 2009	Mady, Kyrgyzstan	Moscow	1976–	Student, tour guide
Satilganov, Aizada	12 Jul 2007	Bishkek, Kyrgyz Republic	Moscow	1982–1988	Student
Satilganov, Nurlanbek	12 Jul 2007	Bishkek, Kyrgyz Republic	Moscow	1982–1988	Student
Serkebaev, Mirbek	3 Aug 2009	Osh, Kyrgyzstan	Leningrad, Moscow	1983–	Trader
Shakiev, Bakyt	8 Aug 2009	Jambyl Raion, Kazakhstan	Leningrad	1976	Dairy farm
Shirinov, Aryan	12 Nov 2007	Pamirs, Tajikistan	Leningrad	1985	Student, martial arts
Somkishvili, David	24 Jul 2011	Kutaisi, Georgia	Moscow	1984–1989	Architecture student
Svanidze, Eliso	24 Jul 2011	Ochamchire, Georgia	Leningrad	1975–1985	Store worker
Temirkulov, Narynbek	11 Jul 2007	Osh Raion, Kyrgyzstan	Moscow	1964–1969	Student
Tsereteli, Fridon	12 Oct 2007	Poti, Georgia	Moscow	1989–	Student, administrator

(continued)

TABLE 1   (continued)

MIGRANT NAME (PSEUDONYM)	INTERVIEW DATE	MIGRANT ORIGIN	MIGRANT DESTINATION	MIGRATION DATES	MIGRANT OCCUPATION
Tursunbaev, Marat	15 May 2007	Samarkand, Uzbekistan	Leningrad	1975–1990	Student, laboratory worker
Usmanova, Dylara	3 Dec 2008	Tashkent, Uzbekistan	Moscow	1959–1975	Graduate student, cared for family
Utiashvili, Lali	29 Nov 2007	Poti, Georgia	Moscow	1979	Agronomist
Voskanyan, Rafael	25 Nov 2007	Yerevan, Armenia	Leningrad	1982–1986	Administrator
Zakirov, Anarbek	9 Aug 2009	Frunze, Kyrgyzstan	Moscow	1978–	Student, militia

unavailable in written sources; determine how state policies were understood and engaged with on the ground; and, carefully, consider emotions and intimate family life.[2] I could probe everyday relationships and investigate the roots of the energy that I encountered on St. Petersburg's and Moscow's streets in 1992. Sadly, I would also seek the foundations of Russian racism that took off at the turn of the 2000s. I was, finally, curious to see how potential subjects would understand the place of the USSR in their lives, more than a decade after its collapse.

Initial interviews with migrants from the Caucasus, Central Asia, and Asian Russia to Leningrad and Moscow fulfilled my expectations and altered my focus. Life stories emerged as far more engaging and important than stories of place; or, perhaps, I grew to understand that lives made places. I realized the broader importance to these individuals, and to the state, of movement, at once geographical and societal; of networks; and of connections between home and away. I grew fascinated as I was told what made a Kyrgyz or an Azerbaijani in a small village decide to leave family and friends and pursue opportunities or profits thousands of kilometers away in the 1960s, 1970s, or 1980s. I listened intently to vivid recollections of first experiences and encounters in Leningrad and Moscow and poignant stories of belonging, or not belonging. I expressed surprise—sometimes openly, during an interview—when two or more subjects, of similar ethnic and social background, faced parallel situations and reacted, or at least recalled their reactions, in dramatically different ways. What makes one brush off an incident of discrimination as a mere distraction to dreams of success, easily forgotten, and another dwell on a quite comparable one to the point of deciding to return home then and to remain haunted by it now? I tried also to make sense of contradictions within interviews, as narrators actively reconstructed their own complicated lives through the lens of their present. Oral histories animated the Soviet Union for me—through my own interviews, as well as through discussions of interviews conducted by Canadian, Kyrgyz, Uzbek, Azerbaijani, and Georgian research assistants and colleagues, all of whom brought their own understandings of the former state and found them transformed.

I ended up compiling seventy-five interviews for this project, of which we used seventy.[3] I began in 2005 with a semi-structured set of open-ended questions that roughly traced migrants' journeys: from their motivations to move to their initial impressions of Leningrad and Moscow, from their study or work life to their everyday encounters with the host society and state. I next asked them explicitly to reflect on their experiences then in the light of their lives now. Personal connections and the Central Eurasian Studies Society Listserv put me in touch with academics or professionals in my target group. Most had attended universities or arrived as part of intellectual or white-collar recruitment or exchange programs to Leningrad or Moscow during the 1970s and 1980s. I conducted interviews in North America, at conferences or by phone. A Carleton University graduate student working on Afghan refugees in St. Petersburg talked to some Tajiks while there, helping me to refine questions for subjects who remained in the former Soviet Union. We both learned lessons: open-ended questions, such as requests to discuss relationships with the host population, could produce the one-word response of "fine" (*normal'no*)—with informants not taking kindly to our efforts at clarification. Subjects did not like us using the term "racism" (*rasizm*), considering it a Western phenomenon. As a result, open-ended questions were accompanied by prods for specific experiences and "discrimination based on national background" replaced "racism." We discovered also that some informants loved to talk much more than others. Some began by offering their "Soviet biography," which could run several minutes; others felt questions on everyday life were excessively personal and never became comfortable discussing their own lives with a stranger. Managing, or coaxing, subjects became an art.

Interviews, especially with open-ended, semi-structured questions, emerged, I learned, as relationships.[4] Before or during an oral history, interviewer and interviewee form, if the process is anywhere near successful, some kind of bond. I worked to ensure this bond was positive. I focused on questions within the survey that engaged my subjects and pursued follow-ups when they wanted to talk (and asked my research assistants to do the same). I was fascinated by how interviewees thoughtfully, sometimes emotionally, rehearsed their own lives in their present. I, and my other interviewers, became implicated in this process. We were foils, perhaps—subjects had specific stories that they might want to tell a young, female Kyrgyz graduate student, for example, as opposed to a mid-career male Canadian professor. Narrative strategies, even if choppy and self-contradictory, emerged when reading transcripts. Soviet and post-Soviet memories and lives acted in concert.

St. Petersburg and Moscow were the next stage for locating oral history subjects. I worked in 2007–2008 with another Canadian research assistant to locate contact information for the ubiquitous diaspora organizations that sprouted in the two cities in the 2000s. We received help from Georgian, Kyrgyz, Uzbek, and Tajik associations. Many of the interview subjects were public figures and comfortable talking about themselves, though some grew impatient after twenty to thirty minutes of a process that normally would take one to two hours. We discovered that these organizations offered up their "success stories," that is, Georgians, Kyrgyz, Uzbeks, or Tajiks who had done well for themselves in the post-Soviet environment and whose Soviet-era stories built up to that success. Another challenge in our interviews with migrants who had remained in the two capitals involved answers and stories that might cross the 1991 divide. We had to keep a sharp ear for details that might indicate the subject was moving forward in time in the 1990s. I realized that the decade from 1990 to 2000—from when shortages of basic goods began in the late perestroika period to Vladimir Putin's presidency—existed for many as one era, recalled for its economic uncertainty and political weakness. My young, female Canadian research assistant also noticed the pleasure her interview subjects took in discussing their "adventures" with Russian women.

As I found other interviews through the "snowball" method, I remarked that our biggest gap consisted of traders and blue-collar workers—in factories, construction, or the service industry—whose presence on Leningrad's and Moscow's streets was frequently remarked on at the time but almost never studied. I found by chance on a 2007 conference trip to Kyrgyzstan a subject who had been a temporary worker (*limitchik*) in 1980s Moscow. Traders remained hard to locate—St. Petersburg and Moscow diaspora organizations did not refer any to us. I discovered that this was not solely, if at all, because they wanted to show off their most respected members. Well-established St. Petersburg and Moscow academics studying current Central Asia and Caucasus traders, much to their own surprise, could find no one to direct me to who was in the two capitals before the late 1990s. The thousands on thousands of seasonal traders in the two post-Soviet cities were of a younger generation. My next interview stage, therefore, involved finding these people in their current homes. Colleagues in Azerbaijan and Kyrgyzstan referred me to students from small towns in the south, whose relatives had traded in 1970s–1980s Leningrad and Moscow. These colleagues and students conducted many of this set of interviews for me in 2009, as subjects preferred to speak Azerbaijani or Kyrgyz rather than Russian. A similar situation occurred two years later. Traders and others who had worked in service sectors located through a colleague in Kutaisi, Georgia, in 2011 preferred to speak their native tongue. The interviews, conducted by young women in Kyrgyzstan or Georgia, had their own flavor. Subjects carefully—and quite helpfully, in terms of offering context for the project overall—explained what life was like in the USSR and how they felt their childhood and youth differed from those growing up today.

I was prepared to encounter nostalgia for the Soviet Union in our interviews, as the phenomenon had already attracted significant scholarly interest. I found similar patterns to those discovered by Svetlana Boym, Daphne Berdahl, Maria Todorova, and others: longing for a form of community that had been lost, one where human relations appeared more important and links to friends and family were closer.[5] My subjects lionized relations in multiethnic dormitories in similar ways as Boym's had regarding their young lives in communal apartments. Nostalgia also related to the "unrelivability" of the past, to the belief that the current, post-Soviet system, in this case, had destroyed elements of the previous regime and society that our subjects considered critical to their sense of identity as well as of success and mobility.[6]

I was less prepared for, and grew fascinated by, my subjects' insistence that the USSR was a meritocracy. Hard work and skill, they argued, would result in prosperity, if not always recognition. In part, this narrative offered a direct contrast to what they saw as a post-Soviet world dominated by large businesses and oligarchs, supported by corrupt and greedy politicians. I believe what underlay their arguments, however, was a different type of nostalgia: for youth, when subjects found ways, through or around the system, to make their own lives. The USSR for them was free, a field for their youthful energies, as opposed to the smaller post-Soviet world dominated by uncertainties and, for most average middle-aged or older citizens, declining living standards. Otto Boele has tied efforts to rehabilitate Leonid Brezhnev and his era—seen since the late 1990s in Russian opinion polls as the time over the past century when life was best—to late middle-aged citizens who felt their youthful contributions to public and private life had been devalued by initial post-Soviet efforts to remove monuments, rename streets, and otherwise deny "their" history.[7] At the same time, oral histories did reveal the 1980s as a more difficult decade, when the seeds for a decline in southern republics had been planted and Leningrad and Moscow grew less friendly to outsiders.

Our subjects, a decade-plus after the collapse, related their experiences within Soviet discursive frameworks. Slogans such as "the friendship of peoples" structured their thoughts on national relations. Common aspirations—if only, now, vicarious ones—remained attached to values linked to the Soviet regime: education, urbanization, mobility, and socialist affection. Serguei Oushakine has noted the failure of post-Soviet Russia to create its own discourse, to effect a new sense of citizenship and bond average citizens to a qualitatively new state.[8] A few of our Caucasus subjects—especially in Azerbaijan, where critiques of Russia's colonial practices were sharpest—did employ a more evident post-Soviet nationalist framework. Even here, these more abstract discussions appeared divorced from their own lives. Does this signal the resiliency of a defunct regime? The USSR's place in a broader, global modernization that continues, albeit unevenly, in its successor states? Or the success of Soviet citizens in making the state and society their own? Oral history work allows us to consider the ways language and ideas persist, and evolve, from the bottom up, and how average people construct their own lives and worlds.

The richness of these oral histories posed challenges as I began to write. Each, as I read it months or years later, existed as a script, with a narrative arc, albeit an improvised and relational one. How could I, or should I, carve these stories into pieces and rob them of so much context? How to account for silences, pauses, and evasions, on the one hand, and for enthusiasm and what might seem to be exaggerations, on the other? How to deal with contradictions, when a subject who claims to have always been treated equally—that it could not be otherwise in the Soviet Union—says, half an hour later, that he or she was a frequent victim of racial discrimination? Such challenges are common, but not unique, to oral historians. Oral histories, like written documents, are narratives, not scripture. There is always a lapse in time between event and product, and a degree of authorial subjectivity, that needs to be accounted for—and which I tried to accomplish, in the main text of the book.[9] In the end, as historians, we have jobs to do. I sought to privilege the voices I had recorded, to make these Soviet citizens actors in their own drama. To best accomplish that, I needed to offer context: whether from other sources, primary or secondary, published or unpublished, or from across the interviews themselves. As I continued my other research through the interview process, I began to comprehend the scale and importance of mobility in the late Soviet Union. The dynamic role played by citizens and migrants of the Caucasus, Central Asia, and Asian Russia caused, or compensated for, gaps in a state, which set, albeit not always intentionally, a broad terrain for personal initiative and in the end was done in by societal energy.

Oral histories are unique sources in many ways, a joint creation of interviewer and interviewee and the product of a constellation of forces that can never be reproduced. The interrogator might be a young Canadian woman or a late middle-aged Azerbaijani man and might have her or his own focus, based on interviews that had come before or gaps that we thought needed filling. The subject might choose to do the interview in his or her native language, Russian, or English and treat it as a formal, academic event or a simple chat—we would always ask if the interview could be recorded or notes taken by hand. He or she might be in a good or bad mood; might be affected by the news of the day or a recent, or not-so-recent, life event; or might be busy or have lots of time to reflect on responses. Answers and thoughts that seem definitive are contingent on all these factors. The five follow-up interviews I did had a different tone, in quite different ways, from the first ones conducted by myself or a research assistant. Agency lies at the heart of the creation as well as the importance of oral histories.

I owe a great debt to those who agreed to participate in this study, who shared their experiences and memories. No other method would have produced the richness of life stories, relationships, and networks that, I believe, makes us rethink the nature of the late Soviet Union. I hope—and in some cases was told—that these interviews also allowed opportunities for my subjects to see their own importance not only as historical actors in the unique social experiment that was the USSR but also as individuals, as sons and daughters, mothers and fathers, friends and citizens, of both the Soviet and post-Soviet worlds.

Notes

ABBREVIATIONS USED IN NOTES

GARF   State Archive of the Russian Federation
RGASPI   Russian State Archive of Social and Political History
TsGAPDK Central State Archive of Political Documentation of the Kyrgyz Republic

INTRODUCTION

1. Pseudonyms are used to identify oral history subjects. Details of the interviews are found in table 1 and the appendix. I use Kyrgyzstan as the more popular term for the Kyrgyz Soviet Socialist Republic. See the note on terminology for further details.

2. Abdul Khalimov, interview, 30 November 2007. Tajikistan refers to the Tajik SSR.

3. Georgia refers to the Georgian SSR.

4. Russia refers to the Russian Soviet Federated Socialist Republic (RSFSR).

5. For a genealogy of the term "stagnation" and sporadic efforts to interrogate it since the USSR's end, see Dina Fainberg and Artemy Kalinovsky, "Introduction: Stagnation and Its Discontents: The Creation of a Political and Historical Paradigm," in *Reconsidering Stagnation in the Brezhnev Era: Ideology and Exchange*, ed. Dina Fainberg and Artemy Kalinovsky (Lanham, MD: Lexington Books, 2016), vii–xix.

6. Morgan Liu, "Urban Materiality and Its Stakes in Southern Kyrgyzstan," *Quaderni storici* 50, no. 2 (2015): 1–24. DOI: 10.1408/81787.

7. On spatial hierarchies in the USSR, see Hilary Pilkington, "'The Future Is Ours': Youth Culture in Russia, 1953 to the Present," in *Russian Cultural Studies*, ed. Catriona Kelly and David Shepherd (Oxford: Oxford University Press, 1998), 378; Olga Vendina, "Social Polarization and Ethnic Segregation in Moscow," *Eurasian Geography and Economics* 43, no. 3 (2002): 216–43. DOI: 10.2747/1538-7216.43.3.216.

8. This volume is a first step in understanding multiethnic integration in central Russian cities in the late USSR. On the unique development of socialist cities within a Western paradigm in other respects, see the articles in the special section "Second World Urbanity: New Histories of the Socialist City," ed. Daria Bocharnikova and Steven E. Harris, *Journal of Urban History* 44, no. 1 (2018): 3–117.

9. On the transnational nature of interethnic, inter-republican mobility, see Lewis H. Siegelbaum and Leslie Page Moch, "Transnationalism in One Country? Seeing and Not Seeing Cross-Border Migration within the Soviet Union," *Slavic Review* 75, no. 4 (2016): 970–86.

10. On the still-understudied role of emotions in Soviet history, see, for example, William M. Reddy, "Emotional Turn? Feeling in Russian History and Culture: Comment," *Slavic Review* 68, no. 2 (2009): 329–34. DOI: 10.2307/27697961.

11. Alexei Yurchak, *Everything Was Forever, Until It Was No More: The Last Soviet Generation* (Princeton, NJ: Princeton University Press, 2005), 19–28.

12. On the evolution of racial ideas, see Quinn Slobodian, ed., *Comrades of Color: East Germany in the Cold War World* (New York: Berghahn Books, 2015), 27. On the connections between racism and postimperial migration, see Catherine Hall and Sonya O. Rose, "Introduction: Being at Home with the Empire," in *At Home with the Empire: Metropolitan Culture and the Imperial World*, ed. Catherine Hall and Sonya O. Rose (Cambridge: Cambridge University Press, 2006), 22–23.

13. Karen E. Fields and Barbara J. Fields, *Racecraft: The Soul of Inequality in American Life* (New York: Verso, 2014), 16.

14. The link between racism and migration from former colonial spaces is discussed in chapter 4. See David Theo Goldberg, "Racial Europeanization," *Ethnic and Racial Studies* 29, no. 2 (2006): 331–64. DOI: 10.1080/01419870500465611.

15. On migrants from southern former Soviet republics in contemporary Russia, see Nikolay Zakharov, *Race and Racism in Russia* (Basingstoke: Palgrave Macmillan, 2015).

16. Monica Boyd, "Family and Personal Networks in International Migration: Recent Developments and New Agendas," *International Migration Review* 23, no. 3 (1989): 639. DOI: 10.2307/2546433.

17. On Soviet dreams, see Donald J. Raleigh, *Russia's Sputnik Generation: Soviet Baby Boomers Talk about Their Lives* (Bloomington: Indiana University Press, 2006). Migrants expressed their own visions of Soviet dreams, as discussed below and in the chapters that follow.

18. Nikolai Bukharin, quoted in Jochen Hellbeck, *Revolution on My Mind: Writing a Diary under Stalin* (Cambridge, MA: Harvard University Press, 2006), 7.

19. On this shift in the USSR, see Moshe Lewin, *The Gorbachev Phenomenon: A Historical Interpretation*, expanded ed. (Berkeley: University of California Press, 1991).

20. On the idea of European superiority taking root among non-European populations, see Meenakshi Thapan, "Imagined and Social Landscapes: Potential Immigrants and the Experience of Migration in Northern Italy," *Economic and Political Weekly* 48, no. 38 (2013): 58.

21. James Millar, "The Little Deal: Brezhnev's Contribution to Acquisitive Socialism," *Slavic Review* 44, no. 4 (1985): 694–706. DOI: 10.2307/2498542.

22. Erik Scott, *Familiar Strangers: The Georgian Diaspora and the Evolution of Soviet Empire* (Oxford: Oxford University Press, 2016), 3.

23. Adeeb Khalid, "Backwardness and the Quest for Civilization: Early Soviet Central Asia in a Comparative Perspective," *Slavic Review* 65, no. 2 (2006): 231–51. DOI: 10.2307/4148591.

24. On linkages between modernization and colonialism in the USSR, see Botakoz Kassymbekova, *Despite Cultures: Early Soviet Rule in Tajikistan* (Pittsburgh: University of Pittsburgh Press, 2016).

25. Matt Bivens, "No Good Will for the Homeless," *Moscow Times* 27 July 1994.

26. On the politics of unrecognition, see Oren Yiftachel, "Critical Theory and 'Gray Space': Mobilization of the Colonized," *City* 13, nos. 2–3 (2009): 240–56. DOI: 10.1080/13604810902982227.

27. *Moskva v tsifrakh* did not include ethnicity as a category in its detailed, annual statistical guidebooks of the late Soviet city.

28. E. B. Bernaskoni, ed., *Moskva—dlia vsekh stolitsa* (Moscow: Moskovskii rabochii, 1982). See also *Moskva: Vchera i segodnia* (Moscow: Moskovskii rabochii, 1978); I. U. Aleksandrovskii, *Moskva: Dialog putevoditel'* (Moscow: Moskovskii rabochii, 1983).

29. Tsentral'noe statisticheskoe upravlenie, *Itogi vsesoiuznoi perepisi naseleniia 1959 goda: RSFSR* (Moscow: Gosstatizdat, 1963), 316.

30. *Itogi vsesoiuznoi perepisi naseleniia 1989 g.* (Moscow: Statistika, 1991), tom 7, chast' 1. Azerbaijan refers to the Azerbaijani SSR.

31. Barbara Anderson and Brian Silver, "Estimating Russification of Ethnic Identity among the Non-Russians of the USSR," *Demography* 20, no. 4 (1983): 461–89. DOI: 10.2307/2061114.

32. Vera Glubova, "Zaboty mnogonatsional'nogo goroda," *Arkhitektura i stroitel'stva Moskvy*, no. 9 (1989): 8.

33. Vendina, "Social Polarization," 228. On collective strategies, see Rina Benmayor and Andor Skotnes, eds., *Migration and Identity* (Oxford: Oxford University Press, 1994), 10.

34. For a full list of the interviews, see table 1.

Loan Receipt
Liverpool John Moores University
Library Services

**Borrower Name: Scarborough, Isaac
HSSISCAR**
Borrower ID: ********

Voices from the Soviet edge : southern
migrants in Leningrad and Moscow /
31111015296997
Due Date: 09/09/2019 23:59:00 BST

Total Items: 1
02/09/2019 12:55

Please keep your receipt in case of
dispute.

35. For example, V. Voronkov and I. Osval'd, eds., *Konstruirovanie etnichnosti: Etnicheskie obshchiny Sankt-Peterburga* (St. Petersburg: Izdatel'stvo "Dmitrii Bulanin," 1998).

36. Benmayor and Skotnes, *Migration and Identity*, 14.

37. The Soviet press, as well as statistics collections and guidebooks, avoided discussion of Leningrad and Moscow as multiethnic cities until 1990. Archives were not structured to organize materials that involved the crossing of republican boundaries. Cynthia Buckley notes, despite a lack of documentation, the "overwhelming evidence for widespread irregular and undocumented migration during the Imperial, Soviet, and post-Soviet periods." Cynthia Buckley, "Introduction: New Approaches to Migration and Belonging in Eurasia," in *Migration, Homeland, and Belonging in Eurasia*, ed. Cynthia Buckley and Blair Ruble (Baltimore: Johns Hopkins University Press, 2008), 7.

38. On the methodological challenges of conducting oral history, see Paul Thompson, *The Voice of the Past: Oral History*, 3rd ed. (Oxford: Oxford University Press, 2000); Donald A. Ritchie, *Doing Oral History: A Practical Guide* (Oxford: Oxford University Press, 2003).

39. For statistics and studies on racial incidents in post-Soviet Russia, see the annual reports of the SOVA Center for Information and Analysis (Moscow), https://www.sova-center.ru/en/ (accessed 25 May 2018).

40. Svetlana Boym, *Common Places: Mythologies of Everyday Life in Russia* (Cambridge, MA: Harvard University Press, 1994), 285.

41. On the linkage between youth and an imagined, defunct state, see Daphne Berdahl, "'(N)ostalgie' for the Present: Memory, Longing, and East German Things," *Ethnos* 64, no. 2 (1999): 192–211. DOI: 10.1080/00141844.1999.9981598.

42. Galina Starovoitova, who became a member of the Congress of People's Deputies in 1989, was a pioneer in this field. See her "Problemy etnosotsiologii inoetnicheskoi gruppy v sovremennom gorode: Na materialakh issledovaniia tatar v Leningrade" (PhD diss., Institut etnografii im. N. N Miklukho-Maklaia, Akademiia nauk SSSR, 1980) and the subsequent book, *Etnicheskaia gruppa v sovremennom sovetskom gorode: Sotsiologicheskie ocherki* (Leningrad: Nauka, 1987).

43. Hein de Haas, "Migration and Development: A Theoretical Perspective," *International Migration Review* 44, no. 1 (2010): 227, https://www.jstor.org/stable/20681751.

1. GLOBAL, SOVIET CITIES

1. On the overlap between the terms "gateway," "global," and "world" in discussions of large Western capital cities, see Michael Samers, "Immigration and the Global City Hypothesis: Towards a Research Agenda," *International Journal of Urban and Regional Research* 26, no. 2 (2002): 389–402. DOI: 10.1111/1468-2427.00386.

2. Doreen Massey, *Space, Place, and Gender* (Minneapolis: University of Minnesota Press, 1994), 6.

3. Jyldyz Nuriaeva, interview, 9 July 2007.

4. Frunze was renamed Bishkek after the end of the Soviet Union.

5. Siegelbaum and Moch, "Transnationalism in One Country?"

6. Kirsten McKenzie, "Britain: Ruling the Waves," in *The Age of Empires*, ed. Robert Aldrich (London: Thames and Hudson, 2007), 128–51.

7. Jennifer Robinson, "Cities in a World of Cities: The Comparative Gesture," *International Journal of Urban and Regional Research* 35, no. 1 (2011): 10. DOI: 10.1111/j.1468-2427.2010.00982.x.

8. Dominic Thomas, *Black France: Colonialism, Immigration, and Transnationalism* (Bloomington: Indiana University Press, 2007), 50.

9. Oren Yiftachel, "Theoretical Notes on 'Gray Cities': The Coming of Urban Apartheid?," *Planning Theory* 8, no. 1 (2009): 92. DOI: 10.1177/1473095208099300.

10. Doreen Massey, *World City* (Cambridge, UK: Polity, 2007); Saskia Sassen, *The Global City: New York, London, Tokyo* (Princeton, NJ: Princeton University Press, 1992).

11. Samers, "Immigration and the Global City Hypothesis," 390.

12. Sassen, *The Global City*.

13. Massey, *Space, Place, and Gender*, 2.

14. See, for example, Anthony D. King, "World Cities: Global? Postcolonial? Postimperial? Or Just the Result of Happenstance?," in *The Global Cities Reader*, ed. Neil Brenner and Roger Keil (London: Routledge, 2006), 319–24.

15. Doreen Massey, "Responsibilities over Distance," in *Globalizing the Research Imagination*, ed. Jane Kenway and Johannah Fahey (London: Routledge, 2009), 73.

16. Jennifer Robinson, "Global and World Cities: A View from Off the Map," *International Journal of Urban and Regional Research* 26, no. 3 (2002): 531–54. DOI: 10.1111/1468-2427.00397.

17. Sarah Hudspith, "Moscow: A Global City? Introduction," *Slavic Review* 72, no. 3 (2013): 457. DOI: 10.5612/slavicreview.72.3.0453.

18. Kate Brown, "Gridded Lives: Why Kazakhstan and Montana Are Nearly the Same Place," *American Historical Review* 106, no. 1 (2001): 17–48. DOI: 10.2307/2652223.

19. Nina Glick Schiller and Ayşe Çağlar, eds., *Locating Migration: Rescaling Cities and Migrants* (Ithaca, NY: Cornell University Press, 2011), 9.

20. Scott, *Familiar Strangers*, 7–8.

21. St. Petersburg was renamed Petrograd in 1914, before becoming Leningrad in 1924.

22. See, for example, Thomas Barrett, "The Remaking of the Lion of Dagestan: Shamil in Captivity," *Russian Review* 53, no. 3 (1994): 353–66. DOI: 10.2307/131191.

23. Iu. V. Bromlei et al., eds., *Etnosotsialnye problemy goroda* (Moscow: Nauka, 1986), 211.

24. V. B. Zhiromskaia, "Etnicheskii sostav naseleniia Moskvy v XVIII–XIX vekakh (istoricheskii aspekt)," in *Moskva mnogonatsional'naia: Istoki, evolutsiia, problemy, sovremennosti*, ed. A. N. Sakharov (Moscow: RAN, 2007), 103–7.

25. Vera Tolz, *Russia's Own Orient: The Politics of Identity and Oriental Studies in the Late Imperial and Early Soviet Periods* (Oxford: Oxford University Press, 2011).

26. On the links between knowledge and empire, see Bernard S. Cohn, *Colonialism and Its Forms of Knowledge: The British in India* (Princeton, NJ: Princeton University Press, 1996). On how these links operated in Russia, see Tolz, *Russia's Own Orient*.

27. Turkestan's representation at the imperial parliament, or duma, consisted of only one duma session—the second, from 1906 to 1907. Deputies from other Muslim regions served through the tsarist collapse, however. Adeeb Khalid, *The Politics of Muslim Cultural Reform: Jadidism in Central Asia* (Berkeley: University of California Press, 1998), 106.

28. Scott, *Familiar Strangers*, 43. On other European cases, see Nicholas Owen, "The Soft Heart of the British Empire: Indian Radicals in Edwardian London," *Past and Present* 220, no. 1 (August 2013): 143–84. DOI: 10.1093/pastj/gtt006; Kelly Duke Bryant, "Social Networks and Empire: Senegalese Students in France in the Late Nineteenth Century," *French Colonial History* 15, no. 1 (2014): 39–66, https://muse.jhu.edu/article/547757.

29. Zhiromskaia, "Etnicheskii sostav," 104.

30. Jeff Sahadeo, "Home and Away: Why the Asian Periphery Matters in Russian History," *Kritika: Explorations in Russian and Eurasian History* 16, no. 2 (2015): 375–88. DOI: 10.1353/kri.2015.0030.

31. Zhiromskaia, "Etnicheskii sostav," 105.

32. Scott, *Familiar Strangers*, 93.

33. Scott, *Familiar Strangers*, 12.

34. Masha Kirasirova, "The 'East' as a Category of Bolshevik Ideology and Comintern Administration: The Arab Section of the Communist University of the Toilers of the East," *Kritika* 18, no. 1 (2017): 7–34. DOI: 10.1353/kri.2017.0001.

35. Kirasirova, "The 'East,'" 21.

36. V. G. Chebotareva, "Moskva—tsentr podgotovki natsional'nykh kadrov dlia soiuznykh i avtonomnykh respublik SSSR, 1920–1930-e gody," in Sakharov, *Moskva mnogonatsional'naia*, 213–19.

37. Kirasirova, "The 'East,'" 8.

38. On the persistence of the colonial economy in the early Soviet period, see Jeff Sahadeo, *Russian Colonial Society in Tashkent, 1865–1923* (Bloomington: Indiana University Press, 2007), 208–28.

39. This assistance is discussed in further detail in chapter 2.

40. Francine Hirsch, *Empire of Nations: Ethnographic Knowledge and the Making of the Soviet Union* (Ithaca, NY: Cornell University Press, 2005), 7–9. The effects of the quota system are detailed in following chapters.

41. Chebotareva, "Moskva—tsentr podgotovki," 246.

42. Kirasirova, "The 'East,'" 29.

43. Adeeb Khalid, *Making Uzbekistan: Nation, Empire, and Revolution in the Early USSR* (Ithaca, NY: Cornell University Press, 2015), 185.

44. Khalid, *Making Uzbekistan*, 242.

45. See Jennifer Anne Boittin, "'Among Them Complicit'? Life and Politics in France's Black Communities, 1919–1939," and Daniel Whittall, "'In This Metropolis of the World We Must Have a Building Worthy of Our Great People': Race, Empire and Hospitality in Imperial London, 1931–1948," in *Africa in Europe: Studies in Transnational Practice in the Long Twentieth Century*, ed. Eve Rosenhaft and Robbie Aitken (Liverpool: Liverpool University Press, 2013), 55–75 and 75–98, respectively.

46. Dina Khapaeva, "Soviet and Post-Soviet Moscow: Literary Reality or Nightmare?," in *Soviet and Post-Soviet Identities*, ed. Mark Bassin and Catriona Kelly (Cambridge: Cambridge University Press, 2012), 172.

47. Z. V. Sikevich, *Peterburzhtsy: Etnonatsional'nye aspekty massovogo soznaniia* (St. Petersburg: Sankt-Peterburgskii gosudarstvennyi universitet, 1995), 10.

48. N. S. Goncharova, "Tatarskoe naselenie Moskvy: Gendernye aspekty," in *Gendernye problemy v obshchestvennykh naukakh*, ed. I. M. Semashko (Moscow: RAN, Institut etnologii i antropologii im. N. N. Miklukho-Maklaia, 2001), 203.

49. Oksana Karpenko, "Byt' 'natsional'nym': Strakh poteriat' i strakh poteriat'sia; Na primere tatar Sankt-Peterburga," in *Konstruirovanie etnichnosti*, ed. Voronkov and Osval'd, 56, 62.

50. I. N. Gavrilova, *Demograficheskaia istoriia Moskvy* (Moscow: Fast-Print, 1997), 185.

51. I. I. Shangina, *Mnogonatsional'nyi Peterburg: Istoriia, religii, narody* (St. Petersburg: Iskusstvo–SPB, 2002), 145.

52. See, for example, Iu. D. Anchabadze and N. G. Volkova, *Staryi Tbilisi: Gorod i gorozhane v XIX veke* (Moscow: Nauka, 1990).

53. Scott, *Familiar Strangers*, 22.

54. Terry Martin, *The Affirmative Action Empire: Nations and Nationalism in the Soviet Union, 1923–1939* (Ithaca, NY: Cornell University Press, 2001), 412, 406–13. See also T. M. Smirnova, *Natsional'nost'—piterskie: Natsional'nye men'shinstva Peterburga i Leningradskoi oblasti v XX veke* (St. Petersburg: Izdatel'stvo "Sudarynia," 2002).

55. N. F. Bugai, "Deportatsiia natsional'nykh men'shinstv iz Moskvy i Moskovskoi oblasti v 1930–1940-e gody," in Sakharov, *Moskva mnogonatsional'naia*, 294.

56. Kimberly Elman Zarecor, "What Was So Socialist about the Socialist City? Second World Urbanity in Europe," *Journal of Urban History* 44, no. 1 (2018): 97. DOI: 10.1177/0096144217710229.

57. Zarecor, "What Was So Socialist?," 97, 107.

58. Rachel Applebaum, "The Friendship Project: Socialist Internationalism in the Soviet Union and Czechoslovakia in the 1950s and 1960s," *Slavic Review* 74, no. 3 (2015): 498. DOI: 10.5612/slavicreview.74.3.484.

59. G. Isaeva, G. Kuleshova, and V. Tsigankov, *Moskva internatsional'naia* (Moscow: Moskovskii rabochii, 1977), 241–42.

60. Kristin Roth-Ey, "'Loose Girls' on the Loose? Sex, Propaganda, and the 1957 Youth Festival," in *Women in the Khrushchev Era*, ed. Melanie Ilič, Susan E. Reid, and Lynne Attwood (Basingstoke: Palgrave Macmillan, 2004), 81.

61. Linda McDowell, "Workers, Migrants, Aliens or Citizens? State Constructions and Discourses of Identity among Post-war European Labor Migrants in Britain," *Political Geography* 22, no. 4 (2003): 865. DOI: 10.1016/j.polgeo.2003.08.002.

62. Rebecca Manley, *To the Tashkent Station: Evacuation and Survival in the Soviet Union at War* (Ithaca, NY: Cornell University Press, 2009).

63. William Fierman, "The Soviet 'Transformation' of Central Asia," in *Soviet Central Asia: The Failed Transformation*, ed. William Fierman (Boulder, CO: Westview, 1991), 19.

64. British and French legislators hesitated to restrict movement in the immediate postwar years, given their need for labor and a desire to maintain imperial connections as the age of formal empire appeared to be ending. Randall Hansen, *Citizenship and Immigration in Post-war Britain* (Oxford: Oxford University Press, 2000), 26. From 1951 to 1966, West Indian residents in London alone grew from 17,000 to 269,000.

65. Artemy Kalinovsky, "Not Some British Colony in Africa: The Politics of Decolonization and Modernization in Soviet Central Asia, 1955–1964," *Ab Imperio*, no. 2 (2013): 191–222. DOI: 10.1353/imp.2013.0044.

66. Masha Kirasirova, "'Sons of Muslims' in Moscow: Soviet Central Asian Mediators to the Foreign East, 1955–1962," *Ab Imperio*, no. 4 (2011): 107. DOI: 10.1353/imp.2011.0003.

67. Kirasirova, "'Sons of Muslims,'" 112. See also Constantin Katsakioris, "Burden or Allies? Third World Students and Internationalist Duty through Soviet Eyes," *Kritika* 18, no. 3 (2017): 539. DOI: 10.1353/kri.2017.0035.

68. On the scale of postwar migration to London, Paris, and other major European cities, see Hansen, *Citizenship and Immigration*; Paul A. Silverstein, *Algeria in France: Transpolitics, Race, and Nation* (Bloomington: Indiana University Press, 2004).

69. Nathalie Moine, "Le système des passeports à l'époque stalinienne: De la purge des grandes villes au morcellement du territoire, 1932–1953," *Revue d'histoire moderne et contemporaine* 50, no. 1 (2003): 148. DOI: 10.3917/rhmc.501.0145.

70. Moine, "Le système des passeports," 150.

71. The Soviet government extended zones where passports were needed to dozens of other cities as well as border areas deemed sensitive and even machine-tractor stations. Gijs Kessler, "The Passport System and State Control over Population Flows in the Soviet Union, 1932–1940," *Cahiers du monde russe* 42, nos. 2–4 (2001): 487, https://www.jstor.org/stable/20174642.

72. Cynthia Buckley, "The Myth of Managed Migration: Migration Control and Market in the Soviet Period," *Slavic Review* 54, no. 4 (1995): 904–5. DOI: 10.2307/2501398.

73. N. A. Tolokontseva and G. M. Romanenkovoi, eds., *Demografiia i ekologiia krupnogo goroda* (Leningrad: Nauka, 1980), 35.

74. Lewis H. Siegelbaum and Leslie Page Moch, *Broad Is My Native Land: Repertoires and Regimes of Migration in Russia's Twentieth Century* (Ithaca, NY: Cornell University Press, 2014), 125.

75. Tova Höjdestrand, "The Soviet-Russian Production of Homelessness," AnthroBase, accessed 30 June 2017, http://www.anthrobase.com/Txt/H/Hoejdestrand_T_01.htm.

76. Matthew Light, "What Does It Mean to Control Migration? Soviet Mobility Policies in Comparative Perspective," *Law and Social Inquiry* 37, no. 2 (2012): 408. DOI:

10.1111/j.1747-4469.2012.01308.x; Dietrich André Loeber, "*Limitchiki*: On the Legal Status of Migrant Workers in Large Soviet Cities," *Soviet and Post-Soviet Review* 11, no. 1 (1984): 301–8. DOI: 10.1163/187633284X00198.

77. Cecil J. Houston, "Administrative Control of Migration to Moscow, 1959–75," *Canadian Geographer* 23, no. 1 (1979): 36. DOI: 10.1111/j.1541-0064.1979.tb00636.x.

78. David Shearer, "Elements Near and Alien: Passportization, Policing, and Identity in the Stalinist State, 1932–1952," *Journal of Modern History* 76, no. 4 (2004): 846. DOI: 10.1086/427570. In 1939, 50 million of 162 million Soviet citizens had internal passports.

79. Azamat Sanatbaev, interview, 14 July 2009.

80. Moine, "Le système des passeports," 163–69; Shearer, "Elements Near and Alien," 862.

81. Roth-Ey, "'Loose Girls,'" 90.

82. V. A. Shpiliuk, *Mezhrespublikanskaia migratsiia i sblizhenie natsii v SSSR* (Lvov, 1975), 118; Bromlei et al., *Etnosotsialnye problemy goroda*, 211.

83. L. V. Makarova, G. F. Morozova, and N. V. Tarasova, *Regional'nye osobennosti migratsionnykh protsessov v SSSR* (Moscow: Nauka, 1986), 79.

84. *Problemy sotsial'nogo razvitiia krupnykh gorodov* (Leningrad: Izdatel'stvo Leningradskogo universiteta, 1982), 48.

85. Alma-Ata is current-day Almaty. Kazakhstan refers to the Kazakh SSR and Uzbekistan refers to the Uzbek SSR.

86. Azamat Sanatbaev, interview, 14 July 2009.

87. Yiftachel, "Critical Theory and 'Gray Space,'" 240.

88. Walter C. Clemens Jr., "Straddling Cultures: An Azeri in Moscow," *Christian Science Monitor*, 12 March 1990.

89. Iohannes Angermiuller, "Ot natsional'nogo patriotizma do etnicheskogo dal'tonizma," in, *Konstruirovanie etnichnosti*, ed. Voronkov and Osval'd, 276.

90. Tsentral'noe statisticheskoe upravlenie, *Itogi vsesoiuznoi perepisi naseleniia 1959 goda*, 316.

91. Bromlei et al., *Etnosotsialnye problemy goroda*, 207.

92. Arif Yunusov, "Azerbaidzhantsy v Rossii—smena imidzha i sotsial'nykh rolei," *Rossiia i musul'manskii mir*, no. 2 (2006): 82.

93. Gerhard Simon, *Nationalism and Policy toward the Nationalities in the Soviet Union: From Totalitarian Dictatorship to Post-Stalinist Society*, trans. Karen Forster and Oswald Forster (Boulder, CO: Westview, 1991), 311–13.

94. Anna Marie Whittington, "Forging Soviet Citizens: Ideology, Stability, and Identity in the Soviet Union, 1930–1991." (PhD diss., University of Michigan, 2018).

95. Aibek Botoev, interview, 8 December 2007; Eliso Svanidze, interview, 24 July 2011.

96. Whittington, "Forging Soviet Citizens," 359.

97. Shuhrat Ikramov, interview, 18 September 2007.

98. Levan Rukhadze, interview, 25 November 2007. Erik Scott notes that Georgians did indeed pay bribes to enter institutions of higher education. Scott, *Familiar Strangers*, 155.

99. Oidin Nosirova, interview, 28 May 2007.

100. Fuad Ojagov, interview, 25 June 2009. The All-Union Academy of Sciences pledged to "render assistance to the scientific branches of the Academies of Sciences of the SSRs." Russian State Archive of Social and Political History (RGASPI), f. 17, op. 132, d. 333, l. 5.

101. Yaacov Ro'i, *Islam in the Soviet Union: From the Second World War to Gorbachev* (New York: Columbia University Press, 2000), 73.

102. Ro'i, *Islam in the Soviet Union*, 653.

103. Ro'i, *Islam in the Soviet Union*, 707.

104. State Archive of the Russian Federation (GARF), f. 6991, op. 4, d. 86, l. 98.

105. Ro'i, *Islam in the Soviet Union*, 75n77.

106. Alexandre Bennigsen et al., *Soviet Strategy and Islam* (New York: Palgrave Macmillan, 1989), 34.

107. GARF, f. 6991, op. 4, d. 99, ll. 5 and 118.

108. Kirasirova, "'Sons of Muslims,'" 107.

109. Dina Zisserman-Brodsky, *Constructing Ethnopolitics in the Soviet Union: Samizdat, Deprivation and the Rise of Ethnic Nationalism* (New York: Palgrave Macmillan, 2003), 32.

110. See, for example, "Guests of Soviet Muslims from the Yemen Arab Republic," *Muslims of the Soviet East*, no. 1 (1985): 16.

111. Meredith Roman, "Making Caucasians Black: Moscow since the Fall of Communism and the Racialization of Non-Russians," *Journal of Communist Studies and Transition Politics* 18, no. 2 (2002): 2. DOI: 10.1080/714003604.

112. Bernaskoni, *Moskva—dlia vsekh stolitsa*, 17.

113. Katsakioris, "Burden or Allies?," 540.

114. Katsakioris, "Burden or Allies?," 544.

115. Roman, "Making Caucasians Black," 6.

116. Aryuna Khamagova, interview, 12 February 2007.

117. D. I. Valentei, ed., *O naselenii Moskvy* (Moscow: Statistika, 1980), 4.

118. Siegelbaum and Moch, *Broad Is My Native Land*, 131.

119. Sassen, *The Global City*, 280.

120. V. I. Perevedentsev, *Molodezh' i sotsial'no-demograficheskie problemy SSSR* (Moscow: Nauka, 1990), 129, 135.

121. Kalinovsky, "Not Some British Colony," 218.

122. On the Hungry Steppe development, see Julia Obertreis, *Imperial Desert Dreams: Cotton Growing and Irrigation in Central Asia, 1860–1991* (Göttingen: V & R Unipress, 2017), 245–366. On the Nurek dam, see Artemy Kalinovsky, "A Most Beautiful City for the World's Tallest Dam: Internationalism, Social Welfare and Urban Utopia in Nurek," *Cahiers du monde russe* 57, no. 4 (2016): 819–46, https://www.cairn-int.info/article-E_CMR _574_0819—a-most-beautiful-city-for-the-world-s.htm.

123. Artemy Kalinovsky, "Central Planning, Local Knowledge? Labor, Population, and the 'Tajik School of Economics,'" *Kritika* 17, no. 3 (2016): 610. DOI: 10.1353/kri.2016.0036; Obertreis, *Imperial Desert Dreams*, 264–72.

124. Kalinovsky, "Central Planning, Local Knowledge?," 610.

125. For one complaint seeking a greater proportion of ethnic Tajiks at the Lenin factory in Frunze, see GARF, f. 56, op. 157, d. 20, l. 10. On Central Asia's human resources, see Makarova, Morozova, and Tarasova, *Regional'nye osobennosti migratsionnykh protsessov*, 75.

126. Aibek Botoev, interview, 8 December 2007.

127. Nancy Lubin, *Labour and Nationality in Soviet Central Asia* (Princeton, NJ: Princeton University Press, 1984), 205.

128. Central State Archive of Political Documentation of the Kyrgyz Republic (TsGAP-DKR), f. 56, op. 157, d. 34, l. 23.

129. On the out-migration of Slavs from Central Asia, see Lubin, *Labour and Nationality*, 47.

130. *Razvitie narodonaseleniia i problemy trudovykh resursov respublik Srednei Azii* (Tashkent: Izdatel'stvo "Fan" UzSSR, 1988), 50.

131. Kalinovsky, "Central Planning, Local Knowledge?," 610.

132. Donna Bahry and Carol Nechemias, "Half-Full or Half-Empty? The Debate over Soviet Regional Equality," *Slavic Review* 40, no. 3 (1981): 366. DOI: 10.2307/2496192.

133. G. M. Maksimov, *Vsesoiuznaia perepis' naseleniia 1970 goda: Sbornik statei* (Moscow: Statistika, 1976), 248–49.

134. Robert A. Lewis, Richard. H. Rowland, and Ralph S. Clem, *Nationality and Population Change in Russia and the USSR: An Evaluation of Census Data, 1897–1970* (New York: Praeger, 1976), 354–81.

135. Kalinovsky, "Central Planning, Local Knowledge?," 588–89.

136. Kalinovsky, "Central Planning, Local Knowledge?," 619.

137. Makarova, Morozova, and Tarasova, *Regional'nye osobennosti migratsionnykh protsessov*, 82.

138. Ajay Patanik, "Agriculture and Rural Out-Migration in Central Asia," *Europe-Asia Studies* 47, no. 1 (1995): 153, https://www.jstor.org/stable/153197.

139. Lubin, *Labour and Nationality*, 59.

140. Moritz Florin, "Faites tomber les murs! La politique civilizatrice de l'ère Brežnev dans les villages kirghiz," *Cahiers du monde russe* 54, nos. 1–2 (2013): 205, https://www.jstor.org/stable/24567694.

141. Florin, "Faites tomber les murs!," 206.

142. Kalinovsky, "Central Planning, Local Knowledge?," 613.

143. Iu. V. Arutiunian and Iu. V. Bromlei, eds., *Sotsial'no-kul'turnyi oblik sovetskikh natsii* (Moscow: Nauka, 1986), 25.

144. Kalinovsky, "Central Planning, Local Knowledge?," 614.

145. Lubin, *Labour and Nationality*, 119.

146. Perevedentsev, *Molodezh'*, 101.

147. Patanik, "Agriculture and Rural Out-Migration," 150; *Razvitie narodonaseleniia*, 75.

148. Cynthia Weber and Ann Goodman, "The Demographic Policy Debate in the USSR," *Population and Development Review* 7, no. 2 (1981): 279–95. DOI: 10.2307/1972624.

149. Murray Feshbach, "Prospects for Outmigration from Central Asia and Kazakhstan in the Next Decade," in *Soviet Economy in a Time of Change: A Compendium of Papers Submitted to the Joint Economic Committee, Congress of the United States* (Washington, DC: Government Printing Office, 1979), 662.

150. William Fierman, "Central Asian Youth and Migration," in *Soviet Central Asia*, ed. Fierman, 255–89.

151. *Razvitie narodonaseleniia*, 111. Fierman, "Central Asian Youth and Migration," 260.

152. Diane Koenker, *Club Red: Vacation Travel and the Soviet Dream* (Ithaca, NY: Cornell University Press, 2013), 227.

153. Makarova, Morozova, and Tarasova, *Regional'nye osobennosti migratsionnykh protsessov*, 86; Anne White, "Internal Migration Trends in Soviet and Post-Soviet European Russia," *Europe-Asia Studies* 59, no. 6 (2007): 902. DOI: 10.1080/09668130701489105.

154. Perevedentsev, *Molodezh'*, 100.

155. Perevedentsev, *Molodezh'*, 149–51.

156. Shearer, "Elements Near and Alien," 871.

157. On the British experience, see Joanna Herbert, *Negotiating Boundaries in the City: Migration, Ethnicity, and Gender in Britain* (London: Routledge, 2008). On continental Europe, see Mark J. Miller and Philip L. Martin, *Administering Foreign-Worker Programs* (Lexington, MA: D. C. Heath, 1982).

158. Houston, "Administrative Control of Migration." 32.

159. Emily Elliott, "Soviet Socialist Stars and Neoliberal Losers: Young Labour Migrants in Moscow, 1971–1991," *Journal of Migration History*, no. 2 (2017): 293.

160. A. V. Baranov, *Sotsial'no-demograficheskoe razvitie krupnogo goroda* (Moscow: Finansy i statistika, 1981), 70.

161. Elliott, "Soviet Socialist Stars," 281.

162. Tatiana Fedotovskaia, "Regulirovanie chislennosti naseleniia—opyt Moskvy," in Valentei, *O naselenii Moskvy*, 60.

163. Perevedentsev, *Molodezh'*, 108.

164. Tolokontseva and Romanenkovoi, *Demografiia i ekologiia krupnogo goroda*, 35.

165. B. S. Khorev, *Urbanizatsiia i demograficheskie protsessi* (Moscow: Finansy i statistika, 1982), 178.

166. B. S. Khorev and V. N. Chapek, *Problemy izucheniia migratsiia naseleniia* (Moscow: Mysl, 1978), 197.

167. George M. Armstrong, "Control of Mobility of Labor in the Soviet Union," *Journal of International and Comparative Law* 3, no. 172 (1982): 191.

168. Shearer, "Elements Near and Alien," 880.

169. Narynbek Temirkulov, interview, 11 July 2007.

170. Houston, "Administrative Control of Migration," 40.

171. Azamat Sanatbaev, interview, 14 July 2009.

172. Anarbek Zakirov, interview, 9 August 2009.

173. On the limited *propiska*, see Loeber, "*Limitchiki.*"

174. Jeremy Azrael, ed., *Soviet Nationality Policy and Practices* (New York: Praeger, 1978), 370.

175. Elliott, "Soviet Socialist Stars," 275.

176. Victor Zaslavsky, *The Neo-Stalinist State: Class, Ethnicity, and Consensus in Soviet Society* (Armonk, NY: M. E. Sharpe, 1982), 144; see also Loeber, "*Limitchiki*," 304.

177. Loeber, "*Limitchiki*," 305.

178. On the number of *limitchiki* who migrated independently in search of work, see Elliott, "Soviet Socialist Stars," 284.

179. Tolkunbek Kudubaev, interview, 15 November 2008.

180. Shuhrat Ikramov, interview, 18 September 2007.

181. Stephen Castles and Mark J. Miller, *The Age of Migration: International Population Movements in the Modern World* (New York: Guilford, 1998), 20.

182. David Lambert and Alan Lester, *Colonial Lives across the British Empire* (Cambridge: Cambridge University Press, 2006), 21–24.

183. Tanja Blokland et al., "Urban Citizenship and the Right to the City: The Fragmentation of Claims," *International Journal of Urban and Regional Research* 39, no. 4 (2015): 655–65. DOI: 10.1111/1468-2427.12259.

2. FRIENDSHIP, FREEDOM, MOBILITY, AND THE ELDER BROTHER

1. Scott, *Familiar Strangers*, 22.

2. Valentei, *O naselenii Moskvy*, 3.

3. Barbara H. Rosenwein, "Worrying about Emotions in History," *American Historical Review* 107, no. 3 (2002): 842. DOI: 10.1086/532498.

4. Christine Evans, "The 'Soviet Way of Life' as a Way of Feeling: Emotion and Influence on Soviet Central Television in the Brezhnev Era," *Cahiers du monde russe* 56, nos. 2–3 (2015): 567, https://www.jstor.org/stable/24567613.

5. Yurchak, *Everything Was Forever*, 19–27.

6. Yurchak, *Everything Was Forever*, 28.

7. Juliane Fürst, "Love, Peace and Rock 'n' Roll on Gorky Street: The 'Emotional Style' of the Soviet Hippie Community," *Contemporary European History* 23, no. 4 (2014): 568, https://doi.org/10.1017/S0960777314000320.

8. Reddy, "Emotional Turn?" 332–334.

9. Yurchak, *Everything Was Forever*, 8.

10. Said Nabiev, interview, 28 November 2007.

11. Nicole Eustace et al., "*AHR* Conversation: The Historical Study of Emotions," *American Historical Review* 117, no. 5 (2012): 1488.

12. On the importance of Nazism in state efforts to bind Soviet citizens through a language of internal and external enemies, see Serhy Yekelchyk, "The Civic Duty to Hate: Stalinist Citizenship as Political Practice and Civic Emotion (Kiev, 1943–53)," *Kritika* 7, no. 3 (2006): 531–32. DOI: 10.1353/kri.2006.0038.

13. Stalin as cited in Martin, *Affirmative Action Empire*, 439.

14. *Pravda*, cited in Ronald Grigor Suny, "The Contradictions of Identity: Being Soviet and National in the USSR and After," in Bassin and Kelly, *Soviet and Post-Soviet Identities*, 25.

15. *Izvestiia*, 8 July 1935. See also Anna Marie Whittington, "Making a Home for the Soviet People: World War II and the Origins of the *Sovetskii Narod*," in *Empire and Belonging in the Eurasian Borderlands*, ed. Krista A. Goff and Lewis H. Siegelbaum. (Ithaca, NY: Cornell University Press, 2019), 147–62.

16. Suny, "The Contradictions of Identity," 29.

17. Golfo Alexopoulos, "Soviet Citizenship, More or Less: Rights, Emotions, and States of Civic Belonging," *Kritika* 7, no. 3 (2006): 488. DOI: 10.1353/kri.2006.0030.

18. Serhy Yekelchyk, *Stalin's Citizens: Everyday Politics in the Wake of Total War* (Oxford: Oxford University Press, 2014), 2.

19. Alexopoulos, "Soviet Citizenship."522–26.

20. Alexopoulos, "Soviet Citizenship," 525.

21. Alexopoulos, "Soviet Citizenship," 527.

22. Yekelchyk, *Stalin's Citizens*, 3.

23. Elizabeth Perry, "Moving the Masses: Emotion Work in the Chinese Revolution," *Mobilization* 7, no. 2 (2002): 112.

24. Khapaeva, "Soviet and Post-Soviet Moscow," 172.

25. On Great Russian chauvinism, see Hélène Carrère d'Encausse, *Le grand défi: Bolcheviks et nations, 1917–1930* (Paris: Flammarion, 1987).

26. Martin, *Affirmative Action Empire*, 441.

27. Isabelle Kaplan, "The *Dekady* of the Art of the Caucasian Republics, 1937–1944" (unpublished manuscript, 2014). An edited version is available at https://drive.google.com /file/d/0B-eSQ2mo0JRxMDZZV3pvUEo5YVE/view (accessed 28 March 2018).

28. Cloé Drieu, *Fictions nationales: Cinéma, empire et nation en Ouzbékistan (1919–1937)* (Paris: Karthala, 2013).

29. Ali Igmen, *Speaking Soviet with an Accent: Culture and Power in Kyrgyzstan* (Pittsburgh: University of Pittsburgh Press, 2012), 111.

30. M. K. Nurmukhamedov, *Iz istorii russko-karakalpakskikh kul'turnykh sviazei* (Tashkent: Izdatel'stvo "Fan" UzSSR, 1974), 63.

31. Said Nabiev, interview, 28 November 2007.

32. Moritz Florin, "Becoming Soviet through War: The Kyrgyz and the Great Fatherland War," *Kritika* 17, no. 3 (2016): 502. DOI: 10.1353/kri.2016.0033.

33. On the millions of Soviet evacuees received in Uzbekistan, see Manley, *To the Tashkent Station*.

34. Florin, "Becoming Soviet through War," 515.

35. On the ideals of pride and sacrifice, see Suny, "The Contradictions of Identity," 32.

36. Farshad Hajiev, interview, 11 November 2007.

37. Jumaboi Esoev, interview, 17 November 2007.

38. Fridon Tsereteli, interview, 12 October 2007.

39. Jasur Haydarov, interview, 23 July 2009.

40. Lowell Tillett, *The Great Friendship: Soviet Historians on the Non-Russian Nationalities* (Chapel Hill: University of North Carolina Press, 1980).

41. Marat Tursunbaev, interview, 15 May 2007.

42. Asylbek Albiev, interview, 8 July 2009.

43. Joseph Stalin, "Toast to the Great Russian People," Seventeen Moments in Soviet History, http://soviethistory.msu.edu/1947-2/eight-hundred-years-of-moscow/eight-hundred-years-of-moscow-texts/toast-to-the-great-russian-people/ (accessed 15 June 2017).

44. Arup Banerji, *Writing History in the Soviet Union: Making the Past Work* (New York: Routledge, 2018), 74–76.

45. Tillett, *The Great Friendship*, 180.

46. Oksana Karpenko, "'Prison of the Peoples' and 'Friendship of Peoples' in Soviet and Post-Soviet History Textbooks of the USSR/Russia," in *Myths and Conflict in the South Caucasus*, vol. 1, *Instrumentalisation of Historical Narratives*, ed. Oksana Karpenko and Jana Javakhishvili (London: International Alert, 2013), 152, https://www.international-alert.org/sites/default/files/Caucasus_MythsConflict_Vol1_EN_2013.pdf.

47. Peter A. Blitstein, "Cultural Diversity and the Interwar Conjuncture: Soviet Nationality Policy in Its Comparative Context," *Slavic Review* 65, no. 2 (2006): 293. DOI: 10.2307/4148593.

48. Whittington, "Making a Home."

49. Florin, "Becoming Soviet through War," 506.

50. Whittington, "Forging Soviet Citizens: Ideology, Stability, and Identity in the Soviet Union," 353–55.

51. Whittington, "Forging Soviet Citizens," 358–59.

52. Mirbek Serkebaev, interview, 3 August 2009.

53. Elmira Nasirova, interview, 11 July 2007.

54. Akmal Bobokulov, interview, 13 November 2007.

55. Bakyt Shakiev, interview, 8 August 2009.

56. Sevda Asgarova, interview, 14 July 2009.

57. Yurchak, *Everything Was Forever*, 85.

58. Abdul Khalimov, interview, 30 November 2007.

59. Martin, *Affirmative Action Empire*, 449.

60. *Pravda*, 2 January 1961.

61. Evans, "The 'Soviet Way of Life,'" 344.

62. Scott, *Familiar Strangers*, 101.

63. The importance of Lenin's mausoleum in migrant incorporation is discussed in chapter 3.

64. See Obertreis, *Imperial Desert Dreams*, 222–30.

65. Jasur Haydarov, interview, 23 July 2009.

66. On the Tashkent earthquake and the city's reconstruction, see Nigel Raab, *All Shook Up: The Shifting Soviet Response to Catastrophes, 1917–1991* (Montreal: McGill-Queens University Press, 2017), 65–122.

67. *Pavil'on Uzbekskoi SSR* (Tashkent: Gosizdat UzSSR, 1961), 61.

68. *Pravda*, 24 February 1980.

69. *Pravda*, 16 June 1980. On the Olympiads, see RGASPI, f. M1, op. 39, d. 642, l. 1.

70. *Pravda*, 16 June 1980.

71. Bernaskoni, *Moskva—dlia vsekh stolitsa*, 11.

72. Bernaskoni, *Moskva—dlia vsekh stolitsa*, 19.

73. Elmira Kafarova, "S Moskvoiu v serdtse," in Bernaskoni, *Moskva—dlia vsekh stolitsa*, 166.

74. Dzh. Tashibekova, "Sovetskoe chudo," in Bernaskoni, *Moskva—dlia vsekh stolitsa*, 244.

75. *Pravda Vostoka*, 1 August 1967.

76. Mirbek Serkebaev, interview, 3 August 2009.

77. Aryan Shirinov, interview, 12 November 2007.

78. Narynbek Temirkulov, interview, 11 July 2007.

79. Scott, *Familiar Strangers*, 163.

80. Yekelchyk, *Stalin's Citizens*, 4.

81. Yuri Slezkine, "The USSR as a Communal Apartment, or How the USSR Promoted Ethnic Particularism," *Slavic Review* 53, no. 2 (1994): 448. DOI: 10.2307/2501300.

82. On emotional performances, see Eustace et al., "*AHR* Conversation," 1497–98.

83. Martin, *Affirmative Action Empire*, 440.

84. Kaplan, "*Dekady.*"

85. Martin, *Affirmative Action Empire*, 440.

86. On the creation of Soviet Central Asian nations, see Arne Haugen, *The Establishment of National Republics in Soviet Central Asia* (Basingstoke: Palgrave Macmillan, 2003).

87. Igmen, *Speaking Soviet with an Accent.*

88. Kaplan, "*Dekady.*"

89. TsGAPDKR, f. 56, op. 10, d. 441, l. 42.

90. TsGAPDKR, f. 56, op. 198, d. 165, ll. 42–43.

91. *Pravda Vostoka*, 5 October 1974.

92. *Pravda Vostoka*, 5 October 1974.

93. TsGAPDKR, f. 42, op. 15, d. 26, l. 42.

94. Scott, *Familiar Strangers*, 207.

95. Kaplan, "*Dekady.*"

96. *Tashkentskaia pravda*, 18 March 1966.

97. *Pravda Vostoka*, 5 January 1974.

98. *Pravda Vostoka*, 1 August 1967.

99. TsGAPDKR, f. 56, op. 198, d. 165, l. 45.

100. *Pravda Vostoka*, 5 October 1974.

101. TsGAPDKR, f. 56, op. 19, d. 165, l. 43.

102. *Pravda Vostoka*, 8 October 1974.

103. TsGAPDKR, f. 42, op. 15, d. 26, l. 7.

104. *Izvestiia*, 22 April 1982.

105. *Izvestiia*, 25 September 1982 and 20 May 1980.

106. Evans, "The 'Soviet Way of Life,'" 559.

107. Armenia refers to the Armenian SSR.

108. Fuad Ojagov, interview, 25 June 2009.

109. Monique Scheer, "Are Emotions a Kind of Practice (And Is That What Makes Them Have a History)? A Bourdieuian Approach to Understanding Emotion," *History and Theory* 51 (May 2012): 193–220. DOI: 10.1111/j.1468-2303.2012.00621.x.

110. See, for example, *Izvestiia*, 27 September 1982.

111. TsGAPDKR, f. 56, op. 198, d. 164, ll. 42–44.

112. TsGAPDKR, f. 56, op. 198, d. 164, l. 46.

113. Abdul Khalimov, interview, 30 November 2007.

114. Aryan Shirinov, interview, 12 November 2007.

115. Aryan Shirinov, interview, 12 November 2007.

116. Meerim Kalilova, interview, 17 July 2009.

117. Jumaboi Esoev, interview, 17 November 2007.

118. Shuhrat Ikramov, interview, 18 September 2007.

119. Yurchak, *Everything Was Forever*, 8.

120. Shuhrat Ikramov, interview, 18 September 2007.

121. Azamat Ormonbekov, interview, 16 July 2007.

122. Jumaboi Esoev, interview, 17 November 2007.

123. Fridon Tsereteli, interview, 12 October 2007.

124. Abdul Khalimov, interview, 30 November 2007.

125. Meerim Kalilova, interview, 17 July 2009.

126. Bolot Oruzbaev, interview, 8 July 2009.

127. Murad Imamaliev, interview, 8 February 2007.

128. Cited in Roman, "Making Caucasians Black," 4.

129. Igmen, *Speaking Soviet with an Accent*, 111.

130. TsGAPDKR, f. 56, op. 10, d. 306, l. 11.

131. Roman, "Making Caucasians Black," 5.

132. Shuhrat Ikramov, interview, 18 September 2007.

133. Farshad Hajiev, interview, 11 November 2007.

134. Erkin Bakchiev, interview, 9 August 2009.

135. Slezkine, "The USSR as a Communal Apartment," 449.

136. Sadig Eldarov, interview, 15 July 2009.

137. Aryuna Khamagova, interview, 12 February 2007.

138. Damira Nogoibaeva, interview, 6 August 2008.

139. Jasur Haydarov, interview, 23 July 2009.

140. Jyldyz Nuriaeva, interview, 9 July 2007.

141. Bakyt Shakiev, interview, 8 August 2009. Kazakhstan refers to the Kazakh SSR.

142. Maia Asinadze, interview, 29 November 2007.

143. Zurab Iashvili, interview, 23 January 2007.

144. Eliso Svanidze, interview, 24 July 2011.

145. Tamriko Otskheli, interview, 27 July 2011.

146. Aryuna Khamagova, interview, 12 February 2007.

147. Sadig Eldarov, interview, 15 July 2009.

148. Tolkunbek Kudubaev, interview, 15 November 2008.

149. Erkin Bakchiev, interview, 9 August 2009.

150. Aisulu Baisalbekova, interview, 26 August 2009.

151. Dylara Usmanova, interview, 3 December 2008.

152. Dina Ataniyazova, interview, 6 December 2008.

153. Dina Ataniyazova, interview, 6 December 2008.

154. Dylara Usmanova, interview, 3 December 2008.

155. Aibek Botoev, interview, 8 December 2007.

156. Abdul Khalimov, interview, 30 November 2007.

157. Farshad Hajiev, interview, 11 November 2007.

158. Elnur Asadov, interview, 5 June 2009.

159. Eliso Svanidze, interview, 24 July 2011.

160. Jyldyz Nuriaeva, interview, 9 July 2007.

161. Yurchak, *Everything Was Forever*, 8.

162. Farshad Hajiev, interview, 11 November 2007.

163. Maia Asinadze, interview, 29 November 2007.

164. Aliya Nurtaeva, interview, 25 October 2006.

165. On state policies toward the development of nations labeled "backward," see Hirsch, *Empire of Nations*.

166. Dina Ataniyazova, interview, 6 December 2008.

167. Aibek Botoev, interview, 8 December 2007.

3. MAKING A PLACE IN THE TWO CAPITALS

1. Akhil Gupta and James Ferguson, "Culture, Power, Place: Ethnography at the End of An Era" in *Culture, Power, Place: Explorations in Critical Anthropology*, ed. Akhil Gupta and James Ferguson (Durham, NC: Duke University Press, 1997), 6–8.

2. Zaslavsky, *The Neo-Stalinist State*, 153–54.

3. The average monthly salary in the mid-1970s was 135 rubles. Siegelbaum and Moch, "Transnationalism in One Country?," 985.

4. Koenker, *Club Red*, 230.

5. David Somkishvili, interview, 24 July 2011.

6. Mirbek Serkebaev, interview, 3 August 2009.

7. Azamat Sanatbaev, interview, 14 July 2009.

8. Elmira Nasirova, interview, 11 July 2007.

9. Eteri Gugushvili, interview, 26 July 2011.

10. Abdul Khalimov, interview, 30 November 2007.

11. Roth-Ey, "'Loose Girls,'" 75–95.

12. Florin, "Faites tomber les murs!," 190–94; Kalinovsky, "A Most Beautiful City," 827.

13. Sergei Abashin, *Sovetskii kishlak: Mezhdu kolonializmom i modernizatsiei* (Moscow: Novoe literaturnoe obozrenie, 2015).

14. Diana Ibañez-Tirado, "'How Can I Be Post-Soviet If I Was Never Soviet?' Rethinking Categories of Time and Social Change—a Perspective from Kulob, Southern Tajikistan," *Central Asian Survey* 34, no. 2 (2015): 195. DOI: 10.1080/02634937.2014.983705.

15. Anarbek Zakirov, interview, 9 August 2009.

16. Farshad Hajiev, interview, 11 November 2007.

17. Aibek Botoev, interview, 8 December 2007.

18. On the exodus of Russians from Central Asian villages in the 1970s and 1980s, see chapter 1. On Russian-language schooling, see chapter 2.

19. Abdul Khalimov, interview, 30 November 2007.

20. Jumaboi Esoev, interview, 17 November 2007.

21. Shuhrat Kazbekov, interview, 13 November 2007.

22. Blair Ruble, *Leningrad: Shaping a Soviet City* (Berkeley: University of California Press, 1990), 144.

23. Bolot Oruzbaev, interview, 8 July 2009.

24. Azamat Sanatbaev, interview, 14 July 2009.

25. Michael Ryan, *Doctors and the State in the Soviet Union* (New York: Palgrave Macmillan, 2016), 20–21.

26. Lali Utiashvili, interview, 29 November 2007.

27. Eljan Jusubov, interview, 5 June 2009.

28. Aibek Botoev, interview, 8 December 2007.

29. Abdul Khalimov, interview, 30 November 2007.

30. Farshad Hajiev, interview, 11 November 2007.

31. Erkin Bakchiev, interview, 9 August 2009.

32. Fuad Ojagov, interview, 25 June 2009.

33. Bruce Grant, "Cosmopolitan Baku," *Ethnos* 75, no. 2 (2010): 123–47. DOI: 10.1080/00141841003753222.

34. Dina Ataniyazova, interview, 6 December 2008.

35. Shuhrat Kazbekov, interview, 13 November 2007.

36. Jyldyz Nuriaeva, interview, 9 July 2007.

37. Leslie Herzberger, *The Rise and Fall of a Thermidorian Society: Why the Soviet Union Came Apart, 1917–1991; A Case Study* (Bloomington, IN: Xlibris, 2007), 248.

38. Bolot Oruzbaev, interview, 8 July 2009.

39. Sadig Eldarov, interview, 15 July 2009.

40. Nino Kvernadze, interview, 23 July 2011. For a discussion of *orgnabor*, see chapter 1.

41. Rasul Asgarov, interview, 12 June 2009.

42. In 1961, the state issued a "decree against avoiding socially useful work," which Asgarov feared might ensnare him. See Alexandra Oberländer, "Cushy Work, Backbreaking

Leisure: Late Soviet Work Ethics Reconsidered," *Kritika* 18, no. 3 (2017): 581. DOI: 10.1353/kri.2017.0036.

43. Vazha Gigulashvili, interview, 23 July 2011.

44. Eteri Gugushvili, interview, 26 July 2011.

45. Alex Koberidze, interview, 2 April 2009.

46. Florin, "Faites tomber les murs!," 205.

47. Authorities in Kyrgyzstan had petitioned to allow its students to attend PTUs in Leningrad as early as 1971. TsAPDKR, f. 56, op. 178, d. 4, l. 57. On the numbers in Leningrad, see Ruble, *Leningrad*, 150.

48. Bakyt Shakiev, interview, 8 August 2009.

49. Aisulu Baisalbekova, interview, 26 August 2009.

50. Aslybek Albiev, interview, 8 July 2009.

51. Tolkunbek Kudubaev, interview, 15 November 2008.

52. The limited residence permit is discussed in chapter 1.

53. Farshad Hajiev, interview, 11 November 2007.

54. Jumaboi Esoev, interview, 17 November 2007.

55. Lali Utiashvili, interview, 29 November 2007.

56. Scott, *Familiar Strangers*.

57. Terenti Papashvili, interview, 25 July 2011.

58. Levan Rukhadze, interview, 25 November 2007.

59. Tamriko Otskheli, interview, 27 July 2011.

60. Levan Rukhadze, interview, 25 November 2007.

61. Angermiuller, "Ot natsional'nogo patriotizma do etnicheskogo dal'tonizma: Armiane Sankt-Peterburga v biograficheskoi perspective," 277.

62. Maia Asinadze, interview, 29 November 2007.

63. Maia Asinadze, interview, 29 November 2007.

64. Gupta and Ferguson, "Beyond 'Culture,'" 12.

65. Rasma Karklins, *Ethnic Relations in the U.S.S.R.: The Perspective from Below* (Boston: Allen & Unwin, 1985), 213.

66. Damira Nogoibaeva, interview, 6 August 2008.

67. Hazi Begirov, interview, 25 June 2009.

68. Jumaboi Esoev, interview, 17 November 2007.

69. These tensions are discussed in chapter 6.

70. Hazi Begirov, interview, 25 June 2009.

71. David Somkishvili, interview, 24 July 2011.

72. Aibek Botoev, interview, 8 December 2007.

73. Aibek Botoev, interview, 8 December 2007. On the Leningrad-Moscow rivalry, see O. I. Vendina, "Moskva i Peterburg: Istoriia ob istorii sopernichestva rossiiskikh stolits," *Politiia* 26, no. 3 (2002): 13–28.

74. Jyldyz Nuriaeva, interview, 9 July 2007.

75. Race and racism is discussed in chapter 4.

76. Marat Tursunbaev, interview, 15 May 2007.

77. Gulnara Alieva, interview, 5 May 2007.

78. Maia Asinadze, interview, 29 November 2007; Akmal Bobokulov, interview, 13 November 2007.

79. Fridon Tsereteli, interview, 12 October 2007.

80. Narynbek Temirkulov, interview, 11 July 2007.

81. Anarbek Zakirov, interview, 9 August 2009.

82. Abdul Khalimov, interview, 30 November 2007.

83. On the Jewish experience in the Soviet Union, see Yuri Slezkine, *The Jewish Century* (Princeton, NJ: Princeton University Press, 2004).

84. Karpenko, "Byt' 'natsional'nym,'" 53.

85. Gulnara Alieva, interview, 5 May 2007.

86. Katsakioris, "Burden or Allies?" See this discussion in chapter 1.

87. Elmira Nasirova, interview, 11 July 2007. Issues of discrimination against Africans are explored in chapter 4.

88. Saule Iskakova, interview, 10 July 2007.

89. Studies of interethnic mobility unsurprisingly consider migrants' ability to speak a host city's language as the strongest correlate for self-described success. See Barry R. Chiswick and Paul W. Miller, "Immigrant Enclaves, Ethnic Goods, and the Adjustment Process," in *From Arrival to Incorporation: Migrants to the U.S. in a Global Era*, ed. Elliott Barkan, Hasia Diner, and Alan M. Kraut (New York: New York University Press, 2007), 89–90. On the importance of language to acculturation, see Jonathan Laurence and Justin Vaisse, *Integrating Islam: Political and Religious Challenges in Contemporary France* (Washington, DC: Brookings Institution Press, 2006), 43.

90. Angermiuller, "Ot natsional'nogo patriotizma," 267.

91. Asylbek Albiev, interview, 8 July 2009.

92. Maia Asinadze, interview, 29 November 2007.

93. Aryuna Khamagova, interview, 12 February 2007.

94. Rafael Voskanyan, interview, 25 November 2007.

95. Gulnara Alieva, interview, 5 May 2007.

96. Jumaboi Esoev, interview, 17 November 2007.

97. On memories of home as a cushioning device, see Peter Kabachnik, Joanna Regulska, and Beth Mitchneck, "Where and When Is Home? The Double Displacement of Georgian IDPs from Abkhazia," *Journal of Refugee Studies* 23, no. 3 (2010): 315–36. DOI: 10.1093/jrs/feq023. On links between home and away, see Giulia Sinatti, "Home Is Where the Heart Abides: Migration, Return and Housing in Dakar, Senegal," *Open House International* 34, no. 3 (2009): 49–55.

98. On "cultural scripts" and their importance in relating home and away, see Ada Ingrid Engebrigtsen, "Kinship, Gender, and Adaptation Processes in Exile: The Case of Tamil and Somali Families in Norway," *Journal of Ethnic and Migration Studies* 33, no. 5 (2007): 727. DOI: 10.1080/13691830701359173.

99. Azamat Sanatbaev, interview, 14 July 2009.

100. Eteri Gugushvili, interview, 26 July 2011.

101. Aryan Shirinov, interview, 12 November 2007.

102. Jumaboi Esoev, interview, 17 November 2007.

103. Farshad Hajiev, interview, 11 November 2007.

104. Marat Tursunbaev, interview, 15 May 2007.

105. Gulnara Alieva, interview, 5 May 2007.

106. Abdul Khalimov, interview, 30 November 2007.

107. Hazi Begirov, interview, 25 June 2009.

108. Shuhrat Kazbekov, interview, 13 November 2007.

109. Farshad Hajiev, interview, 11 November 2007.

110. Irma Balanchivadze, interview, 23 July 2011.

111. David Somkishvili, interview, 24 July 2011.

112. Eliso Svanidze, interview, 24 July 2011.

113. Maia Asinadze, interview, 29 November 2007.

114. Maia Asinadze, interview, 29 November 2007.

115. Sadig Eldarov, interview, 15 July 2009.

116. Damira Nogoibaeva, interview, 6 August 2008.

117. Aryan Shirinov, interview, 12 November 2007.

118. Lali Utiashvili, interview, 29 November 2007.

119. Akmal Bobokulov, interview, 13 November 2007.

120. Steven E. Harris, *Communism on Tomorrow Street: Mass Housing and Everyday Life after Stalin* (Washington, DC: Woodrow Wilson Center Press; Baltimore: Johns Hopkins University Press, 2013).

121. Said Nabiev, interview, 28 November 2007.

122. Zarecor, "What Was So Socialist," 12.

123. Elliott, "Soviet Socialist Stars," 285.

124. On Moscow's housing system, see Timothy Colton, *Moscow: Governing the Socialist Metropolis* (Cambridge, MA: Harvard University Press, 1996), 459–63. See also Mervyn Matthews, *The Passport Society: Controlling Movement in Russia and the USSR* (Boulder, CO: Westview, 1993).

125. Zarecor, "What Was So Socialist," 15.

126. Massey, *Space, Place, and Gender*, 152.

127. On the role of the nation-state in shaping the complex process of balancing ideas and ideals of original and adopted homes, see introduction to *Uprootings/Regroundings: Questions of Home and Migration*, ed. Sara Ahmed et al. (Oxford, UK: Berg, 2003), 4.

128. The literature on dormitory life is scant. See V. N. Gorlov, "Sovetskie obshchezhitiia rabochei molodezhi," *Otechestvennaia istoriia*, no. 5 (2004): 177–80; Sergei Korolev, "The Student Dormitory in the 'Period of Stagnation,'" *Russian Politics and Law* 42, no. 2 (2004): 77–93. DOI: 10.1080/10611940.2004.11066915. On nationality and housing in the USSR and elsewhere, see Richard H. Rowland, "Nationality Population Distribution, Redistribution, and Degree of Separation in Moscow, 1979–1989," *Nationalities Papers* 26, no. 4 (1998): 705–22. On the French system of housing immigrants in suburban *cités*, see Silverstein, *Algeria in France*. On British and U.S. patterns, see Nancy Foner, *In a New Land: A Comparative View of Immigration* (New York: New York University Press, 2005).

129. Chiswick and Miller, "Immigrant Enclaves," 90; Foner, *In a New Land*, 120.

130. Saule Iskakova, interview, 10 July 2007.

131. Aryan Shirinov, interview, 12 November 2007.

132. Murad Imamaliev, interview, 8 February 2007.

133. Farshad Hajiev, interview, 11 November 2007.

134. Anarbek Zakirov, interview, 9 August 2009.

135. Aryuna Khamagova, interview, 12 February 2007.

136. Dina Ataniyazova, interview, 6 December 2008.

137. Maxim Matusevich, "Probing the Limits of Internationalism: African Students Confront Soviet Ritual," *Anthropology of East Europe Review* 27, no. 2 (2009): 24.

138. Katsakioris, "Burden or Allies?," 547–48.

139. Elliott, "Soviet Socialist Stars," 284. Elliott cites a report of the Liublinskii raionnyi komitet narodnogo kontrolia in the Central State Archive of the City of Moscow, f. 974, op. 1, d. 11.

140. Tolkunbek Kudubaev, interview, 15 November 2008.

141. Moscow district reports found working conditions far better than living ones. Elliott, "Soviet Socialist Stars," 285.

142. Terenti Papashvili, interview, 25 July 2011.

143. Narynbek Temirkulov, interview, 11 July 2007.

144. Farshad Hajiev, interview, 11 November 2007.

4. RACE AND RACISM

1. See the discussion in chapter 1.

2. On the link between broader trends of movement in the former British empire and everyday encounters between migrants and the host society, see Joanna Herbert et al.,

"Multicultural Living? Experiences of Everyday Racism among Ghanaian Immigrants in London," *European Urban and Regional Studies* 15, no. 2 (2008): 106. DOI: 10.1177/0969776407087544.

3. Soviet media continually noted the second-class legal status of blacks in the United States, locating examples that stretched throughout the Soviet period. See Charles Quist-Adade, *In the Shadows of the Kremlin and the White House: Africa's Media Image from Communism to Post-Communism* (Lanham, MD: University Press of America, 2001).

4. Goldberg, "Racial Europeanization," 344.

5. Hall and Rose, "Introduction: Being at Home with the Empire," 22–23.

6. Fields and Fields, *Racecraft*, 16.

7. Rogers Brubaker, "Ethnicity, Race and Nationalism," *Annual Review of Sociology* 35 (2009): 22. DOI: 10.1146/annurev-soc-070308-115916.

8. Claire Alexander, "Beyond Black: Re-thinking the Colour/Culture Divide," *Ethnic and Racial Studies* 25, no. 4 (2002): 552–71. DOI: 10.1080/01419870220136637.

9. On the socioeconomic element of racial prejudice in Europe, see Katrine Fangen, Nils Hammarén, and Thomas Johansson, "Margins and Centres," in *Young Migrants: Exclusion and Belonging in Europe*, ed. Katrine Fangen, Thomas Johansson, and Nils Hammarén (Basingstoke: Palgrave Macmillan, 2012), 205.

10. On the idea of European superiority taking root among non-European populations, see Thapan, "Imagined and Social Landscapes," 58.

11. On Soviet spatial hierarchies, see Pilkington, "'The Future Is Ours,'" 378.

12. On hierarchies of power and their effects in situations of migration, see introduction to *Uprootings/Regroundings*, ed. Ahmed et al., 4.

13. On the use of ideas of discipline and dignity to underlie alternate hierarchies, see Michèle Lamont, *The Dignity of Working Men: Morality and the Boundaries of Race, Class, and Immigration* (Cambridge, MA: Harvard University Press, 2000), 172.

14. David Mellor et al., "The Perception of Racism in Ambiguous Scenarios," *Journal of Ethnic and Migration Studies* 27, no. 3 (2001): 474. DOI: 10.1080/13691830124387.

15. Floris Müller has noted in her research in contemporary Europe that even remarks from members of the host society perceived as "harmless compliments," such as on one's language ability, are understood as marking difference. Floris Müller, "Communicating Anti-racism" (PhD diss., University of Amsterdam, 2009), 32.

16. On the act of being classified, see Philomena Essed, *Understanding Everyday Racism: An Interdisciplinary Theory* (London: Sage, 1991), 273. On classification and boundary marking in the Soviet/post-Soviet cases, see Larisa Kosygina, "The Russian Migration Regime and Migrants' Experiences: The Case of Non-Russian Nationals from Former Soviet Republics" (PhD diss., University of Birmingham, 2009).

17. Marat Tursunbaev, interview, 15 May 2007.

18. Katsakioris, "Burden or Allies?," 556.

19. Aryuna Khamagova, interview, 12 February 2007. On the role of Chukchis (an ethnic group from the Soviet north) in Soviet humor, see Emil Draitser *Taking Penguins to the Movies: Ethnic Humor in Russia* (Detroit: Wayne State University Press, 1998), 75–100.

20. The citation continues: "Suddenly Sasha finds herself missing Brooklyn, where people simply called each other motherfucker." Anya Ulinich, *Petropolis* (London: Penguin, 2007), 281.

21. Aryuna Khamagova, interview, 12 February 2007.

22. The host society's focus on relationships between outsider men and local women may stem from the overwhelming majority of early migrants from postcolonial states being male, or may have different, gendered implications that lie beyond this study's scope. On tensions in France and Great Britain, see Paul A. Silverstein, "Thin Lines on the Pavement: The Racialization and Spatialization of Violence in Postcolonial (Sub)Urban

France," in *Gendering Urban Space in the Middle East, South Asia, and Africa*, ed. Martina Rieker and Kamran Ali (New York: Palgrave Macmillan, 2008), 169–205; John Solomos, *Race and Racism in Britain*, 3rd ed. (Basingstoke: Palgrave Macmillan, 2003). On the connection between European and Soviet reactions to interracial dating, see Julie Hessler, "Death of an African Student in Moscow: Race, Politics, and the Cold War," *Cahiers du monde russe* 47, no. 1 (2006): 36–38.

23. Hessler, "Death of an African Student," 34.

24. On the 1958 race riots, see Solomos, *Race and Racism*, 54–55. On Soviet policing, see Nikolai Mitrokhin, *Russkaia partiia: Dvizhenie russkikh natsionalistov v SSSR, 1953–1985 gody* (Moscow: Novoe literaturnoe obozrenie, 2003), 52.

25. Stephen Shenfield, *Russian Fascism: Traditions, Tendencies and Movements*, 2nd ed. (London: Routledge, 2001), 40.

26. Solzhenitsyn, quoted in Hyung-min Joo, "The Soviet Origin of Russian Chauvinism: Voices from Below," *Communist and Post-Communist Studies* 41 (2008): 224, https://doi.org/10.1016/j.postcomstud.2008.03.002.

27. Mitrokhin, *Russkaia partiia*, 47; S. Enders Wimbush, "Great Russians and the Soviet State: The Dilemmas of Ethnic Dominance," in *Soviet Nationality Policy and Practices*, ed. Azrael, 352.

28. Emin Gazyumov, interview, 19 March 2009.

29. Aibek Botoev, interview, 8 December 2007.

30. Karpenko, "Byt′ 'natsional′nym,'" 70.

31. Jyldyz Nuriaeva, interview, 9 July 2007; Gulnara Alieva, interview, 5 May 2007.

32. Anarbek Zakirov, interview, 9 August 2009.

33. Dina Ataniyazova, interview, 6 December 2008.

34. Fuad Ojagov, interview, 25 June 2009.

35. Mitrokhin, *Russkaia partiia*.

36. Mirbek Serkebaev, interview, 3 August 2009.

37. Levan Rukhadze, interview, 25 November 2007; Dea Kochladze, interview, 26 November 2007.

38. Charles Quist-Adade, personal communication, 27 June 2008.

39. Karpenko, "Byt′ 'natsional′nym,'" 48.

40. Parents of different national groups could choose either nationality for their child, but various accounts told of bribes being accepted to have the child declared ethnically Russian. Galina Beliaeva, Denis Draguskii, and Liliia Zotova, "Mnogonatsional′nyi mir Moskvy," *Druzhba narodov*, no. 4 (1993): 147–48.

41. Dina Ataniyazova, interview, 6 December 2008.

42. Fuad Ojagov, interview, 25 June 2009.

43. On the boundedness of the friendship of peoples, as well as its hierarchical nature, see Roman, "Making Caucasians Black." On the biogenetic link, see Karpenko "Byt′ 'natsional′nym,'" 48, 65; Beliaeva, Draguskii, and Zotova, "Mnogonatsional′nyi mir Moskvy," 138.

44. See chapter 1 for this system.

45. Gulnara Alieva, interview, 5 May 2007. On the role of "quotas" for various national groups in Soviet institutes of higher education in Moscow, see Karklins, *Ethnic Relations in the U.S.S.R.*, 110.

46. Azay Husynov, interview, 28 June 2009.

47. Karklins, *Ethnic Relations in the U.S.S.R.*, 92.

48. Shuhrat Ikramov, interview, 18 September 2007.

49. Aryuna Khamagova, interview, 12 February 2007.

50. Goldberg, "Racial Europeanization," 347.

51. Hessler, "Death of an African Student," 37; Katsakioris, "Burden or Allies?," 662.

52. Hessler, "Death of an African Student," 50–54.

53. Katsakioris, "Burden or Allies?," 555.

54. Mitrokhin, *Russkaia partiia*, 63; Quist-Adade, personal communication.

55. See chapter 3. Aibek Botoev, interview, 8 December 2007.

56. Victor Shnirelman, "Migrantofobiia i 'kul'turnyi rasizm,'" *Ab Imperio*, no. 2 (2008): 291.

57. On the tsarist period, see Sahadeo, *Russian Colonial Society in Tashkent*.

58. See Eric Lohr, *Nationalizing the Russian Empire: The Campaign against Enemy Aliens during World War I* (Cambridge, MA: Harvard University Press, 2003); Alan M. Ball, *Russia's Last Capitalists: The Nepmen, 1921–1929* (Berkeley: University of California Press, 1990).

59. On dirty labor in London, see Herbert et al., "Multicultural Living?," 108. On the racialization of the European underclass, see Malcolm Cross and Michael Keith, eds., *Racism, the City and the State* (London: Routledge, 1992).

60. Mitrokhin, *Russkaia partiia*, 62. Mitrokhin notes that this literature revived in a different fashion the myth of Caucasus peoples as exploiting Russians, which had a political bent under Stalin's rule.

61. Draitser, *Taking Penguins to the Movies*, 35–55.

62. Scott, *Familiar Strangers*, 171.

63. *Diaspory: Predstavitel'stva natsional'nostei v Moskve i ikh deiatel'nost'* (Moscow: TsPI, 2003), 3.

64. Mitrokhin, *Russkaia partiia*, 65; Scott, *Familiar Strangers*, 191.

65. Karklins, *Ethnic Relations in the U.S.S.R.*, 92.

66. Elnur Asadov, interview, 5 June 2009.

67. Emin Gazyumov, interview, 19 March 2009.

68. Eljan Jusubov, interview, 5 June 2009.

69. Lena Sawyer, "Voices of Migrants: Solidarity and Resistance," in *Identity, Belonging and Migration*, ed. Gerard Delanty, Ruth Wodak, and Paul Jones (Liverpool: Liverpool University Press, 2008), 241–58.

70. See chapter 1.

71. Essed, *Understanding Everyday Racism*, 77.

72. Thomas, *Black France*, 42.

73. Dea Kochladze, interview, 26 November 2007.

74. Rafael Voskanyan, interview, 25 November 2007.

75. Narynbek Temirkulov, interview, 11 July 2007.

76. Shuhrat Kazbekov, interview, 13 November 2007.

77. Farshad Hajiev, interview, 11 November 2007.

78. Eljan Jusubov, interview, 5 June 2009.

79. Abdul Khalimov, interview, 30 November 2007.

80. Dea Kochladze, interview, 26 November 2007.

81. Bolot Oruzbaev, interview, 8 July 2009.

82. Herbert et al., "Multicultural Living?," 108.

83. Sawyer, "Voices of Migrants," 246.

84. Julie Hessler notes African student efforts to develop a society outside of state structures. After overcoming significant hurdles, the Federation of African Students in the Soviet Union formed in the early 1960s but was never an effective advocate. Hessler, "Death of an African Student," 42–43.

85. Respondents often subsume their experiences within an overall narrative that highlights initial trials followed by success, measured in terms of incorporation with a dominant culture. Kenneth J. Bindas, "Re-remembering a Segregated Past: Race in American Memory," *History and Memory* 22, no. 1 (2010): 125, https://muse.jhu.edu/article/376350;

Janis Wilton, "Identity, Racism, and Multiculturalism: Chinese-Australian Responses," in Benmayor and Skotnes, *Migration and Identity*, 89.

86. Karpenko, "Byt' 'natsional'nym,'" 47.

87. Maia Asinadze, interview, 29 November 2007.

88. On the rise of the Right among ethnic Russians in the USSR and associated prejudice toward Asian populations, see Roman, "Making Caucasians Black"; Alexander Yanov, *The Russian New Right: Right-Wing Ideologies in the Contemporary USSR* (Berkeley: Institute of International Studies, University of California, 1978); John Bushnell, *Moscow Graffiti: Language and Subculture* (Boston: Unwin Hyman, 1990); A. V. Malashenko, F. M. Mukhametshin, and L. R. Siukiiainen, *Musul'mane izmeniaiushcheisia Rossii* (Moscow: ROSSPEN, 2002).

89. On the role of ethnic neighborhoods in creating boundaries between postcolonial migrants and the host society in Europe, see Robert Alzetta, "Building a Home," in *Young Migrants*, ed. Fangen, Johansson, and Hammarén, 174; Cross and Keith, *Racism, the City and the State*.

90. Such attitudes were shared by Russians from outside the capitals, who were also lured by Leningrad's and especially Moscow's relative riches. See Raleigh, *Russia's Sputnik Generation*, 224–28.

91. Damira Nogoibaeva, interview, 6 August 2008.

92. On this linkage in the late imperial and early Soviet eras, see Sahadeo, *Russian Colonial Society in Tashkent*.

93. John Dunlop, *The Faces of Contemporary Russian Nationalism* (Princeton, NJ: Princeton University Press, 2014), 159.

94. More fieldwork is needed to reach strong conclusions. This project did not seek to interview ethnic Russians on intra-ethnic discrimination.

95. Alexander, "Beyond Black," 559.

96. Eljan Jusubov, interview, 5 June 2009. On modernization and the Soviet city, see Lewin, *The Gorbachev Phenomenon*.

97. Jyldyz Nuriaeva, interview, 9 July 2007.

98. Jyldyz Nuriaeva, interview, 9 July 2007.

99. Aryan Shirinov, interview, 12 November 2007.

100. Thapan, "Imagined and Social Landscapes," 58.

101. Goldberg, "Racial Europeanization," 347.

102. Marat Tursunbaev, interview, 15 May 2007.

103. See chapter 1 for the place of Tatars in imperial and early Soviet Moscow.

104. Karpenko, "Byt' 'natsional'nym,'" 52.

105. Fuad Ojagov, interview, 25 June 2009.

106. Bolot Oruzbaev, interview, 8 July 2009.

107. Azamat Sanatbaev, interview, 14 July 2009.

108. On the avoidance of "pure outsiderhood," see Kitty Calavita, *Immigrants at the Margins: Law, Race and Exclusion in Southern Europe* (Cambridge: Cambridge University Press, 2005), 14.

109. On how these stereotypes developed and worked in ethnic humor, see Draitser, *Taking Penguins to the Movies*.

110. On these stereotypes, see Quist-Adade, *In the Shadows of the Kremlin*, 57, 90; Matusevich, "Probing the Limits of Internationalism."

111. Quist-Adade, personal communication.

112. Farshad Hajiev, interview, 11 November 2007.

113. Katsakioris, "Burden or Allies?," 557; Hessler, "Death of an African Student," 36.

114. Katsakioris, "Burden or Allies?," 560; Matusevich, "Probing the Limits of Internationalism."

115. Quist-Adade, *In the Shadows of the Kremlin*, 82.

116. Fuad Ojagov, interview, 25 June 2009; Matusevich, "Probing the Limits of Internationalism."

117. Shuhrat Kazbekov, interview, 13 November 2007.

118. Farshad Hajiev, interview, 11 November 2007.

119. Mitrokhin, *Russkaia partiia*, 62.

120. Aibek Botoev, interview, 8 December 2007.

121. L. V. Ostapenko and I. A. Subbotina, "Problemy sotsial'no-ekonomicheskoi adaptatsii vykhodtsev iz Zakavkaz'ia v Moskve," *Diaspory*, no. 1 (2000): 40–59.

122. Irina L. Isaakyan, "Blood and Soil of the Soviet Academy: Politically Institutionalized Anti-Semitism in the Moscow Academic Circles of the Brezhnev Era through the Life Stories of Russian Academic Emigrants," *Nationalities Papers* 36, no. 5 (2008): 834. DOI: 10.1080/00905990802373520.

123. Gulnara Alieva, interview, 5 May 2007.

124. Sadig Eldarov, interview, 15 July 2009.

125. Azamat Sanatbaev, interview, 11 November 2007. Bakyt Shakiev, interview, 8 August 2009. On hazing in the Soviet army, see Roger R. Reese, *The Soviet Military Experience: A History of the Soviet Army, 1917–1991* (London: Routledge, 2000).

126. Yurchak, *Everything Was Forever*, 85.

127. Elmira Nasirova, interview, 11 July 2007.

128. Nurlanbek Satilganov and Aizada Satilganova, interview, 12 July 2007.

129. Damira Nogoibaeva, interview, 6 August 2008.

130. On language of equality in the West, see Essed, *Understanding Everyday Racism*, 6–21.

131. Romain Garbaye, "British Cities and Ethnic Minorities in the Post-war Era: From Xenophobic Agitation to Multi-ethnic Government," *Immigrants and Minorities* 22, nos. 2–3 (2003): 298–315. DOI: 10.1080/0261928042000244880.

132. Silverstein, *Algeria in France*, 163.

133. Walter J. Nicholls, "Fragmenting Citizenship: Dynamics of Cooperation and Conflict in France's Immigration Rights Movement," *Ethnic and Racial Studies* 36, no. 4 (2013): 611–31. DOI: 10.1080/01419870.2011.626055.

134. On other European cases, see, for example, Calavita, *Immigrants at the Margins*. Elsewhere in Europe, initially only small minorities of migrants had the means or knowledge to use state protections to their advantage. That number has grown significantly over the late twentieth century to today, whereas tools available for post-Soviet migrants have significantly declined.

135. Roman, "Making Caucasians Black," 4.

136. Said Nabiev, interview, 28 November 2007.

137. Maia Asinadze, interview, 29 November 2007.

138. Aliya Nuriaeva, interview, 25 October 2006.

139. See this discussion in chapters 2 and 3.

140. Jumaboi Esoev, interview, 17 November 2007.

141. Terry Martin, "The Russification of the RSFSR," *Cahiers du monde russe* 39, nos. 1–2 (1998): 99–117, https://www.jstor.org/stable/20171076. The emergence of these associations in the late 1980s is discussed in chapter 7.

142. Diane Koenker, personal communication, Urbana, IL, 1994.

143. See Matt Bivens, "No Good Will for Homeless," *Moscow Times*, 27 July 1994.

144. Marat Tursunbaev, interview, 15 May 2007.

145. Marat Tursunbaev, interview, 15 May 2007.

146. Elnur Asadov, interview, 5 June 2009.

147. Fridon Tsereteli, interview, 12 October 2007. On the variety of ethnic jokes in Soviet Russia, which covered groups from Ukrainians to Georgians to Chukchi, see Draitser, *Taking Penguins to the Movies*.

148. Dea Kochladze, interview, 26 November 2007.

149. Aryuna Khamagova, interview, 12 February 2007.

150. Aryuna Khamagova, interview, 12 February 2007.

151. Soviet propaganda to this effect gained currency even before the Second World War and the Cold War. See Maxim Matusevich, "Blackness the Color of Red: Negotiating Race at the US Legation in Riga, Latvia, 1922–33," *Journal of Contemporary History* 52, no. 4 (2017): 832–52. DOI: 10.1177/0022009417723976.

152. Gulnara Alieva, interview, 5 May 2007.

153. Dina Ataniyazova, interview, 6 December 2008.

154. On nostalgia for the USSR, see Serguei Oushakine, "'We're Nostalgic but We're Not Crazy': Retrofitting the Past in Russia," *Russian Review*, 66, no. 3 (2007): 451–82, https://www.jstor.org/stable/20620585; Maria Todorova and Zsuzsa Gille, eds., *Post-Communist Nostalgia* (New York: Berghahn Books, 2010).

155. Thapan, "Imagined and Social Landscapes," 60.

156. On the challenges of using memories in the reconstruction of the past, as well as in the present, see Geoff Eley, "The Past under Erasure? History, Memory, and the Contemporary," *Journal of Contemporary History* 46, no. 3 (2011): 555–73. DOI: 10.1177/002200 9411403342.

157. Aibek Botoev, interview, 8 December 2007.

158. Abdul Khalimov, interview, 30 November 2007.

159. Aijamal Aitmatova, interview, 20 July 2009.

160. Dina Ataniyazova, interview, 6 December 2008.

161. Hazi Begirov, interview, 25 June 2009.

162. Shuhrat Ikramov, interview, 18 September 2007.

163. See chapter 7.

164. The link between racism and migration is explored in Hall and Rose, *At Home with the Empire*; Alexander, "Beyond Black"; Goldberg, "Racial Europeanization."

165. On Western postcolonial migrants' ability to achieve inclusion in Western countries, see Essed, *Understanding Everyday Racism*.

5. BECOMING SVOI: BELONGING IN THE TWO CAPITALS

1. Aryuna Khamagova, interview, 12 February 2007.

2. Aryuna Khamagova, interview, 12 February 2007. On temporary workers (*limit-chiki*), see chapter 1.

3. Aryuna Khamagova, interview, 12 February 2007.

4. Aryuna Khamagova, interview, 12 February 2007.

5. Elliott, "Soviet Socialist Stars," 275–76.

6. Aryuna Khamagova, interview, 12 February 2007.

7. On housing pressures and construction, see Ruble, *Leningrad*, 82, 110.

8. Aryuna Khamagova, interview, 12 February 2007.

9. On the war's role in promoting solidarity among Soviet peoples and citizens, see chapter 2.

10. Aryuna Khamagova, interview, 12 February 2007.

11. Aryuna Khamagova, interview, 12 February 2007.

12. Aryuna Khamagova, interview, 12 February 2007.

13. Raleigh, *Russia's Sputnik Generation*.

14. I also give *svoi* a broader definition than Alena Ledeneva, who links the term to Soviet networks of informal connections or influence, or *blat*. Alena Ledeneva, "*Blat* and

Guanxi: Informal Practices in Russia and China," *Contemporary Studies in Society and History* 50, no. 1 (2008): 122. DOI: 10.1017/S0010417508000078.

15. Oberländer, "Cushy Work, Backbreaking Leisure," 590.

16. Karpenko, "Byt' 'natsional'nym,'" 40–41.

17. Yurchak, *Everything Was Forever*, 103–31.

18. Massey, *Space, Place, and Gender*, 121.

19. On informal networks in the Soviet period, see Alena Ledeneva, *Russia's Economy of Favours: Blat, Networking and Informal Exchange* (Cambridge: Cambridge University Press, 1998).

20. On varieties of migration networks, see Boyd, "Family and Personal Networks"; Nina Glick Schiller, Linda Basch, and Cristina Szanton Blanc, "From Immigrant to Transmigrant: Theorizing Transnational Migration," *Anthropological Quarterly* 68, no. 1 (1995): 48–63. DOI: 10.2307/3317464.

21. On the role of social and state power in migrants' ability to emplace themselves, see Stef Jansen and Staffan Löfving, eds., *Struggles for Home: Violence, Hope, and the Movement of People* (New York: Berghahn Books, 2009).

22. Yurchak, *Everything Was Forever*, 139.

23. Anthony Giddens, *The Constitution of Society* (Berkeley: University of California Press, 1984). On an application of structuration to post-Soviet Moscow, see Kosygina, "The Russian Migration Regime."

24. Jon Goss and Bruce Lindquist, "Conceptualizing International Labor Migration: A Structuration Perspective," *International Migration Review* 29, no. 2 (1995): 317–51. DOI: 10.2307/2546784.

25. Foner, *In a New Land*, 12.

26. Karpenko, "Byt' 'natsional'nym,'" 57–58.

27. Karpenko, "Byt' 'natsional'nym,'" 58.

28. Olga Brednikova and Elena Chikadze, "Armiane Sankt-Peterburga: Kar'ery etnichnosti," in *Konstruirovanie etnichnosti*, ed. Voronkov and Osval'd, 249.

29. Brednikova and Chikadze, "Armiane Sankt-Peterburga," 250.

30. Brednikova and Chikadze, "Armiane Sankt-Peterburga," 250.

31. Angermiuller, "Ot natsional'nogo patriotizma," 278. On Armenian genocide commemoration in the Soviet Union in the 1960s and beyond, see Maike Lehmann, "Apricot Socialism: The National Past, the Soviet Project, and the Imagining of Community in Late Soviet Armenia," *Slavic Review* 74, no. 1 (Spring 2015): 9–31. DOI: 10.5612/slavicreview.74.1.9.

32. Angermiuller, "Ot natsional'nogo patriotizma," 278.

33. Karpenko, "Byt' 'natsional'nym,'" 61, 81. On the opening of Leningrad's mosque, see chapter 1.

34. Ro'i, *Islam in the Soviet Union*, 222.

35. Tamriko Otskheli, interview, 27 July 2011.

36. Terenti Papashvili, interview, 25 July 2011.

37. Robert Eugene Johnson, *Peasant and Proletarian: The Working Class of Moscow in the Late Nineteenth Century* (New Brunswick, NJ: Rutgers University Press, 1979).

38. Vendina, "Social Polarization," 225.

39. Azamat Sanatbaev, interview, 14 July 2009.

40. Saule Iskakova, interview, 10 July 2007.

41. Jyldyz Nuriaeva, interview, 9 July 2007.

42. On this quota system, see chapter 1.

43. Aryan Shirinov, interview, 12 November 2007.

44. Gulnara Alieva, interview, 5 May 2007.

45. Alex Koberidze, interview, 2 April 2009.

46. Gulnara Alieva, interview, 5 May 2007.

47. Aryuna Khamagova, interview, 12 February 2007.

48. Tolkunbek Kudubaev, interview, 15 November 2008.

49. Emily J. Elliott, "Making and Policing Muscovites: Migrant Letters to the Priemnaia of the Supreme Soviet" (paper presented at the Annual Convention of the Association for Slavic, East European, and Eurasian Studies, Chicago, 10 November 2017).

50. Maia Asinadze, interview, 29 November 2007.

51. On this story of Asinadze's arrival in Moscow, see chapter 3.

52. Maia Asinadze, interview, 29 November 2007.

53. Houston, "Administrative Control of Migration," 37.

54. See the discussion on gray zones in chapter 1.

55. Elliott, "Making and Policing Muscovites."

56. Elliott notes an official understanding of reduced labor pools of workers from proximate towns and regions. Chapter 1 discusses the pressures that would drive increasing numbers of Caucasus and Central Asian citizens northward; the effects of this movement are discussed in chapter 7. Elliott, "Making and Policing Muscovites."

57. Elliott, "Making and Policing Muscovites."

58. Zaslavsky and Colton note that marriage was another common way for *limitchiki* to gain permanent status. Zaslavsky, *The Neo-Stalinist State*, 144; Colton, *Moscow*, 463. The role of marriage in gaining status is discussed later in the chapter.

59. Scott, *Familiar Strangers*, 157.

60. Terenti Papashvili, interview, 25 July 2011.

61. Vazha Gigulashvili, interview, 23 July 2011.

62. Eliso Svanidze, interview, 24 July 2011.

63. Irma Balanchivadze, interview, 23 July 2011.

64. Erkin Abdullaev, interview, 26 June 2009.

65. Rasul Asgarov, interview, 12 June 2009.

66. Such cases are discussed in chapter 6.

67. Anarbek Zakirov, interview, 9 August 2009.

68. Perevedentsev, *Molodezh'*, 140.

69. V. I. Moiseenko, ed., *Naselenie Moskvy: Proshloe, nastoiashchee, budushchee* (Moscow: Izdatel'stvo Moskovskogo universiteta, 1992), 47–57.

70. Fuad Ojagov, interview, 25 June 2009.

71. Moiseenko, *Naselenie Moskvy*, 48.

72. Buckley, "The Myth of Managed Migration," 896.

73. Buckley, "The Myth of Managed Migration," 900.

74. Louise Shelley, "The Geography of Soviet Criminality," *American Sociological Review* 45 (1980): 115. DOI: 10.2307/2095246.

75. Loeber, "*Limitchiki*," 301; Shearer, "Elements Near and Alien," 838.

76. Light, "What Does It Mean to Control Migration?," 408.

77. See chapter 1 for this discussion.

78. Some Soviet sociologists criticized "closed city" policies for the aging of vital Soviet cities: see B. S. Khorev and N. P. Matveev, eds., *Rasselenie i dinamika naseleniia Moskvy i Moskovskoi oblasti: Sbornik statei* (Moscow: Moskovskii filial Geograficheskoe obshchestvo, 1981). On Moscow's perpetual labor shortages, see Colton, *Moscow*, 66. Ruble notes that Leningrad purposefully sought outside skilled workers to raise its prestige following the Second World War. Ruble, *Leningrad*, 59.

79. Anarbek Zakirov, interview, 9 August 2009.

80. Bindas, "Re-remembering a Segregated Past," 122.

81. Oidin Nosirova, interview, 28 May 2007.

82. Marat Tursunbaev, interview, 15 May 2007.

83. Bakyt Shakiev, interview, 8 August 2009.

84. Maia Asinadze, interview, 29 November 2007.

85. Maia Asinadze, interview, 29 November 2007.

86. Maia Asinadze, interview, 29 November 2007.

87. Maia Asinadze, interview, 29 November 2007.

88. On "informal microgroups," see Khorev, *Urbanizatsiia i demograficheskie protsessi*, 194. Moshe Lewin labels these "urban microworlds." Lewin, *The Gorbachev Phenomenon*, 66.

89. Karklins, *Ethnic Relations in the U.S.S.R.*, 120.

90. Sarah Ashwin, *Russian Workers: The Anatomy of Patience* (Manchester: Manchester University Press, 1999).

91. Oberländer, "Cushy Work, Backbreaking Leisure," 576.

92. Ashwin, *Russian Workers*, 11.

93. Lali Utiashvili, interview, 29 November 2007.

94. Khorev, *Urbanizatsiia i demograficheskie protsessi*, 191.

95. Rasma Karklins has noted the importance that Soviets placed on the multiethnic basis of Soviet work collectives. Karklins, *Ethnic Relations in the U.S.S.R.*, 129.

96. Lali Utiashvili, interview, 29 November 2007.

97. Levan Rukhadze, interview, 25 November 2007.

98. Azamat Sanatbaev, interview, 14 July 2009.

99. Shuhrat Kazbekov, interview, 13 November 2007.

100. Shuhrat Kazbekov, interview, 13 November 2007.

101. On the *orgnabor* system, see chapter 1.

102. Vazha Gigulashvili, interview, 23 July 2011.

103. Jumaboi Esoev, interview, 17 November 2007.

104. On enterprise-sponsored vacations, see Koenker, *Club Red*.

105. Lali Utiashvili, interview, 29 November 2007.

106. Saule Iskakova, interview, 10 July 2007.

107. Bakyt Nizomov, interview, 27 May 2007.

108. Farshad Hajiev, interview, 11 November 2007.

109. Dea Kochladze, interview, 26 November 2007.

110. Bolot Oruzbaev, interview, 8 July 2009.

111. Levan Rukhadze, interview, 25 November 2007.

112. Farshad Hajiev, interview, 11 November 2007.

113. Elliott, "Making and Policing Muscovites."

114. The national myth of the hardworking migrant in the United States applies more to Europeans who came at the turn of the twentieth century, however, than to the non-white migrants who have since predominated. Foner, *In a New Land*, 207. Dorothy Louise Zinn has noted that Senegalese migrants to Italy constructed an image of themselves as more worldly and knowledgeable than the local population. Dorothy Louise Zinn, "The Senegalese Immigrants in Bari: What Happens When the Africans Peer Back," in *Migration and Identity*, ed. Benmayor and Skotnes, 53–68.

115. Azamat Sanatbaev, interview, 14 July 2009.

116. Angermiuller, "Ot natsional'nogo patriotizma," 270.

117. Bolot Oruzbaev, interview, 8 July 2009.

118. Draitser, *Taking Penguins to the Movies*, 35–55.

119. Emin Gazyumov, interview, 19 March 2009.

120. Elnur Asadov, interview, 5 June 2009.

121. Draitser, *Taking Penguins to the Movies*, 49.

122. Shadulla Agaev, interview, 16 June 2009.

123. Fuad Ojagov, interview, 25 June 2009.

124. Eliso Svanidze, interview, 24 July 2011.

125. Liu, "Urban Materiality," 4.

126. Maia Asinadze, interview, 29 November 2007.

127. Abdul Khalimov, interview, 30 November 2007.

128. Tamriko Otskheli, interview, 27 July 2011.

129. Dina Ataniyazova, interview, 6 December 2008.

130. Dea Kochladze, interview, 26 November 2007.

131. Aibek Botoev, interview, 8 December 2007.

132. Fuad Ojagov, interview, 25 June 2009.

133. Bolot Oruzbaev, interview, 8 July 2009.

134. Mirbek Serkebaev, interview, 3 August 2009.

135. See chapter 2 for discussion of the *dekady*.

136. Lali Utiashvili, interview, 29 November 2007.

137. Mirbek Serkebaev, interview, 3 August 2009.

138. Anarbek Zakirov, interview, 9 August 2009.

139. Claude S. Fischer, *To Dwell among Friends: Personal Networks in Town and City* (Chicago: University of Chicago Press, 1982), 33.

140. Markku Lonkila and Anna-Maria Salmi, "The Russian Work Collective and Migration," *Europe-Asia Studies* 57, no. 5 (2005): 683. DOI: 10.1080/09668130500126452.

141. Ahmed et al., introduction to *Uprootings/Regroundings*, 6. On the broader Soviet phenomenon of holding separate national and Soviet values, see Adeeb Khalid, *Islam after Communism: Religion and Politics in Central Asia* (Berkeley: University of California Press, 2007), chap. 1.

6. LIFE ON THE MARGINS

1. Natalya Chernyshova, "Consumers as Citizens: Revisiting the Question of Public Disengagement in the Brezhnev Era," in *Reconsidering Stagnation*, ed. Fainberg and Kalinovsky, 4.

2. As discussed below, one reason for this increase was corruption at the state level. See Luc Duhamel, "The Last Campaign against Corruption in Soviet Moscow," *Europe-Asia Studies* 56, no. 2 (2004): 187–212. DOI: 10.1080/0966813042000190506.

3. Vladimir J. Treml, *Purchases of Food from Private Sources in Soviet Urban Areas*, Berkeley-Duke Occasional Papers on the Second Economy in the USSR, No. 3 (Durham, NC, 1985), 10.

4. Millar, "The Little Deal."

5. Chernyshova, "Consumers as Citizens," 4.

6. Yiftachel, "Theoretical Notes on 'Gray Cities,'" 88.

7. Yiftachel, "Theoretical Notes on 'Gray Cities,'" 88.

8. Saskia Sassen-Koob, "Recomposition and Peripheralization at the Core," *Contemporary Marxism*, no. 5 (1982): 88–100.

9. Alena Ledeneva notes the extent of informal practices in the late USSR but sees trade primarily as about personal enrichment. Ledeneva, *Russia's Economy of Favours*, 79. Other works that highlight the informal economy from a state perspective include Gregory Grossman, "The 'Second Economy' of the USSR," *Problems of Communism* 26, no. 5 (1977): 25–40. For a piece that uses official statistics to examine household and republic-level variations and gauges the scope of the informal economy, see Byung-Yeon Kim, "Informal Economy Activities of Soviet Households: Size and Dynamics," *Journal of Comparative Economics* 31, no. 3 (2003): 532–51. DOI: 10.1016/S0147-5967(03)00052-0. See also Chernyshova, "Consumers as Citizens."

10. Michael Kearney, "From the Invisible Hand to Visible Feet: Anthropological Studies of Migration and Development," *Annual Review of Anthropology* 15 (1986): 354. DOI: 10.1146/annurev.an.15.100186.001555.

11. Arjun Appadurai defines ethnoscape as "the landscape of persons who constitute the shifting world in which we live: tourists, immigrants, refugees, exiles, guest-workers and other moving groups and persons." Appadurai privileges motion over stability in a globalizing world, which, I argue, included the USSR. Arjun Appadurai, "Disjuncture and Difference in the Global Cultural Economy," in *Theorizing Diaspora: A Reader*, ed. Jana Evans Braziel and Anita Mannur (Malden, MA: Blackwell, 2003), 32.

12. Min Zhou, "Revisiting Ethnic Entrepreneurship: Convergencies, Controversies, and Conceptual Advances," *International Migration Review* 38, no. 3 (2004): 1040–74. DOI: 10.1111/j.1747-7379.2004.tb00228.x. See also Curt H. Stiles and Craig H. Galbraith, eds., *Ethnic Entrepreneurship: Structure and Process* (Amsterdam: Elsevier, 2004).

13. Kalilova and Haydarov alike use the term "second home."

14. Ahmed et al., introduction to *Uprootings/Regroundings*, 1–22.

15. Liisa Malkki, "National Geographic: The Rooting of Peoples and the Territorialization of National Identity among Scholars and Refugees," *Cultural Anthropology* 7, no. 1 (1992): 24–44, https://www.jstor.org/stable/656519.

16. Arutiunian and Bromlei, *Sotsial'no-kul'turnyi oblik sovetskikh natsii*.

17. On the structural inequalities that narrowed these options, see chapter 1.

18. On the Russian exodus from Central Asia, see chapter 1; see also Paul Kolstoe, *Russians in the Former Soviet Republics* (Hong Kong: C. Hurst, 1995), 64–67.

19. On the army's role in forming connections, see chapter 3.

20. Jasur Haydarov, interview, 23 July 2009.

21. Elnur Asadov, interview, 5 June 2009.

22. Scott, *Familiar Strangers*, 169.

23. On the implications of overpopulation in Soviet Central Asian villages, see chapter 1.

24. Aijamal Aitmatova, interview, 20 July 2009.

25. Aijamal Aitmatova, interview, 20 July 2009.

26. Erin Trouth Hofmann and Cynthia Buckley, "Cultural Responses to Changing Gender Patterns of Migration in Georgia," *International Migration* 50, no. 5 (2012): 77–94. DOI: 10.1111/j.1468-2435.2010.00681.x.

27. On "uneven spatiality," see Yiftachel, "Theoretical Notes on 'Gray Cities,'" 89.

28. Koenker, *Club Red*, 2.

29. Ledeneva, *Russia's Economy of Favours*, 101; Chernyshova, "Consumers as Citizens," 5.

30. Luc Duhamel, "Justice and Politics in Moscow, 1983–1986: The Ambartsumyan Case," *Europe-Asia Studies* 52, no. 7 (2000): 1308. DOI: 10.1080/713663133.

31. TsGAPDKR, f. 56, op. 205, d. 17, l. 3.

32. Duhamel, "Justice and Politics in Moscow," 1308.

33. Treml, *Purchases of Food*, 9.

34. Linda J. Cook, *The Soviet Social Contract and Why It Failed: Welfare Policy and Workers' Politics from Brezhnev to Yeltsin* (Cambridge, MA: Harvard University Press, 1993).

35. On the shift toward the informal market as drawing growing numbers of migrants to large industrial cities in the late twentieth century, see Kearney, "From the Invisible Hand," 349.

36. Schiller, Basch, and Szanton Blanc, "From Immigrant to Transmigrant," 48.

37. Aijamal Aitmatova, interview, 20 July 2009.

38. See chapters 1 and 5 for discussions of these residence permits.

39. Elnur Asadov, interview, 5 June 2009.

40. On becoming *svoi*, see chapter 5.

41. Scott, *Familiar Strangers*, 178.

42. Elnur Asadov, interview, 5 June 2009.

43. Arif Yunusov noted that in the 1980s Azerbaijanis began to dominate Moscow's flower markets, taking over from Slavs and Balts. He offers no details, however; whether an accord with the militia was associated with this takeover remains unclear. Yunusov, "Azerbaidzhantsy v Rossii," 113.

44. Elnur Asadov, interview, 5 June 2009.

45. Elnur Asadov, interview, 5 June 2009.

46. Aijamal Aitmatova, interview, 20 July 2009.

47. The difference may well be attributed to the scale of the Azerbaijani flower-selling network. Other Azerbaijani traders interviewed for this study, who were also involved in large networks, offered varying experiences with the militia, however; so it is difficult to draw firm conclusions.

48. Jasur Haydarov, interview, 23 July 2009.

49. Shinder S. Thandi, "Brown Economy: Enterprise and Employment," in *A Postcolonial People: South Asians in Britain*, ed. Nasreen Ali, Virinder S. Kalra, and Salman Sayyid (New York: Columbia University Press, 2008), 229.

50. Schiller, Basch, and Szanton Blanc, "From Immigrant to Transmigrant," 55.

51. Elnur Asadov, interview, 5 June 2009.

52. Aijamal Aitmatova, interview, 20 July 2009.

53. Meerim Kalilova, interview, 17 July 2009.

54. In the 1970s, prices in collective farm markets were about double those in state-run stores. Cook, *The Soviet Social Contract*, 46.

55. James Millar and Elizabeth Clayton, "Quality of Life: Subjective Measures of Relative Satisfaction," in *Politics, Work, and Daily Life in the USSR: A Survey of Former Soviet Citizens*, ed. James Millar (Cambridge: Cambridge University Press, 1987), 43.

56. In 2008, the SOVA research center reported at least 116 deaths and 499 injuries resulting from racism and xenophobia in Russia (excluding the North Caucasus). Alexander Verkhovsky et al., *Xenophobia, Freedom of Conscience and Anti-extremism in Russia in 2008*, trans. I. Salvalieva and S. Rock (Moscow: SOVA Center, 2009).

57. On "black" as an epithet, see chapter 4.

58. Karklins, *Ethnic Relations in the U.S.S.R.*, 21. See chapter 2 for a further discussion on the relationship between ethnicity and territory.

59. Elnur Asadov, interview, 5 June 2009.

60. Yulia Khmelevskaya, personal communication, 31 May 2017.

61. Rasul Asgarov, interview, 12 June 2009.

62. Elnur Asadov, interview, 5 June 2009.

63. See this discussion in chapter 4.

64. On the growing societal challenges that produced street beggars and related phenomena in the 1980s, see Anthony Jones, Walter D. Connor, and David E. Powell, eds., *Soviet Social Problems* (Boulder, CO: Westview, 1991).

65. Two of the nine Azerbaijanis and three of the seven Kyrgyz and Uzbeks interviewed in summer 2009 discussed significant levels of ethnic prejudice in 1970s or 1980s Moscow.

66. Aijamal Aitmatova, interview, 20 July 2009.

67. Aijamal Aitmatova, interview, 20 July 2009.

68. Moscow would periodically send orders to southern republican Communist parties asking for fruits and other goods that were in deficit in the capital. See, for example, TsGAPDKR, f. 56, op. 27, d. 88, l. 5.

69. Chernyshova, "Consumers as Citizens," 5.

70. Jasur Haydarov, interview, 23 July 2009.

71. On Chukchis in ethnic Soviet humor, see Draitser, *Taking Penguins to the Movies*, 75–99.

72. On mumie/shilajit, see Sidney J. Stohs, "Safety and Efficacy of Shilajit (Mumie, Moomiyo)," *Phytotherapy Research* 28, no. 4 (2014): 475–79. DOI: 10.1002/ptr.5018.

73. Mitrokhin, *Russkaia partiia*, 65.

74. On the impact of relationships on identities, see Gupta and Ferguson, "Beyond 'Culture': Space, Identity, and the Politics of Difference," 41–42.

75. On cosmopolitanism, see Malkki, "National Geographic," 38.

76. Elnur Asadov, interview, 5 June 2009.

77. Marianne Kamp, *The New Woman in Uzbekistan: Islam, Modernity, and Unveiling under Communism* (Seattle: University of Washington Press, 2006); Kamp, "The Wedding Feast: Living the New Uzbek Life in the 1930s," in *Everyday Life in Central Asia: Past and Present*, ed. Jeff Sahadeo and Russell Zanca (Bloomington: Indiana University Press, 2007), 103–14.

78. Aijamal Aitmatova, interview, 20 July 2009.

79. Aijamal Aitmatova, interview, 20 July 2009.

80. On the evolution of the Russian nationality as the "older brother" to other Soviet nations, see Tillett, *The Great Friendship*.

81. Aijamal Aitmatova, interview, 20 July 2009.

82. Aijamal Aitmatova, interview, 20 July 2009.

83. Elnur Asadov, interview, 5 June 2009.

84. Jasur Haydarov, interview, 23 July 2009. On the development of stereotypes such as the dishonest Uzbek trader, see Douglas Northrop, "Nationalizing Backwardness: Gender, Empire, and Uzbek Identity," in *A State of Nations: Empire and Nation-Making in the Age of Lenin and Stalin*, ed. Ronald Grigor Suny and Terry Martin (Oxford: Oxford University Press, 2001), 191–220.

85. Jasur Haydarov, interview, 23 July 2009.

86. Elnur Asadov, interview, 5 June 2009.

87. Elnur Asadov, interview, 5 June 2009.

88. Meerim Kalilova, interview, 17 July 2009.

89. Aijamal Aitmatova, interview, 20 July 2009.

90. Jasur Haydarov, interview, 23 July 2009.

91. Jasur Haydarov, interview, 23 July 2009.

92. On links between food and national identity, see Russell Zanca, "Fat and All That: Good Eating the Uzbek Way," in *Everyday Life in Central Asia*, ed. Sahadeo and Zanca, 178–97.

93. On these links in the post-Soviet period, see Madeleine Reeves, "Black Work, Green Money: Remittances, Ritual and Domestic Economies in Southern Kyrgyzstan," *Slavic Review* 71, no. 1 (2012): 108–34. DOI: 10.5612/slavicreview.71.1.0108.

94. On these networks in Georgia, see Scott, *Familiar Strangers*, 163–78.

95. See chapter 3 for these interviews.

96. Elnur Asadov, interview, 5 June 2009.

97. Meerim Kalilova, interview, 17 July 2009.

98. Jasur Haydarov, interview, 23 July 2009.

99. Aijamal Aitmatova, interview, 20 July 2009.

100. Petra Dannecker, "Transnational Migration and the Transformation of Gender Relations: The Case of Bangladeshi Labour Migrants," *Current Sociology* 53, no. 4 (2005): 655–74. DOI: 10.1177/0011392105052720.

7. PERESTROIKA

1. Erkin Bakchiev, interview, 9 August 2009.
2. Erkin Bakchiev, interview, 9 August 2009.
3. Erkin Bakchiev, interview, 9 August 2009.
4. Abdul Khalimov, interview, 30 November 2007.
5. Abdul Khalimov, interview, 30 November 2007.
6. Abdul Khalimov, interview, 30 November 2007.
7. Kirill Nourzhanov and Christian Bleuer, *Tajikistan: A Political and Social History* (Canberra: ANU Press, 2013), 182–83. Witnesses to the violence reported hearing cries of "beat the Russians," and attacks apparently focused on Russian women. The riots prompted a large emigration of Russians and other Slavs from Tajikistan.
8. Abdul Khalimov, interview, 30 November 2007.
9. I understand and define perestroika as a set of behaviors and policies instituted in the Gorbachev era, including glasnost (openness), increased civil liberties, economic reforms, and changes to the Communist Party and political life in the last years of the USSR.
10. On the regional variations of perestroika, see Madeleine Reeves, "'And Our Words Must Be Constructive!' On the Discordances of *Glasnost'* in the Central Asian Press at a Time of Conflict," *Cahiers d'Asie centrale* 26 (2016): 77–110, http://asiecentrale.revues.org /3259.
11. Stephen Kotkin, *Armageddon Averted: The Soviet Collapse, 1970–2000* (Oxford: Oxford University Press, 2001), 173.
12. On the effects of the move to a market economy, see David Lane, *Soviet Society under Perestroika* (London: Routledge, 1992), 15 ff.
13. Scott, *Familiar Strangers*, 198.
14. Reeves, "'And Our Words Must Be Constructive!,'" 78.
15. Aibek Botoev, interview, 8 December 2007.
16. Togrul Mammadov, interview, 6 June 2009.
17. Dea Kochladze, interview, 26 November 2007.
18. Reeves, "'And Our Words Must Be Constructive!,'" 81–86.
19. Rafael Voskanyan, interview, 25 November 2007.
20. On the national movement in Ukraine, see Taras Kuzio, *Ukraine: Perestroika to Independence* 2nd ed. (Basingstoke: Palgrave Macmillan, 2000). See also Rasma Karklins, *Ethnopolitics and Transition to Democracy: The Collapse of the USSR and Latvia* (Washington, DC: Woodrow Wilson Center Press; Baltimore: Johns Hopkins University Press, 1994).
21. David Somkishvili, interview, 24 July 2011.
22. Shuhrat Kazbekov, interview, 13 November 2007.
23. Dea Kochladze, interview, 26 November 2007.
24. On the riot's impact, see Chantal Lemercier-Quelquejay, "Le monde musulman soviétique d'Asie centrale après Alma-Ata (décembre 1986)," *Cahiers du monde russe et soviétique* 32, no. 1 (1991): 117–21, https://www.jstor.org/stable/20170769.
25. See this discussion in chapter 1.
26. See also Isaac Scarborough and Malika Bahovadinova, "Capitalism Fulfills the Final Five-Year Plan: How Soviet-Era Migration Programs Came to Fruition in Post-Soviet Eurasia" in *Eurasia on the Move: Interdisciplinary Approaches to a Dynamic Migration Region*, ed. Marlene Laruelle and Caress Schenk (Washington, DC: The George Washington Central Asia Program, 2018), 1–12. See chapter 1 for a discussion of planning and political decisions regarding regional investment.
27. Scarborough and Bahovadinova, "Final Five-Year Plan," 6.

28. TsGAPDKR, f. 56, op. 257, d. 88, l. 7.

29. TsGAPDKR, f. 56, op. 257, d. 88, l. 8.

30. TsGAPDKR, f. 56, op. 257, d. 8, l. 10. On the out-migration of Russians from Central Asia, see chapter 1.

31. Speech to the Twentieth Party Congress of Tajikistan, 24–25 January 1986, cited in Scarborough and Bahovadinova, "Final Five-Year Plan," 7.

32. TsGAPDKR, f. 42, op. 32, d. 35, l. 17.

33. See chapter 1 for this discussion.

34. TsGAPDKR, f. 42, op. 15, d. 45, l. 13.

35. Makarova, Morozova, and Tarasova, *Regional'nye osobennosti migratsionnykh protsessov*, 95.

36. "Rech' I. B. Usmankhodzhaeva na VII s"ezde uchitelei Uzbekistana," *Pravda Vostoka*, 16 May 1987.

37. On the fear of unemployment in Central Asia as a major theme in the glasnost press, see Fierman, "Central Asian Youth and Migration," 257.

38. "Na rabotu v dal'nie kraia," *Pravda Vostoka*, 22 December 1987.

39. Isaac Scarborough, "(Over)determining Social Disorder: Tajikistan and the Economic Collapse of Perestroika," *Central Asian Survey* 35, no. 3 (2016): 444–45. DOI: 10.1080/02634937.2016.1189679.

40. Kotkin, *Armageddon Averted*, 65.

41. Archie Brown, *Seven Years That Changed the World: Perestroika in Perspective* (Oxford: Oxford University Press, 1991), 613.

42. Ashraf Bayramov, interview, 25 June 2009.

43. G. M. Romanenkova, "Opyt razrabotki programmy 'trud i kadry' Leningrada i Leningradskoi oblasti," in *Demograficheskaia politika v regional'nom razreze*, ed. G. M. Romanenkova (Moscow: Nauka, 1988), 149. On a parallel effort in Moscow, see Elliott, "Soviet Socialist Stars."

44. Cooperatives were legalized enterprises under private ownership, which Gorbachev had expanded in 1987–1988 to retail and service sectors. See Brown, *Seven Years*, 75.

45. Ashraf Bayramov, interview, 25 June 2009.

46. Kemal Jafarov, interview, 25 June 2009.

47. Azamat Sanatbaev, interview, 14 July 2009.

48. David Somkishvili, interview, 24 July 2011.

49. Richard H. Rowland, "Regional Migration in the Former Soviet Union during the 1980s: The Resurgence of European Regions," in *The New Geography of European Migrations*, ed. Russell King (London: Belhaven, 1993), 157.

50. L. V. Ostapenko and I. A. Subbotina, *Moskva mnogonatsional'naia. Starozhily i migranty: Vmeste ili riadom?* (Moscow: Rossiiskii universitet druzhba narodov, 2007), 14.

51. Moiseenko, *Naselenie Moskvy*, 77.

52. Perevedentsev, *Molodezh'*, 117.

53. Gulnara Alieva, interview, 5 May 2007.

54. Donna Bahry, "Society Transformed? Rethinking the Social Roots of Perestroika," *Slavic Review* 52, no. 3 (1993): 512–54. DOI: 10.2307/2499722.

55. Luc Duhamel, *The KGB Campaign against Corruption in Moscow, 1982–1987* (Pittsburgh: University of Pittsburgh Press, 2010).

56. Duhamel, *The KGB Campaign*, 163.

57. Postanovlenie [Decree] 21 August 1986, "On Measures to Improve the Populations of Leningrad and Moscow with Fruits and Vegetables and Potatoes," TsAPDKR, f. 56, op. 257, d. 144, l. 54.

58. Mirlan Musabekov, interview, 10 August 2009.

59. On cooperative enterprises, see Brown, *Seven Years*, 75.

60. Deborah Adelman, *The "Children of Perestroika": Moscow Teenagers Talk about Their Lives and the Future* (Armonk, NY: M. E. Sharpe, 1992), 165.

61. Ostapenko and Subbotina, *Moskva mnogonatsional'naia*, 37.

62. Yunusov, "Azerbaidzhantsy v Rossii," 164.

63. Shuhrat Kazbekov, interview, 13 November 2007.

64. Karpenko, "Byt' 'natsional'nym,'" 82.

65. GARF, f. 1661, op. 11, d. 7, l. 5.

66. L. Babaeva and E. Nazarchuk, "Ezhemesiachnyi opros '*AiF*' iiun' 1988 g.: Punkt 5, natsional'nost'," *Argumenty i fakty*, 4 June 1988.

67. Babaeva and Nazarchuk, "Ezhemesiachnyi opros '*AiF*.'"

68. Dina Rome Spechler, "Russian Nationalism and Soviet Politics," in *The Nationalities Factor in Soviet Politics and Society*, ed. Lubomyr Hajda and Mark Beissinger (Boulder, CO: Westview, 1990), 288.

69. Jumaboi Esoev, interview, 17 November 2007.

70. Viktor Astaf'ev, *The Catching of Gudgeons in Georgia*, quoted in Draitser, *Taking Penguins to the Movies*, 37.

71. Robert Horvath, *The Legacy of Soviet Dissent: Dissidence, Democratisation and Radical Nationalism in Russia* (London: RoutledgeCurzon, 2005), 160.

72. Rasma Karklins, "Nationality Policy and Ethnic Issues in the USSR," in *Politics, Work, and Daily Life*, ed. Millar, 326.

73. Matusevich, "Probing the Limits of Internationalism."

74. Adelman, *"Children of Perestroika,"* 97.

75. Bushnell, *Moscow Graffiti*, 152n81.

76. On the appearance of neo-Nazi organizations, see Adelman, *"Children of Perestroika,"* 87; Lane, *Soviet Society under Perestroika*, 116.

77. Lane, *Soviet Society under Perestroika*, 212.

78. Charles King, *The Ghost of Freedom: A History of the Caucasus* (Oxford: Oxford University Press, 2008), 213.

79. E. I. Koman and E. O. Khabenskaia, "Stanovlenie instituta natsional'no-kul'turnoi avtonomii v stolichnom megapolise," in *Etnicheskie protsessi v stolichnom megapolise* (Moscow: RAN, 2008), 46.

80. Iu. V. Arutiunian, "Armiane-moskvichi: Sotsial'nyi portret po materialam etno-sotsiologicheskogo issledovaniia," *Sovetskoe etnografiia*, no. 2 (1991): 3–16.

81. Brednikova and Chikadze, "Armiane Sankt-Peterburga," 241.

82. Community leaders, as discussed in chapter 5, organized annual, albeit small-scale, commemorations from the late 1960s.

83. Arutiunian, "Armiane-moskvichi," 5.

84. Arutiunian, "Armiane-moskvichi," 8.

85. Koman and Khabenskaia, "Stanovlenie instituta natsional'no-kul'turnoi avtonomii," 45.

86. Brednikova and Chikadze, "Armiane Sankt-Peterburga" 247.

87. Eteri Gugushvili, interview, 26 July 2011.

88. See also *Diaspory: Predstavitel'stva natsional'nostei v Moskve*.

89. Koman and Khabenskaia, "Stanovlenie instituta natsional'no-kul'turnoi avtonomii," 15.

90. "Zaboty mnogonatsional'naia goroda," *Arkhitektura i stroitel'stvo* (Moscow), no. 9 (1989).

91. "Zaboty mnogonatsional'naia goroda."

92. On the congress, see Kotkin, *Armageddon Averted*, 75; David R. Marples, "Revisiting the Collapse of the USSR," *Canadian Slavonic Papers* 53, nos. 2–4 (2011): 463. DOI: 10.1080/00085006.2011.11092684.

93. Said Nabiev, interview, 28 November 2007.

94. Dina Ataniyazova, interview, 6 December 2008.

95. Elliott, "Soviet Socialist Stars," 285.

96. On the Baku events, see King, *The Ghost of Freedom*, 212–15.

97. Fuad Ojagov, interview, 25 June 2009.

98. Thomas de Waal, *The Caucasus: An Introduction* (Oxford: Oxford University Press, 2010), 113.

99. Hodzhamamat Umarov, "Regional'nye osobennosti proiavleniia protivorechii sotsialisticheskoi ekonomiki," *Izvestiia Akademiia nauk Tadzhikskoi SSR, Seriia: Filosofiia, ekonomika, pravovedenie*, no. 3 (1989): 29, cited in Kalinovsky, "Central Planning, Local Knowledge?," 618.

100. Brown, *Seven Years*, 111.

101. On *bomzhi*, see David Remnick, *Lenin's Tomb: The Last Days of the Soviet Empire* (New York: Random House, 1993), 200–202; Jeni Klugman, ed., *Poverty in Russia: Public Policy and Private Responses* (New York: World Bank, 1997).

102. Shuhrat Kazbekov, interview, 13 November 2007.

103. Aibek Botoev, interview, 8 December 2007.

104. Colton, *Moscow*, 463.

105. Mitrokhin, *Russkaia partiia*. On "going to the people," see John Dunlop, "Russian Nationalism Today: Organizations and Programs," *Nationalities Papers* 19, no. 2 (1991): 146–66.

106. Laura Belin, "The Russian Media in the 1990s," *Journal of Communist Studies and Transition Politics* 18, no. 1 (2002): 139–60. DOI: 10.1080/13523270209696371.

107. Beliaeva, Draguskii, and Zotova, "Mnogonatsional'nyi mir Moskvy," 143.

108. "Petition to Russian Patriots: Pamiat Forms National Front," pamphlet, 16 July 1989, cited in *Anti-Semitism and Nationalism at the End of the Soviet Era*, ed. Boris Belenkin (Leiden: Brill, 1999).

109. *Russkie vedomosti*, no. 3 (1991). The newspapers discussed in this section are part of the collection of primary documents in Belenkin, ed., *Anti-Semitism and Nationalism*.

110. The Pale of Settlement (Cherta osedlosti) emerged under Catherine the Great to restrict Jewish residence and activities to regions that mainly came under Russian control during the eighteenth-century partitions of Poland.

111. For analysis of the 1989 census, see Barbara Anderson and Brian Silver, "Growth and Diversity of the Population of the Soviet Union," *Annals of the American Academy of Political and Social Science* 1, no. 510 (1990): 155–77. DOI: 10.1177/0002716290510001012.

112. Many suspected at the time that census figures had been manipulated to "ensure" Russians' majority status.

113. John L. H. Keep, *Last of the Empires: A History of the Soviet Union, 1945–1991* (Oxford: Oxford University Press, 1995), 385.

114. By this time, Russian nationalists had mounted a campaign to return the name of Leningrad to St. Petersburg. A referendum to make this change in June 1991 was successful.

115. *Russkoe delo*, no. 4 (1991).

116. *Nardonoe delo*, no. 8 (1991).

117. *Golos Rossii*, no. 1 (1991).

118. *Nashe vremia*, no. 5 (1991).

119. *Russkaia gazeta*, no. 1 (1992).

120. *Golos Rossii*, no. 3 (1992).

121. Tamriko Otskheli, interview, 27 July 2011.

122. William Moskoff, *Hard Times: Impoverishment and Protest in the Perestroika Years; The Soviet Union, 1985–1991* (Armonk, NY: M. E. Sharpe, 1993).

123. Moskoff, *Hard Times*, 47–51.

124. Eteri Gugushvili, interview, 26 July 2011.

125. Eteri Gugushvili, interview, 26 July 2011.

126. Abdul Khalimov, interview, 30 November 2007.

127. Eljan Jusubov, interview, 5 June 2009.

128. Matusevich, "Probing the Limits of Internationalism," 30.

129. Dina Ataniyazova, interview, 6 December 2008.

130. Erkin Bakchiev, interview, 9 August 2009.

131. Azamat Sanatbaev, interview, 14 July 2009.

132. Kemal Jafarov, interview, 25 June 2009.

133. Olga Brednikova and Oleg Pachenkov, "Azerbaidzhanskie torgovtsy v Peterburge: Mezhdu 'voobrazhaemymi soobshchestvami' i 'pervichnymi gruppami,'" *Diaspory*, no. 1 (2001): 131–47.

134. Elliott, "Soviet Socialist Stars," 295.

135. Azamat Sanatbaev, interview, 14 July 2009.

136. Abdul Khalimov, interview, 30 November 2007.

137. Vladimir Zhirinovsky as cited in Viktor Grebenshikov, "Profile: A Clown That Everyone Is Now Taking Seriously," *Los Angeles Times*, 10 December 1991.

138. Maia Asinadze, interview, 29 November 2007.

139. Jumaboi Esoev, interview, 17 November 2007.

140. Akmal Bobokulov, interview, 13 November 2007. On the Uzbek friendship society, see *Diaspory: Predstavitel'stva natsional'nostei v Moskve*, 75.

141. Aryan Shirinov, interview, 12 November 2007.

142. Beliaeva, Draguskii, and Zotova, "Mnogonatsional'nyi mir Moskvy," 134.

143. Koman and Khabenskaia, "Stanovlenie instituta natsional'no-kul'turnoi avtonomii," 45.

144. Beliaeva, Draguskii, and Zotova, "Mnogonatsional'nyi mir Moskvy," 134–48.

145. Beliaeva, Draguskii, and Zotova, "Mnogonatsional'nyi mir Moskvy," 143–45.

146. Beliaeva, Draguskii, and Zotova, "Mnogonatsional'nyi mir Moskvy," 146.

147. Eteri Gugushvili, interview, 26 July 2011.

148. Terenti Papashvili, interview, 25 July 2011.

149. Erkin Bakchiev, interview, 9 August 2009.

150. Brown, *Seven Years*, 6.

CONCLUSION

1. Madeleine Reeves, "Clean Fake: Authenticating Documents and Persons in Migrant Moscow," *American Ethnologist* 40, no. 3 (2013): 508–24. DOI: 10.1111/amet.12036.

2. Stuart Hall, "The Local and the Global: Globalization and Identity," in *Culture, Globalization and the World-System: Contemporary Conditions for the Representation of Identity*, ed. Anthony D. King (Basingstoke: Macmillan, 1991), 24.

3. Mike Phillips and Trevor Phillips, *Windrush: The Irresistible Rise of Multi-racial Britain* (London: HarperCollins, 2009).

4. On halting but sometimes successful efforts of Muslim minorities to gain social and political power in Western Europe, see Sarah Hackett, *Foreigners, Minorities and Integration: The Muslim Immigrant Experience in Britain and Germany* (Manchester: Manchester University Press, 2013).

5. Vazha Gigulashvili, interview, 23 July 2011.

6. Irma Balanchivadze, interview, 23 July 2011.

7. Anarbek Zakirov, interview, 9 August 2009.

8. David Somkishvili, interview, 24 July 2011.

9. For an older but more detailed analysis of abuse faced by post-Soviet migrants, see Human Rights Watch, *"Are You Happy to Cheat Us?" Exploitation of Migrant Construction*

Workers in Russia (New York: Human Rights Watch, 2009), https://www.hrw.org/report/2009/02/10/are-you-happy-cheat-us/exploitation-migrant-construction-workers-russia. In 2008, the SOVA research center reported at least 116 deaths and 499 injuries resulting from racism and xenophobia in Russia (excluding the North Caucasus). These numbers have fallen to fewer than 6 deaths and 71 overall victims in 2017. SOVA Center, "Old Problems and New Alliances: Xenophobia and Radical Nationalism in Russia, and Efforts to Counteract Them in 2016," https://www.sova-center.ru/en/xenophobia/reports-analyses/2017/05/d36995/ (accessed 3 July 2017). An analysis of this decrease lies far beyond the scope of this study, but belated state efforts to prosecute leaders of nationalist organizations play a strong role. Madeleine Reeves notes that the lessened threat of physical violence is not matched by any greater ease of avoiding exploitation or harassment. Reeves, "Clean Fake," 509.

10. Farshad Hajiev, interview, 11 November 2007.

11. On Central Asian and Caucasus migrants' efforts to claim these cities and overcome discrimination, see, for example, Olga Kornienko et al., "Financial and Emotional Support in Close Personal Ties among Central Asian Migrant Women in Russia," *Social Networks* 53, no. 2 (2018): 125–35. DOI: 10.1016/j.socnet.2017.04.006; Sergei Abashin, "Movements and Migrants in Central Asia," *The Russian Reader* (blog), https://therussianreader.com/2015/07/15/sergei-abashin-movements-and-migrants-in-central-asia/ (accessed 20 June 2018).

APPENDIX

1. Sahadeo, *Russian Colonial Society in Tashkent*.

2. On the possibilities of oral history, see Paul Thompson, "The Voice of the Past: Oral History," in *The Oral History Reader*, ed. Robert Perks and Alistair Thomson, 3rd ed. (New York: Routledge, 2016), 34–39.

3. In a few cases, it turned out that informants had lived in Leningrad / St. Petersburg only after 1991 or that their experiences were with other European cities in the USSR. We generally would conduct such interviews to gather information, but did not use them in the final product.

4. On interviews as relationships, see Alessandro Portelli, "The Peculiarities of Oral History," *History Workshop Journal* 12, no. 1 (1981): 96–107. DOI: 10.1093/hwj/12.1.96.

5. Berdahl, "'(N)ostalgie' for the Present"; Boym, *Common Places*; Todorova and Gille, *Post-Communist Nostalgia*.

6. On this phenomenon, see Barbara Shircliffe, "'We Got the Best of That World': A Case for the Study of Nostalgia in the Oral History of School Segregation," *Oral History Review* 28, no. 2 (2001): 59–84, https://www.jstor.org/stable/3675778.

7. Otto Boele, "Remembering Brezhnev in the New Millennium: Post-Soviet Nostalgia and Local Identity in the City of Novorossiisk," *Soviet and Post-Soviet Review* 38, no. 1 (2011): 3–29. DOI: 10.1163/187633211X564157.

8. Oushakine, "'We're Nostalgic but We're Not Crazy.'"

9. Portelli, "The Peculiarities of Oral History."

Bibliography

ARCHIVES

Central State Archive of the City of Moscow (Tsentral'nyi Gosudarstvennyi Arkhiv Goroda Moskvy)

Central State Archive of Political Documentation of the Kyrgyz Republic (Tsentral'nyi Gosudarstvennyi Arkhiv Politicheskoi Dokumentatsii Kirgizskoi Respubliki) (TsGAPDKR)

Russian State Archive of Social and Political History (Rossiiskoi Gosudarstvennyi ArkhivSotsial'no-Politicheskoi Istorii) (RGASPI)

State Archive of the Russian Federation (Gosudarstvennyi Arkhiv Rossiiskoi Federatsii) (GARF)

NEWSPAPERS AND PERIODICALS

Argumenty i fakty
Arkhitektura i Stroitel'stva
Chasy
Christian Science Monitor
Golos Rossii
Izvestiia
Los Angeles Times
Moscow Times
Moskovskii komsomolets
Muslims of the Soviet East
Narodnoe delo
Nashe vremia
Pravda
Pravda Vostoka
Russkaia gazeta
Russkie vedomosti
Russkoe delo
Tashkentskaia pravda

PUBLISHED SOURCES

Abashin, Sergei. "Movements and Migrants in Central Asia." *The Russian Reader* (blog). Accessed 20 June 2018. https://therussianreader.com/2015/07/15/sergei-abashin -movements-and-migrants-in-central-asia/.

——. *Sovetskii kishlak: Mezhdu kolonializmom i modernizatsiei*. Moscow: Novoe literaturnoe obozrenie, 2015.

Adelman, Deborah. *The "Children of Perestroika": Moscow Teenagers Talk about Their Lives and the Future*. Armonk, NY: M. E. Sharpe, 1992.

Ahmed, Sara, Claudia Castañeda, Anne-Marie Fortier, and Mimi Sheller, eds. *Uprootings/Regroundings: Questions of Home and Migration*. Oxford, UK: Berg, 2003.

Aldrich, Robert, ed. *The Age of Empires*. London: Thames and Hudson, 2007.

Aleksandrovskii, I. U. *Moskva: Dialog putevoditel'*. Moscow: Moskovskii rabochii, 1983.

Alexander, Claire. "Beyond Black: Re-thinking the Colour/Culture Divide." *Ethnic and Racial Studies* 25, no. 4 (2002): 552–71. DOI: 10.1080/01419870220136637.

Alexopoulos, Golfo. "Soviet Citizenship, More or Less: Rights, Emotions, and States of Civic Belonging." *Kritika: Explorations in Russian and Eurasian History* 7, no. 3 (2006): 487–528. DOI: 10.1353/kri.2006.0030.

Ali, Nasreen, Virinder S. Kalra, and Salman Sayyid, eds. *A Postcolonial People: South Asians in Britain*. New York: Columbia University Press, 2008.

Anchabadze, Iu. D., and N. G. Volkova. *Staryi Tbilisi: Gorod i gorozhane v XIX veke*. Moscow: Nauka, 1990.

Anderson, Barbara, and Brian Silver. "Estimating Russification of Ethnic Identity among the Non-Russians of the USSR." *Demography* 20, no. 4 (1983): 461–89. DOI: 10.2307/2061114.

———. "Growth and Diversity of the Population of the Soviet Union." *Annals of the American Academy of Political and Social Science* 1, no. 510 (1990): 155–77. DOI: 10.1177/0002716290510001012.

Applebaum, Rachel. "The Friendship Project: Socialist Internationalism in the Soviet Union and Czechoslovakia in the 1950s and 1960s." *Slavic Review* 74, no. 3 (2015): 484–507. DOI: 10.5612/slavicreview.74.3.484.

Armstrong, George M. "Control of Mobility of Labor in the Soviet Union." *Journal of International and Comparative Law* 3, no. 172 (1982): 173–92.

Arutiunian, Iu. V. "Armiane-moskvichi: Sotsial'nyi portret po materialam etnosotsio-logicheskogo issledovaniia." *Sovetskoe etnografiia*, no. 2 (1991): 3–16.

Arutiunian, Iu. V., and Iu. V. Bromlei, eds. *Sotsial'no-kul'turnyi oblik sovetskikh natsii*. Moscow: Nauka, 1986.

Ashwin, Sarah. *Russian Workers: The Anatomy of Patience*. Manchester: Manchester University Press, 1999.

Azrael, Jeremy, ed. *Soviet Nationality Policy and Practices*. New York: Praeger, 1978.

Bahry, Donna. "Society Transformed? Rethinking the Social Roots of Perestroika." *Slavic Review* 52, no. 3 (1993): 512–54. DOI: 10.2307/2499722.

Bahry, Donna, and Carol Nechemias. "Half-Full or Half-Empty? The Debate over Soviet Regional Equality." *Slavic Review* 40, no. 3 (1981): 366–83. DOI: 10.2307/2496192.

Ball, Alan M. *Russia's Last Capitalists: The Nepmen, 1921–1929*. Berkeley: University of California Press, 1990.

Banerji, Arup. *Writing History in the Soviet Union: Making the Past Work*. New York: Routledge, 2018.

Barkan, Elliott, Hasia Diner, and Alan M. Kraut, eds. *From Arrival to Incorporation: Migrants to the U.S. in a Global Era*. New York: New York University Press, 2007.

Barrett, Thomas. "The Remaking of the Lion of Dagestan: Shamil in Captivity." *Russian Review* 53, no. 3 (1994): 353–66. DOI: 10.2307/131191.

Bassin, Mark, and Catriona Kelly, eds. *Soviet and Post-Soviet Identities*. Cambridge: Cambridge University Press, 2012.

Belenkin, Boris, ed. *Anti-Semitism and Nationalism at the End of the Soviet Era*. Leiden: Brill, 1999.

Beliaeva, Galina., Denis Draguskii, and Liliia Zotova. "Mnogonatsional'nyi mir Moskvy." *Druzhba narodov*, no. 4 (1993), 134–48.

Belin, Laura. "The Russian Media in the 1990s." *Journal of Communist Studies and Transition Politics* 18, no. 1 (2002): 139–60. DOI: 10.1080/13523270209696371.

Benmayor, Rina, and Andor Skotnes, eds. *Migration and Identity*. Oxford: Oxford University Press, 1994.

Bennigsen, Alexandre, Paul Henze, George Tanham, and S. Enders Wimbush. *Soviet Strategy and Islam*. New York: Palgrave Macmillan, 1989.

Berdahl, Daphne. "'(N)ostalgie' for the Present: Memory, Longing, and East German Things." *Ethnos* 64, no. 2 (1999): 192–211. DOI: 10.1080/00141844.1999.9981598.

Bernaskoni, E. B., ed. *Moskva—dlia vsekh stolitsa*. Moscow: Moskovskii rabochii, 1982.

Bindas, Kenneth J. "Re-remembering a Segregated Past: Race in American Memory." *History and Memory* 22, no. 1 (2010): 113–34. https://muse.jhu.edu/article /376350.

Blitstein, Peter A. "Cultural Diversity and the Interwar Conjuncture: Soviet Nationality Policy in Its Comparative Context." *Slavic Review* 65, no. 2 (2006): 273–93. DOI: 10.2307/4148593.

Blokland, Talja, Christine Hentschel, Andrej Holm, Henrik Lebuhn, and Talia Margalit. "Urban Citizenship and the Right to the City: The Fragmentation of Claims." *International Journal of Urban and Regional Research* 39, no. 4 (2015): 655–65. DOI: 10.1111/1468-2427.12259.

Bocharnikova, Daria, and Steven E. Harris, eds. "Second World Urbanity: New Histories of the Socialist City." Special section, *Journal of Urban History* 44, no. 1 (2018): 3–117.

Boele, Otto. "Remembering Brezhnev in the New Millennium: Post-Soviet Nostalgia and Local Identity in the City of Novorossiisk." *Soviet and Post-Soviet Review* 38, no. 1 (2011): 3–29. DOI: 10.1163/187633211X564157.

Boyd, Monica. "Family and Personal Networks in International Migration: Recent Developments and New Agendas." *International Migration Review* 23, no. 3 (1989): 638–70. DOI:10.2307/2546433.

Boym, Svetlana. *Common Places: Mythologies of Everyday Life in Russia*. Cambridge, MA: Harvard University Press, 1994.

Braziel, Jana Evans, and Anita Mannur, eds. *Theorizing Diaspora: A Reader*. Malden, MA: Blackwell, 2003.

Brednikova, Olga, and Oleg Pachenkov. "Azerbaidzhanskie torgovtsy v Peterburge: Mezhdu 'voobrazhaemymi soobshchestvami' i 'pervichnymi gruppami.'" *Diaspory*, no. 1 (2001): 131–47.

Brenner, Neil, and Roger Keil, eds. *The Global Cities Reader*. London: Routledge, 2006.

Bromlei, Iu. V., et al., eds. *Etnosotsialnye problemy goroda*. Moscow: Nauka, 1986.

Brown, Archie. *Seven Years That Changed the World: Perestroika in Perspective*. Oxford: Oxford University Press, 1991.

Brown, Kate. "Gridded Lives: Why Kazakhstan and Montana Are Nearly the Same Place." *American Historical Review* 106, no. 1 (2001): 17–48. DOI: 10.2307/2652223.

Brubaker, Rogers. "Ethnicity, Race and Nationalism." *Annual Review of Sociology* 35 (2009): 21–42. DOI: 10.1146/annurev-soc-070308-115916.

Bryant, Kelly Duke. "Social Networks and Empire: Senegalese Students in France in the Late Nineteenth Century." *French Colonial History* 15, no. 1 (2014): 39–66. https://muse.jhu.edu/article/547757.

Buckley, Cynthia. "The Myth of Managed Migration: Migration Control and Market in the Soviet Period." *Slavic Review* 54, no. 4 (1995): 896–916. DOI: 10.2307/2501398.

Buckley, Cynthia, and Blair Ruble, eds. *Migration, Homeland, and Belonging in Eurasia*. Baltimore: Johns Hopkins University Press, 2008.

Bushnell, John. *Moscow Graffiti: Language and Subculture*. Boston: Unwin Hyman, 1990.

Calavita, Kitty. *Immigrants at the Margins: Law, Race and Exclusion in Southern Europe*. Cambridge: Cambridge University Press, 2005.

Carrère d'Encausse, Hélène. *Le grand défi: Bolcheviks et nations, 1917–1930*. Paris: Flammarion, 1987.

Castles, Stephen, and Mark J. Miller. *The Age of Migration: International Population Movements in the Modern World*. New York: Guilford, 1998.

Clemens, Walter C., Jr. "Straddling Cultures: An Azeri in Moscow." *Christian Science Monitor*, 12 March 1990.

Cohn, Bernard S. *Colonialism and Its Forms of Knowledge: The British in India*. Princeton, NJ: Princeton University Press, 1996.

Colton, Timothy. *Moscow: Governing the Socialist Metropolis*. Cambridge, MA: Harvard University Press, 1996.

Cook, Linda J. *The Soviet Social Contract and Why It Failed: Welfare Policy and Workers' Politics from Brezhnev to Yeltsin*. Cambridge, MA: Harvard University Press, 1993.

Cross, Malcolm, and Michael Keith, eds. *Racism, the City and the State*. London: Routledge, 1992.

Dannecker, Petra. "Transnational Migration and the Transformation of Gender Relations: The Case of Bangladeshi Labour Migrants." *Current Sociology* 53, no. 4 (2005): 655–74. DOI: 10.1177/0011392105052720.

de Haas, Hein. "Migration and Development: A Theoretical Perspective." *International Migration Review* 44, no. 1 (2010): 227–64. https://www.jstor.org/stable /20681751.

Delanty, Gerard, Ruth Wodak, and Paul Jones, eds. *Identity, Belonging and Migration*. Liverpool: Liverpool University Press, 2008.

de Waal, Thomas. *The Caucasus: An Introduction*. Oxford: Oxford University Press, 2010.

Diaspory: Predstavitel'stva natsional'nostei v Moskve i ikh deiatel'nost'. Moscow: TsPI, 2003.

Draitser, Emil. *Taking Penguins to the Movies: Ethnic Humor in Russia*. Detroit: Wayne State University Press, 1998.

Drieu, Cloé, *Fictions nationales: Cinéma, empire et nation en Ouzbékistan (1919–1937)*. Paris: Karthala, 2013.

Duhamel, Luc. "Justice and Politics in Moscow, 1983–1986: The Ambartsumyan Case." *Europe-Asia Studies* 52, no. 7 (2000): 1307–29. DOI: 10.1080/713663133.

——. *The KGB Campaign against Corruption in Moscow, 1982–1987*. Pittsburgh: University of Pittsburgh Press, 2010.

——. "The Last Campaign against Corruption in Soviet Moscow." *Europe-Asia Studies* 56, no. 2 (2004): 187–212. DOI: 10.1080/0966813042000190506.

Dunlop, John. *The Faces of Contemporary Russian Nationalism*. Princeton, NJ: Princeton University Press, 2014.

——. "Russian Nationalism Today: Organizations and Programs." *Nationalities Papers* 19, no. 2 (1991): 146–66.

Eley, Geoff. "The Past under Erasure? History, Memory, and the Contemporary." *Journal of Contemporary History* 46, no. 3 (2011): 555–73. DOI: 10.1177/0022009411403342.

Elliott, Emily J. "Making and Policing Muscovites: Migrant Letters to the Priemnaia of the Supreme Soviet." Paper presented at the Annual Convention of the Association for Slavic, East European, and Eurasian Studies, Chicago, 10 November 2017.

——. "Soviet Socialist Stars and Neoliberal Losers: Young Labour Migrants in Moscow, 1971–1991." *Journal of Migration History*, no. 2 (2017): 274–300.

Engebrigtsen, Ada Ingrid. "Kinship, Gender, and Adaptation Processes in Exile: The Case of Tamil and Somali Families in Norway." *Journal of Ethnic and Migration Studies* 33, no. 5 (2007): 727–46. DOI: 10.1080/13691830701359173.

Essed, Philomena. *Understanding Everyday Racism: An Interdisciplinary Theory*. London: Sage, 1991.

Etnicheskie protsessi v stolichnom megapolise. Moscow: RAN, 2008.

Eustace, Nicole, Eugenia Lean, Julie Livingston, Jan Plamper, William M. Reddy, and Barbara H. Rosenwein. "*AHR* Conversation: The Historical Study of Emotions." *American Historical Review* 117, no. 5 (2012): 1487–1531.

Evans, Christine. "The 'Soviet Way of Life' as a Way of Feeling: Emotion and Influence on Soviet Central Television in the Brezhnev Era." *Cahiers du monde russe* 56, nos. 2–3 (2015): 543–69. https://www.jstor.org/stable/24567613.

Fainberg, Dina, and Artemy Kalinovsky, eds. *Reconsidering Stagnation in the Brezhnev Era: Ideology and Exchange*. Lanham, MD: Lexington Books, 2016.

Fangen, Katrine, Thomas Johansson and Nils Hammarén, eds. *Young Migrants: Exclusion and Belonging in Europe*. Basingstoke: Palgrave Macmillan, 2012.

Fields, Karen E., and Barbara J. Fields. *Racecraft: The Soul of Inequality in American Life*. New York: Verso, 2014.

Fierman, William, ed. *Soviet Central Asia: The Failed Transformation*. Boulder, CO: Westview, 1991.

Fischer, Claude S. *To Dwell among Friends: Personal Networks in Town and City*. Chicago: University of Chicago Press, 1982.

Florin, Moritz. "Becoming Soviet through War: The Kyrgyz and the Great Fatherland War." *Kritika* 17, no. 3 (2016): 495–516. DOI: 10.1353/kri.2016.0033.

——. "Faites tomber les murs! La politique civilizatrice de l'ère Brežnev dans les villages kirghiz." *Cahiers du monde russe* 54, nos. 1–2 (2013): 187–211. https://www.jstor.org/stable/24567694.

Foner, Nancy. *In a New Land: A Comparative View of Immigration*. New York: New York University Press, 2005.

Fürst, Juliane. "Love, Peace and Rock 'n' Roll on Gorky Street: The 'Emotional Style' of the Soviet Hippie Community." *Contemporary European History* 23, no. 4 (2014): 565–87. DOI: 10.1017/S0960777314000320.

Garbaye, Romaine. "British Cities and Ethnic Minorities in the Post-war Era: From Xenophobic Agitation to Multi-ethnic Government." *Immigrants and Minorities* 22, nos. 2–3 (2003): 298–315. DOI: 10.1080/0261928042000244880.

Gavrilova, I. N. *Demograficheskaia istoriia Moskvy*. Moscow: Fast-Print, 1997.

Giddens, Anthony. *The Constitution of Society*. Berkeley: University of California Press, 1984.

Glubova, Vera. "Zaboty mnogonatsional'nogo goroda." *Arkhitektura i stroitel'stva Moskvy*, no. 9 (1989): 8.

Goldberg, David Theo. "Racial Europeanization." *Ethnic and Racial Studies* 29, no. 2 (2006): 331–64. DOI: 10.1080/01419870500465611.

Gorlov, V. N. "Sovetskie obshchezhitiia rabochei molodezhi." *Otechestvennaia istoriia*, no. 5 (2004): 177–80.

Goss, Jon, and Bruce Lindquist. "Conceptualizing International Labor Migration: A Structuration Perspective." *International Migration Review* 29, no. 2 (1995): 317–51. DOI: 10.2307/2546784.

Grant, Bruce. "Cosmopolitan Baku." *Ethnos* 75, no. 2 (2010): 123–47. DOI:10.1080/00141841003753222.

Grossman, Gregory. "The 'Second Economy' of the USSR." *Problems of Communism* 26, no. 5 (1977): 25–40.

Gupta, Akhil, and James Ferguson, eds. "Beyond 'Culture': Space, Identity, and the Politics of Difference." In *Culture, Power, Place: Exploration in Critical Anthropology*. Durham, NC: Duke University Press, 1997, 33–51.

Hackett, Sarah. *Foreigners, Minorities and Integration: The Muslim Immigrant Experience in Britain and Germany.* Manchester: Manchester University Press, 2013.

Hajda, Lubomyr, and Mark Beissinger, eds. *The Nationalities Factor in Soviet Politics and Society.* Boulder, CO: Westview, 1990.

Hall, Catherine, and Sonya O. Rose, eds. *At Home with the Empire: Metropolitan Culture and the Imperial World.* Cambridge: Cambridge University Press, 2006.

Hansen, Randall. *Citizenship and Immigration in Post-war Britain.* Oxford: Oxford University Press, 2000.

Harris, Steven E. *Communism on Tomorrow Street: Mass Housing and Everyday Life after Stalin.* Washington, DC: Woodrow Wilson Center Press; Baltimore: Johns Hopkins University Press, 2013.

Haugen, Arne. *The Establishment of National Republics in Soviet Central Asia.* Basingstoke: Palgrave Macmillan, 2003.

Hellbeck, Jochen. *Revolution on My Mind: Writing a Diary under Stalin.* Cambridge, MA: Harvard University Press, 2006.

Herbert, Joanna. *Negotiating Boundaries in the City: Migration, Ethnicity, and Gender in Britain.* London: Routledge, 2008.

Herbert, Joanna, Jon May, Jane Wills, Kavita Datta, Yara Evans, and Cathy McIlwaine. "Multicultural Living? Experiences of Everyday Racism among Ghanaian Immigrants in London." *European Urban and Regional Studies* 15, no. 2 (2008): 103–17. DOI: 10.1177/0969776407087544.

Herzberger, Leslie. *The Rise and Fall of a Thermidorian Society: Why the Soviet Union Came Apart, 1917–1991; A Case Study.* Bloomington, IN: Xlibris, 2007.

Hessler, Julie. "Death of an African Student in Moscow: Race, Politics, and the Cold War." *Cahiers du monde russe* 47, no. 1 (2006): 33–64.

Hirsch, Francine. *Empire of Nations: Ethnographic Knowledge and the Making of the Soviet Union.* Ithaca, NY: Cornell University Press, 2005.

Hofmann, Erin Trouth, and Cynthia Buckley. "Cultural Responses to Changing Gender Patterns of Migration in Georgia." *International Migration* 50, no. 5 (2012): 77–94. DOI: 10.1111/j.1468-2435.2010.00681.x.

Höjdestrand, Tova. "The Soviet-Russian Production of Homelessness." AnthroBase. Accessed 30 June 2017. http://www.anthrobase.com/Txt/H/Hoejdestrand_T_01.htm.

Horvath, Robert. *The Legacy of Soviet Dissent: Dissidence, Democratisation and Radical Nationalism in Russia.* London: RoutledgeCurzon, 2005.

Houston, Cecil J. "Administrative Control of Migration to Moscow, 1959–75." *Canadian Geographer* 23, no. 1 (1979): 32–44. DOI: 10.1111/j.1541-0064.1979.tb00636.x.

Hudspith, Sarah. "Moscow: A Global City? Introduction." *Slavic Review* 72, no. 3 (2013): 453–57. DOI: 10.5612/slavicreview.72.3.0453.

Human Rights Watch. *"Are You Happy to Cheat Us?" Exploitation of Migrant Construction Workers in Russia.* New York: Human Rights Watch, 2009. https://www.hrw.org/report/2009/02/10/are-you-happy-cheat-us/exploitation-migrant-construction-workers-russia.

Ibañez-Tirado, Diana. "'How Can I Be Post-Soviet If I Was Never Soviet?' Rethinking Categories of Time and Social Change—a Perspective from Kulob, Southern Tajikistan." *Central Asian Survey* 34, no. 2 (2015): 190–203. DOI: 10.1080/02634937.2014.983705.

Igmen, Ali. *Speaking Soviet with an Accent: Culture and Power in Kyrgyzstan.* Pittsburgh: University of Pittsburgh Press, 2012.

Ilič, Melanie, Susan E. Reid, and Lynne Attwood, eds. *Women in the Khrushchev Era.* Basingstoke: Palgrave Macmillan, 2004.

Isaakyan, Irina L. "Blood and Soil of the Soviet Academy: Politically Institutionalized Anti-Semitism in the Moscow Academic Circles of the Brezhnev Era through the Life Stories of Russian Academic Emigrants." *Nationalities Papers* 36, no. 5 (2008): 833–59. DOI: 10.1080/00905990802373520.

Isaeva, G., G. Kuleshova, and V. Tsigankov. *Moskva internatsional'naia*. Moscow: Moskovskii rabochii, 1977.

Itogi vsesoiuznoi perepisi naseleniia 1989 g. Tom 7, chast' 1. Moscow: Statistika, 1991.

Jansen, Stef, and Staffan Löfving, eds. *Struggles for Home: Violence, Hope, and the Movement of People*. New York: Berghahn Books, 2009.

Johnson, Robert Eugene. *Peasant and Proletarian: The Working Class of Moscow in the Late Nineteenth Century*. New Brunswick, NJ: Rutgers University Press, 1979.

Jones, Anthony, Walter D. Connor, and David E. Powell, eds. *Soviet Social Problems*. Boulder, CO: Westview, 1991.

Joo, Hyung-min. "The Soviet Origin of Russian Chauvinism: Voices from Below." *Communist and Post-Communist Studies* 41 (2008): 217–42. DOI:10.1016/j.postcomstud.2008.03.002.

Kabachnik, Peter, Joanna Regulska and Beth Mitchneck. "Where and When Is Home? The Double Displacement of Georgian IDPs from Abkhazia." *Journal of Refugee Studies* 23, no. 3 (2010): 315–36. DOI: 10.1093/jrs/feq023.

Kalinovsky, Artemy. "Central Planning, Local Knowledge? Labor, Population, and the 'Tajik School of Economics.'" *Kritika* 17, no. 3 (2016): 585–620. DOI: 10.1353/kri.2016.0036.

——. "A Most Beautiful City for the World's Tallest Dam: Internationalism, Social Welfare and Urban Utopia in Nurek." *Cahiers du monde russe* 57, no. 4 (2016): 819–46. https://www.cairn-int.info/article-E_CMR_574_0819—a-most-beautiful-city-for-theworld-s.htm.

——. "Not Some British Colony in Africa: The Politics of Decolonization and Modernization in Soviet Central Asia, 1955–1964." *Ab Imperio*, no. 2 (2013): 191–222. DOI: 10.1353/imp.2013.0044.

Kamp, Marianne. *The New Woman in Uzbekistan: Islam, Modernity and Unveiling under Communism*. Seattle: University of Washington Press, 2006.

Kaplan, Isabelle. "The *Dekady* of the Art of the Caucasian Republics, 1937–1944." Unpublished manuscript, 2014. https://drive.google.com/file/d/0B-eSQ2mo0JRxMDZZV3pvUEo5YVE/view.

Karklins, Rasma. *Ethnic Relations in the U.S.S.R.: The Perspective from Below*. Boston: Allen & Unwin, 1985.

——. *Ethnopolitics and Transition to Democracy: The Collapse of the USSR and Latvia*. Washington, DC: Woodrow Wilson Center Press; Baltimore: Johns Hopkins University Press, 1994.

Karpenko, Oksana, and Jana Javakhishvili, eds. *Myths and Conflict in the South Caucasus*. Vol. 1, *Instrumentalisation of Historical Narratives*. London: International Alert, 2013. https://www.international-alert.org/sites/default/files/Caucasus_MythsConflict_Vol1_EN_2013.pdf.

Kassymbekova, Botakoz. *Despite Cultures: Early Soviet Rule in Tajikistan*. Pittsburgh: University of Pittsburgh Press, 2016.

Katsakioris, Constantin. "Burden or Allies? Third World Students and Internationalist Duty through Soviet Eyes." *Kritika* 18, no. 3 (2017): 539–67. DOI: 10.1353/kri.2017.0035.

Kearney, Michael. "From the Invisible Hand to Visible Feet: Anthropological Studies of Migration and Development." *Annual Review of Anthropology* 15 (1986): 331–61. DOI: 10.1146/annurev.an.15.100186.001555.

Keep, John L. H. *Last of the Empires: A History of the Soviet Union, 1945–1991*. Oxford: Oxford University Press, 1995.

Kelly, Catriona, and David Shepherd, eds. *Russian Cultural Studies*. Oxford: Oxford University Press, 1998.

Kenway, Jane, and Johannah Fahey, eds. *Globalizing the Research Imagination*. London: Routledge, 2009.

Kessler, Gijs. "The Passport System and State Control over Population Flows in the Soviet Union, 1932–1940." *Cahiers du monde russe* 42, nos. 2–4 (2001): 477–503. https://www.jstor.org/stable/20174642.

Khalid, Adeeb. "Backwardness and the Quest for Civilization: Early Soviet Central Asia in a Comparative Perspective." *Slavic Review* 65, no. 2 (2006): 231–51. DOI: 10.2307/4148591.

——. *Islam after Communism: Religion and Politics in Central Asia*. Berkeley: University of California Press, 2007.

——. *Making Uzbekistan: Nation, Empire, and Revolution in the Early USSR*. Ithaca, NY: Cornell University Press, 2015.

——. *The Politics of Muslim Cultural Reform: Jadidism in Central Asia*. Berkeley: University of California Press, 1998.

Khorev, B. S. *Urbanizatsiia i demograficheskie protsessi*. Moscow: Finansy i statistika, 1982.

Khorev, B. S., and V. N. Chapek. *Problemy izucheniia migratsiia naseleniia*. Moscow: Mysl, 1978.

Khorev, B. S., and N. P. Matveev, eds. *Rasselenie i dinamika naseleniia Moskvy i Moskovskoi oblasti: Sbornik statei*. Moscow: Moskovskii filial Geograficheskoe obshchestvo, 1981.

Kim, Byung-Yeon. "Informal Economy Activities of Soviet Households: Size and Dynamics." *Journal of Comparative Economics* 31, no. 3 (2003): 532–51. DOI: 10.1016/S0147-5967(03)00052-0.

King, Anthony D., ed. *Culture, Globalization and the World-System: Contemporary Conditions for the Representation of Identity*. Basingstoke: Macmillan, 1991.

King, Charles. *The Ghost of Freedom: A History of the Caucasus*. Oxford: Oxford University Press, 2008.

King, Russell, ed. *The New Geography of European Migrations*. London: Belhaven, 1993.

Kirasirova, Masha. "The 'East' as a Category of Bolshevik Ideology and Comintern Administration: The Arab Section of the Communist University of the Toilers of the East." *Kritika* 18, no. 1 (2017): 7–34. DOI: 10.1353/kri.2017.0001.

——. "'Sons of Muslims' in Moscow: Soviet Central Asian Mediators to the Foreign East, 1955–1962." *Ab Imperio*, no. 4 (2011): 106–32. DOI: 10.1353/imp.2011.0003.

Klugman, Jeni, ed. *Poverty in Russia: Public Policy and Private Responses*. New York: World Bank, 1997.

Koenker, Diane. *Club Red: Vacation Travel and the Soviet Dream*. Ithaca, NY: Cornell University Press, 2013.

Kolstoe, Paul. *Russians in the Former Soviet Republics*. Hong Kong: C. Hurst, 1995.

Kornienko, Olga, Victor Agadjanian, Cecilia Menjivar, and Natalia Zotova. "Financial and Emotional Support in Close Personal Ties among Central Asian Migrant Women in Russia." *Social Networks* 53, no. 2 (2018): 125–35. DOI: 10.1016/j.socnet.2017.04.006.

Korolev, Sergei. "The Student Dormitory in the 'Period of Stagnation.'" *Russian Politics and Law* 42, no. 2 (2004): 77–93. DOI: 10.1080/10611940.2004.11066915.

Kosygina, Larisa. "The Russian Migration Regime and Migrants' Experiences: The Case of Non-Russian Nationals from Former Soviet Republics." PhD diss., University of Birmingham, 2009.

Kotkin, Stephen. *Armageddon Averted: The Soviet Collapse, 1970–2000.* Oxford: Oxford University Press, 2001.

Kuzio, Taras. *Ukraine: Perestroika to Independence.* 2nd ed. Basingstoke: Palgrave Macmillan, 2000.

Lambert, David, and Alan Lester. *Colonial Lives across the British Empire.* Cambridge: Cambridge University Press, 2006.

Lane, David. *Soviet Society under Perestroika.* London: Routledge, 1992.

Laruelle, Marlene, and Caress Schenk, eds. *Eurasia on the Move: Interdisciplinary Approaches to a Dynamic Migration Region.* Washington, DC: George Washington Central Asia Program, 2018.

Laurence, Jonathan, and Justin Vaisse. *Integrating Islam: Political and Religious Challenges in Contemporary France.* Washington, DC: Brookings Institution Press, 2006.

Ledeneva, Alena. "*Blat* and *Guanxi*: Informal Practices in Russia and China." *Contemporary Studies in Society and History* 50, no. 1 (2008): 118–44. DOI: 10.1017/S0010417508000078.

——. *Russia's Economy of Favours:* Blat, *Networking and Informal Exchange.* Cambridge: Cambridge University Press, 1998.

Lehmann, Maike. "Apricot Socialism: The National Past, the Soviet Project, and the Imagining of Community in Late Soviet Armenia." *Slavic Review* 74, no. 1 (Spring 2015): 9–31. DOI: 10.5612/slavicreview.74.1.9.

Lemercier-Quelquejay, Chantal. "Le monde musulman soviétique d'Asie centrale après Alma-Ata (décembre 1986)." *Cahiers du monde russe et soviétique* 32, no. 1 (1991): 117–21. https://www.jstor.org/stable/20170769.

Lewin, Moshe. *The Gorbachev Phenomenon: A Historical Interpretation.* Expanded ed. Berkeley: University of California Press, 1991.

Lewis, Robert A., Richard H. Rowland, and Ralph S. Clem. *Nationality and Population Change in Russia and the USSR: An Evaluation of Census Data, 1897–1970.* New York: Praeger, 1976.

Light, Matthew. "What Does It Mean to Control Migration? Soviet Mobility Policies in Comparative Perspective." *Law and Social Inquiry* 37, no. 2 (2012): 395–429. DOI: 10.1111/j.1747-4469.2012.01308.x.

Liu, Morgan. "Urban Materiality and Its Stakes in Southern Kyrgyzstan." *Quaderni storici* 50, no. 2 (2015): 1–24. DOI: 10.1408/81787.

Loeber, Dietrich André. "*Limitchiki*: On the Legal Status of Migrant Workers in Large Soviet Cities." *Soviet and Post-Soviet Review* 11, no. 1 (1984): 301–8. DOI: 10.1163/187633284X00198.

Lohr, Eric. *Nationalizing the Russian Empire: The Campaign against Enemy Aliens during World War I.* Cambridge, MA: Harvard University Press, 2003.

Lonkila, Markku, and Anna-Maria Salmi. "The Russian Work Collective and Migration." *Europe-Asia Studies* 57, no. 5 (2005): 681–703. DOI: 10.1080/09668130500126452.

Lubin, Nancy. *Labour and Nationality in Soviet Central Asia.* Princeton, NJ: Princeton University Press, 1984.

Makarova, L. V., G. F. Morozova, and N. V. Tarasova. *Regional'nye osobennosti migratsionnykh protsessov v SSSR.* Moscow: Nauka, 1986.

Maksimov, G. M. *Vsesoiuznaia perepis' naseleniia 1970 goda: Sbornik statei.* Moscow: Statistika, 1976.

Malashenko, A. V., F. M. Mukhametshin, and L. R. Siukiiainen. *Musul'mane izmeniai-ushcheisia Rossii.* Moscow: ROSSPEN, 2002.

Malkki, Liisa. "National Geographic: The Rooting of Peoples and the Territorialization of National Identity among Scholars and Refugees." *Cultural Anthropology* 7, no. 1 (1992): 24–44. https://www.jstor.org/stable/656519.

Manley, Rebecca. *To the Tashkent Station: Evacuation and Survival in the Soviet Union at War.* Ithaca, NY: Cornell University Press, 2009.

Marples, David R. "Revisiting the Collapse of the USSR." *Canadian Slavonic Papers* 53, nos. 2–4 (2011): 461–73. DOI: 10.1080/00085006.2011.11092684.

Martin, Terry. *The Affirmative Action Empire: Nations and Nationalism in the Soviet Union, 1923–1939.* Ithaca, NY: Cornell University Press, 2001.

——. "The Russification of the RSFSR." *Cahiers du monde russe* 39, nos. 1–2 (1998): 99–117. https://www.jstor.org/stable/20171076.

Massey, Doreen. *Space, Place, and Gender.* Minneapolis: University of Minnesota Press, 1994.

——. *World City.* Cambridge, UK: Polity, 2007.

Matthews, Mervyn. *The Passport Society: Controlling Movement in Russia and the USSR.* Boulder, CO: Westview, 1993.

Matusevich, Maxim. "Blackness the Color of Red: Negotiating Race at the US Legation in Riga, Latvia, 1922–33." *Journal of Contemporary History* 52, no. 4 (2017): 832–52. DOI: 10.1177/0022009417723976.

——. "Probing the Limits of Internationalism: African Students Confront Soviet Ritual." *Anthropology of East Europe Review* 27, no. 2 (2009): 19–39.

McDowell, Linda. "Workers, Migrants, Aliens or Citizens? State Constructions and Discourses of Identity among Post-war European Labor Migrants in Britain." *Political Geography* 22, no. 4 (2003): 863–86. DOI: 10.1016/j.polgeo.2003.08.002.

Mellor, David, Gai Bynon, Jerome Maller, Felicity Cleary, Alex Hamilton, and Lara Watson. "The Perception of Racism in Ambiguous Scenarios." *Journal of Ethnic and Migration Studies* 27, no. 3 (2001): 473–88. DOI: 10.1080/13691830124387.

Millar, James. "The Little Deal: Brezhnev's Contribution to Acquisitive Socialism." *Slavic Review* 44, no. 4 (1985): 694–706. DOI: 10.2307/2498542.

——, ed. *Politics, Work, and Daily Life in the USSR: A Survey of Former Soviet Citizens.* Cambridge: Cambridge University Press, 1987.

Miller, Mark J., and Philip L. Martin. *Administering Foreign-Worker Programs.* Lexington, MA: D. C. Heath, 1982.

Mitrokhin, Nikolai. *Russkaia partiia: Dvizhenie russkikh natsionalistov v SSSR, 1953–1985 gody.* Moscow: Novoe literaturnoe obozrenie, 2003.

Moine, Nathalie. "Le système des passeports à l'époque stalinienne: De la purge des grandes villes au morcellement du territoire, 1932–1953." *Revue d'histoire moderne et contemporaine* 50, no. 1 (2003): 145–69. DOI: 10.3917/rhmc.501.0145.

Moiseenko, V. I., ed. *Naselenie Moskvy: Proshloe, nastoiashchee, budushchee.* Moscow: Izdatel'stvo Moskovskogo universiteta, 1992.

Moskoff, William. *Hard Times: Impoverishment and Protest in the Perestroika Years; The Soviet Union, 1985–1991.* Armonk, NY: M. E. Sharpe, 1993.

Moskva: Vchera i segodnia. Moscow: Moskovskii rabochii, 1978.

Müller, Floris. "Communicating Anti-racism." PhD diss., University of Amsterdam, 2009.

Nicholls, Walter J. "Fragmenting Citizenship: Dynamics of Cooperation and Conflict in France's Immigration Rights Movement." *Ethnic and Racial Studies* 36, no. 4 (2013): 611–31. DOI: 10.1080/01419870.2011.626055.

Nourzhanov, Kirill, and Christian Bleuer. *Tajikistan: A Political and Social History.* Canberra: ANU Press, 2013.

Nurmukhamedov, M. K. *Iz istorii russko-karakalpakskikh kul'turnykh sviazei.* Tashkent: Izdatel'stvo "Fan" UzSSR, 1974.

Oberländer, Alexandra. "Cushy Work, Backbreaking Leisure: Late Soviet Work Ethics Reconsidered." *Kritika* 18, no. 3 (2017): 569–90. DOI: 10.1353/kri.2017.0036.

Obertreis, Julia. *Imperial Desert Dreams: Cotton Growing and Irrigation in Central Asia, 1860–1991.* Göttingen: V & R Unipress, 2017.

Ostapenko, L. V., and I. A. Subbotina. *Moskva mnogonatsional'naia. Starozhily i migranty: Vmeste ili riadom?* Moscow: Rossiiskii universitet druzhba narodov, 2007.

——. "Problemy sotsial'no-ekonomicheskoi adaptatsii vykhodtsev iz Zakavkaz'ia v Moskve." *Diaspory,* no. 1 (2000): 40–59.

Oushakine, Serguei. "'We're Nostalgic but We're Not Crazy': Retrofitting the Past in Russia." *Russian Review* 66, no. 3 (2007): 451–82. https://www.jstor.org/stable /20620585.

Owen, Nicholas. "The Soft Heart of the British Empire: Indian Radicals in Edwardian London." *Past and Present* 220, no. 1 (August 2013): 143–84. DOI: 10.1093/pastj/ gtt006.

Patanik, Ajay. "Agriculture and Rural Out-Migration in Central Asia." *Europe-Asia Studies* 47, no. 1 (1995): 147–69. https://www.jstor.org/stable/153197.

Pavil'on Uzbekskoi SSR. Tashkent: Gosizdat UzSSR, 1961.

Perevedentsev, V. I. *Molodezh' i sotsial'no-demograficheskie problemy SSSR.* Moscow: Nauka, 1990.

Perks, Robert, and Alistair Thomson, eds. *The Oral History Reader.* 3rd ed. New York: Routledge, 2016.

Perry, Elizabeth. "Moving the Masses: Emotion Work in the Chinese Revolution." *Mobilization* 7, no. 2 (2002): 111–28.

Phillips, Mike, and Trevor Phillips. *Windrush: The Irresistible Rise of Multi-racial Britain.* London: HarperCollins, 2009.

Portelli, Alessandro. "The Peculiarities of Oral History." *History Workshop Journal* 12, no. 1 (1981): 96–107. DOI: 10.1093/hwj/12.1.96.

Problemy sotsial'nogo razvitiia krupnykh gorodov. Leningrad: Izdatel'stvo Leningradskogo universiteta, 1982.

Quist-Adade, Charles. *In the Shadows of the Kremlin and the White House: Africa's Media Image from Communism to Post-Communism.* Lanham, MD: University Press of America, 2001.

Raab, Nigel. *All Shook Up: The Shifting Soviet Response to Catastrophes, 1917–1991.* Montreal: McGill-Queens University Press, 2017.

Raleigh, Donald J. *Russia's Sputnik Generation: Soviet Baby Boomers Talk about Their Lives.* Bloomington: Indiana University Press, 2006.

Razvitie narodonaseleniia i problemy trudovykh resursov respublik Srednei Azii. Tashkent: Izdatel'stvo "Fan" UzSSR, 1988.

Reddy, William M. "Emotional Turn? Feeling in Russian History and Culture: Comment." *Slavic Review* 68, no. 2 (2009): 329–34. DOI: 10.2307/27697961.

Reese, Roger R. *The Soviet Military Experience: A History of the Soviet Army, 1917–1991.* London: Routledge, 2000.

Reeves, Madeleine. "'And Our Words Must Be Constructive!' On the Discordances of Glasnost' in the Central Asian Press at a Time of Conflict." *Cahiers d'Asie centrale* 26 (2016): 77–110. http://asiecentrale.revues.org/3259.

——. "Black Work, Green Money: Remittances, Ritual and Domestic Economies in Southern Kyrgyzstan." *Slavic Review* 71, no. 1 (2012): 108–34. DOI: 10.5612/slavicreview.71.1.0108.

——. "Clean Fake: Authenticating Documents and Persons in Migrant Moscow." *American Ethnologist* 40, no. 3 (2013): 508–24. DOI: 10.1111/amet.12036.

Remnick, David. *Lenin's Tomb: The Last Days of the Soviet Empire*. New York: Random House, 1993.

Rieker, Martina, and Kamran Ali, eds. *Gendering Urban Space in the Middle East, South Asia, and Africa*. New York: Palgrave Macmillan, 2008.

Ritchie, Donald A. *Doing Oral History: A Practical Guide*. Oxford: Oxford University Press, 2003.

Robinson, Jennifer. "Cities in a World of Cities: The Comparative Gesture." *International Journal of Urban and Regional Research* 35, no. 1 (2011): 1–23. DOI: 10.1111/j.1468-2427.2010.00982.x.

——. "Global and World Cities: A View from Off the Map." *International Journal of Urban and Regional Research* 26, no. 3 (2002): 531–54. DOI: 10.1111/1468-2427.00397.

Ro'i, Yaacov. *Islam in the Soviet Union: From the Second World War to Gorbachev*. New York: Columbia University Press, 2000.

Roman, Meredith. "Making Caucasians Black: Moscow since the Fall of Communism and the Racialization of Non-Russians." *Journal of Communist Studies and Transition Politics* 18, no. 2 (2002): 1–27. DOI: 10.1080/714003604.

Romanenkova, G. M., ed. *Demograficheskaia politika v regional'nom razreze*. Moscow: Nauka, 1988.

Rosenhaft, Eve, and Robbie Aitken, eds. *Africa in Europe: Studies in Transnational Practice in the Long Twentieth Century*. Liverpool: Liverpool University Press, 2013.

Rosenwein, Barbara H. "Worrying about Emotions in History." *American Historical Review* 107, no. 3 (2002): 821–45. DOI: 10.1086/532498.

Rowland, Richard H. "Nationality Population Distribution, Redistribution, and Degree of Separation in Moscow, 1979–1989." *Nationalities Papers* 26, no. 4 (1998): 705–21.

Ruble, Blair. *Leningrad: Shaping a Soviet City*. Berkeley: University of California Press, 1990.

Ryan, Michael. *Doctors and the State in the Soviet Union*. New York: Palgrave Macmillan, 2016.

Sahadeo, Jeff. "Home and Away: Why the Asian Periphery Matters in Russian History." *Kritika* 16, no. 2 (2015): 375–88. DOI: 10.1353/kri.2015.0030.

——. *Russian Colonial Society in Tashkent, 1865–1923*. Bloomington: Indiana University Press, 2007.

Sahadeo, Jeff, and Russell Zanca, eds. *Everyday Life in Central Asia: Past and Present*. Bloomington: Indiana University Press, 2007.

Sakharov, A. N., ed. *Moskva mnogonatsional'naia: Istoki, evolutsiia, problemy, sovremennosti*. Moscow: RAN, 2007.

Samers, Michael. "Immigration and the Global City Hypothesis: Towards a Research Agenda." *International Journal of Urban and Regional Research* 26, no. 2 (2002): 389–402. DOI: 10.1111/1468-2427.00386.

Sassen, Saskia. *The Global City: New York, London, Tokyo*. Princeton, NJ: Princeton University Press, 1992.

Sassen-Koob, Saskia. "Recomposition and Peripheralization at the Core." *Contemporary Marxism*, no. 5 (1982): 88–100.

Scarborough, Isaac. "(Over)determining Social Disorder: Tajikistan and the Economic Collapse of Perestroika." *Central Asian Survey* 35, no. 3 (2016): 439–63. DOI: 10.1080/02634937.2016.1189679.

Scheer, Monique. "Are Emotions a Kind of Practice (And Is That What Makes Them Have a History)? A Bourdieuian Approach to Understanding Emotion." *History and Theory* 51 (May 2012): 193–220. DOI: 10.1111/j.1468-2303.2012.00621.x.

Schiller, Nina Glick, Linda Basch, and Cristina Szanton Blanc. "From Immigrant to Transmigrant: Theorizing Transnational Migration." *Anthropological Quarterly* 68, no. 1 (1995): 48–63. DOI: 10.2307/3317464.

Schiller, Nina Glick, and Ayşe Çağlar, eds. *Locating Migration: Rescaling Cities and Migrants*. Ithaca, NY: Cornell University Press, 2011.

Scott, Erik. *Familiar Strangers: The Georgian Diaspora and the Evolution of Soviet Empire*. Oxford: Oxford University Press, 2016.

Semashko, I. M., ed. *Gendernye problemy v obshchestvennykh naukakh*. Moscow: RAN, Institut etnologii i antropologii im. N. N. Miklukho-Maklaia, 2001.

Shangina, I. I. *Mnogonatsional'nyi Peterburg: Istoriia, religii, narody*. St. Petersburg: Iskusstvo–SPB, 2002.

Shearer, David. "Elements Near and Alien: Passportization, Policing, and Identity in the Stalinist State, 1932–1952." *Journal of Modern History* 76, no. 4 (2004): 835–81. DOI: 10.1086/427570.

Shelley, Louise. "The Geography of Soviet Criminality." *American Sociological Review* 45 (1980): 111–22. DOI: 10.2307/2095246.

Shenfield, Stephen. *Russian Fascism: Traditions, Tendencies and Movements*. 2nd ed. London: Routledge, 2001.

Shircliffe, Barbara. "'We Got the Best of That World': A Case for the Study of Nostalgia in the Oral History of School Segregation." *Oral History Review* 28, no. 2 (2001): 59–84. https://www.jstor.org/stable/3675778.

Shnirelman, Victor. "Migrantofobiia i 'kul'turnyi rasizm.'" *Ab Imperio*, no. 2 (2008): 287–324.

Shpiliuk, V. A. *Mezhrespublikanskaia migratsiia i sblizhenie natsii v SSSR*. Lvov, 1975.

Siegelbaum, Lewis H., and Leslie Page Moch. *Broad Is My Native Land: Repertoires and Regimes of Migration in Russia's Twentieth Century*. Ithaca, NY: Cornell University Press, 2014.

——. "Transnationalism in One Country? Seeing and Not Seeing Cross-Border Migration within the Soviet Union." *Slavic Review* 75, no. 4 (2016): 970–86. DOI: 10.5612/slavicreview.75.4.0970.

Sikevich, Z. V. *Peterburzhtsy: Etnonatsional'nye aspekty massovogo soznaniia*. St. Petersburg: Sankt-Peterburgskii gosudarstvennyi universitet, 1995.

Silverstein, Paul A. *Algeria in France: Transpolitics, Race, and Nation*. Bloomington: Indiana University Press, 2004.

Simon, Gerhard. *Nationalism and Policy toward the Nationalities in the Soviet Union: From Totalitarian Dictatorship to Post-Stalinist Society*. Translated by Karen Forster and Oswald Forster. Boulder, CO: Westview, 1991.

Sinatti, Giulia. "Home Is Where the Heart Abides: Migration, Return and Housing in Dakar, Senegal." *Open House International* 34, no. 3 (2009): 49–56.

Slezkine, Yuri. *The Jewish Century*. Princeton, NJ: Princeton University Press, 2004.

——. "The USSR as a Communal Apartment, or How the USSR Promoted Ethnic Particularism." *Slavic Review* 53, no. 2 (1994): 414–52. DOI: 10.2307/2501300.

Slobodian, Quinn, ed. *Comrades of Color: East Germany in the Cold War World*. New York: Berghahn Books, 2015.

Smirnova, T. M. *Natsional'nost'—piterskie: Natsional'nye men'shinstva Peterburga i Leningradskoi oblasti v XX veke*. St. Petersburg: Izdatel'stvo "Sudarynia," 2002.

Solomos, John. *Race and Racism in Britain*. 3rd ed. Basingstoke: Palgrave Macmillan, 2003.

SOVA Center. "Old Problems and New Alliances: Xenophobia and Radical Nationalism in Russia, and Efforts to Counteract Them in 2016." Accessed 3 July 2017. https://www.sova-center.ru/en/xenophobia/reports-analyses/2017/05/d36995/.

Soviet Economy in a Time of Change: A Compendium of Papers Submitted to the Joint Economic Committee, Congress of the United States. Washington, DC: Government Printing Office, 1979.

Starovoitova, Galina. *Etnicheskaia gruppa v sovremennom sovetskom gorode: Sotsio-logicheskie ocherki*. Leningrad: Nauka, 1987.

———. "Problemy etnosotsiologii inoetnicheskoi gruppy v sovremennom gorode: Na materialakh issledovaniia tatar v Leningrade." PhD diss. Institut etnografii im. N. N Miklukho-Maklaia, Akademiia nauk SSSR, 1980.

Stiles, Curt H., and Craig S. Galbraith, eds. *Ethnic Entrepreneurship: Structure and Process*. Amsterdam: Elsevier, 2004.

Stohs, Sidney J. "Safety and Efficacy of Shilajit (Mumie, Moomiyo)." *Phytotherapy Research* 28, no. 4 (2014): 475–79. DOI: 10.1002/ptr.5018.

Suny, Ronald Grigor, and Terry Martin, eds. *A State of Nations: Empire and Nation-Making in the Age of Lenin and Stalin*. Oxford: Oxford University Press, 2001.

Thapan, Meenakshi. "Imagined and Social Landscapes: Potential Immigrants and the Experience of Migration in Northern Italy." *Economic and Political Weekly* 48, no. 38 (2013): 55–64.

Thomas, Dominic. *Black France: Colonialism, Immigration, and Transnationalism*. Bloomington: Indiana University Press, 2007.

Thompson, Paul. *The Voice of the Past: Oral History*. 3rd ed. Oxford: Oxford University Press, 2000.

Tillett, Lowell. *The Great Friendship: Soviet Historians on the Non-Russian Nationalities*. Chapel Hill: University of North Carolina Press, 1980.

Todorova, Maria, and Zsuzsa Gille, eds. *Post-Communist Nostalgia*. New York: Berghahn Books, 2010.

Tolokontseva, N. A., and G. M. Romanenkovoi, eds. *Demografiia i ekologiia krupnogo goroda*. Leningrad: Nauka, 1980.

Tolz, Vera. *Russia's Own Orient: The Politics of Identity and Oriental Studies in the Late Imperial and Early Soviet Periods*. Oxford: Oxford University Press, 2011.

Treml, Vladimir J. *Purchases of Food from Private Sources in Soviet Urban Areas*. Berkeley-Duke Occasional Papers on the Second Economy in the USSR, No. 3. Durham, NC, 1985.

Tsentral'noe statisticheskoe upravlenie. *Itogi vsesoiuznoi perepisi naseleniia 1959 goda: RSFSR*. Moscow: Gosstatizdat, 1963.

Ulinich, Anya. *Petropolis*. London: Penguin, 2007.

Umarov, Hodzhamamat. "Regional'nye osobennosti proiavleniia protivorechii sotsialisticheskoi ekonomiki." *Izvestiia Akademiia nauk Tadzhikskoi SSR, Seriia: Filosofiia, ekonomika, pravovedenie*, no. 3 (1989).

Valentei, D. I., ed. *O naselenii Moskvy*. Moscow: Statistika, 1980.

Vendina, Olga. "Moskva i Peterburg: Istoriia ob istorii sopernichestva rossiiskikh stolits." *Politiia* 26, no. 3 (2002): 13–28.

———. "Social Polarization and Ethnic Segregation in Moscow" *Eurasian Geography and Economics* 43, no. 3 (2002): 216–43. DOI: 10.2747/1538-7216.43.3.216.

Verkhovsky, Alexander, et al. *Xenophobia, Freedom of Conscience and Anti-extremism in Russia in 2008*. Translated by I. Salvalieva and S. Rock. Moscow: SOVA Center, 2009.

Voronkov, V., and I. Osval'd, eds. *Konstruirovanie etnichnosti: Etnicheskie obshchiny Sankt-Peterburga*. St. Petersburg: Izdatel'stvo "Dmitrii Bulanin," 1998.

Weber, Cynthia, and Ann Goodman. "The Demographic Policy Debate in the USSR." *Population and Development Review* 7, no. 2 (1981): 279–95. DOI: 10.2307/1972624.

White, Anne. "Internal Migration Trends in Soviet and Post-Soviet European Russia." *Europe-Asia Studies* 59, no. 6 (2007): 887–911. DOI: 10.1080/09668130701489105.

Whittington, Anna Marie. "Forging Soviet Citizens: Ideology, Stability and Identity in the Soviet Union, 1930–1991." PhD. diss., University of Michigan, 2018.

——. "Making a Home for the Soviet People: World War II and the Origins of the *Sovetskii Narod*." In *Empire and Belonging in the Eurasian Borderlands*, edited by Krisa A. Goff and Lewis H. Siegelbaum. Ithaca, NY: Cornell University Press, 2019, 147–62.

Yanov, Alexander. *The Russian New Right: Right-Wing Ideologies in the Contemporary USSR*. Berkeley: Institute of International Studies, University of California, 1978.

Yekelchyk, Serhy. "The Civic Duty to Hate: Stalinist Citizenship as Political Practice and Civic Emotion (Kiev, 1943–53)." *Kritika* 7, no. 3 (2006): 529–56. DOI: 10.1353/kri.2006.0038.

——. *Stalin's Citizens: Everyday Politics in the Wake of Total War*. Oxford: Oxford University Press, 2014.

Yiftachel, Oren. "Critical Theory and 'Gray Space': Mobilization of the Colonized." *City* 13, nos. 2–3 (2009): 240–56. DOI: 10.1080/13604810902982227.

——. "Theoretical Notes on 'Gray Cities': The Coming of Urban Apartheid?" *Planning Theory* 8, no. 1 (2009): 88–100. DOI: 10.1177/1473095208099300.

Yunusov, Arif. "Azerbaidzhantsy v Rossii—smena imidzha i sotsial'nykh rolei." *Rossiia i musul'manskii mir* (164), no. 2 (2006).

Yurchak, Alexei. *Everything Was Forever, Until It Was No More: The Last Soviet Generation*. Princeton, NJ: Princeton University Press, 2005.

Zakharov, Nikolay. *Race and Racism in Russia*. Basingstoke: Palgrave Macmillan, 2015.

Zarecor, Kimberly Elman. "What Was So Socialist about the Socialist City? Second World Urbanity in Europe." *Journal of Urban History* 44, no. 1 (2018): 95–117. DOI: 10.1177/0096144217710229.

Zaslavsky, Victor. *The Neo-Stalinist State: Class, Ethnicity, and Consensus in Soviet Society*. Armonk, NY: M. E. Sharpe, 1982.

Zhou, Min. "Revisiting Ethnic Entrepreneurship: Convergencies, Controversies, and Conceptual Advances." *International Migration Review* 38, no. 3 (2004): 1040–74. DOI: 10.1111/j.1747-7379.2004.tb00228.x.

Zisserman-Brodsky, Dina. *Constructing Ethnopolitics in the Soviet Union: Samizdat, Deprivation and the Rise of Ethnic Nationalism*. New York: Palgrave Macmillan, 2003.

Index

101st kilometer, 7, 21, 111

Abkhazia, 23, 45, 46, 60, 184
"acceleration" (*uskorenie*), 173
admissions, university. *See* quota system: by
  nationality (higher education admissions)
advertisements, employment, 29, 32, 75.
  See also message boards, Moscow
Aeroflot, 74, 143–44
Afghanistan, 77, 90
Africa, Cold War competition for, 18–19, 25–26
African-Americans, 15, 89, 93, 104, 112, 131
African students: challenges of Soviet life for,
  91; in Europe, 14, 16, 19, 105–6, 109–10;
  privileges of, 107, 182; protests by, 99; racism
  against, 91, 93–96, 98–99, 107, 189–91; in
  USSR, 11, 15–16, 67, 82, 105–9, 113, 205
AIDS, 172, 189
airports, 67–68, 79, 80, 198
air travel, 66–67, 77, 143, 157. *See also* Aeroflot
Aitmatov, Chingiz, 90
alcoholism, 85, 125, 137–38, 140, 142, 189.
  See also drinking
Alma-Ata, Kazakhstan, 21, 174
Andijon, Uzbekistan, 2, 155, 166
Andropov, Yuri, 153, 199
anti-racism, 25, 110
Aragvi restaurant, Moscow, 44, 100, 180
Ararat restaurant, Moscow, 44
Arbat, Moscow, 129, 156
army service, 32–33, 61, 76–78, 83, 96, 109,
  143; Russian-language acquisition during,
  22, 42, 69, 74, 78, 124. *See also* demobilized
  soldiers; networks: army-based
Arutiunian, Iu. V, 29, 149, 183
Asia: Cold War competition for, 3, 19, 26;
  idea of, 6, 72; students and migrants from,
  11, 15–16, 19
Astaf'ev, Viktor, 182

backward nations, 15–16, 30, 40, 54
backwardness, 21, 30, 72, 100, 105, 149, 162
Baku, Azerbaijan, 2, 22, 72, 139–40, 143, 173;
  1990 violence in, 172, 186–87; economic
  difficulties in, 1, 147, 151, 162, 166; education

in, 23, 55, 74, 87, 98, 123; flower-selling
  networks based in, 74–75, 128, 152, 154–55,
  160
Baku restaurant, Moscow, 43
Baltic Fleet, 2, 88
Beria, Laventii, 20
birthrates, differential, 28–29, 31, 32, 96, 176,
  177. *See also* demographic imbalances
blacks (*chernye*), 5, 7, 93–97, 100–101, 105–6,
  114–15, 158, 160, 172, 195
Bolshoi Drama Theater, Leningrad, 117
Bolshoi Theater, Moscow, 144
Brezhnev, Leonid, 28, 50, 151, 197–98, 212
bribery, 91, 98, 127–28
Broido, G. I., 15
Bromlei, Iu. V., 22, 29
Bukharin, Nikolai, 38

census, 8, 178; of 1912, 15; of 1959, 22; of 1970,
  28, 96; of 1979, 29, 190; of 1989, 8, 189–90
Central Statistical Administration, 29
China, 15, 53, 56, 67, 190
Chokay, Mustafa, 14
Christianity, 4, 17, 98, 134, 144, 183
citizenship: friendship of peoples and, 37, 52,
  57, 101–2; pride in, 42–43, 94, 185; Soviet,
  6–7, 11, 39, 78, 110–11, 115, 198
Citizenship Act, 1938, 38–39
Cold War, 3, 13, 18–19, 25, 27, 30, 82, 107,
  165, 205
collective farms, 2, 20, 45, 68–69, 74, 150;
  overemployment on, 28–29, 175. *See also*
  networks: collective-farm based
colonialism: Soviet, 27, 58–59, 72, 213; tsarist,
  41–42, 59; Western, 10, 12, 41, 91, 112, 115
communal housing, 78, 117–18, 125, 129,
  142, 212
Communist Party, 38, 49, 50, 88, 96, 124, 143;
  corruption in, 153; education and, 42, 45; in
  Kazakhstan, 173; in Kyrgyzstan, 27, 47, 49,
  73, 175, 177–78; perestroika and, 171–73,
  179, 185–86, 192–93; schools, 22, 43; in
  Tajikistan, 176
Communist University of the Toilers of the
  East, 15–16